# European Integration and Competitiveness

NEW HORIZONS IN INTERNATIONAL BUSINESS

**General Editor: Peter J. Buckley**
Professor of Managerial Economics
Management Centre, University of Bradford

This series is aimed at the frontiers of international business research. Each volume tackles key problem areas in international political economy. The study of international business is important not least because it gives researchers the opportunity to innovate in theory, technique, empirical investigation and interpretation. The area is fruitful for interdisciplinary and comparative research. This series is established as a central forum for the presentation of new ideas in international business.

New Directions in International Business
Research Priorities for the 1990s
*Edited by Peter J. Buckley*

Europe and the Multinationals
Issues and Responses for the 1990s
*Edited by Stephen Young and James Hamill*

Multinational Enterprises in the World Economy
Essays in Honour of John Dunning
*Edited by Peter J. Buckley and Mark Casson*

Multinational Investment in Modern Europe
Strategic Interaction in the Integrated Community
*Edited by John Cantwell*

The Growth and Evolution of Multinational Enterprise
Patterns of Geographical and Industrial Diversification
*R.D. Pearce*

Multinational Enterprise and Public Policy
A Study of the Industrial Countries
*A.E. Safarian*

Transnational Corporations in Southeast Asia
An Institutional Approach to Industrial Organization
*Hans Jansson*

European Integration and Competitiveness
Acquisitions and Alliances in Industry
*Edited by Frédérique Sachwald*

# European Integration and Competitiveness

## Acquisitions and Alliances in Industry

Edited by Frédérique Sachwald

Edward Elgar

First published as *L'Europe et la globalisation. Acquisitions et accords dans l'industrie*, by Masson Éditeur, Paris.

© 1993, IFRI, Masson, Paris.

© Frédérique Sachwald 1994

Published by
Edward Elgar Publishing Limited
Gower House
Croft Road
Aldershot
Hants GU11 3HR
England

Edward Elgar Publishing Company
Old Post Road
Brookfield
Vermont 05036
USA

**British Library Cataloguing in Publication Data**
European Integration and Competitiveness: Acquisitions and Alliances in Industry. –
(New Horizons in International Business Series)
I. Sachwald, Frédérique. II. Series
338.5

**Library of Congress Cataloguing in Publication Data**
European integration and competitiveness: acquisitions and alliances in industry/
Frédérique Sachwald, editor.
p. cm. (New horizons in international business)

1. International business enterprises — Europe — Case studies. 2. Vertical integration — Europe — Case studies. 3. Competition, International — Case studies.
I. Sachwald, Frédérique. II. Series.
HD2844, I567, 1994
338.8'884 — dc20

93 – 34133

ISBN 1 85278 965 4

CIP

Printed and Bound in Great Britain by
Hartnolls Limited, Bodmin, Cornwall.

# Contents

# Contributors

*Etienne de Banville*. Research fellow, Centre National de la Recherche Scientifique, France.

*Martin Bloom*. Associate fellow, Royal Institute of International Affairs, UK.

*Jean-Jacques Chanaron*. Research fellow, Centre National de la Recherche Scientifique, France.

*Mike Hobday*. Research fellow, Science Policy Research Unit, University of Sussex, UK.

*Isabelle Joinovici*. Research assistant, Institut Français des Relations Internationales, France.

*Frédérique Sachwald*. Senior research fellow, Institut Français des Relations Internationales, France.

*Peter de Wolf*. Associate Professor in Economics of industrial organization, Rotterdam School of Management, Erasmis University, Netherlands.

# Acknowledgements

This research project has been supported by a grant from the National Institute for Research Advancement (Tokyo).

Victoire Auguste-Dormeuil, Carine Barco and Isabelle Joinovici have been successively my assistants on this project and this research owes much to their efficient cooperation.

I want to thank Pierre Jacquet, Lynn Mytelka, Françoise Nicolas, Manuel Santhiago, Margaret Sharp, Anita Tiraspolsky and Graham Vickery, who have made useful comments on different chapters of this work.

Some of the sectoral chapters have benefited from interviews with firms or from non-published data. I want to collectively thank the different persons and institutions which have been helpful. For more detailed acknowledgements, see the specific chapters (either inside or at the end, after the bibliography).

This project has been conducted at IFRI. I am particularly grateful to Véronique Bernas, Dominique Briet and Valérie Dupré for their efficient documentation service. Corinne Ponsart, with help from Catherine Risset, has prepared the typescript; I want to thank both of them.

F. S.

# Introduction

## Frédérique Sachwald

At the beginning of the 1980s, the countries from the European Community suffered from Eurosclerosis. Europe was then caught in the crisis that followed the second oil shock. The crisis spread over the entire industrial countries, but the situation was considered as more serious in the case of the EC. Indeed, the macroeconomic component of Eurosclerosis was not the most important; structural aspects and in particular a weak record in terms of competitiveness were considered as particularly worrying. At the beginning of the decade, the European Commission, viewing competitiveness as a largely structural question, had advocated in particular the creation of a true European industrial space.[1] Indeed, the Single Market scheme was largely devised as a set of measures in favour of competitiveness.

At the end of the 1980s, Europe was optimistic again — over-optimistic. The Single Market, which has been taken very seriously by firms, has played an important part in this wave of Europtimism. The crisis at the beginning of the 1990s shows that the achievement of the internal market, which is indeed largely on the way, will suffice to ensure European competitiveness. This book discusses this question from a specific point of view, that of firms' strategies, and more particularly external growth operations.

## OBJECTIVES

The objective of the book is twofold. From a theoretical point of view, it is to contribute to the analysis of the determinants of competitiveness. In this respect it identifies the interactions between firms' competitiveness and national competitiveness as fundamental. From the empirical point of view, the objective is to show how firms, and European firms in particular, have resorted to external growth operations (mergers, acquisitions and alliances of various sorts) to implement their strategies and strengthen their competitiveness. This perspective is particularly interesting since external growth operations have been one of the main instruments of firms' strategies during the 1980s. They have been used in particular to adapt to the prospective consequences of the Single Market.

From the point of view of firms' strategies, the Single Market has to be considered in a more general context. Firms have been quite rapidly convinced of the potential consequences of the Single Market, but while globalization progressed, it could certainly not be the only item on their agenda. This general perspective leads to a more modest appreciation of the consequences of the Single Market itself for European competitiveness.

## READER'S GUIDE

The first chapter considers the main logic behind the Single Market scheme and its prospective consequences. It shows that these positive effects may be altered, firstly if concentration were to threaten the efficiency gains from the unified market and secondly if globalization were to distract firms' strategies from regional integration. These questions are examined from the point of view which has been chosen for the entire book, that is to say external growth operations, and more specifically mergers, acquisitions and joint ventures.

The second chapter exposes the theoretical point of view which underlies the general approach. It discusses the definition of the notion of competitiveness and the contribution of economics to its understanding. It shows that the gaps in the analysis of competitiveness have to be related to the representation of the process of competition itself and, eventually, to the theory of the firm and of its development. This chapter thus explains the importance given to firms' strategies in the empirical studies of this book.

Readers who are not interested in theory can skip the second chapter. They should however look at it if they want to know the precise meaning given to the notion of competitiveness in this book.[2]

The six sectoral studies constitute the core of the book. Their general format is the following. They start with an analysis of the competitive game in each sector. They then assess the competitive position of Europe and European firms, as well as the prospective consequences of the Single Market. They focus on firms' strategies and more particularly on the role of external growth operations which are studied in detail. The sectoral chapters give various indicators of competitiveness; they are complemented in this respect with a statistical appendix which calculates an indicator of competitiveness for all the industries.

The general format did not lead to similar studies on the different sectors, mainly because the industries which have been chosen have specific characteristics. The industries have been chosen so as to offer quite a wide spectrum of sectoral characteristics and of competitive positions for European firms. They are: automobile, automobile components, chemicals, pharmaceuticals, electronic components, consumer electronics.

A general conclusion compares external growth strategies in the different sectors and discusses their role with respect to both the Single Market and globalization.

## NOTES

1. *La compétitivité des industries de la Communauté*, Commission des Communautés Européennes, Luxembourg, 1982.
2. This discussion is situated at the beginning of Chapter 2.

# 1. European Competitiveness, the Single Market and Globalization

## Frédérique Sachwald

The Single Market has been conceived as an answer to Eurosclerosis and, fundamentally, to the lack of competitiveness of European firms. The perspective was mostly internal, that is internal to the EC since the objective was to really complete the Common Market, which actually remained too fragmented as the result of numerous and complex non-tariff barriers.[1] The rationale was to provide European firms with a unified market so that they would be able to exploit large potential economies of scale. Moreover the liberal perspective of the Single Market was to ensure that competition would boost European firms' performances. This chapter explores the different aspects of this internal logic and introduces the external perspective.

The chapter examines the internal logic of the Single Market. It explores the possible tensions between the exploitation of economies of scale and the negative consequences that concentration can induce on the process of competition (section 1.1). Innovation policy is examined as exemplary of the dynamic between intra-European cooperation and competition, which were brought by the Single Market scheme. Section 1.3 questions the internal perspective of the Single Market by stressing the importance of the process of globalization for European firms' strategies; the achievement of the Single Market may not be sufficient to ensure their competitiveness.

Both the internal and the external perspectives are illustrated by the mergers, acquisitions and cooperative agreements which have been one of the main routes to prepare for the Single Market, and more generally one of the main instruments used by firms to implement their strategies during the 1980s.

## 1.1 HOW DOES THE SINGLE MARKET FOSTER COMPETITIVENESS?

The Single Market is largely an exercise in deregulation, the objective being to erase the various obstacles to a true common market. Defragmentation of the markets has been considered as a mighty instrument to favour European firms' competitiveness. The main route to more efficiency is the exploitation of economies of scale, economies of scope and possible economies of learning.

This section exposes the rationale which the Commission has put forward and then considers the possible conflicts with one other central priority of the European Community: free trade and free competition.

### 1.1.1 Economies of Scale versus Fragmentation

The Commission has produced a number of studies to analyse the consequences of the Single Market on European economies and more particularly on competitiveness. Several generations of such studies can be identified.

In 1988, the Commission published studies on the 'cost of non-Europe'[2] which served as background to the Cecchini report (Cecchini 1988). These contributions should be seen as an evaluation of the potential gains from the Single Market. The sectoral studies, which served as inputs to the macro-economic simulation, evaluated the importance of the various barriers to mobility within Europe. They estimated the costs of reduced mobility and the costs incurred by administrative controls. The main part of the exercise, however, was to evaluate the potential gains from economies of scale. These have been estimated for a large number of sectors by Pratten (1988). He used the so-called 'method of the engineer', which relies on estimates from engineers in each sector and which is not very well suited to take into account either technical progress or organizational aspects.[3] Then the sectoral studies have been able to use Pratten's estimates to evaluate the potential cost reductions which the Single Market could bring. The rationale has been the following. The Single Market, by giving access to a larger unified market should enable European firms to benefit from as yet unattainable economies of scale. They should thus become more efficient and gain market share, both within the Community and in external markets.

The estimates of the Cecchini report were rough and, again, only dealt with potential effects; many obstacles can come between potential technical economies of scale and real achievements. Moreover, one could expect other cost reductions by taking into account economies of scope[4] or dynamic effects.

The Commission then proposed a new series of studies which analysed the consequences of the Single Market by sector and by country (Buigues and Ilzkovitz 1988; Buigues, Ilzkovitz and Lebrun 1990). The objective was to show which sectors and nations would be most affected by the process. Sectoral differences are of course linked to the degree of fragmentation of the European market before the operation of the Single Market and more generally to various structural characteristics. Buigues and Ilzkowitz (1988) analysed the prospective sensitivity to the Single Market by combining three main criteria: the importance of non-tariff barriers, price differentials and the degree of openness to intra-Community trade.[5] According to this study, the Single Market should have few consequences for sectors in which non-tariff barriers are low, such as watches, sugar, iron ore, steel tubes or musical instruments. It should also have few consequences in sectors in which non-tariff barriers are moderate but intra-Community trade is low (the hypothesis being that these industries have a national scope) or national price differentials and economies of scale are low. On the contrary, the combination of moderate non-tariff barriers and high price differentials between the European countries should give more importance to the Single Market, as in the case of the automobile sector. Buigues and Ilzkovitz (1988) thus identify 40 sectors for which the Single Market should bring substantial changes; they represent 50 per cent of the value added in the European industry.[6]

Mayes (1991) coordinated a series of detailed studies on the evolution of industries since the launching of the Single Market. In comparison with the previous works, it analyses the actual evolution, as opposed to potential gains, and adopts a dynamic perspective. It shows that generalization about the process is very difficult given the diversity of the industrial sectors. However, two interesting general remarks can be made. First, the degree of openness to extra-European trade and relations in general plays a fundamental role. In a number of cases, it is essential to take foreign competition into account, which was not the case of most of the studies on the 'cost of non-Europe'.[7] Foreign competition explains that, in a number of sectors, the Single Market is only one of the important evolutions that firms' strategies have to take into account.[8] Second, Mayes considers that the clearest response by firms to the Single Market has been to increase external growth operations within Europe. This second point can be discussed; the question is whether European firms directed their external growth operations (mergers, acquisitions and cooperative agreements) mainly to Europe or more generally to the world. Section 1.3 deals with this question.

Firms have intensively resorted to external growth during the 1980s, which is bound to have consequences on the competitive game in a number of sectors and could thus complicate the Single Market scenario. The background studies to the Cecchini report (1988) tended to conclude that the Single Market would both bring cost reductions through economies of scale and lower prices because of such reductions. In a number of sectors, there should be more numerous large firms able to offer their products on a European scale, which should increase competition. Moreover, in sectors where economies of scale are large, the increase in European firms' competitiveness could enable them to enlarge their world market shares. This smooth logical chain going from a more unified market to more competitiveness implies that competition is not hindered, while increased concentration may lessen the degree of competition.

The Commission has recognized that concentration could be a danger for the operation of the Single Market. It published a study which proposed criteria to identify the industry in which concentration could threaten the competition process and European efficiency (Jacquemin, Buigues and Ilzkovitz 1989). Here again, the authors combine several criteria: the rate of growth of demand, the rate of import penetration, the importance of economies of scale and the technological content of products. The combination of these criteria yields four different types of competitive environment which the authors use to assess the consequences of further concentration. Table 1.1 shows this classification. Industries are divided into four groups. In group 1, concentration would be detrimental to competition without prospective efficiency gains; the situation is reversed in group 3. In group 4, the situation is ambiguous; concentration should bring efficiency gains, but may also threaten competition. In group 2, which is constituted of mature industries, concentration between European firms would not be dangerous to the extent that external competition is strong; moreover, concentration does not seem to be the most appropriate strategy.

A comparison between the results on the prospective consequences of the Single Market and on sectoral competitive structures enables us to identify the industries in which concentration may be the most harmful to the process of competition. Using the results of two of the above studies (Buigues and Ilzkovitz 1988 and Jacquemin, Buigues and Ilzkovitz, 1989), these industries are the following: railway materials, electrical cables, sweets, chocolate and pasta.[9] In other sectors where the Single Market should have important consequences, the study by Jacquemin, Buigues and Ilzkovitz (1989) considers that concentration should not be harmful, essentially because they are already quite open to international trade: pharmaceuticals, computers, telecommunication equipment, cars, aeroplanes and helicopters, consumer electronics. According to Table 1.1, concentration should enable European firms to become stronger on international markets.

### 1.1.2  The Risk of Concentration and Competition Policy

The Treaty of Rome asserts the need for a system of undistorted competition (art. 3f in particular) and the Commission has powerful means to control the competitive process. A whole chapter (in part 3 of the Treaty) is dedicated to 'rules on competition'; it deals with firms' behaviour, including public ones (arts. 85–90), with dumping within the Community (art. 91) and with state aids (arts. 92–94). The importance given to competition policy in the Treaty results from the very rationale of the Common Market, which is founded on liberal principles. Moreover, free trade has been conceived as instrumental

*Table 1.1    Sectoral Typology with Respect to Concentration*

| Group | Sectors | Characteristics |
|---|---|---|
| 1 | Construction materials<br>Metal products<br>Paints, coatings<br>Furniture<br>Paper products<br>Rubber products<br>Tobacco | Mature or declining sectors<br>Little open to international trade<br>Low technology or slow<br>  evolution<br>Low economies of scale |
| 2 | Iron-smelting<br>Industrial and agricultural<br>  machinery<br>Leather and leather products; furs,<br>  textiles, clothes<br>Wooden products<br>Paper and paperboard<br>Jewels<br>Toys<br>Musical instruments | Mature or declining sectors<br>Widely open to international<br>  trade; cases of strong<br>  competition from developing<br>  countries<br>Low economies of scale or<br>  economies already exploited<br>Low technology or internationally<br>  diffused<br>High fragmentation in some cases<br>  (toys, furs...) |
| 3 | Advanced materials<br>Chemicals, pharmaceuticals<br>Data processing, office equipment<br>Telecommunications<br>Electronics<br>Automobile<br>Aeronautics<br>Scientific instruments | Sectors in the development phase<br>Open to international trade<br>Strong competition from<br>  industrial countries<br>High economies of scale<br>High R&D expenditure, rapidly<br>  evolving technologies |
| 4 | Boilers<br>Cables, electrical equipment<br>Railway equipment<br>Shipyards<br>Some foodstuff sectors<br>  (confectionery, chocolate,<br>  pasta) | Mature sectors<br>Few intra-European exchanges,<br>  fragmentation due to norms and<br>  regulations<br>High economies of scale<br>Low to middle technology |

*Source*: Jacquemin, Buigues and Ilzkovitz (1989)

in the construction of the European space (Dumez and Jeunemaître 1991). As a consequence, neither firms nor national States were to be allowed to elevate or maintain barriers to free competition within Europe. This is why the European competition policy, contrary to national policies, addresses both firms' behaviours and states' policies in favour of national firms.[10]

The Single Market scheme has induced the Commission to reinforce its competition policy. The Commission has forcefully developed the argument that Europe would reap the full benefits of 1992 only if competition were carefully fostered. In this perspective, it has considered that a stronger competition policy was one of the main instruments to promote European firms' competitiveness, both on the internal market and worldwide. The Commission has thus worked to implement competition policy in a more transparent and more rigorous way (Sachwald 1991). However, the most important innovation has been the adoption of the regulation on mergers in December 1989.[11]

Until very recently, the Commission could control uncompetitive behaviour from firms by using art. 85 of the Treaty on alliances between firms and art. 86 on abuse of dominant position. However, the Commission had not been endowed with a specific tool to control mergers and acquisitions. Historically, this important gap can be explained by the absence of worries about concentration in Europe when the Common Market was designed, and by national resistance from member states having merger control as part of their national competition policies afterwards. Moreover, in Europe, relationships between the state and firms have been traditionally quite intricate; intervention *vis-à-vis* industry has been considered as a way to achieve various economic, social and regional goals. This, in part, reflects an emphasis on competition as a process rather than as the mechanism of the invisible hand achieving the optimal allocation of resources (George and Jacquemin 1990).

During the 1960s, both individual countries and European authorities were generally convinced that European firms were too small to stand foreign competition (Geroski and Jacquemin 1985; Hölzler 1990). Then, the United States were the main competitor, and American firms being generally much larger than European ones, the objective was to build larger, more efficient and more powerful firms. This can be summarized as the 'American challenge complex'.[12] The economic rationale behind this quest for size mainly rested on economies of scale. The 1960s and the beginning of the 1970s saw rapid progress in European integration and a wave of mergers and acquisitions. However, economic results in the following period showed that concentration does not necessarily bring competitiveness.

Disappointing results of concentration and the importance of the phenomenon have contributed to the attention given to merger control in Europe during the 1970s, both in individual countries and at the European level. Since the 1970s, the Commission has worked at controlling concentrations; it tried to have a regulation passed on the subject, but also resorted to arts. 85 and 86 in some cases (George and Jacquemin 1990; Sachwald 1991). The regulation was finally adopted by the Council in 1989.

The main features of the regulation on mergers are similar to those of the first 1973 proposal, even if the latter has been progressively transformed along the negotiation route. The regulation deals with the case of operations with a 'Community dimension'. The latter is defined by several criteria:

'(a) the aggregate world-wide turnover of all the undertakings concerned is more than ECU 5,000 million, and (b) the aggregate Community-wide turnover of each of at least two of the undertakings concerned is more than ECU 250 million, unless each of the undertakings concerned achieves more than two-thirds of its aggregate Community-wide turnover within one of the same Member states.' (Art. 1, para. 2)

Concentrations[13] with a Community dimension have to be notified to the Commission.

The criteria to be used to appraise concentrations have of course been a critical issue. As for any competition policy, the central question was the choice between an appraisal on the sole consideration of competition and an appraisal taking other matters of public interest into consideration. Earlier drafts of the regulation contained the possibility of an 'efficiency defence', but this feature met with strong opposition from some member states. They feared that European competition policy could serve for industrial strategy purposes, to choose 'European champions' for example (George and Jacquemin 1990).

Article 2 of the regulation, which states the elements of appraisal of concentrations, puts the emphasis on preserving effective competition. A concentration should not 'create or strengthen a dominant position as a result of which effective competition would be significantly impeded in the Common Market or in a substantial part of it'. But one may wonder whether the article does not allow for some arbitration in the case of efficiency gains from concentration. In its first paragraph it gives a list of elements to take into account. Most of them relate to the evaluation of the degree of competition. Among these are the structure of markets, the actual and potential competitors, or the existence of barriers to entry. In this same section, the article also mentions as a basis for appraisal 'the development of technical and economic progress' adding 'provided that it is to consumers' advantage and does not form an obstacle to competition'. This wording may appear somewhat confusing. Moreover, if the emphasis on competition is quite clear in the text of the regulation, in the preambles and in the declarations of the Council upon its acceptance of the regulation, there are references to defence of competitiveness.

Hölzler (1990) underlines the compromises which were necessary to reach a decision on the regulation. George and Jacquemin (1990) also recognize that the final regulation has suffered from the compromises which it had to go through. However, they are convinced that 'the emphasis is unambiguously on preserving and developing effective competition' and that this will lead in practice to the defence of efficiency, which includes dynamic efficiency gains. Indeed, the reference to technical and economic progress with the provision that competition is not hindered can be interpreted as allowing for an appraisal of dynamic efficiency gains. In this perspective, the regulation would retain competition as the only reference, while going beyond static considerations.

The answer to the question of the efficiency defence also lies in the implementation of the regulation. So far (April 1992) there have been very few cases to judge upon. Between September 1990 and the end of that year, there were twelve notifications; in 1991, 63; and during the first three months of 1992, eleven. There has been only one refusal[14] and three cases for which the authorization was conditional. In the case of refusal, the De Havilland case, the Commission has considered the potential cost gains which a larger firm could enjoy, but has judged that they were negligible; and there was thus no scope for arbitration. Nor, of course, was it the case when the Commission has ruled that a merger or acquisition did not constitute a dominant position. After a little more than a year and a half, the Commission has not met with all the possible cases and its interpretation of the regulation is certainly not definitive. However, it seems that its interpretation corresponds to the text in the emphasis which it puts on competition. Even with this strict interpretation, the rate of refusal has been very low. In these conditions, the conflicts between competition and competitiveness on this ground may be very limited.

During the 1980s, the Commission reinforced the control of competition within the Community, both with respect to firms' behaviour and to state aids.[15] The question is whether this achievement could not be somewhat contradictory with the main rationale for the Single Market which, as we have seen above, rests on reaping potential economies of scale. Indeed, in order to exploit economies of dimension, firms largely resort to concentration — even if some possible cost reductions can result from a better organization within Europe after a number of barriers have been removed. The Commission has considered competition policy as one of the main instruments to ensure that the benefits of the Single Market will be transmitted to the consumer. But, to a certain extent, competition policy could also threaten the process by opposing concentrations aiming at larger economies of scale (Jenny 1991).

### 1.1.3 European Innovation Policy

The question of the arbitration between cooperation and competition has been raised very generally in the case of innovation and innovation policy. For Margaret Sharp (1991), Community policies for advanced technology exemplify the 'dialectic of 1992', where collaborative schemes interact with the central feature of the Single Market which is deregulation.

During the 1980s, technology has been one of the great battlefields on which to improve European competitiveness. European weaknesses had been identified in high-tech sectors and Europe was considered as inefficient at transforming science and ideas into innovations. The completion of the internal market has not been specifically aimed at innovation, but the Single Act does introduce new provisions in this respect. Competition policy has also adapted to the specific needs of cooperative research.

The Treaty of Rome does not give the EC specific responsibilities to foster the development of technologies.[16] The Single European Act adds a title (VI, arts. 130f–130q) to the original treaty on research and technological development. According to article 130f para.1, 'the Community's aim shall be to strengthen the scientific and technological basis of European industry and to encourage it to become more competitive at international level'. The Single European Act mentions the actions which the Community should be taking in this respect. It insists in particular on the promotion of cooperation between European firms, but also universities and research institutes. It also lays down an implementation mechanism. It mainly consists of a 'multiannual framework programme' (art. 130i) which lays down the objectives, establishes priorities and fixes the financial amounts deemed necessary. The framework programme is to be implemented through specific projects developed within each activity (art. 130k). Finally, the Single Act specifies that the Community should take into account the relationships between the promotion of innovation and 'the establishment of the internal market and the implementation of common policies, particularly as regards competition and trade' (art. 130f para. 3).

Since the 1980s, the perception that Europe achieved poor technological performances[17] has induced a number of initiatives both at national and Community levels. In this respect ESPRIT (European Strategic Programme of Research in Information Technology, 1983–94) has been an important step. It was taken to counteract Europessimism and pioneered a new attitude towards what should be done.[18] In particular, it gave a significant role to industrialists, both in the very conception of the programme and in the choice and definition of the different research projects, by adopting a bottom-up approach. Another innovation was the introduction of the notion of 'pre-competitive research', that is research which is necessary to develop innovations, but which has no immediate commercial applications. This notion, in implying that cooperation was not on a commercial basis, had two advantages: it avoided conflicts with the European competition policy and made cooperation between potential competitors easier.[19] However, it should be noted that parts of the ESPRIT project have gone beyond pre-competitive research.[20]

ESPRIT had started before the Single Act was signed and was well under way when the first framework programme was adopted in 1987. ESPRIT has been integrated into the framework programme — information technology is actually the area which has received the largest amounts of funding within the programmes (1987–91 and 1990–94).

The projects developed within the framework programmes have largely followed the format adopted by ESPRIT. The bottom-up logic is even more strongly asserted by EUREKA projects. EUREKA, the idea of which was originally launched by President Mitterrand in 1985 to answer the American Star Wars programme, is actually an umbrella mechanism to foster cooperation between European firms.[21] The initiative of the projects, which addresses the competitive end of R&D, belongs to firms; they propose their cooperative research to the board of EUREKA in order to obtain its label. However, unlike the framework programme, EUREKA is not a centralized mechanism; funds are distributed by national authorities or the Community when it participates in a project, such as in the case of JESSI.[22]

The financial effort from the Community remains quite limited. The projected expenditures of the second framework programme (ECU 5700 million) represents only 4 per cent of the total civilian R&D funding from the twelve countries and 3 per cent of the EEC budget (*Usine Nouvelle*, 4/4/ 1991). However, various evaluations of the European programmes have concluded that they have had substantial results (Laredo and Callon 1991; Mytelka 1991). Evaluations mainly underline two types of achievements: the programmes restored confidence in European capabilities and triggered widespread cooperation between firms.[23]

Nevertheless, and for ESPRIT in particular, cooperation has been considered as ambiguous. Indeed, increased cooperative research between European firms was one of the objectives of the programmes but, at a certain point, cooperation may become collusion or even outright concentration. The Big Twelve of European information technology, which have been associated with the idea of ESPRIT, have also been its most important participants.[24] Over the period 1984–88, 50 per cent of ESPRIT's budget has been allocated to the Big Twelve (Mytelka, 1991). In general, funds from ESPRIT did not represent a large share of the R&D spending of large companies, however, their weight in the programme meant that they largely shaped its content. The role of large companies in ESPRIT has led to fears that the programme could be captured by these firms, and that they would be transformed into European champions, while national champions had been judged as inefficient.

Mytelka (1991) examined the data on collaborative research within ESPRIT in detail. She shows that the Big Twelve largely shaped the programme, but concludes that the latter has had a global positive impact on the European information technology industry. Her comment on the role taken by smaller firms tends to show that they did gain from ESPRIT. Their participation meant an opportunity to access new knowledge and means to innovate, even if projects were often led by the large firms. The consequences in terms of the degree of competition are difficult to assess, however. It seems that ESPRIT has helped overcome some types of barriers to entry, but the creation of networks, both between the largest European firms and around them by cooperation with smaller firms may have constituted other barriers to entry. Moreover, there have been a number of mergers and acquisitions in the sector during the 1980s (Mayes 1991).

European competition policy has specifically examined the question of collaborative research. During the 1980s, cooperative research agreements have become much more frequent; this has been a quite general phenomenon, not confined to Europe.[25] The theoretical analysis of cooperative agreements has also become richer and more qualified.[26] European competition policy has taken these developments into account.

Article 85 para. 1 prohibits agreements and practices which aim at preventing, restricting or distorting competition within the Common Market. The main such practices include price-fixing, market-sharing, restrictions in supply and the tying of sales. The prohibited agreements are void, but can be exempted from sanctions if they 'contribute to improving the production or distribution of goods or to promoting technical and economic progress' (art. 85 para. 3). Exemption is conditional; the agreement must allow consumers 'a fair share of the resulting benefit' and must not eliminate competition for a substantial part of the products in question (art. 85 para. 3). Thus art. 85 provides for a trade-off between an increase in market power and efficiency gains. Economic theory and competition policy practice have shown that it is quite difficult to identify and evaluate the efficiency consequences of firms' behaviour. Decisions thus do not rest on unambiguous analysis.

The Commission has used 'block exemptions' to rationalize the process of decision (Lovergne 1989). A block exemption concerns an entire category of agreements for which there exists a presumption of market failure.[27] When the Commission has decided a block exemption, the agreements do not have to be notified individually any more; they are considered as generally acceptable. Thus the Commission avoids scrutinizing each case. By limiting the scope of discretionary power, it may increase the credibility of the policy (George and Jacquemin 1990).

The Commission has decided block exemptions for R&D and intellectual property agreements. It has recognized the specific problems due to the public good characteristics of research (see Chapter 2). In 1968, in a notice dealing with cooperation between firms, the Commission mentioned that agreements which have R&D as their sole objective do not fall under art. 85 para 1.[28] In December 1984, the Commission issued a block exemption for certain categories of agreements in R&D matters.[29] More specifically, it explicitly extends its favourable attitude to some types of agreements involving joint exploitation of the research results.

Thus during the 1980s, the Commission has been endowed with specific means to implement the recommendations of the Single Act with respect to research and innovation. European innovation policy consists mostly in encouraging cooperation between firms from the Community, both financially and through a special treatment from competition law. In so doing the Community considers that technology and innovation do require a specific treatment within the main rationale of the Single Market scheme which emphasizes the role of competition. But, as was again confirmed by the debate on the orientation of European competition policy in Spring 1992, the support for research should remain at the pre-competitive stage, and not get nearer to the market.[30]

Innovation also exemplifies the other challenge to European policies in favour of competitiveness: globalization. Several studies on the cooperative research agreements struck by European firms have insisted on the fact that the partners are largely non-European. This was the case before the launching of the European programmes (GEST 1986); the new programmes did stimulate intra-Community collaborations, but European firms still very often look for partners in the United States and Japan. This question is considered more generally in the next section.

## 1.2   GLOBALIZATION VERSUS INTEGRATION?

European competitiveness has constituted one of the main motivations of the Single Market. As we have seen above, the rationale largely rested on the exploitation of economies of dimension made possible by the access to a large unified market. In this perspective, the evaluations of the consequences of the Single Market by the Commission insisted on the reorganization of European firms on a European basis; in the fields of research and technology, the Commission has forcefully fostered cooperation between European firms. The question is whether this European perspective is the only relevant one and whether the international point of view would not shed a different light on the relationship between the Single Market and European competitiveness. The question seems quite natural after a decade of globalization. Indeed, during the 1980s, economies have become more deeply interdependent and internationalization may have qualitatively changed.[31]

During the 1980s, firms have resorted both to internal and external growth to stand up to the crisis and then to implement more aggressive strategies and conquer markets. They have invested heavily internally to update their

productive capabilities. However, external growth has gained more importance as a source of spending during the decade.[32] External growth has been
widely used to conquer foreign markets. Foreign direct investment has
grown very rapidly; between 1985 and 1990, it grew more rapidly than
world trade (UN 1991). Among the Triad, cross-border mergers and acquisitions (M&A) grew more rapidly than other forms of direct investment
(Bleeke *et al.* 1990) and see Figure 1.1. So, on a very general basis, data tend
to show that M&A have been one of the main instruments used by firms to
implement their strategies. Studies on cooperative agreements also conclude
that they have played an increasing role.[33]

The 1980s wave of mergers and acquisitions[34] has been worldwide in
scope, but an assessment of the role of international operations depends on
their relative importance. Unfortunately, a detailed examination of mergers,
acquisitions and cooperative agreements is made difficult by the lack of
adequate data. The discussion below uses available data to assess more
specifically the role played by cross-border operations in the case of Europe.

*Figure 1.1    Large European firms' M&A and joint ventures, in number of
operations*

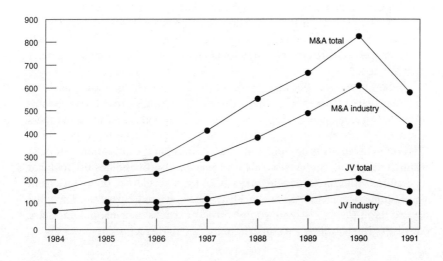

*Source*: Reports on competition policy, EC. See below for a discussion of these data.

### 1.2.1 Mergers and Acquisitions

Numerous studies either examine domestic M&A, or cross-border M&A, or direct investment in general. As just said, all have increased, but it is important to compare the evolution of the different types of operations. We focus here on the comparison between domestic and different types of cross-border M&A in order to capture the tendencies in terms of internationalization.

It is important to emphasize that data on M&A can be quite different according to the indicator used; more specifically, data in terms of numbers of operations differ from data in terms of value. Unfortunately, neither can be considered as totally accurate, indeed, the value of transactions is not always disclosed and data in value are thus incomplete. One should also emphasize the problems in collecting data; there is no single source which gathers national and cross-border data, there is no single source to provide an international perspective.

Between 1984 and 1989 foreign acquisitions by Japanese firms grew from 31 to 63 per cent of the total number of Japanese M&A; the corresponding figures for M&A in value are 94 and 95 per cent.[35] Japan is an exception; in the United States and Europe, M&A remain mostly domestic.[36] For the United States, over the period 1985–89, both in terms of numbers and value, domestic deals represented more than 80 per cent of the total, with a tendency to decline slowly.[37] In Germany, the number of domestic M&A still represented well over half the total at the end of the 1980s.[38] In France, the number of domestic acquisitions represented 57 per cent of the total in 1990 and 64 per cent in 1991; the corresponding percentages for the value of transactions were respectively 44 and 38.[39] In the UK in 1990, domestic M&A represented 70 per cent of the total number of transactions, and 56 per cent in value.[40]

According to Bleeke *et al.* (1990), for the European Community, between 1984 and 1989, cross-border M&A (including intra-EC cross-border operations) as a percentage of total M&A was reduced both in terms of numbers (from 33 to 28 per cent) and in terms of value (from 49 to 46 per cent). These figures differ from those published by the European Community in its annual report. According to Table 1.2, at the end of the 1980s, national operations still represented the majority of the total number of operations in the Community; in 1990 their share had gone down to 42 per cent. The table shows that the relative share of domestic operations depends on the sector considered; it has decreased quicker in the case of industry.

Table 1.2    Mergers, acquisitions and majority holdings from EEC firms\*, domestic
operations as % of total number of operations\*\*

|              | 1985 | 1986 | 1987 | 1988 | 1989 | 1990 |
|--------------|------|------|------|------|------|------|
| Total        | 70   | 64   | 70   | 57   | 53   | 42   |
| Industry     | 70   | 64   | 70   | 56   | 47   | 39   |
| Distribution | 88   | 82   | 82   | 70   | 91   | 60   |
| Banks        | 55   | 48   | 63   | 68   | 61   | 57   |
| Insurance    | 47   | 42   | 61   | 35   | 45   | 35   |

\*    The 1000 largest European firms
\*\* That is, domestic, intra-community and international operations
*Source*: calculations from EC Reports on competition policy

Table 1.3    Scope of mergers, acquisitions and majority holdings from EEC firms
(industry and services)\*, % of total number of operations

|                 | 1985 | 1986 | 1987 | 1988 | 1989 | 1990 |
|-----------------|------|------|------|------|------|------|
| National        | 70   | 64   | 70   | 57   | 53   | 42   |
| Intra-Community | 22   | 22   | 22   | 26   | 34   | 38   |
| International   | 78   | 14   | 8    | 16   | 13   | 20   |

\*    See note to Table 1.2
*Source*: calculations from EC Reports on competition policy

The Commission classifies the operations according to the partners and
records intra-Community operations. Table 1.3 calculates the share by
geographical distribution of the operations from these data. It shows that the
reduction in the share of domestic operations has not been to the sole benefit
of the intra-Community operations. It is the share of international operations
which has increased the most: by 150 per cent while that of intra-
Community operations has increased by 72 per cent. Moreover, it has to be
underlined that the sample of firms used by the Commission is biased in
favour of the external operations in general since it consists of the largest
firms from the Community (see note to Table 1.2). This certainly reduces the
proportion of domestic operations as compared with that in the total population of firms, which may explain the differences between the figures from
the Commission and those quoted above since the latter include operations

involving smaller firms. It is more difficult to assert the bias with respect to the distribution between intra-Community and international operations. Besides, the operations which are taken into account by the Commission underestimate the share of international operations for another reason. Indeed, the Commission labels 'international' the acquisitions of European firms by non-European ones, and thus does not take into account the reverse operations (say a French firm buying an American one). This unilateral accounting introduces all the larger a bias that European firms have been active buyers across the Atlantic during the 1980s.

A more complete source confirms this analysis. According to Securities Data Corp., in 1989, extra-European M&A represented 38 per cent of the M&A involving European companies in value (and 29 per cent in number of operations).[41] European firms have spent $6 bn on M&A in non-EC countries in 1985 and more than $33 bn in 1989. From these different data, one can quite safely hypothesize that the increase in intra-Community operations has not been the most important phenomenon in the strategy of large European firms.

Table 1.4 proposes the same figures as Table 1.3 for the manufacturing sector only. It shows that the share of domestic operations has decreased more rapidly in industry.[42]

*Table 1.4    Scope of mergers, acquisitions and majority holdings from EEC firms industry\*, % of total number of operations*

|                  | 1985 | 1986 | 1987 | 1988 | 1989 | 1990 | 1991 |
|------------------|------|------|------|------|------|------|------|
| National         | 70   | 64   | 70   | 56   | 47   | 39   | 41   |
| Intra-Community  | 21   | 23   | 25   | 29   | 40   | 41   | 37   |
| International    | 9    | 13   | 6    | 15   | 13   | 20   | 22   |

\*   See note to Table 1.2
*Source*: calculations from EC Reports on competition policy

### 1.2.2  Inter-Firm Agreements

Cooperative ventures have become an important phenomenon during the 1980s. Collaborations between firms and various types of alliances certainly do not date back to the 1980s. Joint ventures have for example long been quite common in sectors such as aluminium (Stuckey 1983) or in forest products (Globerman and Schwindt 1986). However, the evolution of the competitive game since the 1970s, in general and more particularly in specific sectors, has led to the multiplication of collaborative ventures.

Statistics on the evolution of cooperative agreements are even more difficult to gather than statistics on mergers and acquisitions for two types of
reason. First, there is no single definition of cooperative agreements, and
they are indeed quite varied; they comprise in particular the different forms
of joint ventures, more or less extensive agreements, with or without equity
participation. Moreover, they can address each of the functions of firms, or a
set of these functions. Cooperative research has been at the forefront during
the 1980s, but numerous collaborative agreements also concern distribution
and production. So, heterogeneity is a first source of difficulty. The identification of the agreements is the second one. Mergers and acquisitions are
much more visible because stock changes hands. It is also why joint
ventures are the most visible of the cooperative agreements.[43]

To be more precise, the following is a general definition of a cooperative
agreement (or ventures): a transaction where at least one of the parties is a
firm and which can be described as being intermediate between the market
(exchange through the price mechanism) and the firm (internal exchange).[44]

Empirical studies on cooperative agreements have not always used the
same definition, which explains certain variations in the results.[45] However,
as a whole, the literature on the subject shows a clear tendency to rapid
growth since the 1970s. There are three types of studies: general cross-
sectoral studies and studies on a particular sector or function such as R&D.

General studies tend to be the least precise because they rely on the financial press and cannot complement their information with more detailed
information. This kind of analysis has shown clear upward trends. Hergert
and Morris (1988), using a database which has been compiled from public
announcements reported in the *Economist* and *Financial Times* over the
period 1975–86 (as of mid-1986, there were 839 agreements in the base),
show a clear upward trend between 1979 and 1986. The agreements between
firms from the US and from the EC grew more quickly than between the US
and Japan or the EC and Japan. Marity and Smiley (1983) had produced one
of the first empirical studies on this subject. They concentrated on agreements struck during the year 1980, but complemented their data with
interviews which showed that managers were conscious both of the need for
cooperation and of the upward trend. Since then, numerous enquiries have
confirmed these attitudes from managers.

Sectoral studies have been able to analyse the progression of cooperative
agreements in much more detail.[46] These studies differ in their method and
in their coverage, but they show a general upward tendency. The explanations and the conditions of this evolution differ, however, and it seems very
important to have a sectoral approach.

Studies on cooperative agreements to fulfil specific functions have also
been important. They show that cooperative research is a significant motiva-
tion, even if it is not the only one.[47] It seems that cooperative agreements are

particularly numerous in high-tech sectors (GEST 1986; Mowery 1988). This is due to the role played by innovation in the competitive game (see Chapter 2) and to the benevolent attitude of public authorities (Dussauge, Garrette and Ramanantsoa 1988; Sachwald 1990c).

The Commission publishes general statistics on joint ventures which are based on the general press and on more specialized publications. Table 1.5 shows that the largest firms from the EEC have entered more and more joint ventures during the 1980s. It also shows that industry represents about 70 per cent of the total during the period.

*Table 1.5   Number of new joint ventures involving the largest EC firms*

|          | 1983 | 1984 | 1985 | 1986 | 1987 | 1988 | 1989 | 1990 | 1991 |
|----------|------|------|------|------|------|------|------|------|------|
| Total    | –    | –    | 100  | 102  | 121  | 164  | 183  | 210  | –    |
| Industry | 46   | 69   | 82   | 81   | 90   | 111  | 129  | 156  | 127  |

*Source*: Reports on the competition policy from the EEC

As in the case of M&A, the increase in cooperative agreements between European firms during the 1980s has to be interpreted in the general context referred to above. Cooperation between European firms has been advocated on the same grounds as M&A: efficiency and competitiveness. In the case of cooperative agreements, R&D has been more particularly stressed.

At the beginning of the 1980s, European firms seemed to cooperate insufficiently; they often concluded agreements with American and Japanese firms. The Commission as well as several European governments have interpreted this situation as the result of the fragmentation of the European economic space. So, one of the objectives of the Single Market has been to favour collaboration within the Community. It is explicitly mentioned in the Single Act in the case of research (art. 130f) and advocated by the Cecchini report (1988, Chapter 5). The rationale is the following. As globalization progresses and cooperative agreements are one of the responses from firms, cooperation between European firms is necessary to strengthen them and to develop strong European networks able to compete with Japanese and American firms. Two questions then arise. Do European firms cooperate insufficiently? Will the Single Market favour intra-European cooperation?

At the beginning of the 1980s, intra-European cooperations (including domestic ones) represented over 50 per cent of the total for the four largest EC countries. Intra-European cooperations represented more than 50 per cent of international cooperations for France and Germany and a little less for Italy, and around 40 per cent for the UK.[48] Data from the Commission show that the proportion of intra-European cross-border joint ventures has increased, even though it tends to fluctuate from year to year. This tendency has been generally to the detriment of national operations (see Table 1.6).

*Table 1.6    Share of the different types of joint ventures, % of total\**

|  | National | | Intra-EC | | International | |
|---|---|---|---|---|---|---|
|  | Total | Industry | Total | Industry | Total | Industry |
| 1985 | 53 | 49 | 18 | 18 | 29 | 33 |
| 1988 | 46 | 40 | 27 | 28 | 27 | 31 |
| 1990 | 29 | 26 | 38 | 35 | 35 | 38 |

\*    Grand total; total in the column refers to the total of the different sectors (services and industry) for each geographical extension
*Source*: calculations from EC Reports on competition

Joint ventures, like mergers and acquisitions, have become more European and the Single Market scheme has certainly been an active factor in this evolution. But it does not necessarily mean that intra-European cooperations are or will be the most dynamic category of alliances. This question can be explored by analysing the functions of the different types of external growth operations.

Joint ventures are generally not firms' first choice when they become multinational, especially if they intend to conduct a whole range of activities abroad (production and distribution in particular). They usually prefer to control the operations of their foreign units and joint ventures appear as the result of specific constraints, which have often to do with national regulations in foreign countries or with high risks.[49]

If joint ventures are second-best solutions when direct investment in independent operations or acquisitions is considered as impossible or impractical, they should occur between relatively distant partners. In this perspective, Kay (1991) has hypothesized that joint ventures should be relatively more useful for international operations than for domestic ones. Intra-European operations can be considered as the middle ground in this respect, but the Single Market should render them more comparable to national ones.[50] According to this reasoning, the Single Market should diminish the attractiveness of intra-European joint ventures relative to intra-European mergers and acquisitions. Table 1.7 uses the ratio of joint ventures to M&A as an indicator of the propensity to cooperate.[51]

*Table 1.7    Propensity to cooperate\* for European firms from industry, 1984–91*

|               | 1984  | 1986  | 1988  | 1990  | 1984/91** |
|---------------|-------|-------|-------|-------|-----------|
| National      | 0.31  | 0.23  | 0.21  | 0.17  | 0.21      |
| EEC           | 0.37  | 0.38  | 0.28  | 0.21  | 0.25      |
| International | 1.04  | 0.90  | 0.60  | 0.48  | 0.70      |

\*  Number of joint ventures over the number of M&A and majority holdings
\*\* Average over the period 1984–91
*Source*: calculations from EC Reports on competition policy

Table 1.7 shows two remarkable patterns. First, the propensity to co-operate consistently decreases with the degree of market completion, which tends to confirm the above hypothesis. Second, the ratio decreases during the period, whatever the type of partners. This may be due to the fact that the decade has experienced a merger wave, and mergers have become relatively easier.[52]

The patterns are similar in the case of high-tech industries defined as the set of electrical, mechanical, chemical and computer sectors. This result can seem quite paradoxical since the Community has deployed important efforts to foster intra-European cooperative research. Several types of explanation can be proposed. First, the above definition of high-tech sectors is quite broad since it includes entire industries when only part of them are really high-tech. Second, joint ventures are probably not the mostly used type of transaction to operate cooperative research. There are a number of cooperative agreements which are more flexible or more adapted to large numbers of partners (as is often the case in research).[53] In this respect, the general figures from the Commission on joint ventures certainly do not reflect the entire cooperative activities from European firms. Finally, in a number of cases, European firms prefer cooperating in research with American and Japanese firms. This is more particularly the case when Europe is relatively weak, such as in electronics. This is also more generally the case because complementarities may be stronger between very different firms. In parti-cular, the national origin of a firm has an influence on its capacity to innovate and on its fields of excellence.[54]

## 1.3    CONCLUSION

This chapter has discussed the objectives of the Single Market from two perspectives: the internal rationale and the international environment.

From the internal perspective, it showed that the main rationale of the Single Market, to create a more competitive European industry, that is by deregulation and homogenization of rules aiming at economies of dimension, has been strongly complemented with support for innovative activities. Both routes may endanger the competitive game. In this respect, the Commission has reinforced its competition policy; it is now able to control the operations of concentration and the exercise of dominant position, as well as to monitor cooperative agreements.[55] However, the analysis discussed possible cases of arbitration between the logic of deregulation on the one hand, and that of support for innovation and the build-up of competitive strengths on the other hand.

This chapter also showed that the main logic of the Single Market may be countered by the evolution of the world economy, and in particular by the development of globalization. Globalization means that European firms consider the Single Market as only one of the factors in their strategies. As a result, firms' strategies may not obey the plan of the Single Market which focused on intra-European restructuring. In this respect, the EC as a whole is confronted with the same questions as national states, and in particular with the fact that there are more and more sources of discrepancies between national competitiveness and firms' competitiveness. This chapter has focused on one of them, that is, cross-border external growth.

The above developments also mentioned large sectoral differences, which is quite logical since external growth operations are instruments to implement firms' strategies. It is why this book has chosen to compare different sectors in order to analyse firms' strategies during the 1980s and to relate them to the Single Market project. Chapter 2 explains this choice from a theoretical point of view.

# NOTES

1.  As has been the case for the GATT process, tariff barriers have proved much easier to eliminate. The traditional non-tariff barriers like quotas have also been rapidly eliminated within the EC.
2.  There are sixteen background reports on the cost of non-Europe; some are mentioned in the bibliography to this chapter under EC as the author.
3.  For a discussion of the notion of economies of scale and of the different methods of evaluation, see in particular Sachwald (1989).
4.  Some studies use the term economies of scale as a general term for different types of economies of dimension, and in particular economies of scope; the distinction is not always obvious. In the automobile industry, for example, if a firm organizes its production lines so that it can lengthen the series of certain elements while keeping some differentiation in the final products, it takes advantage of economies of scope. But this result is obtained by achieving economies of scale on the production of the common elements.
5.  Openness to external trade is also important though; see below.
6.  For another work on the identification of the sensitive sectors, see BIPE (1989).
7.  In the case of the automobile industry, for example, it may be interesting to evaluate potential

economies of scale, but the crucial point is to examine the strategy of the European firms with respect to Japanese performances (see Chapter 3 on the automobile industry in this volume).

8. This fact has already been recognized by a number of sectoral studies. See for example Crespy (1990) and Sachwald (1990c).
9. It should be noted that the two studies do not use the same industrial classification.
10. There are a number of descriptions of the European competition policy. See in particular George and Jacquemin (1990), Montagnon (1990), Sachwald (1991).
11. Regulation (EEC) no. 4064/89 of 21 December 1989.
12. The book by J.-J. Servan-Schreiber, *The American challenge* (1967) is often quoted as a reminder of the way the problem was perceived in Europe at the time.
13. Mergers and acquisitions are concentrations. Some joint ventures can also be considered as concentrations; concentrative joint ventures perform on a lasting basis all the functions of an autonomous economic entity; see art. 3 of the merger regulation and Renault/Volvo case in 1990.
14. Affair no. IV/M.053 — Aérospatiale-Alénia/de Havilland — for which the decision was given on 2 October 1991.
15. This section has mainly dealt with the question of concentration.The Commission has also worked on other firms' behaviours (arts. 85 and 86) as well as on states' behaviours; see in particular Montagnon (1990); Sachwald (1991).
16. On the contrary, the Euratom Treaty and the European Coal and Steel Community Treaty provide a legal basis for European action on science and technology development.
17. Even if they were only perceived as such. For evaluations, see in particular Sachwald (1990c); Freeman, Sharp and Walker (1991).
18. Discussions on the concept of such a programme had started in 1979–80. On the birth of ESPRIT from this perspective, see in particular Sharp (1991).
19. The notion has been criticized as being vague; the tactical interpretation given here transforms this shortcoming into an advantage.
20. According to Mytelka (1991), the objectives (functions) of 35 per cent of ESPRIT 1 projects and 48 per cent of ESPRIT 2 projects were either specific application research or standardization.
21. EUREKA is not an EEC mechanism; it applies to European countries more generally.
22. For details on this programme, see Chapter 6 on electronic components in this volume.
23. The objective here is not to present an evaluation of European R&D policy; on this question see in particular Laredo and Callon (1991); Freeman *et al.* (1991); Mytelka (1989).
24. When ESPRIT started, the list was the following: ICL, GEC, Plessey, AEG, Nixdorf, Siemens, Thomson, Bull, CGE, Olivetti, STET and Philips.
25. Intra-European agreements were not the most frequent. For data see below, section 1.3.
26. This question will be dealt with in the next Chapter 2; for a study from the Commission, see Jacquemin, Lammerant and Spinoit (1986).
27. Regulation 17/65 (2 March 1965) authorizes the Commission to make block exemptions.
28. JO C75 (29/7/1968) and JO C84 (28/8/1968), see the 14th Report on competition policy (EEC 1985).
29. The regulation is valid for the period between 1 March 1985 and December 1997. Regulation (EEC) no. 418/85; JO L 53 (22/2/1985).
30. On this debate, see in particular Europolitique (11/4/1992, 1/5/1992), as well as Chapters 6 and 4 on electronic components and automobile components in this volume.
31. The objective here is not to give a precise definition or to evaluate the degree of globalization. The sectoral chapters give indications on specific industries, though. For further analysis on this question, see in particular OECD, 1991.
32. For data on the French case for example, see Bavay and Beau (1990).
33. See Marity and Smiley (1983); GEST (1986); Jacquemin, Lammerant and Spinoit (1986); Chesnais (1988); Mowery (1988); Mytelka (1986, 1991); Sachwald (1990a, b, c).
34. For elements on the different waves of M&A, see in particular Chandler (1990) (historical data back to the nineteenth century); Geroski and Vlassopoulos (1990); Prot and Rosen (1990).
35. Bleeke *et al.* (1990) and Yamaichi Securities figures quoted in *Financial Times* (18/10/1990). The figures include majority and minority acquisitions; value corresponds to the sum of disclosed values (value is not always disclosed).

36. On this point, see also Geroski and Vlassopoulos (1990).
37. Figures vary slightly according to sources, but the share of domestic deals is always of this magnitude. For two different sources, see Bleeke *et al.* (1990) and Securities Data Corporation quoted in *Le Figaro* (29/6/1990).
38. Figures slightly differ according to sources. According to Burckhardt (1991), the number of domestic M&A represented 57 per cent of the total in 1987 and 54 per cent in 1990. According to figures from M&A International, quoted in *Financial Times* (7/1/1991), they represented 68 per cent both in 1989 and 1990. The number of domestic M&A represented 66% of the total in 1991 according to *Fusions & Acquisitions (2/1992)*.
39. Calculations from *Fusions & Acquisitions* (1/1992).
40. Calculations from *Fusions & Acquisitions (7–8/1991)*.
41. Calculations from data quoted in *Le Figaro* (29/6/1990).
42. The relatively small difference can be partially explained by the fact that industry represents about two-thirds of the total number of operations.
43. The term 'joint venture' has often been used to designate agreements in general.
44. For theoretical aspects, see Chapter 2 in this volume.
45. For example, the fact that Ghemawat, Porter and Rawlinson (1986) do not find an upward trend in cooperative agreements may be due to the wide definition which they chose. In particular, it includes licences, which can be considered as market transactions.
46. See, in particular, Mowery (1988); Mytelka (1991).
47. See some data on this question in Marity and Smiley (1983); Chesnais (1988); see also sectoral studies.
48. For high-tech sectors, see GEST (1986); Delapierre (1991).
49. Chapter 2 deals with the theoretical explanations of cooperative agreements between firms.
50. Kay (1991) quotes surveys on the motives for cooperation of European firms which show that the persistent fragmentation of the Common Market constitutes one of the main incentives to cooperation.
51. This ratio is derived from the 'aversion ratio' of Kay (1991) which divides the number of mergers by the number of joint ventures.
52. See above on the evolution of M&A during the 1980s.
53. On this point, see Sachwald (1990a) and examples in the sectoral chapters in this book.
54. On this type of questions see Chapter 2 and the references therein.
55. The chapter has emphasized the fact that cooperative research benefits from a special treatment.

# BIBLIOGRAPHY

Bavay, F. and Beau D. (1990), 'L'efficacité des stratégies de croissance externe', *Cahiers économiques et monétaires*, no. 35, Banque de France.

BIPE (1989), 'L'Europe en 1993', *Problèmes Economiques*, 5 May.

Bleeke, J., Isono, J., Ernst, D. and Weinberg, D. (1990), 'The shape of cross-border M&A', *The McKinsey Quarterly*, Winter.

Buigues, P. and Ilzkovitz, F. (1988),'Les enjeux sectoriels du marché intérieur', *Revue d'Economie Industrielle*, 3rd trim.

Buigues, P., Ilzkovitz, F. and Lebrun, J.-F. (1990), 'The impact of the internal market by industrial sector: the challenge for the Member states', *European Economy*, May.

Cecchini, P. (1988), *Le Défi*, Flammarion, Paris.

Chandler, A. (1990), *Scale and Scope: The dynamics of industrial capitalism*, Belknap.

Chesnais, F. (1988), 'Les accords de coopération technique entre firmes indépendantes', *STI/Revue*, OECD, Dec.

Crespy, G. (1990), *Marché unique, marché multiple*, Economica, Paris.

Delapierre, M. (1991), 'Les accords inter-entreprises, partage ou partenariat?', *Revue d'Economie Industrielle*, 1ˢᵗ trim.

Dumez, H. and Jeunemaître, A. (1991), 'Décomposition, recomposition des souverainetés: les politiques de concurrence en Europe', *Politiques et management public,* Sept.

Dussauge, P., Garrette, B. and Ramanantsoa, B. (1988), 'Stratégies relationnelles et stratégies d'alliances technologiques', *Revue Française de Gestion*, March–May.

Freeman, C., Sharp, M. and Walker, W. (eds.) (1991), *Technology and the future of Europe*, Pinter Publishers.

George, K. and Jacquemin, A. (1990), 'Competition policy in the European Community', in W. Comanor *et al.* (eds), *Competition policy in Europe and North America: Economic issues and institutions*, Harwood Academic Publishers.

Geroski, P. and Jacquemin, A. (1985), 'Industrial change, barriers to mobility and European industrial policy', *Economic Policy*, no. 1

Geroski, P. and Vlassopoulos, A. (1990), 'European merger activity: a response to 1992', in *Continental mergers are different*, Centre for Business Strategy, London Business School.

GEST (1986), *Grappes technologiques. Les nouvelles stratégies d'entreprises*, McGraw-Hill.

Ghemawat, P., Porter, M. and Rawlinson, R. (1986), 'Patterns in international coalition activity' in Porter, M., *Competition in Global Industries*, Harvard Business School Press, London.

Globerman, S. and Schwindt, R. (1986) 'The organization of vertically related transactions in the Canadian forest products industries', *Journal of Economic Behavior and Organization*, 7.

Hergert, M. and Morris, D. (1988), 'Friends in International Collaborative Venture Agreements' Contractor, F. and Lorange P. (eds), *Cooperative Strategies in International Business,* Lexington Books.

Hölzler, H. (1990), 'Merger control', in P. Montagnon (ed.), *European competition policy*, Royal Institute for International Affairs/Pinter, London

Jacquemin, A., Lammerant, M. and Spinoit, B. (1986), *Compétition européenne et coopération entre entreprises en matière de recherche-développement*, Document, Commission des Communautés européennes, Bruxelles.

Jacquemin, A., Buigues, P. and Ilzkovitz, F. (1989), 'Concentration horizontale, fusions et politique de la concurrence dans la Communauté européenne', *Economie Européenne,* May.

Jenny, F. (1991), *Europe after 1992. Competition and Competition Policy*, mimeo.

Kay, N. (1991), 'Industrial collaborative activity and the completion of the Single Market', *Journal of Common Market Studies*, June.

Laredo, P. and Callon, M. (1991), 'Les états nationaux ont-ils encore la maîtrise de leur politique de la recherche et de la technologie?', *Politiques et management public*, June.

Lovergne, J. (1989), 'La réglementation de la concurrence', *Annales des Mines*, February.

Marity, P. and Smiley, R. (1983), 'Cooperative agreements and the organization of industry', *Journal of Industrial Economics*, Oct.

Mayes, D. (1991), *The European challenge*, Harvester Wheatsheaf.

Montagnon, P. (ed.) (1990), *European competition policy*, Royal Institute for International Affairs/Pinter, London.

Mowery, D. (ed.) (1988), *International Collaborative Ventures in US Manufacturing*, Ballinger.

Mytelka, L. (1986), 'La gestion de la connaissance dans les entreprises multinationales... Vers la formation d'oligopoles technologiques', *Economie Prospective Internationale*, 3rd trim.

Mytelka, L. (1989), 'Les alliances stratégiques au sein du programme européen ESPRIT', *Economie Prospective Internationale*, 1st trim.

Mytelka, L. (ed.) (1991), *Strategic partnerships. States, firms and international competition*, Pinter, London.

OECD (1991), *TEP, Le cycle des conférences internationales*, Paris.

Pratten, C. (1988), 'A survey of economies of scale', in *Research on the Cost of Non-Europe, Basic Findings*, vol. 2, Commission of the European Community, Brussels.

Prot, B. and Rosen, M. (1990), (sous la direction de) *Le retour du capital*, Odile Jacob.

Sachwald, F. (1989), *Ajustement sectoriel et adaptation des entreprises. Le cas de l'industrie automobile*, CEPII, May.

Sachwald, F. (1990a), 'Les accords dans l'industrie automobile. Une analyse en termes de coûts de transaction', *Economie Prospective Internationale*, 1st trim.

Sachwald, F. (1990b), 'Les accords dans l'industrie automobile. La poursuite de la concurrence par d'autres moyens', *Economie Prospective Internationale*, 2nd trim.

Sachwald, F. (1990c), 'La compétitivité européenne: nations et entreprises', *RAMSES 91*, IFRI/Dunod, Paris.

Sachwald, F. (1991), 'Competition policy and competitiveness in Europe in the 80s', *T5 Occasional papers*, Tokyo Club Foundation for Global Studies, Tokyo.

Sharp, M. (1991), 'The Single Market and European Technology policies', Freeman, C., Sharp, M. and Walker, W. (eds.), *Technology and the future of Europe*, Pinter Publishers.

Stuckey, J. (1983), *Vertical integration and joint ventures in the aluminium industry*, Harvard University Press.

UN (1991), *World investment report 1991: the Triad in foreign direct investment*, United Nations Centre on Transnational Corporations.

# 2. Competitiveness and Competition: which Theory of the Firm?

## Frédérique Sachwald

Since the end of the 1970s, there has been a renewal in the analysis of national competitiveness. In particular, its structural and microeconomic components have been explored more closely. This evolution has led to more explicit examination of the build-up of competitiveness by firms, which in turn has induced questions about the representation of firms in economic theory.

The analysis of the process of competition, and in particular the different sorts of 'imperfect competition', have also led to questions about the firm itself: as has the exploration of innovation.

It thus seems interesting to deal with these different developments from the perspective of the theory of the firm. This is the objective of this chapter. It shows that the analysis of the formation of competitiveness rests on a sound understanding of the competitive processes and thus on the theoretical representation of the firm.

The first section deals with the different analyses of competitiveness and stresses the interactions with the representation of competitive processes. Section 2.2 presents the different approaches to competition. Section 2.3 proposes elements of a theory of the firm which would be compatible with a comprehensive analysis of competitiveness.

## 2.1 THE ANALYSIS OF COMPETITIVENESS

The notion of competitiveness explored here concerns firms. Competitiveness is the capability of firms to face competition successfully. In this sense, competitiveness is often identified with market share gains (or at least their successful defence). However, a firm should not endanger its future development and financial situation in order to gain market share, and market share indicators should be supplemented with other indicators, of profitability in particular, in order to offer a general assessment. Thus, for firms, competitiveness is a more or less general assessment of their performances; even if market share indicators are used to yield instant evaluations.

   The idea of competitiveness is also commonly used for nations, but the transposition of the idea at the macroeconomic level is fraught with difficulties. There is however a quite clear parallel with the two tier definition given to firms' competitiveness above. First, a competitive economy can be considered as one which gains market share which, in this case means either on export markets or on its internal market (import penetration is limited or reduced). But of course the balance of trade is not the only indicator to consider; a competitive economy must be able to grow and to raise the standards of living of its people. A complete definition of national competitiveness must take these different aspects into consideration. Thus, national competitiveness can be defined as the capability to produce and sell competitive products and services (both on national and foreign markets)[1] while increasing real revenues. In this perspective, as for the microeconomic level, the evaluation of competitiveness implies a quite comprehensive assessment of economic performance. In fact, such a definition establishes strong links between competitiveness and productivity.
   The objective of this section is twofold: first, to explore the meaning of competitiveness both at the microeconomic and macroeconomic level; second, to analyse the relationships between firms' competitiveness and national competitiveness.

### 2.1.1 The Macroeconomic Perspective

For a country, competitiveness is an essential macroeconomic stake. If an economy is competitive, its performances are such that openness to trade represents an opportunity and not a binding constraint. In France, the question of the 'external constraint' has been widely debated among economists and policy makers. The idea was that French macroeconomic policy was 'constrained' by external trade imbalances, which themselves resulted from an insufficient level of competitiveness. The equilibrium of the balance of trade is not a final objective, but large and persistent deficits may constitute a source of constraint for economic policy. Competitiveness, through its consequences on the balance of trade, is an instrument to loosen the external constraint. From this point of view, competitiveness clearly appears as a performance indicator.
   Competitiveness has played a larger role as industrial economies have become more open to international trade.[2] Hence the importance of measuring competitiveness and to understand its build-up.
   Traditionally, macroeconomic competitiveness has been defined as price competitiveness.[3] This approach has had to face two types of problems. The first has to do with the measure of prices. Export prices result from the addition of a number of costs incurred along the production and distribution lines. The objective has been to identify the sources of differences among

countries. Unfortunately, the costs which have been the easiest to measure, that is labour costs, have become less relevant (Lorino 1989). In particular, it has become less justified to identify competitiveness with the level of labour costs (Mathis, Mazier and Rivaud-Danset 1988; OECD 1992). The second problem is the relevance of price competitiveness itself as the main if not the sole component of competitiveness. A number of studies have questioned the relationships between exports and prices (Turpin 1989b; Sachwald 1990c; OECD 1992). One of the objectives was to explain why cost increases in Germany or Japan did not lead to reductions in market share, even if in a number of cases price increases did follow cost increases.

Competitiveness, as a capability to gain market share, has two main constituents: prices and the various qualities of products. Besides quality in the common sense, one has to take into account the various characteristics attached to the products such as the degree of novelty, the design, or distribution networks and after-sales service. All these qualities have been progressively recognized as determinants of export performance (as well as of sales on the internal market). One of them has become more prominent: innovativeness. Given these results, the determinants of competitiveness have become much more difficult to analyse. Indeed, the analysis has to deal not only with price competitiveness, but also with 'structural competitiveness'. This term has been coined to summarize the set of non price determinants of competitiveness (Fouquin 1988; OECD 1992).

The notion of structural competitiveness is quite similar to that of competitiveness as it has been defined above, that is to say, an indicator of general performance. The notion of structural competitiveness tends to emphasize sources of competitiveness. It is not just the composition of trade which brings competitiveness, but the structure of the economy. The notion of structural competitiveness brings the question of the formation of competitiveness much more to the forefront. Moreover, the analyses of structural competitiveness have often led to a holistic conception of the formation of competitiveness; competitiveness is the result of multiple interactions within national economies and in this respect, it also has a systemic nature. Some nations are more competitive because of the higher efficiency of their whole system of production (including their capability to innovate). This approach to competitiveness immediately reintroduces firms as crucial actors; one of the main components of structural competitiveness is the set of relationships between firms and their national environment.

Section 2.1.3 deals with the relationships between firms' competitiveness and national competitiveness. Before that, section 2.1.2 examines the contribution of international trade theory to the analysis of competitiveness.

## 2.1.2  The Evolution of International Trade Theory

Paradoxical as it may seem, international trade theory has contributed relatively little to the analysis of competitiveness. This section argues that competitiveness was of little relevance within the framework of traditional trade theory. More recent developments bring international trade theory closer to the analysis of competitiveness.

### 2.1.2.1  Competitiveness as a tautology

For a long time, international trade theory (mainly neo-classical trade theory) has considered that the question of competitiveness was irrelevant. Indeed, comparative advantage[4] implied that national exports would be competitive. Moreover, when the theory bases comparative advantage on national resource endowments as in the Heckscher-Ohlin model (in this case: capital and labour), the production process itself disappears. More exactly, the theory then directly links resource endowments and comparative advantage through a production function. The process of production is thus extremely simplified and can obscure the problems which may exist in establishing a relationship between resource endowments and trade performances.[5]

International trade theory has demonstrated that countries should specialize according to their comparative advantage.[6] As a consequence, the notion of specialization has gained considerable importance. Effective specialization patterns (i.e. the sectoral composition of trade) have been considered as the result of the working of the comparative advantage mechanism. Moreover, since comparative advantages are difficult to measure, specialization has been used as a proxy. In such a context, specialization has become, in itself, an indicator of competitiveness.

France has offered an interesting example of the approach described above. Since the 1970s, numerous studies have concluded that the French economy is insufficiently competitive. The structure of trade has been examined, with two main conclusions. First, the geographical destinations of exports were unfavourable; up to the beginning of the 1980s, French exports relied too much on slow growth markets, such as Africa (Holcblat and Tavernier 1989, Turpin 1989b). Second, the sectoral composition of exports was also unfavourable. A first consideration is quite straightforward: exports were not concentrated in the fastest growing sectors. The second point is related to trade theory. French exports were not sectorally concentrated; France exported a little of many categories of products — it exhibited an intrasectoral specialization (Turpin 1989a). According to the theory of international trade, (inter)sectoral specialization is a sign that a country exploits its comparative advantage (and is competitive as a result). Thus France was judged as insufficiently specialized to be competitive. It was compared with

Germany and Japan which both exhibited strong specializations and high trade surpluses (Lafay and Herzog 1989; Turpin 1989a).

The question is whether the lack of specialization can really be identified as a source of weakness or whether it is merely part of a wider diagnosis (Sachwald 1989b; 1990).

### 2.1.2.2 Paradoxes

The traditional international trade theory has been at odds with a number of empirical results, especially since the 1950s. The first of these is the Leontief paradox which resulted from the fact that the United States exhibited a composition of its external trade in contradiction with the predictions of international trade theory. Briefly, it exported goods with a relatively high labour intensity and imported goods with relatively low labour intensity. One of the results of the subsequent studies was to show the importance of the quality of labour (with the notion of human capital) and more generally of knowledge and innovation in the determination of international trade flows.

The existence of intra-industry trade constitutes another paradox. Indeed, if trade flows obey comparative advantage, exchanges should be inter-sectoral (cars against food) and not intrasectoral (cars against cars). The measure of intra-industry trade is difficult; the main problems have been to define the relevant extent of the industry and to devise an appropriate indicator.[7] Beyond these methodological problems, several studies in the 1980s have shown that intra-industry trade does exist on a substantial scale and has tended to increase since the 1970s. One possible explanation of intra-industry trade could be intra-industry specialization. Certain segments of an industry could require different resources than others. A rather obvious example is high and low quality goods, or more or less sophisticated goods within a sector (cars for example). But, if such intra-industry specialization exists, it relies on quite subtle differences and the relationship with factor endowments is less direct. In particular, differentiation rests on the quality or innovativeness of products and the relevant endowments are the set of technological capabilities and production techniques which both evolve over time.

Finally, one can also consider that the very existence of multinational companies is a paradox within orthodox international trade theory since one of the main hypotheses of the theory is that resources (factors) are immobile.[8]

The paradoxes revealed by empirical studies have underlined the short-comings of international trade theory. The latter can be classified into four main categories, which are related to the hypotheses of the theory: first, the hypothesis of perfect competition; second, the absence of technical progress or innovation; third and more generally, the absence of production as a process (and not a black box); and finally, the hypothesis of immobility of production factors. The 'new international trade theory' has worked on some of these restrictive hypotheses, and in particular on the modelling of the competitive process and the productive process.

### 2.1.2.3 The new international trade theory

The term 'new international trade theory' has been coined in order to underline the departure of a growing number of models from the traditional hypotheses which have been briefly recalled above.

The new international trade theory has been made possible because of the development of the 'new industrial economics'. What was new in new industrial economics was its methodology. Since the 1970s, industrial economics has built more rigorous models, using microeconomic and game theory techniques to explore imperfect competition (Jacquemin 1985). These developments have been essential for the introduction of imperfect competition into international trade theory. Krugman (1990) has underlined how crucial this was because of the strong interdependence between economies of scale and imperfect competition.

The introduction of increasing returns into international trade models has probably been the most important development. Economies of scale (and of scope) are pervasive in modern economies, moreover they are often combined with economies of learning. A number of the pioneer articles on the new international trade theory have explored the consequences of the introduction of economies of scale as characteristic of the production of exporting countries. The most striking result was that economies of scale can determine 'non-comparative-advantage trade' flows (Krugman 1979; 1990). Intra-industry trade and specialization find here at least one explanation. A number of models have shown that comparative and non-comparative-advantage trade can coexist, thus explaining the coexistence of inter- and intra-industry trade. Interactions between oligopolistic firms on segmented markets have also been identified as a possible motive for trade, in the absence of both comparative advantage and economies of scale (Brander and Spencer 1985).

The results of the development of the new international trade theory are quite important both with respect to the representations of international trade and to trade policy.

New international trade theory modifies the representation of trade and offers explanations of some of the paradoxes presented above. The introduction of economies of scale and imperfect competition result in a more satisfying picture in that it is nearer to the existing modes of production and competition.[9] Apart from the demonstration of a logic for non-comparative-advantage trade, the new features of the production process reintroduce history into the analysis of trade and can give a more important and complex role to innovation. In the presence of economies of scale and of learning, cumulative production becomes a source of cost advantage: through these mechanisms, the fact that some production has been started early in time becomes an advantage in international trade (first mover advantage). This of course is even more important in the case of innovation.

New international trade theory has led to interesting conclusions with respect to policy matters. Here again economies of scale and learning have been central. If the quantity produced and the cumulative production through time are sources of competitive advantage on international markets, as opposed to natural factor endowments in the traditional theory, there may be a role for economic policy. In fact the debate has largely concerned trade policy. Some models have shown that under certain circumstances of imperfect competition and economies of scale, protectionist measures may be economically justified.[10] These new trade policies have been qualified as 'strategic'; the term refers to the fact that they are intended to modify the behaviour of the competitors (firms or other states). The basic idea is that when there are economies of scale and imperfect competition, there are also pure profits and the objective of state intervention is then to modify the conditions of appropriation of these profits through profit-shifting. The theoretical results are interesting, but there has been much debate about their applicability. One conclusion is that the conditions under which the strong result in favour of free trade are quite restrictive (Krugman 1986; Richardson 1989; Stegeman 1989).

The new international trade theory yields interesting results and, to a certain extent, complements the traditional theory. Yet, some developments also threaten the traditional construction and its remarkable consistency (Sachwald 1989b; Ravix 1991). Moreover, the new theory does not provide answers to all the paradoxes mentioned above and does not explain the construction of competitiveness.

### 2.1.2.4 Back to absolute advantage?

We have seen above that in the world of comparative advantage, competitiveness was, in a way, necessary. This does not mean that the two notions are synonymous. Comparative advantage introduces a comparison between products within a nation; competitiveness compares the ability of nations to sell similar products on international markets. As a capability to gain market share, competitiveness is much more akin to absolute advantage. In the history of economic thought, comparative advantage has traditionally been considered as an advance with respect to absolute advantage.[11] It seems that when some of the restrictive hypotheses of the traditional trade theory are abandoned, and in particular when characteristics of the production process such as economies of dimension and innovation are introduced, absolute advantage comes back as a determinant of trade.

The importance of the twin notions of absolute advantage and competitiveness is reinforced when the hypothesis of factor immobility is abandoned. Factors are mobile, as evidenced by the existence and development of multinational companies. In such a world, it is more difficult to represent the nation as a block of factors and to determine precisely the correspondence between these factors and trade flows as does the theory of international trade. First, the existence of multinational companies gives much more importance to firms as productive entities, which may be more or less independent of the endowments of their nation of origin. Second, the specific role of firms is reinforced by the cumulative characteristics of the production and innovation processes. These considerations underline the relevance of the analysis of competitiveness as a structural feature of national economies, including a whole set of relationships between firms and their national environment.

### 2.1.3 Competitiveness of Firms and Nations

The discussion above (section 2.1.1) has considered competitiveness as a rather encompassing performance indicator.[11'] It seems particularly important to adopt a holistic perspective on competitiveness when analysing its development; indeed, competitiveness depends on the efficiency of the production system as a whole, compared with that of the competitors. As explained above, this perspective is relevant for both firms and nations. This section shows that the analysis of the relationships between the competitiveness of firms and national competitiveness is essential to understand each of them. It explores these relationships as a fundamental component of structural competitiveness.

The interaction between the competitiveness of firms and nations can be summarized as follows. The firms which operate in a nation determine the competitiveness of that nation. Conversely, firms are largely dependent upon their environment for their development and in this respect a number of structural characteristics of the nation of origin may be crucial (even for firms which become multinational). Obvious as they may seem, these interactions have taken a long time to be recognized as central to the analysis of competitiveness.[12] Moreover, the analysis must go beyond this general principle and try to qualify these interactions. Finally, it is necessary to examine the consequences of globalization on the analysis: in any industrial country, there are both numerous units from multinational companies, as well as units of the national firms located abroad.

The task for analysis is thus huge. Indeed, it hinges on searches into two related black boxes of economic theory: the nation as a block of factors and the firm as a production function.[13] Each of these two black boxes is a complex territory to explore and their interactions are numerous and continuous. The central point to explore is production: what are the conditions of production and the conditions of its evolution, including innovation? The authors who have tackled the question with this perspective have given an important role to firms, but have at the same time discussed their interactions with the general national environment.[14]

It is interesting to note that a number of contributions on the analysis of competitiveness have, in a way, reversed the question. Starting from the question of national competitiveness, they quickly turn to the question of the role of the national environment in the constitution of firms' competitiveness. This reformulation of the question is explicitly discussed in the book by Porter, *The competitive advantage of nations*.[15] The approach taken results from the fact that, competitiveness being defined as an indicator of effectiveness and productivity, production processes are now at the core of the analysis. Firms are the main actors of production and if their operations are not reduced to a function automatically transforming input into output, the analysis must span from inside the firm to its relationships with its environment.[16]

The work by Porter (1990) is very interesting since it relates the approach to a specific methodology. It can be summarized as an attempt to integrate elements from the theory of international trade, industrial economics and management theory. Porter draws conclusions from his previous work on firms' competitiveness (1980; 1985) to analyse national competitiveness; in particular, he extends the examination of the relationships of firms with their environment. This is why, he explains, the relevant scope of analysis is the sector. The core of the analysis presents the different factors which influence the competitive performance of a firm within a sector. Porter (1990) identifies four sets of national attributes which constitute a system through their interactions and which form the environment of firms.

Two sets of attributes are hardly new; they relate to factor and demand conditions. The factor conditions are akin to the notion of factor endowments of international trade theory. However, for Porter, the notion of factors is larger and can evolve; in particular, it explicitly comprises the characteristics of the labour force and infrastructures. The demand conditions describe the nature and size of the home market, and in particular its degree of sophistication. Economists have also identified the importance of demand conditions in international trade. The role of market size is linked to economies of dimension (understood in a wide sense, to include scale, scope and learning effects). The role of the specific characteristics of national demand has also been analysed as a determinant in international trade. This is linked to the fact that trade is fuelled by differences; specific national consumption leads to the corresponding pattern of supply from national firms and thus influences the pattern of trade and specialization.[17] The pattern of national demand has been more particularly emphasized for its role in the innovation process. Vernon (1966) has established a strong relationship between a sophisticated national demand (in the United States), innovation and exports.[18]

The two other sets of factors are newer, or more exactly, they belong to the analysis of competition within industrial sectors, and not to traditional analyses of competitiveness. They relate on the one hand to the competitive conditions and on the other hand to the relationships between one industry and its business partners, which Porter labels the 'related and supporting industries'. The analysis of the competitive conditions takes into account the structural characteristics of the industry and firms' strategies. Porter insists on the strength of rivalry between companies. He identifies rivalry as a strong incentive to competitiveness and contends that it is influenced by national conditions. He mentions in particular the case of Japan where the most competitive industries are populated with numerous firms (in automobiles for example). The importance of 'related and supporting industries' is due to the fact that the whole process of production and distribution should be taken into account in order to analyse competitiveness. In this perspective strong and efficient relationships with suppliers and distributors is a competitive asset. Beyond day-to-day work, these relationships have become increasingly important to achieve innovation.[19]

The four sets of factors form a system (the 'diamond') the working of which Porter (1990) describes in detail and illustrates with case studies. The main interest of this presentation is that it brings together several determinants of competitiveness which had been previously identified separately. As said above, it is particularly clear for the factor and demand conditions. Moreover, it brings together the analyses of three hitherto separated fields: the theory of international trade, industrial economics and managerial science. The result is a particularly rich system with numerous interactions; indeed, the system is sketched as a set of boxes which represent the four types of factors and which all interact reciprocally. However, when compared with simpler explanations like that of international trade theory, the system does not yield a clear hierarchy between the different factors. The analysis is particularly complex because the hierarchy depends on the industries.

The complexity is a characteristic which is common to the different holistic analyses of competitiveness. Some are even more encompassing than that of Porter, which starts from the competitive environment of firms. This is the case for example of the book by A. d'Iribarne which analyses the structure of the French productive system and insists on the role of human resources. In particular, he shows that the evolution of the organization of production depends on adequate education and training. In addition, the author also relates these evolutions to national social structures.

The analysis of competitiveness has become richer but has not become a new unified and clearly structured region of economic theory — it may never be. However, important results have been obtained. One is crucial: the relationships between the development of competitiveness by firms and nations permanently interact, and this feature should be central to the analysis. The work by Porter (1990) is a good example since it starts from firms' competitiveness and draws on both economic and managerial analyses. It thus clearly shows the importance of the analysis of the process of competition to deal with competitiveness. The two following sections explore these questions further.

## 2.2   THE ANALYSIS OF COMPETITION

The analysis of the competitive processes has also evolved and its evolution can be compared to that of the analysis of competitiveness. This section shows that this parallel relies on the representation of the firm. It also considers the consequences on competition policies.

### 2.2.1   Industrial Economics

The traditional analysis of competition belongs to the field of industrial economics[20] and relates to microeconomics, even if it does not use its rigorous framework. In microeconomic models, firms maximize profit and consequently sectoral structures are 'natural' and efficient. This logic is quite clear in the case of perfect competition which does not leave much choice to firms in terms of behaviour. Oligopolistic structures give more ambiguous results.[21]

Inspired by microeconomics, industrial economics largely developed around the structure-conduct-performance paradigm. This paradigm explains that in an industry, market structure induces typical firms' behaviours, which themselves result in foreseeable performances (prices, profitability). This sequence is quite well known, even if its complete description involves numerous elements and can vary from one author to another; Figure 2.1 reproduces the diagram proposed by Scherer (1980).

This figure enables us to see that some of the basic conditions or market structure features can in fact be manipulated by firms or governments. Let us mention for example the category of barriers to entry. The latter designate the different factors such as economies of scale or different types of regulations which inhibit the entry of new firms into a sector, and thus protect the incumbents. Figure 2.1 represents certain retroactions with dotted lines. However, they are not really integrated in the analysis, which insists on structural determinism.[22]

*Figure 2.1    A model of industrial organization analysis*

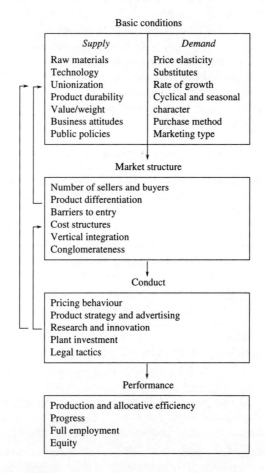

Basic conditions

| *Supply* | *Demand* |
|---|---|
| Raw materials | Price elasticity |
| Technology | Substitutes |
| Unionization | Rate of growth |
| Product durability | Cyclical and seasonal |
| Value/weight | character |
| Business attitudes | Purchase method |
| Public policies | Marketing type |

Market structure

Number of sellers and buyers
Product differentiation
Barriers to entry
Cost structures
Vertical integration
Conglomerateness

Conduct

Pricing behaviour
Product strategy and advertising
Research and innovation
Plant investment
Legal tactics

Performance

Production and allocative efficiency
Progress
Full employment
Equity

*Source:* Scherer (1980)

Industrial economics has long been dominated by the structure-conduct-performance paradigm. Its strength largely comes from the rather direct relationship which it establishes between market structure and performance. As explained above in the case of international trade theory, the process of production (not the production function) as well as firms' strategies are not really considered within this framework of analysis. This general standpoint has not been disturbed with the more recent developments around the notion of contestable markets. Briefly summarized, a contestable market is one on which entry and exit by firms is totally free. This point of view interestingly underlines the importance of barriers to entry and sunk cost, but the conditions for free competition are hardly less restrictive than in the traditional case of pure competition.[23]

Industrial economics has evolved and its explorations of various imperfect competition situations have served as a basis for the new international trade models mentioned above. Industrial economics has also explored relatively new areas. In this respect, the analysis of innovation has probably been at the root of many of the newest developments and has greatly contributed to a new point of view which puts the process of production itself at the centre of the analysis (section 2.3).

### 2.2.2 The Theoretical Foundations of Competition Policy

The evolution of industrial economics can be observed from the point of view of competition policy since the former has served as a theoretical basis for the latter.

#### 2.2.2.1 Concentration

Traditional industrial economics constitutes the theoretical foundations of competition policy. The influence of industrial organization may be partially due to its consequences in terms of competition policy: the behaviours which diminish collective welfare, as maximized by perfect competition, can be eradicated by altering the structure which 'naturally' generates them.[24]

Traditionally, the welfare loss due to imperfect competition is analysed with reference to the 'deadweight loss' due to the existence of a monopoly as opposed to perfect competition.[25] This analysis relies on a number of hypotheses; it can be taken as a starting point in order to identify the supplementary relevant parameters.[26] Quality is a case in point; in order to ensure a given level of quality for their products and services, firms may impose some restrictions on competition at the level of distribution. This is due to the specific characteristics of certain intangible assets such as goodwill (Comanor *et al.* 1990).

The specific properties of knowledge have also generally led to special legal provisions. Knowledge can be considered as a collective good: it can be applied to several classes of problems without losing its integrity[27] and it can be used simultaneously by several agents. This means that ownership may become a serious problem: if an innovation can be implemented by several producers, its 'inventor' only partially owns it and cannot benefit from all the monopoly rents, which of course reduces the incentive to invest in research.The problem of ownership of knowledge has been tackled by the regulation of property rights through patents and licences.

Competition policy may also take into account the possible evolution of costs which can result from a modification of the market structure. This has traditionally been the role of the trade-off considerations, the objective of which is to examine to what extent some restriction on competition is accompanied by more efficient structures of production.[28]

The role of competition policy of course greatly differs according to the durability of monopoly rents. If potential competition is considered as strong, any inefficient market power will be successfully threatened; in other words, market power is transitory.[29] The comparison between the different representations of the competitive process largely hinges on barriers to entry. A careful examination of barriers to entry and of their development shows that they can be conceived as central to the competitive game; competition is exercised as much through barriers to entry as through prices. Strategic behaviours, which are aimed at influencing the behaviour of competitors, largely depend on the existence of barriers to entry.[30] But the analysis is very much more complex than that of Figure 2.1; barriers to entry are market structures only in the short term, they can be manipulated by firms as part of their strategy.

Large economies of scale and other technological features can constitute barriers to entry. Innovation is also a prominent source of barriers to entry. In this perspective, it seems important to analyse the process by which barriers to entry are created. Section 2.3 proposes such an analysis and shows that it entails a different representation of the firm itself.

### 2.2.2.2 Transaction cost theory

Transaction cost theory has proposed a new point of view on industrial organization, with consequences for the conception of competition policy.

The objective of transaction cost economics is to explain the choice between different types of transactions (or organization).[31] The point of view is quite different from that of microeconomics or industrial economics. Two hypotheses are crucial. First, the individual is considered as less competent, unable to be totally informed and to consider all the possible options before taking a decision; we are in the world of 'bounded rationality'. Moreover, individuals may adopt opportunistic behaviours, that is, given the opportunity, they may cheat.

Second, the firm is considered as a 'governance structure' rather than a production function (Williamson 1986). This means that the main aspect to analyse is organizational, rather than technical. Williamson explains that the basic unit of analysis is the transaction (rather than the firm or the individual). Williamson (1985) defines a transaction as the transfer of a good or service across a 'technologically-separable interface'. For example, a transaction occurs between two firms when one supplies the other; that transaction would occur under different conditions if the firm integrated the supplier. In this sense, transactions are not limited to exchanges between firms.

The process of competition has been a significant area of application for transaction cost economics. Transaction cost economics analyses the different organizational moves taken by firms and tries to explain their rationality. This contrasts with traditional economics which focuses on the structural characteristics of markets. Let's take the example of vertical integration. Vertical integration can be considered as a way to concentrate, and to reduce the scope for competition through markets. Transaction cost economics adopts a different perspective; it examines the degree of efficiency of different organizational and legal arrangements. It then shows that vertical integration can result from efficiency considerations. It can be the case for example when there may be opportunistic behaviour between two non-integrated companies.

Acquisition, leading to vertical or horizontal concentration, may also be a source of efficiency for technical reasons. Traditional theory has considered the case of economies of scale (and more recently economies of scope). Efficiency improvements also often result from the reorganization of transactions within the new entity. In such cases, specific assets are often involved. Cohen (1983) defines 'specific' or 'internal' resources as those to which the firm attributes more value than the market does. The degree of specificity can be summarized by the difference between the market value of the resource and its present value for the firm. The difference results from the combination of resources with information which is internal to the firm. By itself, information generated by the firm has little value; it has to be incorporated with assets, but through this operation, the latter gain a superior value too.

Transaction cost theory shows that when specific assets are involved in a transaction the latter becomes more risky, which means that markets are less efficient. Specific assets — such as know-how or dedicated equipment — often require complex contracts, or even long-term cooperative agreements between the transacting parties. In extreme cases, specific assets may require vertical integration. Transaction cost theory explains how the specific character of certain resources leads to the adoption of particular organizational forms. The firm is one of them (vertical integration), but the theory can also be useful in understanding such choices as joint ventures and various types of cooperative agreements, or even decisions with respect to the internal organization of the firm. Widely understood the notion of transaction cost thus enables us to elaborate links between the assets of the firm, its internal organization and its modes of acquiring new resources.

## 2.3   IN SEARCH OF A THEORY OF THE FIRM

Sections 2.1 and 2.2 have shown that economic theory does not provide a
satisfactory framework for analysis to understand the evolution of competitiveness. It appears that the central question is the representation of the
process of competition and, eventually, of firms. This section considers the
theory of the firm in this perspective. The central point is a shift in the focus
of the analysis from the sectoral characteristics to the specific situation of
firms within their sector, and in particular with respect to the process of
production and its evolution. As a consequence, this section draws on
several strands of literature, and in particular the economics of innovation
and management science.

A careful examination of the notion of barrier to entry enables us to
understand better the foundation of firms' specific features. Then, the
analysis of the creation and development of these features leads to a radical
revision of the representation of the firm.

### 2.3.1   From Barriers to Entry to Competitive Barriers

In the structure-conduct-performance paradigm, barriers to entry belong to
sectoral structures (Figure 2.1). Barriers to entry are built by firms and they
can thus be interpreted differently.

There are several definitions of barriers to entry (Sachwald 1989b); the
notion generally expresses the fact that established firms enjoy a relatively
protected position because, in order to penetrate the market, potential
competitors incur higher cost — which can be due to economies of scale or
to regulations for example. At one point in time, in a static perspective,
barriers to entry do constitute a source of structural asymmetry between
firms. However, in a dynamic perspective, firms can attempt to use the
sources of barriers to entry to create and manipulate asymmetries. Thus,
barriers to entry have been examined as part of firms' strategies of deter-
rence; in particular they can prevent costly price wars (Jacquemin 1985).

The notion of barriers to entry has been extended to explore the question
of intra-sectoral heterogeneity. Caves and Porter (1977) oppose the 'traditional approach' which considers that within a sector, size is the only
economically relevant variable characteristic. The hypothesis of identical
firms enables us to consider barriers to entry as structural characteristics.
But, in such a framework, product differentiation becomes difficult to
analyse.[32] Caves and Porter divide sectors into 'groups' within which firms
have common characteristics. Firms recognize that they are more interdependent within their group than with firms from other groups of the
industry. The approach does not amount to a redefinition of the frontiers of

industries, since firms also recognize a stronger interdependence within each sector than with other sectors.

Intrasectoral heterogeneity explains that it is less difficult to penetrate certain segments and that potential entrants elaborate sequential entries, beginning with a less protected 'group'.[33] Entry into a sector enables a firm to accumulate experience, to launch investments and so on. The advantages attached to previous participation in the industry explain why entry into a particular segment is often attempted by firms from the same industry which diversify. These advantages also benefit foreign firms, which can be in a better position to penetrate a national market than domestic firms alien to the industry (Jacquemin 1982; Owen 1983).

The exploration of the notion of barrier to entry is proving a channel to reinterpret the competitive process. In particular, strategic manipulation of barriers to entry establishes an influence of firms' behaviour on sectoral structures (using the categories in Figure 2.1).

The same type of reasoning applies to 'mobility barriers' within sectors. From the point of view of competition analysis, it seems judicious to regroup the different types of barriers under the general heading of 'competitive barriers'. The expression may seem paradoxical. It is so only in the traditional framework which does not allow competition to play through qualitative factors. Barriers to price competition are omnipresent, but firms also resort to other means than prices to compete. Competitive barriers are both obstacles to and means of competition. Thus, the notion of competitive barriers leads to a radical questioning of the competitive pattern. Moreover, it opens a new domain of investigation: how do firms develop barriers and how do they overcome others? The answer is in the establishment of dynamic relationships between firms' specific characteristics and competitive barriers. The economist should therefore penetrate inside firms, and add to industrial economics a theory of the firm.

### 2.3.2 Firms as Sets of Resources and Competences

Two types of questions have led us to focus on the evolution of the firm, of its capabilities in relationship with the process of competition: innovation and the growth of firms. In both cases, authors have often departed from the tradition of industrial economics (Sachwald 1989b). The central point of this section is to show that the analysis of these evolutionary matters leads us to see the firm as a set of competences, which have to be built.

As early as 1959, in her book *The theory of the growth of the firm,* Edith Penrose gave a crucial role to firms' specific characteristics. She considers that, in order to study the process of growth, it is necessary to allow firms to possess a whole array of attributes, which make it difficult to represent them with simple cost and revenue curves. She proposes a definition of the firm to take account of both its main function and its organization as a distinctive unit: a firm is a set of productive resources, the allocation of which is organized by administrative decisions.

The direct inputs are not the resources themselves but the services which resources yield (Penrose 1959). This conception explains why a firm can produce for various markets. The condition is simply that the different products require services and combinations of services available from the resources of the firms.[34] In this perspective, efficient multiproduct firms appear as quite trivial phenomena.[35] Moreover, firms develop specific characteristics by combining resources and services in order to produce various goods.

Edith Penrose has also broken new ground with her concept of the evolution of resources. She examines the case of human resources and insists on the role of 'experience'. The members of a team learn to work in a specific environment and by so doing develop the efficiency of the group itself. Progress by the team is due in particular to the development of confidence, which enables better circulation of information and easier coordination. The importance of experience in building an efficient team results from the modes of transmission of knowledge. Some 'objective' pieces of knowledge can be expressed formally, making it possible to transmit and learn them through various types of documents. A second type of knowledge can only be acquired through personal experience because it is largely tacit.

Knowledge is specific in the sense of transaction cost theory (see section 2.2.2.2) since partners often have to incur specific investments in order to acquire a piece of knowledge and to be able to use it efficiently. For example, knowledge transfers often necessitate important investment in human resources so as to disseminate the new techniques and information within the firm. The problem is particularly acute in the case of tacit knowledge, which is little or not at all codified and which has to be transmitted through experience. This is the case with the important category of know-how, for example. In such circumstances, transactions in knowledge are costly since they may require elaborate contracts and long-term relationships between the parties.

Since the 1960s, with the development of large firms and the increasing role played by scientific knowledge and technology, the question of transfers has become very important to understand the evolution of firms' competitiveness. Several authors have insisted on the role played by the organization of the firm in this respect. Edith Penrose's notion of 'experience' can be compared with David Teece's 'organizational knowledge' (Teece 1982). Nelson and Winter (1982) underline the fact that within an organization, a large part of actions are answers to signals from the organization. Often the regular and flexible working of activity is dependent upon the fact that knowledge is not made explicit during the process of decision. The 'routines' which are developed in this way constitute the basis of the 'organizational memory' (Nelson and Winter 1982; Teece 1982).[36] Routines are favourable to collective work, and thus to all sorts of learning. In so doing they prominently participate in the creation of the firms' specific charateristics.

Considered together, the above developments underline the fact that, beyond firms' resources, it is their evolution and their usage which make them fundamental variables in the analysis. The crucial point is to understand the mechanisms by which firms use their resources to build 'competences'.[37] Teece, Pisano and Shuen (1990) have thus put learning processes at the centre of their 'dynamic capabilities approach'. The firm is presented as a space of learning, the quality of which depends on the internal organization of the process. Beyond the organizational question, learning by the firm is constrained by two types of factors. First, previous accumulation of knowledge can lock the firm into unfavourable patterns of thinking or research paths.[38] The firm learns, but progressively it builds on its history, and can be trapped by it. This very general remark should allow for discontinuities, of which the history of large firms gives examples (Chandler 1962; Abernathy 1978; Cayez 1988). Second, the development of firms' capabilities is hampered by the need for external contributions. In order to learn or innovate, the firm needs to call on complementary resources. This is only possible if the relevant resources exist somewhere, but, beyond this point of departure, there are many problems to solve before successful use can be made of them. Such problems arise even before the resources are to be integrated: they need to be identified and valued, the firm has to decide upon the most suitable way to gain control of them (purchase, cooperative agreement and so on).[39] Then, a fundamental point is that the firm has a limited capacity to absorb new resources.

The concept of the firm as a set of competences leads us to change the focus of research on the development of competitiveness. In particular, this perspective gives a great importance to organizational aspects, both for internal relations and for the interactions of the firm with the environment (suppliers, competitors, regulations, and so on). More generally, reflection on the firm and competitiveness tends to draw the theory out of the strict domain of industrial economics. Because of the nature of the factors which have been progressively put forward, the theory of the firm has to call on management and history in particular.[40] Moreover, the firm as an organization has to become integrated into a complex environment, which reinforces the need for various points of view.

## 2.4  CONCLUSION

This chapter has been mostly devoted to the explanation of the development of competitiveness. In this respect the record is not entirely satisfactory. The interactions between the firm, conceived as a set of competences, and the development of national competitiveness have been identified as a fundamental area for research. These interactions are to be studied in two ways: to understand the development of firms' competitiveness and to examine the connections with the national environment.

The concept of the firm as a set of competences perpetually evolving enables us to deal with dynamic questions, and in particular with the development of competitiveness. But this concept introduces methodological problems. The economist, when deprived of statistical regularity and of the possibility to consider a sector as homogeneous, cannot directly relate the technical characteristics of production, firms' behaviours and economic performances. He/she has to turn to new methods and call for the cooperation of other disciplines. Technical and organizational considerations become more relevant, and history has more important a contribution to make to the analysis.[41] Moreover, the analysis of the integration of the firm with its environment also requires new knowledge on the social aspects of learning, and work in particular. The relevant information is particularly varied and complex; hence the methodological difficulties.

Competitiveness has become a central economic issue, which has induced closer analysis. This has resulted in further complexity as well as doubts about the capacity of traditional economic methods to understand the problem. According to the above developments, economic research should strengthen its efforts in two directions. First, the theory of the firm should certainly stay on the agenda; in particular, the notion of competences or capabilities has to be worked on. Second, it seems that a better comprehension of the interactions between firms' competitiveness and national competitiveness very much depends on empirical studies, which should tackle various specific points and try several methods. Such efforts should enable us to better understand the interactions between national endowments and characteristics on the one hand and firms' specific competences on the other. The analysis of competitiveness should thus benefit from reflection on a similar question being led by researchers on innovation processes.[42] The analysis of multinational companies' behaviour should also be explored with the objective of explaining what they transfer and what they bring from one country to another.[43]

The empirical chapters of this book aim at contributing to this broad research agenda. They focus on external growth operations as one of the means to control and use new resources. In this way they deal with one aspect of the growth of competitiveness.

# NOTES

1. With the hypothesis that if the different markets are open, that there is a reasonable degree of free trade.
2. Historically, there has been a correlation between the movements of internationalization and the preoccupation of competitiveness.
3. Which for international trade comprises the price of goods and the exchange rate.
4. A country has a comparative advantage for a product A if it is relatively more efficient to produce A than other products. In a world of free trade, countries export products for which they have a comparative advantage and import those for which they have a comparative disadvantage. In such a world products should always find their right price and market share.
5. The discussion of the formation of comparative advantage leads to the question of the production function, see below.
6. And thus according to their resources if technology is not allowed to differ between countries (Hekcher-Ohlin).
7. On these questions, see in particular Grubel (1979); Greenaway (1986); Abd-El-Rahman (1986); Sachwald (1989a,b).
8. As a consequence the theoretical analysis of multinational companies has developed largely outside the main international trade theory. See in particular Caves (1982); Dunning (1981; 1988).
9. There are also drawbacks. In particular, since there may be no links between the resources of a country and its exports and imports, the direction of trade is not determined, as it was within traditional international trade theory.
10. On these questions, see in particular Brander and Spencer (1984); Krugman (1984; 1986).
11. The first has been forged by Ricardo. Before him, A. Smith had considered absolute advantage as a basis for trade.
11'. Krugman (1994) has argued that in this sense competitiveness is actually close to productivity
12. See the discussion above of international trade theory. For a discussion of the evolution of the conception of competitiveness, see in particular Sachwald (1989b; 1990); OECD (1992).
13. There is a strong parallel between the two functions; they result from the hypotheses of economic theory. The firm is described as a production function which transforms inputs into outputs, and the nation is described as a set of factor endowments which, through the production functions (of firms) are transformed into products.
14. Among the abundant literature and for various approaches, see in particular Mistral (1983); Chesnais (1986); Dertouzos, Lester and Solow (1989); d'Iribarne (1989); Porter (1990); Sachwald (1990); Delmas (1991); OECD (1992). See also section 2.2.
15. It is also the case of Dertouzos, Lester and Solow (1989); Delmas (1991), for example.
16. Section 2.3 deals with the related question of the representation of the firm and its working.
17. This argument had been proposed by Linder in the 1960s.
18. The analysis addressed more particularly the question of multinational companies. After exports, firms would transfer production to less developed countries.
19. This is due both to the demanding rhythm of innovation and to the fact that new technologies and methods often require the cooperation of several disciplines which may be disseminated in different firms. On these debated questions, see for example OECD (1992).
20. Or more exactly to industrial organization which designates the 'traditional' mainstream in industrial economics (Sachwald 1989b).
21. Oligopolistic situations have been explored with game theory and in particular with models of non-cooperative games. For reviews, see Scherer (1986); Schmalensee (1988).
22. There exist differences between authors as to what extent they take firms' behaviours into account (Scherer 1980).
23. On the notion of contestable market, see Baumol and Panzar (1982); for a critical discussion, see in particular Sachwald (1989a).
24. For a discussion of the idea of natural market structure (as meaning a direct link between the underlying conditions of competition and the structure of the market) and its application in industrial economics (including the newer therory of contestable markets), see in particular Sachwald (1989b).
25. $W = 1/2 \ (^{\wedge}P.^{\wedge}Q) = L \ (1/2.Pm \ Qm) = (1/2.Pm \ Qm)/e$ where $W$ is the deadweight loss, $Pm$ and

$Qm$ the price and quantity monopoly values, $L$ the price cost margin (Lerner index) and $e$ the price elasticity of demand. See for example Ordover (1990); Hay and Morris (1979).
26. The discussion which follows refers to the case of monopoly; it could be extended to that of oligopolies.
27. But not without costs, see below, section 2.3.
28. For the case of the European competition policy, see Chapter 1 in this volume.
29. This is the case in particular in the theory of contestable markets (on which there are no entry or exit barriers) and that of the Chicago school. On the contrary, in limit pricing models, barriers to entry allow the persistence of monopoly pricing above pure competition.
30. For developments on this aspect of the industrial economics literature, see in particular Jacquemin (1985).
31. This brief presentation draws in particular from Coase (1937); Williamson (1981; 1985; 1986). For empirical applications, see for example Monteverde and Teece (1982); Stuckey (1983); Pisano (1990); Sachwald (1990a).
32. For example, in the case of monopolistic competition, identical firms produce differentiated products.
33. The low quality end for example (see the case of the Japanese in the auto industry).
34. Richardson (1972) presents a similar analysis by connecting firms' capabilities and the types of activities in which they engage.
35. Multiproduct firms are more difficult to develop in the traditional framework. On this point, see Baumol and Panzar (1982); Teece (1980; 1982); Sachwald (1989b).
36. The notion of routine is to be compared with Edith Penrose's 'experience'.
37. Competences result from a set of technological skills, but also complementary assets and organizational routines. This notion is used in a number of papers, among which are Dosi, Teece and Winter (1990); Cantwell (1990); Teece, Pisano and Shuen (1990).
38. The economic literature has developed the notion of 'technological paradigm' (Dosi 1982). Teece, Pisano and Shuen (1990) refer to 'path dependencies' of a firm. Abernathy (1978) has shown an interest in this type of consideration in his study of the automobile industry.
39. Various economic analyses of innovation have dealt with these questions; see Teece (1987). For an application to the automobile sector, see Sachwald (1990a, 1990b); for other sectors see Mowery (1988).
40. Management science has also been criticized for strong reference to rational behaviour and maximizing procedures, but this discussion goes beyond this chapter. See Lorino (1989).
41. In this respect, the economics of technology and innovation offer an interesting exemple of the evolution of analysis.
42. In this respect, see for example Dosi, Pavitt and Soete (1990); Nelson (1990).
43. See in particular Cantwell (1990); Patel and Pavitt (1990).

# BIBLIOGRAPHY

Abd-El-Rahman, K. (1986), 'Réexamen de la définition et de la mesure des échanges croisés de produits similaires entre nations', *Revue Economique*, 1.

Abernathy, W. (1978), *The productivity dilemma*, The Johns Hopkins University Press, Baltimore.

Baumol, W. and Panzar, J. W. (1982), *Contestable markets and the theory of industry structure,* Harcourt Brace Jovanovich.

Brander, J. and Spencer, B. (1984), 'Tariff protection and imperfect competition', in H. Kierzkowski (ed.), *Monopolistic competition and international trade*, Oxford University Press.

Brander, J. and Spencer, B. (1985), 'Export subsidies and international market share rivalry', *Journal of International Economics,* 18.83–100.

Cantwell, J. (1990), *The technological competence theory of international production and its implications*, mimeo, Reading University.

Caves, R. (1982), *Multinationals and economic analysis*, Cambridge University Press.

Caves, R. and Porter, M. (1977), 'From entry barriers to mobility barriers', *Quarterly Journal of Economics.*

Cayez, P. (1988), *Rhône-Poulenc 1895–1975*, Armand Colin/Masson, Paris.

Chandler, A. (1962), *Strategy and Structure,* MIT Press, Cambridge.

Chesnais, F. (1986), 'Science, technologie et compétitivité', *STI Revue,* OECD, Autumn.

Coase, R. (1937), 'The nature of the firm', *Economica.*

Cohen, W. (1983), 'Investment and industrial expansion', *Journal of Economic Behavior and Organization,* 4.

Comanor, W., George, K., Jacquemin, A., Jenny, F., Kantzenbach, E., Ordover, J. and Waverman, L. (1990), *Competition policy in Europe and North America: Economic issues and institutions*, Harwood Academic Publishers.

Delmas, P. (1991), *Le maître des horloges*, Odile Jacob.

Dertouzos, M., Lester, R. and Solow, R. (1989), *Made in America*, MIT Press, Cambridge.

Dosi, G. (1982) 'Technological paradigms and technological trajectories. A suggested interpretation of the determinants and directions of technical change', *Research Policy,* vol. 11.

Dosi, G., Pavitt, K. and Soete, L. (1990), *The economics of technical change and international trade*, Harvester Wheatsheaf.

Dosi, G., Teece, D. and Winter, S. (1990), 'Les frontières des entreprises: vers une théorie de la cohérence de la grande entreprise', *Revue d'Economie Industrielle*, no. 51, 1st trim.

Dunning, J. (1981), *International production and the multinational enterprise*, George Allen and Unwin, London.

Dunning, J. (1988), *Explaining international production*, Unwin Hyman.

Fouquin, M. (sous la direction de) (1988), *Industrie mondiale: la compétitivité à tout prix*, CEPII/Economica, Paris.

Greenaway, M. (1986), *The economics of intra-industry trade*, Basil Blackwell, Oxford.

Grubel, H. and Loyd, L. (1975), *Intra-Industry Trade*, MacMillan.

Hay, D. and Morris, D. (1979), *Industrial Economics*, Oxford University Press.

Holcblat, N. and Tavernier, J.-L. (1989), 'Entre 1979 et 1986, la France a perdu des parts de marché industriel', *Economie et Statistique,* 1–2.

Iribarne (d'), A. (1989), *La compétitivité, défi social, enjeu éducatif*, Presses du CNRS, Paris.

Jacquemin, A. (1982), 'Imperfect market structure and international trade', *Kyklos,* 1.

Jacquemin, A. (1985), *Sélection et pouvoir dans la nouvelle économie industrielle*, Cabay-Economica.

Krugman, P. (1984), 'Import protection as export promotion: International competition in the presence of oligopolies and economies of scale', in H. Kierzkowski (ed.), *Monopolistic competition and international trade,* Oxford University Press.

Krugman, P. (ed.) (1986), *Strategic trade policy and the new international economics*, MIT Press, Cambridge.

Krugman, P. (1990), *Rethinking international trade theory*, MIT Press, Cambridge.

Krugman, P. (1994), 'Competitiveness: A Dangerous Obsession', Foreign Affairs, March-April 1994.

Lafay, G. and Herzog, C. (1989), *La fin des avantages acquis,* CEPII/Economica.

Lorino, P. (1989), *L'Economiste et le manager*, La Découverte.

Mathis, J., Mazier, J. and Rivaud-Danset, D. (1988), *La compétitivité industrielle*, Dunod, Paris.

Mistral, J. (1983), *Competitiveness of the productive system and international specialisation*, OECD, DSTI 7.

Monteverde, K. and Teece, D. (1982), 'Supplier switching costs and vertical integration in the automobile industry', *Bell Journal of Economics*.

Mowery, D. (1988), 'Collaborative Ventures between US and Foreign Manufacturing Firms: an Overview', in D. Mowery (ed.), *International Collaborative Ventures in US Manufacturing*, Ballinger, Hagerstown.

Nelson, R. (1990), What is public and what is private about technology? CCC, Working Paper no. 90-9, University of California, Berkeley.

Nelson, R. and Winter, S. (1982), *An evolutionary theory of economic change*, Harvard University Press.

OECD (1992), *Technology and the economy. The key relationships*, TEP, Paris.

Ordover, J. (1990), *Economic foundations of competition policy*, Harwood Academic Publishers.

Owen, N. (1983), Economies of scale, *Competitiveness, and trade patterns within the European Community*, Clarendon Press, Oxford.

Patel, P. and Pavitt, K. (1990), *Large firms in the production of the world's technology: an important case of Non-Globalisation*, mimeo, Sussex University, May.

Penrose, E. (1959), *The theory of the growth of the firm*, Basil Blackwell, Oxford.

Pisano, G. (1990), 'The R&D boundaries of the firm', *Administrative Science Quarterly*, March.

Porter, M. (1980), *Competitive strategy,* Macmillan, London.

Porter, M. (1985), *Competitive advantage, The Free Press,* New York.

Porter, M. (1990), *The competitive advantage of nations*, Macmillan, London.

Richardson, G. (1972), 'The organisation of industry', *Economic Journal*, 9.

Richardson, J. (1989), 'Etat des recherches empiriques sur la libéralisation des échanges dans des conditions de concurrence imparfaites: vue d'ensemble', *Revue économique de l'OCDE*, Spring.

Sachwald, F. (1989a), *Ajustement sectoriel et adaptation des entreprises, le cas de l'industrie automobile*, document de travail, CEPII, June.

Sachwald, F. (1989b), *Des dotations factorielles à la compétitivité: le rôle des entreprises, Cahier de l'IFRI*, no. 4, IFRI.

Sachwald, F. (1990a), 'Les accords dans l'industrie automobile: une analyse en termes de coûts de transaction', *Economie prospective internationale*, CEPII, La Documentation française, Paris, 1st trim.

Sachwald, F. (1990b), 'Les accords dans l'industrie automobile: la poursuite de la concurrence par d'autres moyens', *Economie et prospective internationale*, CEPII, La Documentation française, Paris, 2nd trim.

Sachwald, F. (1990c), 'La compétitivité européenne: nations et entreprises', *RAMSES 1991*, IFRI/DUNOD, Paris.

Scherer, F. (1980), *Industrial Market structure and economic performance*, Rand MacNally College.

Scherer, F. (1986), 'On the current state of knowledge in industrial organization', in H. Jong and W. Shepherd (eds), *Mainstream in industrial organization*, Kluwer Academic Press Publishers, Dordrecht/Boston.

Schmalensee, R. (1988), 'Industrial Economics: an overview', *Economic Journal*, 9.

Stegeman, K. (1989), 'Policy rivalry among industrial states: what can we learn from models of strategic trade policy?', *International Organization*, Winter.

Stuckey, J. (1983), *Vertical integration and joint ventures in the aluminium industry*, Harvard University Press.

Teece, D. (1980), 'Economies of scope and the scope of the firm', *Journal of Economic Behavior and Organization*, 9.

Teece, D. (1982), 'Towards an economic theory of the multiproduct firm', *Journal of Economic Behavior and Organization*, 3.

Teece, D. (1987), 'Capturing Value from Technological Innovation: Integration, Strategic Partnering, and Licensing Decisions' in B. Guile and H. Brooks (eds), *Technology and Global Industry*, National Academy Press.

Teece, D., Pisano, G. and Shuen, A. (1990), 'Firm capabilities, resources, and the concept of strategy', mimeo, University of California at Berkeley, September.

Turpin, E. (1989a), 'Le commerce extérieur français: une spécialisation industrielle fragile', *Economie et statistique*, February.

Turpin, E. (1989b) 'Heurs et malheurs du solde industriel, les entreprises à l'épreuve des années 80', *INSEE*.

Vernon, R. (1966), 'International Investment and International Trade in the Product Cycle', *Quarterly Journal of Economics*, May.

Williamson, O. (1981), 'The modern corporation: origins, evolution, attributes', *Journal of Economic Literature*, 12.

Williamson, O. (1985), *The Economic institutions of capitalism*, The Free Press, New York.

Williamson, O. (1986),'Vertical integration and related variations on a transaction cost economics theme, in Stiglitz, J. and Mathewson, G. (eds.), *New developments in the analysis of market structures*, MacMillan, London.

# 3. The Automobile Industry

## Frédérique Sachwald

In the automobile industry the competitive game was quite stable in the United States and Europe until the 1970s. From the end of the 1960s a number of elements combined to unsettle the game. The rate of growth of demand was that of a mature industry, but a number of characteristics did not correspond with the predictions of the product cycle model.[1] In particular, there were strong new entrants and the pace of innovation tended to increase. As a result, the 1980s appeared as a period of transition during which the industry has had to adapt to a new competitive game. This 'dematurity' phase was characterized in particular by a renewal of the production paradigm, by a more rapid rhythm of innovation and by progress towards globalization.

During the 1980s, cooperative agreements have been increasing, which was a rather new phenomenon for the automobile industry; during the second half of the decade there were also a number of acquisitions. This chapter analyses the role of external growth operations in firms' strategies. Given their originality and their remarkable growth, cooperative agreements are particularly scrutinized. One important question is whether they have been an adaptation tool in a period of transition or whether they correspond to a new but now relatively stable competitive game.

In order to explain the challenges which firms have been facing since the 1980s, the first two sections present the production system and the competitive game in the automobile industry up to the 1970s (3.1) and the different elements of disruption (3.2). The third part then briefly draws conclusions as to the strategic agenda. Section 3.4 analyses the role of cooperative agreements and acquisitions in the implementation of strategies. It shows that each type of operation was used for specific objectives. Section 3.5 considers the geographical distribution of the operations and the position of European firms within the network of alliances.

## 3.1   TRADITIONAL CHARACTERISTICS OF THE INDUSTRY

### 3.1.1   The Production System

Born at the end of the nineteenth century, the car industry has been one of the most important ones during the twentieth, not only because it was one of the largest (in terms of turnover or employment), but also because it epitomized mass production. The automobile production system and its evolution have been carefully studied (Abernathy 1978; Altshuler *et al.* 1984; Womack, Jones and Roos 1990); the objective here is only to recall the main characteristics of mass production, the paradigm for car production from the 1920s to the 1970s.[2]

Mass production does not simply mean that huge numbers of products are being manufactured. For each firm, mass production is a system formed by the interaction between strategy, products, organization and human resources. Moreover, beyond the single company, mass production also implies specific relationships between firms, and especially with respect to suppliers. To summarize briefly, the strategy is to offer relatively cheap products by exploiting economies of scale. The objective of mass production implies both product standardization and dedicated, high-yield machinery which requires extreme division of tasks. As a consequence, low qualified workers fulfil fragmented and repetitive tasks on assembly lines; responsibilities and initiatives are largely pushed up the hierarchy through foremen, engineers and managers.

As a system mass production, once stabilized, reinforced itself. Thus the manufacture of cars has become the most obvious example of the 'productivity dilemma'. Abernathy (1978) coined this expression to summarize the necessary arbitration between productivity and flexibility within the mass production system. Ford has been the first to suffer from the inflexibility of the system it had created. In the 1920s Ford produced only one model, the Ford T, and it was unable to react quickly to the evolution of demand (Abernathy 1978; Roos 1990). At the end of the 1920s, General Motors became the largest automobile company by succeeding in introducing some differentiation into mass production (Sloan 1963). But the quest for economies of scale remained a general feature of automobile production. One of the main features of General Motors' innovations in the management of mass production was the combination of model differentiation with the use of common mechanical components, which enabled the exploitation of economies of scale and economies of scope.

The question of economies of scale has often been thought about too narrowly. Observations and calculations for the automobile industry concentrated on manufacturing operations in their existing organization. The question then was: what would be the change in cost if the factory or the firm (the distinction was not always made clearly) were to produce $x$ times more (with similar techniques)? Not surprisingly, relying on different starting points, studies arrived at different results, in particular with respect to the supposedly 'optimum scale' of a firm, that from which cost reductions due to size become negligible.[3] This variability can be explained by the fact that calculations did not take the whole firm into consideration and thus could not relate size to product strategy and organization.[4]

The preoccupation with scale as such has largely abated since the beginning of the 1980s when automobile production began to be seen as a system and not merely as the sum of assembly lines and other isolated manufacturing operations. In fact, firms never used the strict theoretical notion of economies of scale. In this respect, it is useful to contrast economies of scale with the notion of break-even point. The break-even point is the level of production from which the firm begins to make profits; it establishes a relationship between the margin made on variable costs and fixed costs. It is thus a global accounting notion; it takes into consideration the whole production process, including indirect costs. With such a notion, size is not the only relevant parameter to act on. In the logic of mass production, it may be thought that the only way to reduce costs is to increase the level of turnover. But, if a firm is able to question its production system, it may consider other changes in order to increase productivity and reach a lower break-even point. This is exactly what a number of car makers did at the beginning of the 1980s. For Renault and PSA, the break-even point, which was at 2 million cars a year, has been brought down to 1.2 million at the end of the 1980s; for VW, it has been lowered from 2.5 million to 1.7 million (Caput 1989).

Mass production has been deeply entrenched in the Western automobile industry. Robotization and flexible automation have suggested that the productivity dilemma engendered by mass production may be altered (Gerwin and Tarondeau 1984). The Japanese production techniques have questioned mass production much more radically.

### 3.1.2 Competitive Positions

The automobile was born in Europe, but European domination was short-lived. The United States took the lead as early as 1907 and its production progressed very rapidly after that date, especially after the introduction of the Ford T in 1908 (Roos 1990). In 1920s, the United States accounted for about 90 per cent of total automobile production (Altshuler *et al.* 1984).

Until the 1970s, the automobile industry has been essentially American and European. The American domination weakened after the Second World

War, *vis-à-vis* European producers from the 1950s on, but also *vis-à-vis* Japanese producers at the end of the 1960s. The import share on the American market began to steadily increase from 1955 onwards.

Figure 3.1 shows the decline in the American share of world car production. It also shows that the United States, Europe and Japan have progressively become equal producers.

*Figure 3.1　Share of world motor vehicle production by region, 1955–89*

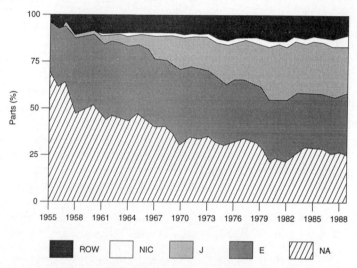

*Note*: This figure includes all vehicles produced within the three major regions, by all companies operating in those regions. In addition, it groups the production of the newly industrializing countries and of the rest of the world.

NA　= North America: United States and Canada
E　　= Western Europe, including Scandinavia
J　　= Japan
NIC　= Newly industrializing countries, principally Korea, Brazil, and Mexico
ROW = Rest of the world, including the Soviet Union, Eastern Europe, and China
*Source*: Altshuler *et al.* (1984)

From the 1950s on, trade was progressively liberated. This movement first benefited the Europeans who traded between themselves and with the United States. American producers were already multinationals and exports from the United States were low. Figure 3.2 shows the evolution of the structure of automobile exports; the larger share taken by Japanese producers has mainly been compensated by the reduction in the European share. It also underlines the fact that, for production, there are really only three important regions (intra-European exchanges are included).

*Figure 3.2    Regional origin of automobile exports, in cumulative %*

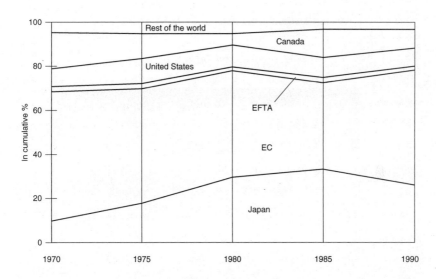

*Source*: calculations from the database CHELEM (CEPII)

In the different regions, automobile production has traditionally been quite concentrated. When the industry was born, there were numerous firms, but their number rapidly declined in the United States and in Europe. In Europe there remained a larger number of firms because the isolation of national markets protected diversity through segmentation. In Japan, the number of firms is also traditionally higher in the automobile industry. However, in comparison with other sectors, the industry can be considered as quite concentrated. Table 3.1 lists the world leading automobile firms.

The table shows that few firms acccount for a large part of production. The world automobile production is quite concentrated; in 1986, the largest firm represented 19 per cent of world production and the first four firms totalled 50 per cent.

Table 3.2 details the degree of sales concentration for different countries and for the EC. The degree of sales concentration is also quite high, but generally lower than that of production.[5] It tends to decrease, due to Japanese competition in particular.

*Table 3.1    World automobile companies*

| Groups | Cars | Trucks | Total production | Rank for total production |
|---|---|---|---|---|
| General Motors | 5 483 000 | 1 942 000 | 7 425 000 | 1 |
| Ford | 3 725 000 | 1 816 000 | 5 441 000 | 2 |
| Toyota | 4 231 000 | 1 289 000 | 5 520 000 | 3 |
| Nissan | 2 416 000 | 769 000 | 3 185 000 | 4 |
| VAG* | 2 880 571 | 172 881 | 3 053 452 | 5 |
| Fiat | 2 353 000 | 281 000 | 2 634 000 | 6 |
| Peugeot SA | 1 989 405 | 245 506 | 2 234 911 | 7 |
| Honda | 1 840 000 | 160 000 | 2 000 000 | 8 |
| Chrysler | 944 934 | 954 463 | 1 899 397 | 9 |
| Renault | 1 513 651 | 329 509 | 1 843 160 | 10 |
| Mazda | 1 432 000 | 321 000 | 1 753 000 | 11 |
| Mitsubishi | 1 051 000 | 524 000 | 1 575 000 | 12 |
| Suzuki | 618 788 | 377 370 | 996 158 | 13 |
| Mercedes-Benz | 588 206 | 250 189 | 838 395 | 14 |
| Vaz | 560 000 | 070 000 | 730 000 | 15 |
| Hyundai | 557 683 | 118 384 | 676 067 | 16 |
| Isuzu | 203 974 | 409 093 | 613 067 | 17 |
| Fuji Heavy | 350 335 | 196 434 | 546 769 | 18 |
| BMW | 519 660 | | 519 660 | 19 |
| Rover | 438 158 | 035 920 | 474 078 | 20 |
| Volvo | 369 797 | 059 272 | 429 069 | 21 |
| Kia | 222 125 | 199 574 | 421 699 | 22 |

*    Volkswagen-Audi-Seat
*Source*: Comité des Constructeurs Français d'Automobiles, quoted in *Les Echos*,
       16 October 1991.

*Table 3.2    Sales concentration in some countries*\*

|  | Share of the first firm (%) | Share of the first four firms (%) | Herfindahl Index[\*\*] | Number of firms equivalent[\*\*] |
|---|---|---|---|---|
| **United States** | | | | |
| 1975 | 44.30 | 84.90 | 0.27 | 3.61 |
| 1980 | 46.40 | 77.50 | 0.26 | 3.80 |
| 1985 | 40.90 | 77.40 | 0.25 | 4.41 |
| 1990 | 35.20 | 75.00 | 0.20 | 5.20 |
| **Japan** | | | | |
| 1975 | 39.20 | 83.20 | 0.26 | 3.77 |
| 1980 | 37.30 | 82.00 | 0.24 | 4.13 |
| 1985 | 42.60 | 83.50 | 0.26 | 3.79 |
| 1990 | 37.10 | 75.70 | 0.21 | 4.83 |
| **EC** | | | | |
| 1975 | 15.30 | 51.50 | 0.09 | 10.52 |
| 1980° | 15.50 | 57.00 | 0.10 | 9.35 |
| 1985 | 15.40 | 52.30 | 0.09 | 10.40 |
| 1990 | 14.30 | 53.70 | 0.10 | 9.99 |
| **Germany** | | | | |
| 1975 | 28.00 | 68.80 | 0.15 | 6.45 |
| 1980 | 30.30 | 67.50 | 0.15 | 6.57 |
| 1985 | 28.60 | 66.20 | 0.14 | 7.06 |
| 1990 | 25.60 | 60.90 | 0.12 | 8.03 |
| **France** | | | | |
| 1975 | 37.40 | 84.10 | 0.26 | 3.81 |
| 1980 | 40.50 | 86.70 | 0.31 | 3.28 |
| 1985 | 34.70 | 77.20 | 0.22 | 4.56 |
| 1990 | 33.10 | 78.10 | 0.21 | 4.75 |
| **Italy** | | | | |
| 1975 | 65.50 | 83.60 | 0.44 | 2.25 |
| 1981 | 57.90 | 84.40 | 0.36 | 2.74 |
| 1985 | 58.70 | 82.80 | 0.37 | 2.71 |
| 1990 | 52.40 | 80.80 | 0.31 | 3.22 |
| **UK** | | | | |
| 1975 | 31.00 | 67.30 | 0.16 | 6.23 |
| 1980 | 30.70 | 67.00 | 0.16 | 6.40 |
| 1985 | 26.50 | 63.00 | 0.13 | 7.52 |
| 1990 | 25.30 | 64.50 | 0.13 | 7.82 |
| **Spain** | | | | |
| 1975 | 48.20 | 98.30 | 0.33 | 2.98 |
| 1980 | 39.20 | 100.00 | 0.29 | 3.44 |
| 1985 | 33.70 | 90.70 | 0.23 | 4.26 |
| 1990 | 18.60 | 63.50 | 0.11 | 9.93 |

\*    Calculations use the number of cars registered.
\*\*   In each case, estimates include firms which total more than 10 000 registrations; EC does not include Greece.
°    1981 for Italy, 1982 for the Netherlands.
*Source*: calculations on figures from CCFA and *Automotive News*

For a long period, the industry was moderately internationalized. By the 1920s, Ford and General Motors had production units in numerous countries; this internationalization of the American producers was reinforced in the 1930s as European countries tried to protect their infant automobile industry (Sachwald 1989b). European producers also built international operations, but on a much smaller scale. Producers from industrialized countries have manufacturing operations in developing countries, but here again, the importance of these operations remains rather limited. So, until the 1970s, national markets are relatively protected from foreign cars, be it from exports or from multinational production units. Moreover, in Europe, automobile imports often come from other European countries.[6]

## 3.2   INGREDIENTS FOR A CRISIS

Since the end of the 1970s, the traditional characteristics of the automobile industry have been dramatically altered, which has led to a period of crisis. This section analyses the different components of the crisis in order to identify the adaptation requirements and hence the resources firms need.

### 3.2.1  The Evolution of Demand

In the 1970s, three causes combined to decrease demand for cars. The automobile industry is generally quite sensitive to the general level of demand. So, of course, the industry was hurt by the consequences of the first oil shock. Moreover, oil shocks have constituted a specific cause of lower demand for cars; they gave rise to fears about the future of the automobile industry. These fears have abated, but the increase in gas prices has had an effect on the cost of using cars. Thus oil shocks have reinforced the longer term tendency towards demand saturation.[7]

Since the 1970s in industrial countries, demand for cars is mainly for renewal. This has consequences both on the rate of growth and on the type of products. The long-term demand growth rate is at best equal to the GDP growth rate, expectations being even lower for the United States (Roos 1990). From a qualitative point of view, demand has become more complex to satisfy. Since the rate penetration is high or very high, demand largely concerns replacement or second vehicles. In such circumstances, clients are more demanding in terms of quality and sophisticated features; they also tend to yield more easily to fashion or to very specific types of vehicles like sports cars. The automobile market thus presents features of a 'mature' product.[8] These different evolutions have combined with the consequences of oil shocks, and in particular the interest in smaller cars, to trigger product renewal and differentiation.

## 3.2.2 Supply: The Japanese Challenge

On the supply side the challenge is obviously the triumphal entry of Japan.[9] Traditionally, entry on a market is discussed in the case of firms. In economic history there have been a number of cases of entry by countries, that is by several firms from the same country. Their collective entry is generally linked with a specific resource linked to their country. In the past, the resources have often been 'natural'; they were what international trade theory has labelled 'national factor endowments'. In the case of the Japanese automobile industry, the strength is not a resource but rather a capability; the Japanese challenge is organizational. This rather original asset has long been misunderstood by traditional producers in the industry (see section 3.3).

Japanese automobile production was negligible until the 1960s (100000 vehicles in 1956 - Roos 1990). Production was essentially directed at the domestic market until the end of the 1960s. Japan really became the third pole of world automobile production in the 1970s. During the decade, Japanese production increased much more rapidly than that from other regions. In 1980, it exceeded that of the United States; it was the case again until 1983, and then from 1987.[10] The share of Japanese producers in world automobile exports grew rapidly from 1970-85 (see Figure 3.2 above). Table 3.3 shows the evolution of the rate of penetration by Japanese brands on the main car markets.

*Table 3.3   Share of Japanese brands in total registrations, %*

| Countries | 1970 | 1975 | 1980 | 1984 | 1988 | 1991 |
|-----------|------|------|------|------|------|------|
| US | 3.7 | 9.4 | 21.3 | 18.3 | 21.3 | 30.2 |
| Germany | 0.1 | 1.7 | 10.4 | 11.6 | 25.5 | 25.3 |
| UK | 0.4 | 9.0 | 11.9 | 11.1 | 11.4 | 10.7 |
| France | 0.2 | 1.5 | 2.9 | 3.0 | 2.9 | 4.0 |
| Spain | – | – | – | 0.6 | 0.9 | 2.3 |
| Italy | a | a | 0.1 | 0.2 | 0.9 | 2.6 |
| Portugal | 10.7 | 20.5 | 7.5 | 8.5 | 7.8 | 9.2 |
| Greece | – | – | 49.2 | 30.9 | 38.9 | 31.6 |
| Belgium | 4.9 | 16.5 | 24.7 | 20.1 | 21.0 | 22.3 |
| Netherlands | 3.1 | 15.5 | 25.7 | 22.0 | 27.7 | 27.8 |
| Norway | 11.4 | 28.3 | 39.1 | 33.5 | 39.3 | 45.1 |
| Sweden | 0.7 | 6.5 | 12.1 | 15.0 | 25.5 | 25.3 |
| Austria | 0.9 | 5.4 | 19.2 | 27.0 | 33.1 | 28.7 |

[a]   Less than 0.1%

*Sources*: CCFA, *Les Echos* 6/2/1991, *Le Journal de l'Automobile* no. 337

These data show the seriousness of Japanese inroads during the 1970s; after so long a domination, in a few years American and European producers are revealed as uncompetitive. Their reactions and their relative positions are analysed below in section 3.3.

The strength of Japanese automobile manufacturers lies in their original production system. As for mass production, the objective here is to characterize the Japanese system and not to analyse it in detail, which has already been done.[11] We begin with a comparison between the Japanese type of production system and mass production. The comparison is quite depressing for mass production: Japanese car makers often reach higher scores for all the relevant indicators; they simultaneously achieve high levels of productivity, quality and product mix complexity. These achievements are reflected in the characteristics of the products they offer. Since the 1970s, Japanese cars have been praised for their moderate prices, their high quality standards and their very diversified production.

The MIT programme has worked on a standardization of the different manufacturing steps in car production and on a set of indicators to characterize the different production systems (Womack, Jones and Roos 1990). The use of these indicators yields a strong opposition between mass production and the Japanese way. Table 3.4 uses this box score to show that the Japanese producer is more productive, achieves a higher level of quality and uses both less inventories and less assembly space.

*Table 3.4    GM Framingham assembly plant vs Toyota Takaoka assembly plant, 1986*

|  | GM Framingham | Toyota Takaoka |
|---|---|---|
| Gross assembly hours per car | 40.7 | 18.0 |
| Adjusted assembly hours per car | 31.0 | 16.0 |
| Assembly defects per 100 cars | 130.0 | 45.0 |
| Assembly space per car | 8.1 | 4.8 |
| Inventories of parts (average) | 2 weeks | 2 hours |

*Note*:    Gross assembly hours per car are calculated by dividing total hours of effort in the plant by the total number of cars produced. 'Adjusted assembly hours per car' incorporates the adjustments in standard activities and product attributes described in the test. Defects per car were estimated from the J.D. Power Intital Quality Survey for 1987. Assembly space per car is square feet per vehicle per year, corrected for vehicle size. Inventories are a rough average for major parts.

*Source*:    Womack, Jones and Roos (1990)

According to these findings, Japanese producers do more with less. This remarkable capability led the MIT team to label the Japanese system 'lean production', a whole system relating strategy, product, organization and management.[12] The objective is to produce the right product, at the right time and at the right quality level. With these objectives, the organization of production is quite different. It aims at producing different types of cars with relatively short series at acceptable costs. Flexibility is the name of the game. This objective is easier to reach if the assembly line can rely on components without defects. Very generally good quality all along the production chain is a formidable way to save on costs (repair costs and lower stocks). The search for quality and flexibility has entailed a high degree of cooperation along the entire production chain, both within the factory itself and with its suppliers. Coordination extends beyond production, in particular to conception. Japanese producers manage to produce new car models much more rapidly than their competitors thanks to a process of development which integrates the different parts of the production and engineering process very early on.

### 3.2.3  Innovation in a Mature Industry

As explained above, for a long time competition had been rather stable in the automobile industry. In the 1970s, both demand and supply conditions were dramatically altered. These evolutions have interacted with a renewal of the role of innovation in the competitive game. Moreover, innovation has concerned products and processes.

On the supply side, lean production may be considered as the main innovation (section 3.2.2). Apart from this organizational innovation, the automobile industry has experienced process innovations related to data processing. As in other industries, and often to a greater extent, this type of innovation has been wide-ranging. The most spectacular aspects have been robotization and other automated devices such as computer aided design or manufacture. Communication systems within firms and companies have also been an important source of innovation. In a number of cases, interdependences between process innovations and organizational aspects have been very clear. For example, robotization has underlined the need for strong communication between the services responsible for the conception of machinery and those responsible for manufacturing.

Product innovations have also been quite numerous, even if the fundamental 'production paradigm' (Abernathy 1978), that is the internal combustion engine, has not altered. A first set of innovations has related to energy consumption. The oil shocks have revealed the need to save on energy and of course the automobile was one of the main battlegrounds. Car makers have been obliged to innovate in this field both because of market pressure and because of governmental regulations in industrial countries. Several routes have been pursued simultaneously: car weight reductions, more efficient engines and better aerodynamic characteristics. In turn these research directions have led to numerous improvements and innovations. New materials such as aluminium, plastics and composites have contributed to lighten cars. Engine electronic control has been a source of gas saving. More recently, environmental worries have constituted a new area for innovation. Research is directed at long-term radical solutions such as the electric car or at shorter term solutions such as the catalytic converter.

The second set of innovations is more related to the improvement of quality and performance. From the producer's point of view the means to do this are nevertheless similar. Electronics have pervaded most of the functions. For example, various devices aim at increasing control and security (ABS).

Of course, product and process innovations are related. In particular, a number of innovations in processes are required to implement product innovations. This is the case in the use of plastics and composites, since the automobile industry had traditionally used metallurgical techniques. The renewal of the importance of innovation has meant substantial increases in R&D spending, both by car makers and suppliers.[13]

## 3.3  THE STRATEGIC AGENDA

Since the mid-1970s, the automobile industry has seen a number of its fundamental characteristics change. To summarize, this could be seen as a 'dematuring' process.[14] This idea accounts for both the renewal of the innovation process and the evolution of the competitive game. In such circumstances, the strategic agenda had to be revised.

During the 1980s automobile firms and their respective countries have been obliged to assess their strengths and weaknesses closely and decide new strategies. Identification of the central problem, the evolution of the production paradigm, has been quite slow and adequate strategies difficult to both decide and implement. Globalization has also progressively become a central issue.

### 3.3.1  Relative Competitive Positions

Section 3.2 has described the Japanese production system as much more efficient than mass production and showed that it has been a significant competitive weapon on world markets. Since the 1970s, Japanese producers have rapidly conquered international markets, whether the indicator is the share in world production (Figure 3.1) or in world exports (Figure 3.2).

Thus, during the 1970s and 1980s American and European competitive positions have weakened *vis-à-vis* the Japanese. However, apart from this general trend, positions between competitors have been diverse. Two main methods are used here to evaluate the competitive position of firms: first, market share data, and second, more direct evaluation of the relative efficiency in manufacturing.

Table 3.3 showed the evolution of the rate of penetration by Japanese brands on the main car markets. This rate began to grow earlier in the United States and has reached higher levels; in 1980, it was already over 20 per cent. In Europe, the competitiveness of Japanese producers cannot be directly confirmed by their rate of penetration on the markets, which are protected. There are clearly two categories of countries. In countries where there is no national car maker such as Austria or Greece, the Japanese market share has early reached very high levels. In countries where there are national companies the progress has been much slower. This is due to two types of factors. First, traditionally, automobile markets were characterized by a relatively high level of brand loyalty, which tended to benefit national producers. In turn, this brand loyalty interacted with the fact that markets were relatively protected and fragmented. Second, a number of European markets were protected by non-tariff barriers in the 1970s — the United States gained protection in the 1980s (see section 3.2.3). On average, figures in Table 3.3 confirm Japanese competitive strength but the differences in trade policies between countries makes it difficult to compare relative positions.

The fact that European firms often have difficulty penetrating foreign markets, and more particularly the markets of their Triad rivals, is another indication of Europe's weak competitive position. There are of course differences within European firms. In particular, specialist producers have had some successes on the American and Japanese markets.[15]

Productivity is a fundamental determinant of competitiveness and its evaluation provides an interesting indicator of competitiveness. For the automobile industry, productivity comparisons are particularly delicate to operate. International comparisons are always difficult. One other classical problem is to compare equivalent products, both in terms of characteristics and quality. In the automobile industry, the problem is made even more complex by the fact that firms have quite different rates of vertical integration.[16] For example, Japanese companies have traditionally had a low rate of vertical integration. Given the discrepancies in the rates of integration, it is not very meaningful to calculate figures such as the number of cars produced by employee or the turnover by employee.

The IMVP has chosen to compare 'equivalent' production operations between different assembly factories. The programme has devoted a lot of thought to methodological questions and showed how intricate they are

(Krafcik 1988). Their detailed evaluation of assembly operations can be criticized since they have chosen specific ways to compare different operations (such as the assembly of different cars or the fact that different factories include more or less operations). However, they have elaborated a series of indicators to evaluate the efficiency of production with a consistent method and such an effort has no equivalent so far. The indicators have been very helpful in comparing mass production and lean production systems (see section 3.2). They can also be used to compare the efficiency of car makers. Figure 3.3 compares the productivity of the volume car makers from the Triad.

*Figure 3.3    Assembly plant productivity, volume producers, 1989*

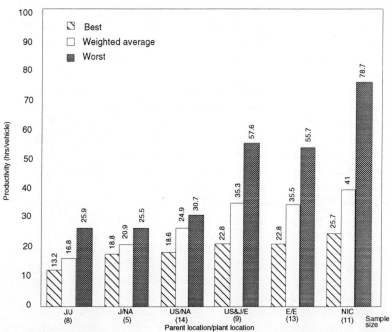

*Note*:  Volume producers include the American 'Big Three': Fiat, PSA, Renault, and Volkswagen in Europe; and all of the companies from Japan.

    J/J    = Japanese-owned plants in Japan

    J/NA   = Japanese-owned plants in North America, including joint venture plants with American firms

    US/NA  = American-owned plants in North America

    US&J/E = American- and Japanese-owned plants in Europe

    E/E    = European-owned plants in Europe

    NIC    = Plants in newly industrializing countries: Mexico, Brazil, Taiwan, and Korea

*Source*: Womack, Jones and Roos (1990)

The figure shows the weak position of Europe as a location. Within the Triad, producers from Europe, both Europeans and American subsidiaries, tend, on average, to be less productive. North America achieves better performance, both for American producers and Japanese transplants. These results are valid both on average and for the worst producer of each sample, which is much less productive in Europe. On average, Japanese car manufacturers in Japan are the most productive. As predicted by the analysis of the lean production system, productivity goes along with quality. The data from the IMVP research programme show that European manufacturers achieve the lowest levels of quality. Moreover, the evaluations which have been made for luxury car producers show similar results: European producers, despite their high reputation for the production of this type of car, reveal very low levels of efficiency on both criteria (Womack, Jones and Roos 1990).

The above evaluations of European producers' efficiency may look alarming. The IMVP method has been criticized and the results have been contested. Helmer (1991) for example considers that the method is biased in favour of Japanese manufacturers and that corrections reduce their cost advantage to 2 to 5 per cent of the ex-factory price of cars.[17] The precise evaluation of the relative efficiency of the various car manufacturers remains an empirical question to be worked on, but there is a general agreement on the Japanese advantage. This agreement is rooted in their market performance as well as in the analysis of the strong consistency of their production system.[18] European manufacturers score better on innovativeness, but all the producers are convinced that innovation is a strong weapon in the competitive game and all invest heavily in the technology race.

### 3.3.2 European Integration and Globalization

The 1980s have often been considered as the decade of globalization (as discussed in Chapter 1). Moreover, the automobile industry has largely served as an example. In section 3.1.2, the automobile industry was characterized as moderately internationalized. Since the mid-1970s, it has become much more so and has acquired certain characteristics of a globalized industry. But the movement was certainly not smooth and constant. Japanese producers have largely fuelled the movement, at least in part because they faced important obstacles on the route to exports.

#### 3.3.2.1 Neo-protectionism, integration and globalization

One of the first reactions to the Japanese challenge has been quite traditional. The hypothesis (sincere or not) was that Japanese producers operated under such different conditions that confrontation was unfair. Consequently, a number of countries resorted to protection. The evolution of trade policies in the automobile industry is quite exemplary. The industry followed the various tariff reductions organized by GATT from the 1950s to the 1970s, as well as the more radical reductions within the European Community. Since then, the industry has been one of the most concerned by neo-protectionist tendencies.[19] The main contentious issues have related to Japanese exports, both to the United States and to European countries. In particular, since the 1970s, they have had to face voluntary export restraints (some countries, like Italy, also have more long established quotas). But Japan has also been accused of benefiting from protection, in particular through its intricate distribution system.

Since the first reaction of the industry has been to seek protection, it was logical that it would resist further internationalization. This explains the protracted negotiations about EEC external trade policy after the completion of the Single Market; indeed the opening of markets is going to be the most important consequence of the Single Market for the car industry. The scheme aims at the free circulation of goods within the Community. In the case of cars, it means that no national market will be able to benefit from stricter access conditions than other EEC members. For example, France is protected from Japanese exports by a very low quota (3 per cent). However, Belgium has no restriction of this sort, and cars travel freely between France and Belgium.[20] The solution is obvious: export cars to Belgium, and then from Belgium to France. Concerns on the part of the protected countries have induced delays in the completion of the Single Market, which depends on the adoption of harmonization measures on a number of technical questions (Sachwald 1989b; 1990c). In July 1991, Japan and the European Commission agreed on a European voluntary export restraint to open the Single Market progressively. From 1993–99, Japanese penetration into EC markets should be around 16 per cent. But the agreement remains rather unclear. In particular, Japanese and Europeans do not agree on the question of the transplants; should their production be included in the quota or not?[21]

Protectionist measures against Japanese exports have accelerated the internationalization of the Nippon car makers. As American producers did in the 1920s and 1930s, Japanese car makers have decided to produce abroad. The sheer size of the Japanese automobile industry and the appreciation of the Yen have certainly contributed to the evolution of a growing share of international production. But trade impediments have been strong incentives to go ahead both soon and on a large scale. In turn, their relative inexperience with international production has induced Japanese car makers to look for ways to become acquainted with foreign markets and minimize risks. These solutions will be explored in section 3.4. Table 3.5 lists Japanese manufacturing operations in Europe and the United States.

*Table 3.5  Japanese car makers' production facilities in Europe and the United States*

| Car maker | Location | Starting date | Products | Capacity, in '000s |
|---|---|---|---|---|
| Honda | Marysville/US | 1982 | Accord, Civic | 360 |
| | Anna/US | 1986 | Engines | 360 |
| | Alliston/Ca | 1986 | Civic, Accord | 80 |
| | East Liberty/US | 1989 | Civic, Acura | 140 |
| | Swindon/UK | 1989 | Engines | 70, 92:240 |
| | Swindon | 1992 | Synchro | 94:100 |
| Toyota/GM (NUMMI) | Fremont/US | 1984 | Corolla, Geo Prizm, pick-up | 250, 91:320 |
| Toyota | Cambridge/Ca | 1988 | Corolla | 75 |
| | Georgetown/US | 1988 | Camry | 200, 93:400 |
| | Georgetown/US | 1990 | Engines, components | n.a |
| | Burnaston/UK | 1992 | Carina II | 95:100, 98:200 |
| | Shotton/UK | 1992 | Engines | 98:200 |
| Nissan | Volos/Grèce | 1980 | Car, pick-up | 36 |
| | Smyrna/US | 1983/85* | Sunny, pick-up | 240, 92:440 |
| | Smyrna/US | 1992 | Engines | 150 |
| | Sunderland/UK | 1986 | Bluebird, 89:Primera, 92: Micra | 80, 92:200 |
| | Decherd | 1996 | Engines, components | 300 |
| Mazda | Flat Rock/US | 1987 | MX6, 89:626, Ford Probe | 240 |
| Fuji Heavy/Isuzu (Subaru-Isuzu Automotive) | Lafayette/US | 1989 | Car, pick-up | 150, 93:240 |
| Mitsubishi/Chrysler (Diamond Star) | Bloomington/US | 1988 | Sport cars, 91:Mirage | 240 |
| Suzuki/GM (CAMI) | Ingersoll/Ca | 1989 | Cars, 4×4 | 200 |
| Mitsubishi/Volvo (Nederland Car)° | Amsterdam/NL | 1991 | Cars | 96:200 |

\*   In 1983 the factory produced only pick-ups and started to produce cars in 1985.
°   In 1991, Mitsubishi took a third of the capital of the company, the other two-thirds belong to Volvo and the Dutch government.
*Sources*: CCFA (Répertoire mondial), press, documents from firms.

In the 1980s, it became increasingly clear that Japanese exports constituted a permanent feature of the competitive game and would be
progressively coupled with international production in the United States and
in Europe. Foreign direct investment by Japanese companies in industrial
countries has induced resistance from indigenous car makers and from some
governments. In the case of the automobile industry, one bone of contention
has been the level of the local content of delocalized production. This question has given rise to quarrels, in Europe in particular, but they will not
prevent the progression of the Japanese movement. Once car makers have
been convinced that protection was, sooner or later, going to be lifted, they
started to devise strategic responses. They are of course directed towards
efficiency improvements, but also towards globalization.

### 3.3.2.2 Towards globalization

During the 1980s, the automobile industry has been considered as one of the
most globalized sectors. Indeed, internationalization has intensified through
a higher level of trade and through foreign direct investments. However, if
globalization goes beyond and means a qualitative change, the fact that
internationalization is deeper and implies changes for most aspects of the
process of production, the automobile industry can only be described as in
the process of globalizing. Moreover, it seems that the different car makers
have chosen divergent strategies in this respect. Some of the Japanese manufacturers may well aim at a globalized system of production; on the contrary,
during the 1980s, Europeans have tended to retreat from a number of their
international operations, in the United States in particular.

For the firm, globalization has been opposed to the good old multi-
nationalization (Porter 1986) or to glocalization (Ruigrok, Tulder and Baven
1991). To take these different contributions into account, though briefly, one
can describe a global company as having worldwide operations and seeking
to integrate all its activities on a worldwide basis. This, for example, would
exclude a multinational company which organizes its foreign subsidiaries
relatively independently. The question of the degree and means of integration of the different national and regional operations has always been
important for multinational companies and the automobile industry with its
early internationalization is no exception.

In the 1970s, preoccupation with economies of scale had gone so far as to
lead to the notion of 'world car'. This notion has never been precisely
defined, but the idea was to conceive a car for the world, to propose a
common design and to use common components to manufacture for world
markets. Moreover, in order to benefit from both economies of scale and
cost differentials, the ideal was to specialize production units around the
world. Actually, no world car ever existed. Ford was the company which
seemed to be trying to implement the concept with the Escort. But the car

was neither engineered nor produced for the world; the American and European versions were different and only a few components were common (Bordenave and Lung 1988).

During the 1980s, the internationalization of design was seen quite differently. The objective was not to design a car for the entire world, but to draw on the worldwide knowledge of markets to both adapt the models to the markets and to use good ideas in different places. For production, worldwide rationalization has remained on the agenda, but account must be taken of lean production techniques. They require quite close cooperation with suppliers, and the different manufacturing units need a sophisticated environment. (This is the case for a number of modern industries.)

Globalization has been considered as a necessary strategic move since competition became global. During the 1980s the car makers from the Triad have become closer competitors. Also, close adaptation to local markets requires good information networks, and probably some production operations in the different regions. Nevertheless, the need for a truly global organization of each car manufacturer may be questioned. It is not the objective of this chapter to deal in depth with this question.[22]

### 3.3.3 Strategic Options

Given the evolution of the competitive game explained in section 3.2 and the context of the 1980s as it has been briefly sketched above, the strategic agenda for the decade was quite heavy for automobile manufacturers.

For Japanese car makers, the objective was to organize in order to benefit from their productive efficiency. This meant selling more on foreign markets which, in turn, required a higher level of international manufacturing. Japanese producers thus tended to internationalize rapidly, in particular because direct investment could not be for final assembly only and because of the high degree of sophistication of automobile markets.

For American producers, the first objective was to defend their market share on their home ground. They progressively understood that to be more efficient and more imaginative it meant enormous changes. For General Motors and Ford, it was also important to improve the efficiency of their European subsidiaries.

The situation was more diverse in Europe. For volume producers, the efficiency problem was also very acute, but the different national markets were more protected. Production was also more diversified and, in some respects, more similar to that of the Japanese. Intra-European competition was an important factor, especially in the perspective of the Single Market, and it also seemed important for firms to become more internationalized beyond Europe and towards the American market in particular. For most of the decade specialist producers such as BMW, Mercedes or Saab benefited from their very strong image which commanded high prices; efficiency questions have come to the forefront only recently.

The identification of the central problem, that is the necessary evolution (if not revolution) of the production system, has been progressing, both in Europe and in the US. Strategies have followed, and thus several steps can be identified; each step has been associated with specific external growth operations.


## 3.4   THE ROLE OF COOPERATIVE AGREEMENTS AND ACQUISITIONS

Since the end of the 1970s, numerous cooperative agreements have been concluded between automobile manufacturers while this type of operation had been quite rare during previous periods (Sachwald 1989a; 1990b). Table 3.6 illustrates this tendency by considering the number of agreements concluded each year and the evolution of the stock of agreements. The calculations rely on a database, Auto-JV, which is described in the appendix to this chapter.

*Table 3.6   Number of new cooperative agreements per year and evolution of stock*

| Year | New agreements[*] | Stock of agreements | New agreements between car makers[**] |
|---|---|---|---|
| 1980 | 7 | 27 | 5 |
| 1981 | 3 | 30 | 3 |
| 1982 | 4 | 34 | 2 |
| 1983 | 10 | 44 | 7 |
| 1984 | 7 | 51 | 6 |
| 1985 | 4 | 53 | 4 |
| 1986 | 15 | 65 | 11 |
| 1987 | 15 | 79 | 12 |
| 1988 | 13 | 86 | 11 |
| 1989 | 13 | 97 | 12 |
| 1990 | 14 | 109 | 12 |
| 1991 | 10 | 117 | 9 |
| 1992° | 10 | 126 | 10 |

[*]   Agreements in which there is at least one car maker
[**]   Agreements uniquely between car makers, i.e. excluding agreements with suppliers and with firms not in the auto industry
°   As of July 1992
*Source*: own database, Auto-JV

The first column shows the number of agreements which have been concluded during each year between car makers and either other car makers or other partners; the last column only counts the agreements between car makers. The second column gives the number of agreements in stock each year; it thus takes into account the end of some of the agreements.

Other sectors show much more numerous cooperative agreements. However, one should take into account the high degree of concentration of the automobile industry, which means that there are few actors. This is only true for car makers; in the component sector, there are both more actors and more agreements (see Chapter 4 in this volume).

At the beginning of the 1980s, there were no acquisitions between car makers; their number has grown during the second half of the decade. Table 3.7 shows this change by listing acquisitions since the 1970s.

*Table 3.7   Acquisitions within the automobile industry, 1974–90*

| Year | Acquiring firm | Acquired firm/type of operation |
| --- | --- | --- |
| 1974 | Peugeot | Citroën |
| 1975 | Volvo | Volvo  lifts its participation in DAF Auto to 75%; in 1981, it sells 70% to the Dutch state; in 1990, formation of a joint venture with Mitsubishi |
| 1978 | PSA | European subsidiaries of Chrysler |
| 1979 | Renault | 46.4% of AMC (control) |
| 1985 | Innocenti | Maserati |
| 1986 | Fiat | Alfa Romeo |
| 1986 | GM | Lotus |
| 1986 | Volkswagen | SEAT, VW first bought 55% |
| 1987 | Chrysler | AMC (bought from Renault) |
| 1987 | Chrysler | Lamborghini |
| 1987 | Ford | AC Cars (50.7%), production of prototypes |
| 1987 | Ford | Aston Martin (75%) |
| 1988 | Fiat | Ferrari (buys 40% which complements the stock bought in 1969) |
| 1989 | Ford | Jaguar (OPA) |
| 1990 | GM | Saab (50%) |

*Source*: own database, Auto-MA

The analysis of the whole set of car makers' external growth operations reveals four main types of objectives, which are examined in turn: to penetrate new markets, to increase the efficiency of production, by lowering costs and by implementing new techniques, to enlarge the scope of production with niche vehicles, and to innovate.

### 3.4.1  Penetrate Foreign Markets

Firms have resorted to different means to penetrate foreign markets, including exports and direct investment. Cooperative agreements have played a prominent role in this endeavour.

The most important movement has been the penetration of American and European markets by Japanese producers. The latter resorted to cooperative agreements, both to export more cars and to produce locally. At first, they progressed through exports. In the automobile industry, selling cars requires a specialized distribution network which is both expensive and quite lengthy to establish. To sell in foreign countries, these costs are compounded with risks. In such conditions, the new entrant may look for less expensive and/or less risky solutions. It may first use the services of an independent distributor, if such outlets exist; it may also try to find a local ally. This last solution has been used by a number of Japanese producers. The simplest way to proceed was to have the foreign cars distributed through the network of an American car maker. This has been the case of Mitsubishi cars which have been distributed in the United States through Chrysler network, according to a 1970 agreement. But in most cases, American firms distributed Japanese cars through their networks after having applied their own badge on the vehicles. Mitsubishi has used this means of distribution with Chrysler since a 1971 agreement. Isuzu has supplied General Motors with vehicles to sell in the United States under GM badges since 1972; from 1989 on, Isuzu has also been a supplier to the new GM network, Geo. Recently, Ford and Mazda agreed on a new type of cooperation by which the Japanese partner can sell in the United States without meeting tariff barriers: according to the 1991 agreement, Ford will manufacture a pick-up for Mazda to sell in the United States.

As explained above, in the 1980s Japanese car manufacturers have had to produce abroad on a large scale; they have opened production facilities, first in the United States and then in Europe. They basically had to choose from three types of solutions: build greenfield operations and run them as part of their world business, buy existing facilities, or collaborate with local producers. Here again, because of the sheer size of the necessary investment and the risks, they mostly chose the collaborative solution, at least as a first step.

In 1982 Honda was the first Japanese car maker to build a production facility in one of the large automobile producing countries (Table 3.5). This early start can be explained by the peculiar position of Honda which, given its relatively weak domestic position as a late comer, badly needed international markets.[23] Next was Toyota which chose a less risky solution by teaming with General Motors. In 1983 they agreed on the constitution of a joint venture, New United Motor Manufacturing Inc. (NUMMI) which would produce Toyota cars in a GM facility. According to the agreement, both firms could sell a proportion of the cars under their badges. Production started in 1984; the agreement has been signed for a period of twelve years, and Toyota will control the venture after 1996. This joint venture has been an important learning experience for Toyota which has been in charge of the management; managers have gained experience in teaching to Americans Toyota's production techniques. Toyota then decided to go it alone for its next American ventures; the firm opened two assembly units in 1988, one in the United States and one in Canada. It also opened a motor and components unit in the United States in 1990.

Mitsubishi and Chrysler have agreed to the constitution of a production joint venture in 1985, the Diamond Star. Diamond Star started production in 1988 and supplied cars to both Chrysler and Mitsubishi; in 1991, Mitsubishi took full control of the venture. In 1986, General Motors and Suzuki agreed to create a joint venture (CAMI) to produce cars in Canada. The factory started production in 1989. For Mazda, the relationship with the American partner is somewhat different. In 1985, the partners signed an agreement allowing Ford to buy up to 50 per cent of Mazda's future production at its Flat Rock factory (United States). Production started in 1987 with a common model derived from the Mazda 626.

The European expansion of Japanese producers occurred somewhat later. Nissan led the march with the construction of a production unit in the UK which started production in 1986. Nissan made a traditional greenfield investment; it had already started to produce in Greece with local partners on a small scale (1980) and in the United States (1985).[24] Honda started production in the UK as part of its cooperation with Rover. In 1983, the two partners agreed to develop in common a new executive car, which would have two different versions. The agreement provided for the assembly of each version by both producers. Production of the Honda Legend and Rover 800 started in 1986, but common production was stopped after 1988. In 1986 an agreement was signed by which Rover would build a small number of Honda Ballade in its Longbridge facility (production was about 4000 per year). In this instance, Rover was used as a subcontractor by Honda. This type of cooperation was repeated for the Honda Concerto from 1989 on. Honda has also decided to produce in the UK by itself. Its first factory which produces motors opened in 1989; its first assembly facility started production at the end of 1992.

Thus the different types of cooperative agreements into which Japanese car makers entered in order to either sell or produce in the United States and Europe answer two broad sets of preoccupations. The first is related to the learning process about local conditions and the second to risk attached to large new operations.

Conversely, cooperative agreements have also been used to penetrate the Japanese market. The Japanese automobile market is considered particularly difficult to enter. Two barriers to entry are often mentioned: the intricate distribution system and the very high prices of land in large towns. For a time American and European producers shrank from the difficulty, but recently it has become more and more important to be present on the sophisticated and demanding Japanese market. Foreign producers do not consider production in Japan, but even for distribution alone, they have mostly chosen to cooperate with a local firm (see Box 3.1).

*Box 3.1    Agreements between Japanese car makers and other producers for distribution in Japan\**

| – | GM/Isuzu | Isuzu distributes GM models (including Opel since 1988) in Asia, and in particular in Japan as part of their wider alliance (see Box 3.2). |
|---|---|---|
| 1987 | GM/Suzuki | From 1988, Suzuki's network distributes GM cars in Japan. |
| – | Ford/Mazda | Mazda distributes Ford models in Japan as part of their wider alliance (see Box 3.2). |
| 1987 | Mitsubishi/ Mercedes | Project of joint venture which will be abandoned. In 1990, Mitsubishi agrees to distribute Mercedes models in Japan. |
| 1988 | PSA/Mazda | Mazda distributes Citroën models in Japan. |
| 1989/ 1990 | Fiat/Mazda | Mazda distributes Lancia models in Japan from 1990 on. |
| 1990 | Chrysler/Honda | Honda distributes Jeep models in Japan. |
| 1991 | VW/Toyota | Toyota distributes VW models in Japan from 1992 on. |

\*   There was a number of small-scale agreements in the 1960s which are not dealt with.
*Source*: own database

### 3.4.2  Increase Efficiency

For American and European producers, the main challenge was to increase efficiency and, more exactly, as explained above, to learn a quite different mode of production.

Car makers did not all diagnose the death of mass production at once. They all took quite a long time to accept that they would have to rethink their mode of production. Moreover, quite typically, once an organization agrees on such a radical diagnosis, the treatment is both long and painful. It is why, even if Western firms progressively took lessons in lean production, they also maintained the more traditional option of low-cost delocalization. Besides, even if mass production has proved a weaker system than lean production, scale considerations remain relevant in the automobile industry, and some firms have considered that they should increase their scale, or at least the scale of certain of their operations.

### 3.4.2.1 Learning lean production

A production system is complex and largely dependent on ingrained routines followed by numerous actors. As such, it cannot really be implemented by reading a blueprint; it needs to be learnt progressively (see Chapter 2). So, in order to pass from mass production to lean production, car makers not only needed to observe and understand the workings of the new model, but also to train in it. Ideally, the learning process would include training with a master. Masters in lean production are the Japanese and a number of volume producers attempted to learn from them through cooperative agreements. The arrangements have been quite diverse. Box 3.2 briefly describes the cases of substantial long-term relationships between American and Japanese producers; they include the agreements aimed at lean production, but their objective is to show the width of the general relationships.

General Motors was the first to register for courses. NUMMI has been mentioned above (section 3.4.1) and Toyota's motives explained; the Japanese producer wanted both to observe automobile manufacturing in the United States and to go around import restrictions. As for its American partner, it wanted to experiment lean production and to rapidly add a small car to its range. In this perspective, Toyota has been in charge of NUMMI's management; senior managers with operational responsibilities have come from Toyota. NUMMI has been observed carefully after a number of years of operation and results are quite striking.[25] NUMMI uses a former General Motors facility which had been closed in 1982. When the joint venture started in 1984, only minor modifications were made to the buildings and most of the workforce had been with GM previously. Despite these *a priori* unfavourable conditions, NUMMI has shown high levels of both productivity and product quality.[26] These results are due to the fact that Toyota has tried to implement lean production at NUMMI.

Performance at NUMMI contributed to show that lean production could be imported. The problem for General Motors was to draw the right lessons from NUMMI. For GM, the objective was not to allow Toyota to produce efficiently in the United States, but to learn how to achieve better manufacturing itself by observation. Womack (1988) explains the techniques which have been used by GM to observe NUMMI and transfer know-how to its own manufacturing facilities. Fifteen GM managers work at NUMMI for periods of three years. The idea is to use the 'NUMMized' managers to implement lean production techniques at GM. General Motors has also established a liaison office which documents NUMMI's techniques. These elements are complemented with a programme for management trainees from GM to undertake research projects at NUMMI as part of their curriculum. These techniques of transfer do work, but a major problem is that NUMMI is small relative to GM, which means that GM has very few managers with hands-on experience of lean production.

*Box 3.2   Wide-ranging cooperative agreements between American and Japanese firms*

---

*Chrysler/Mitsubishi*

Cooperation started in 1970 with commercial agreement by which Chrysler distributed Mitsubishi models in the US.

In 1971 Mitsubishi Motors Corp. was created as a joint venture between Mitsubishi Heavy Industries (85%) and Chrysler (15%). From then on, Chrysler imported and sold Mitsubishi cars and small trucks; for example, in 1986, 10% of Chrysler sales in the US were due to Mitsubishi cars. Mitsubishi also supplies Chrysler with components, including engines.

In 1985, the two partners created a 50/50 joint venture, the Diamond Star Motors Corp. in the US. It produces Mitsubishi models to be sold through both distribution networks.

Cooperation has not been very successful. Chrysler first increased its participation to 22% (1985), but it cut it sharply in 1989 (to 12%) in a period of financial difficulties. The relationship has been maintained but, in 1991, Mitsubishi bought Chrysler's part of the Diamond Star. Besides, Mitsubishi has concluded an alliance with Daimler Benz which could be very important.

*Ford/Mazda*

In 1979 Toyo Kogyo (Mazda cars) took over Ford Industries Ltd (Japanese subsidiary); as a consequence Ford received 24% of Toyo Kogyo. Firms cooperate in various fields: technical exchanges, distribution and component supplies.

In 1983, Ford commissioned Mazda to engineer the new version of the Escort; Ford was responsible for the body and Mazda for mechanics. The car was launched in 1990 as a 'global car' — it is assembled in a dozen countries.

In 1985, it was agreed that Ford could buy up to 50% of Mazda's Flat Rock factory which began production in 1987 (see Table 3.5).

In 1987, the partners decided to step up their mutual part supply, standardize major parts for their new models and reorganize their part supply bases in South Korea and Taiwan. The objectives were to lower costs and increase flexibility in the choice of production sites for components. In 1989, Mazda decided to buy Ford engines for its Flat Rock factory, to increase local content.

Ford also supplies cars to Mazda for its American network. Since 1990, Mazda has bought Ford Explorer, a four-wheel drive leisure vehicle. In 1991, firms agreed on a contract by which Mazda would buy a small pick-up from Ford. It will enable Ford to produce longer series and Mazda to sell pick-ups without incurring the 25% tariff. Finally, Mazda supplies Ford with cars which are sold in Japan through Mazda's network, Autorama.

The two partners are also linked through their participations in Kia; Ford owns 10% of the Korean car maker and Mazda.

For production and supply, Ford has learnt Mazda's methods. The collaboration between Ford and Mazda is successful and exchanges tend to be both ways; this does not mean that it is exclusive — Ford is one of the most active car makers in terms of cooperative agreements.

*General Motors/Isuzu*

In 1971, GM took a participation of 34% in Isuzu (it then increased to 40%). At the time no precise project was announced, but collaboration developed. From 1972, GM sold an Isuzu pick-up as a Chevrolet; GM uses Isuzu's network in South East Asia. The firms collaborated on the development of the Isuzu Gemini which was derived from the Opel Kadett. GM and Isuzu also have technical exchanges and collaborate for component supply. Since 1988, GM Mexico has supplied Isuzu with V6 engines for light commercial vehicles which are assembled either in Japan or in Isuzu/Fuji Heavy joint venture in the US. Since the same date, Isuzu has distributed Opel models in Japan.

Since 1984, Isuzu has supplied GM with cars (Geo Storm and Metro) which are sold in the US.

In 1987 the partners created IBC vehicles in the UK; GM has 60% of the joint subsidiary which is managed by Isuzu; it produces light commercial vehicles and, since 1991, a leisure utility vehicle developed by Isuzu.

Finally, the partners have created General Motors Egypt where GM has 31% and Isuzu 20%; it first produced commercial vehicles and should produce cars in 1993.

Ford has chosen a more diffuse way to learn from its Japanese partner. Ford and Mazda have been partners since 1979 and have developed one of the most complete and successful relationships of the automobile industry.

Ford and Mazda have been cooperating on most areas of automobile production and distribution. In particular, they have been working on development, component supply and production. Ford thus has opportunities to learn lean production techniques through different projects bearing on various aspects of automobile manufacturing. For example, Ford's plant at Wayne outside Detroit has been remodelled after Mazda's plant at Flat Rock (*The Economist* 14/4/1990). That plant manufactures the new Escort model which is based on the Mazda 323 (see Box 3.3). Ford's learning process is less visible than GM's through NUMMI, but it also seems that it has so far been more efficient. Ford has achieved large improvements in productivity and has implemented a number of lean production features.

The relationship between Rover and Honda is also a long-term and wide ranging one — the evolution of the relationship between the two companies is described in Box 3.3 The relative strengths of the partners differ substantially from the previous case; this probably explains the slower development of the relationship. In 1979 the first collaboration was a licence agreement by which Rover could produce a car developed by Honda. However, the relationship has developed over the years and Rover has been able to learn much from Honda.

*Box 3.3    Cooperation between Honda and Rover (previously British Leyland)*

---

Cooperation started in 1979 with a licence agreement for production of a car developed by Honda, production of the Triumph Acclaim began in 1981.

In 1983 they agreed to develop a new model in common. The executive car was to have two versions with some common characteristics. Both versions were to be produced by Honda in Japan and Rover in the UK. Common production of the Rover 800/Honda Legend, which started in 1986, stopped in 1988 and objectives were not reached. In 1985 they decided to develop a new car in common, along similar lines as the previous agreement. (The Honda Concerto/Rover 200-400).

In 1986, Rover agreed to build the Honda Ballade in its Longbridge factory in order to use spare capacity; the contract was renewed in 1989 for the Honda concerto (for 40000 cars a year).

In 1989 Honda took 20% of Rover.

In 1991 the companies signed a memorandum of understanding which provides for a number of new common projects:

– collaboration on the development of three new models;

– organization of a common strategy of component supply for models manufactured in the UK by both companies;

– establishment of formal relations by which Rover will have access to Honda's production units in Japan and North America in order to learn engineering and production techniques;

– Rover will set up a stamping unit at Swindon which will become Honda's main European supplier for metallic panels.

---

Rover and Honda have been working together on product development. The collaboration itself enabled Rover to issue new models with relatively little investment, but in the process, Rover also learnt new methods (Bertodo 1990). Firms also collaborated on component supply and on production. Things have been rather informal; the two companies' latest agreement provides for a more formal process of learning. The memorandum of understanding signed in October 1991 aims at organizing Rover's access to Honda's factories in Japan and North America so that Rover can learn the latter's engineering and production techniques.

### 3.4.2.2 European producers in search of scale

During the 1960s and 1970s European producers, in conformity with mass production, sought to increase their scale of operation. They resorted to acquisitions in a number of cases (see Table 3.7), but also to cooperative agreements particularly, in the case of expensive models.

Renault and Peugeot had agreed on a framework of cooperation in 1966, an 'association' the aim of which was to study the possibilities of achieving economies of scale for a number of components. Two joint ventures for component manufacturing were born of the association.[27] In 1971, the two partners created a joint venture with Volvo to develop a V6 engine.

In 1979, Renault and Volvo entered a cooperation to develop components and share a Renault platform. The agreement was made when Renault took a 10 per cent participation in Volvo (which was sold back in 1983 and 1985). The ambitious programme of the partners was not realized, but, the partners did develop close cooperation on certain components and Renault supplied Volvo with engines and gearboxes. In 1981, the two firms also signed an agreement by which Volvo distributes Renault models in Scandinavia (renewed in 1988).

In 1990, Renault and Volvo agreed on a comprehensive collaboration involving technical and industrial cooperation. The importance of this new venture is attested by cross-capital participations. Renault acquired 10 per cent of Volvo AB, 25 per cent of Volvo Car and 45 per cent of Volvo Truck; conversely, Volvo acquired 20 per cent of Renault and 45 per cent of Renault Vehicles Industriels, the truck subsidiary. The objective is to create strong relationships and benefit from synergies while remaining independent; one main objective is to reduce costs.[28]

Since the agreement, numerous collaborative steps have been taken. The two partners have created coordination committees on cars and trucks, as well as one on strategic issues. In 1990, they created a joint venture (ARA) to monitor common research projects. They also cooperate in purchasing and share some components. Cooperation has rapidly progressed in the field of supply. In 1991 the supply directions of both firms have created a common monitoring committee. In 1992, 20 per cent of the FF 70 bn worth external supplies are made in common (*Le Nouvel Economiste* 22/5/1992). In October 1991, Volvo agreed to buy 1 million engines from Renault over a ten-year period. The two partners have also tightened their relationships in the field of distribution. Finally, they exchange information and coordinate their attitude on questions such as quality.

The success of this relatively young alliance as well as the respective competitive positions of the two companies fuelled rumours of merger at the beginning of 1992.[29] This outcome seemed logical given the numerous collaborative links which have been forged. The traditional preoccupation with economies of scale remains, but the two companies had also thought about the different products and geographical complementarities. The ideal long-term result would have been to create a global European car maker with a large scope of production and the capability to be present on the US market[30], but the merger project was cancelled in 1993.

### 3.4.2.3 Cost-led delocalization

Delocalization in low-cost countries has two traditional types of objectives, which are often both present. The first has to do with costs and the second with market access. Indeed, developing countries often require that multi-national companies manufacture a certain percentage of product locally to grant market access. Under such conditions, production in developing countries has very often entailed agreements between governments or public companies and car makers. This section does not deal with these relationships in detail, the objective is rather to observe that operations in peripheral regions are also concerned by cooperative agreements and to underline the fact that during the 1980s, access for low-cost localizations has tended to favour the acquisition route.

As a general tendency, during the 1980s delocalization in developing countries has been rather limited. This option has appeared as much less powerful than lean production to reduce costs, largely because automobiles are sophisticated products, both in terms of marketing and in terms of production techniques. The most telling example in this respect is South Korea. At the beginning of the 1980s, South Korea's successes in the auto-mobile sector were remarkable and some thought that it might become a new Japan, that the car industry could well follow the textile pattern and be a good example of the product life cycle. But the Korean successes have been short lived, because of wages increases, but more importantly because of quality problems.

Cost-led delocalization has in fact focused on Europe. Spain, and to a lesser extent Portugal, have been the first two countries seized on by car makers. Firms mostly chose the direct investment route, either in greenfield sites or through acquisitions. American and European firms have invested in new production sites. Japanese companies have taken participations in local firms. Volkswagen has used a cooperative agreement as a step towards complete acquisition of SEAT in Spain. This agreement, which lasted from 1982–86 when Volkswagen acquired SEAT, served as a trial ground; this intermediary step constituted a sort of insurance against risk.

Acquisitions and cooperations in production sites have also been largely used to manufacture in Eastern Europe. Things started in a rather confused way, in Russia and Poland for example.[31] But, in general, negotiations have often been similar to those between car makers and developing countries' governments. They are thus quite different from agreements between car makers which are largely competitors.

In conclusion, it appears that the search for low-cost production sites in developing countries is only a complementary solution in the whole globalization project.[32] Low cost should not mean low quality, so that companies must control quality anywhere in the world. Low-cost sites tend to be integrated in the world networks which are progressively set up by companies, especially for component supply. The main example is Korea. American companies are related to Korean firms, either directly as General Motors through its joint venture with Daewoo, or indirectly through a Japanese partner, as for Ford and Chrysler. More generally when two partners become closer, when they cooperate on component supply and on a number of production operations, they tend to include their different sites around the world in the network. This is the case with Ford and Mazda in particular; their cooperation includes relationships with Kia from Korea.

### 3.4.3 Enlarge the Scope of Production

Since the 1980s, because of the combined effect of demand for sophistication, which is favoured by marketing policies, and technical evolutions, product diversification has tended to increase on automobile markets. This diversification has two parts. Japanese producers have increased the rhythm of model renewal and all producers have been carefully nurturing the so-called 'niches'. Sports cars are in a way traditional niches and most car makers have endeavoured to produce some. The same is true for luxury cars in general. Two main new types of niche products have made rapid inroads: four-wheel drive leisure vehicles and the newer all-purpose vehicles such as the Espace model from Renault.

The acquisition of resources to complement volume production with niche vehicles has resorted to different means according to the type of niche. For traditional ones the tendency has been acquisition of specialist producers which have had financial difficulties during the decade. Table 3.7 lists these acquisitions for the 1980s. American volume producers have been the most active; they needed these prestigious brands more than the European firms which have often acquired similar brands in earlier periods and more than the Japanese, whose production techniques enabled them to diversify more flexibly into short series.

On the contrary, cooperative agreements have been preferred for the newer niches. The agreements have first concerned distribution. There have been agreements for the distribution of the Jeep model (which belonged first to AMC and then to Chrysler) by Renault in Europe and of the Pajero model from Mitsubishi by Mercedes. Since the end of the 1980s, there has been a series of agreements to develop, produce and distribute 4×4 and all-purpose vehicles. In 1989, Ford and Nissan decided to cooperate for a 4×4 vehicle, and GM and Suzuki for a leisure/utility vehicle. In 1990, there were four agreements of this type. Chrysler and Steyr (Austria) created a joint venture to produce the Voyager model for Europe. Chrysler also agreed with Honda for the latter to distribute the Jeep model in Japan. Ford agreed to supply Mazda with the Explorer model, which Mazda will sell in the US under the name Navajo. As part of a larger alliance, Mitsubishi and Mercedes agreed to cooperate on a 4×4 vehicle, the definition of the cooperation has progressed in 1991, but all the details are not known yet. Finally, the joint venture between Renault, Toyota and Mitsui in Colombia will produce a Toyota 4×4 model. In 1991, Ford and Volkswagen reached an agreement for the common production of an all-purpose vehicle in Portugal.

A parallel can be drawn between this type of agreements and those which are aimed at producing small trucks such as pick-ups. The latter include the one between GM and Isuzu, or Fiat and PSA, for example.

The difference in the modes of control over the production of niche and specialized vehicles can be due to two types of considerations. The first has to do with production volumes. The higher the prospective market, the more likely the acquisition. On the contrary, for very short series, all the more if they are considered quite risky, some sort of cooperative agreement tends to be preferred. This is of course the case for 4×4 vehicles which may be a fashion fad. The second type of consideration is related to goodwill. In the automobile industry, reputation is a fundamental asset and some prestigious brands may be sought after uniquely for this purpose. American producers which have been widely criticized for their design wanted to appropriate the image of luxury which has been attached to some prestigious European specialist producers such as Lamborghini or Jaguar. But typically, such an appropriation cannot be operated through agreement and requires acquisition.

### 3.4.4 Innovate

Since the 1970s, the automobile industry has experienced a renewal of innovation. We saw that organizational innovation is a crucial aspect; section 3.4.1 showed that the diffusion of lean production is a long and complicated process which relies in part on cooperative agreements. This section focuses on technical innovation.

The current importance of innovation has meant an increase in R&D spending. Moreover, for both process and product innovation, car makers have had to enter new fields of competences. In such circumstances the question is whether to integrate the assets which deliver the relevant competences or whether it is more efficient to just use them without appropriation (Sachwald 1990a; 1990d). The second type of solution can be pursued either by buying technical knowledge on a market, through licences or by directly buying a component which integrates the innovative feature, or by establishing some sort of closer and long-term relationship through a cooperative agreement. The solutions chosen by the automobile manufacturers have differed according to the type of innovation and to their traditions in terms of vertical integration. This section deals with these different means and shows that innovation has been one of the factors which has forcefully fostered new relationships of car makers with their different partners.

### 3.4.4.1  To control new technologies

There have been very few cases where the automobile industry has been able to acquire high-tech companies in order to appropriate their knowledge. Moreover, they have involved two types of actors: aeronautics and electronics companies on one side and American car makers on the other. At the beginning of the 1980s, American car makers were convinced that innovation required direct access to the relevant technologies. And they thought that there could be important synergies with aerospace technologies. In this instance, aerospace was considered as merely in advance of the automobile industry; one day its technologies would arrive in everybody's car. This reasoning is actually quite typical of the American innovation system which has experienced tremendous successes with its military research leading the way since the 1940s. The problem is that the relationships between military and civilian research have become weaker, and more varied.

The Big Three have acquired high-tech companies to boost their innovative capability. GM bought Hughes Aircraft in 1985, Chrysler bought Gulfstream in 1985 and Electrospace Systems in 1987; as for Ford, it had controlled Ford Aerospace for thirty years.[33] GM bought Electronic Data System in 1984 and Ford BDM, a military research business, in 1988.

For Chrysler and Ford this strategy has largely failed and they sold their acquisitions at the end of the decade. From a Chrysler executive's point of view: 'there were no opportunities to take anything practical from aerospace and apply it to mass production of cars'. GM's record is harder to assess. The automobile company has tried various ways to draw technologies from Hughes and EDS and a number of projects have been launched. However, it is difficult to know whether it would not have been cheaper to buy the corresponding technologies.

In Europe there are well established relationships between certain aerospace companies and automobile manufacturers, such as Saab, but synergies are not considered important. In 1989 Daimler-Benz bought MBB, but technological synergies did not appear central to the venture, even if a number of common projects was envisioned (*Les Echos* 15/2/90). Diversification and financial or even political factors also account for some acquisitions such as that of MBB by Daimler or that of Rover by British Aerospace.

### 3.4.4.2 Cooperative research

Most of the time, car makers have preferred cooperation to integration in order to use new technologies in which they had no experience.

Since the 1970s, there has been a number of cooperative projects to develop either components such as engines and transmissions, or car models. The database Auto-JV counts thirteen such cooperative agreements between car makers. Auto-JV also identifies some licence agreements between car makers.[34] Generally speaking there are quite numerous agreements with respect to knowledge exchanges, especially as part of larger cooperations. On the other hand, there are only few cooperative pre-competitive research projects between car makers alone, and without public funding. Box 3.4 lists the three research agreements which have been signed between car makers during the 1980s[35]; one of them has developed by incorporating more numerous partners and can be considered as three successive agreements.

*Box 3.4    Pre-competitive research cooperations between car makers*

---

*1980 Joint Research Committee*
Partners: Fiat, PSA, Renault, Rover, Volvo, Volkswagen. Daimler-Benz joined in 1988 and BMW in 1990.
Objectives: cooperation on pre-competitive research projects with coordination from the Joint Committee which is a light structure. One of the objectives is to avoid duplicating a number of projects. Since 1980, the JRC has been working on numerous projects; there has been a tendency for the number of projects to increase (from about five to six at the beginning of the decade to about 25 at the beginning of the 1990s). The projects often involve universities, but much more rarely suppliers.

*1988 Automotive Composites Consortium*
Partners: GM, Ford, Chrysler
Objectives: consortium to monitor research on composite materials. The projects can be conducted either collectively or separately by the partners.

*1990 Associates in Advanced Research (ARA)*
Partners: Renault, Volvo
Objectives: conceive, organize and control the future advanced research projects of the two companies.

---

Looking at these cooperations, which were relatively new in the 1980s (Sachwald 1990b), it is easy to see that the types of partners differ from those of other agreements. In particular, they involve more numerous partners and firms from the same country or the same region. This is due to the fact that cooperation is 'pre-competitive' and that it can be implemented even with the nearest competitors.

But the very limited number of cooperative agreements of this type indicates that car makers have relatively little to exchange. Most research agreements organize cooperation with partners from other industries. There are two large categories of projects dealing with new areas. The first brings together several car makers within a large project which may include many partners and is at least partially financed by public funds. Box 3.5 lists the eight projects of this kind.

The second type of cooperative research projects brings together a car maker and one or several partners from other industries without public funding. The database Auto-JV numbers a dozen agreements of this sort. They mostly use simple contracts but some create a joint venture. Innovation, as part of the process of development and production, constitutes one of the main areas in which relationships with suppliers have evolved. Since vertical integration tends to diminish and since component suppliers are given more responsibilities in terms of product development, they become major partners in the innovation process. This source of innovation depends on the relationships established with suppliers and, in turn, on the innovativeness of the component industry. These subjects are dealt with in the chapter on automobile components (Chapter 4).

## 3.5   EUROPEAN FIRMS FACING GLOBALIZATION

The previous section has shown that car makers have actively used external growth operations to implement their strategies. This shows the importance of cooperative agreements, especially in a period of restructuring, but does not give a general evaluation by company. This section focuses on the situation of European firms. By adopting the point of view of external growth operations, it shows that European firms tend to be less internationalised[36] than their American and Japanese competitors, or, more precisely, they tend to concentrate on the European markets.

### 3.5.1  The Geographical Distribution of External Growth Operations

Table 3.7 above lists the acquisitions in the automobile industry since the mid-1970s. It shows that European car makers have mostly acquired companies or divisions in Europe. There is actually only one exception, the control

*Box 3.5      Research agreements with public support*

---

*1980 Groupement Scientifique des Moteurs (GSM)*
*Partners: PSA, Renault, Institut Français du Pétrole*
Objectives: cooperation in order to study engines and carburation.

*1986–94 PROMETHEUS (Program for European Traffic with Highest Efficiency and Unprecedented Safety)*, a EUREKA project
*Partners: Daimler-Benz (chiefly responsible), BMW, Fiat, Porsche, PSA, Renault, Rover, Saab, Volvo, VW; about 100 suppliers and 70 research organizations.*
Objectives: to develop electronics related to the car and traffic flow. It is divided into seven sub-programs (three in industrial research and four in fundamental research).

*1986–91 CARMAT,* EUREKA project
*Partners: PSA (chiefly responsible), fourteen other firms from different specialities (BASF, ICI, Saint-Gobain, etc.), two public institutes.*
Objectives: to examine the possibilities of conceiving a vehicle with new materials which would be competitive both in terms of cost and efficiency.

*1987 AGATA,* EUREKA project
*Partners: PSA (chiefly responsible), Volvo, Daimler-Benz, Pechiney, Microturbo, Office National d'Etudes et de Recherches Appliquées.*
Objectives: conception by the year 2000 of a gas turbine engine. It should be highly efficient and generate as little as possible pollution by using new metallic materials and ceramics.

*1988–98 Moonlight project*
*Partners: Toyota, Nissan, Mitsubishi, Japan Auto Research Institute.*
Objectives: research on ceramics and their use in gas turbine engines. The project is part of the Moonlight project which also includes a research group on electrical cars.

*1990 Moteur propre (clean engine)*
*Partners: PSA, Renault, suppliers (Solex, Siemens-Bendix, Valeo, etc.) and public institutes (IFP, AFME, CEA, CNRS, etc.).*
Objectives: innovations in order to face future environmental regulations and in particular the clean engine (low consumption and emissions); to explore several possibilities while focusing on non-pollution (as opposed to depollution through the catalytic converter).

*1990 MOSAIC (Matériaux Optimisés pour une Structure Automobile Innovant la Conception)*, EUREKA project
*Partners: Renault (chiefly responsible), Sollac, Ciba-Geigy, DSM, Hydro-Aluminium, Montedipe, Montedison.*
Objectives: innovative conception of cars in order to answer the environmental challenge; to produce vehicles which optimize the properties of different types of materials.

*1991 Electrical batteries*
*Partners: GM, Ford, Chrysler, American government (50% of the budget).*
Objectives: to develop advanced technologies for electrical car batteries. Twelve-year project.

of AMC (US) by Renault, which only lasted from 1979–87 since Renault sold its stake to Chrysler in 1987. The European pattern contrasts with that of the American car makers which acquired a number of small European firms at the end of the 1980s. The main difference on the side of cooperative agreements is the substantial role played by Japanese car makers.

*Table 3.8   Geographical distribution of cooperative agreements, in %*

| Between firms from | All types | Type of agreements | |
| | | Between car makers | Between car makers and active in 1992 |
| --- | --- | --- | --- |
| EC/EC | 19.4 | 12.5 | 12.7 |
| EC/EFTA | 11.1 | 10.8 | 7.8 |
| EC/US | 4.2 | 5.0 | 3.9 |
| EC/Japan | 17.4 | 20.0 | 18.6 |
| US/Japan | 26.4 | 30.8 | 32.3 |
| US/US | 5.5 | 5.0 | 4.9 |
| Japan/Japan | 2.8 | 2.5 | 2.9 |
| Japan/Asia | 4.9 | 5.8 | 6.9 |
| With Eastern Europe | 2.8 | 3.3 | 3.9 |

*Source*: calculations from Auto-A

Table 3.8 gives the geographical distribution of the cooperative agreements from the database. The table shows that there have been relatively few cooperative agreements among EC car makers. Moreover, among these cooperations, a number are between domestic firms, which leaves a very small number of international cooperations within the EC (only eight out of fifteen EC operations). There has been more cooperation with suppliers and firms from outside the automobile industry (such as chemical or electronics companies). These results are unchanged if we only consider the agreements which were still active in 1991; this means that cooperation between EC car makers has not increased during the 1980s. Besides, despite the extensive cooperation between Renault and Volvo, the share of agreements between car makers from EC and EFTA countries has tended to decrease during the period. In 1992, the cooperative agreements between European car makers (from EC and EFTA) represented 20.5 per cent of the total.

European car makers are quite naturally led to cooperation in domains which are more and more regulated by the EEC, such as environmental and security questions; they also cooperate with suppliers and firms from other sectors on research. It seems quite sensible to find new solutions only once, especially since R&D costs tend to increase rapidly. At present, research is the field where European firms cooperate the most. This pattern can be explained by the so-called 'pre-competitive' character of research; otherwise, European car makers are close competitors. This discrepancy between the two types of cooperation does not exist for other types of agreements, and in particular for the most important categories, that is EC/Japan and US/Japan. If we only consider agreements between car makers, Japanese firms are central in the general pattern: 67 per cent of all international cooperations (i.e. excluding domestic cooperations) between car makers involve Japanese firms, as against 47 per cent for European firms (EC) and 43 per cent for American firms.

European firms' external growth operations are thus concentrated on Europe. Moreover, European cooperative agreements with non-European firms tend to be of limited scope.This is consonant with their general strategy. Indeed, during the 1980s, European firms have tended to retreat from a number of markets, and more particularly from the United States.[37] Luxury firms have exported a great deal to the US for a time, but have been hard hit by the recession which started at the end of the decade.

### 3.5.2  The Functional Distribution of Cooperative Agreements

A classification of the agreements by function enables us to deal with the objectives of cooperation.[38] Such a classification has already been used in section 3.4; the objective here is to try to assess the importance of the different cooperations. The database is helpful since it gives the number of agreements between the same partners, and then the types of functions which are concerned.

A rough classification by importance leads to three groups of cooperative agreements. In the first group there are only agreements of limited importance (distribution in one country for example) which usually take place between occasional partners. In the second category, two partners may have a couple of agreements together, but their cooperation remains limited. This is the case of Fiat and PSA, for example, which cooperate in a number of projects, either as sole partners (joint design of a motor, joint venture for small commercial vehicles) or with other European partners (in the case of research). The third category consists of the most important agreements, those which could be considered as most strategic. Their number is quite limited; Table 3.9 lists them. The table gives the number of important cooperative agreements between the companies but cannot trace all the steps of the cooperation, which are not always recorded with specific agreements.[39]

*Table 3.9    Strategic alliances between car makers*°

| Partners | Number of agreements | Financial arrangement | Cooperation in: |
|---|---|---|---|
| GM/Isuzu | 9 | GM owns 38% of Isuzu | Knowledge, production, supply, distribution, several countries |
| Chrysler/ Mitsubishi | 7 | Chrysler owns 12.1% of Mitsubishi | Production, supply, distribution, mainly US |
| Ford/ Mazda | 8 | Ford owns 24% of Mazda | Knowledge, production, supply, distribution, several countries |
| Honda/ Rover | 8 | Honda owns 20% of Rover | Knowledge, production, supply, distribution, mainly Europe and Japan |
| Renault/ Volvo | 7 | Renault owns 10% of Volvo AB; Volvo 20% of Renault* | Knowledge, supply, quality, distribution. The agreement tends to operate coordination between countries. |

°   For details on the agreements, see text; in particular, Boxes 3.3 and 3.4.
*   There are also specific participations for the car and truck divisions; see above.
*Source*: Auto-A

Table 3.9 shows that strategic alliances fit the general pattern of cooperation. In particular, Japanese firms are heavily represented and European firms cooperate within Europe (here between the EC and EFTA). The strategic alliances, as well as some important agreements from the second category, such as those between GM and Toyota, and Ford and Nissan, result in strong links between American and Japanese firms. Moreover, the strategic alliances between American and Japanese firms which are listed in the table are complemented with alliances with Korean firms (GM and Daewoo; Ford as well as Mazda with Kia; Mitsubishi with Hyundaï). On the contrary, European firms have only shallower links with firms from the other poles of the Triad. The relationship between Rover and Honda is an exception, but Rover plays the weaker part.

## 3.6   CONCLUSION

This conclusion comes back on two points: first, the confrontation of the experience of the automobile industry in terms of external growth with theoretical developments; second, the position of European firms within the networks of triadic alliances.

The experience of the automobile industry tends to corroborate the analysis of cooperative agreements in terms of transaction costs. Indeed, once a firm has a strategic objective, it chooses the type of agreement to enter into according to transaction cost considerations. In particular, it is quite obvious that the most ambitious cooperations involve financial participation (Renault/Volvo, for example). Common production often implies a joint venture (NUMMI for example), while cooperative research can be achieved through much lighter structures and contractual arrangements.[40] Moreover, when the objectives are all encompassing or when the appropriation is considered as necessary, firms prefer to acquire a company. Acquisitions have not been very numerous in the automobile industry, one of the reasons being that it was already quite concentrated. This consideration leads to the strategic aspect of external growth operations.

Transaction cost analysis is very useful once the strategic options have been considered, but this chapter has shown that cooperative agreements as well as acquisitions are used to implement strategic options and the latter thus constitute the most important point to examine. From this perspective, it appears that cooperative agreements offer very useful tools in periods of adaptation and restructuring. This is due to their flexibility and their reversibility, two properties which contrast with acquisitions, which can be much more costly.

During the 1980s, the automobile industry has had to confront several challenges. Firms from all the regions of the Triad had to adapt quickly to the evolution of the competititve game, even if their competences and, as a consequence, their needs differed. In such a context cooperative agreements have been an important source of flexibility. A large number of the agreements in the automobile industry have to do with learning. Apart from cooperative research, learning is the objective of numerous cooperations: learning new production methods (from the Japanese), learning about the business environment in a foreign country (in the US or in Europe), cooperating on the development of a new product (such as niche vehicles). Moreover, information exchange is of course part of all the important alliances (Renault/Volvo, Ford/Mazda, etc.).[41]

Cooperative agreements are now quite numerous in the automobile industry[42] and they have to be considered in order to analyse the competitive game. First, some sets of alliances can amount to networks and, more generally, some types of alliances can impact on the degree of concentration of the industry. Second, alliances appear as one of the instruments to adapt to the process of globalization.

This chapter has shown that European firms have used cooperative agreements differently from American and Japanese firms. As a result, they appear relatively more isolated. Their cooperations with Japan in particular are quite limited in scope.[43] This situation corresponds to the strategic choice of most European companies during the 1980s, that is to concentrate on Europe. How much of a handicap this could be depends on the progress of globalization. So far, and despite the fact that the automobile industry has often been considered as one of the most globalized, globalization is only just underway. Firms are in quite different situations, even among the Japanese producers. Nevertheless, globalization should continue its progress in the automobile industry. For Europe, it means that its markets will be more open to various competitors.

The probable increase in the degree of competition on European markets has two consequences for European firms. First, they have to go on with their efforts to increase their efficiency (including the qualitative aspect). Second, they have to take steps in order to penetrate foreign markets. In this endeavour, they may want to use cooperative agreements, either with other European firms[44] or on different markets. More generally, globalization and product differentiation should make certain cooperative ventures attractive if not vital.

## APPENDIX: Data on External Growth Operations involving Car Makers

This chapter relies on two data banks which have been constructed by the author: Auto-MA on mergers and acquisitions and Auto-A on cooperative agreements.

### The Operations

The operations in Auto-MA are those which involve control (more than 30 per cent).

The operations in Auto-A are diverse. They include all formal cooperative agreements. The latter can take different legal shapes: joint venture, minority holdings, cooperative agreement without equity. They fulfil various functions: production, distribution, research, technological transfer, supply (including cars supplied in OEM).

Some agreements develop over time; examples include GM/Isuzu or Renault/Volvo. In these cases, in order to take into account the different aspects of the cooperation and its overall importance, the database includes one entry for each new development. Even with this feature, the database does not provide a case study for these wide cooperations.

**The partners**

The data have been collected for car makers from industrial countries and Korea. Operations in developing countries are not recorded, except if they involve two partners from industrial countries (e.g. Autolatina).

A number of agreements between car makers and suppliers on forms from other industries are included. (For operations within the automobile component sector, see Chapter 4.)

**The sources**

Both banks have been progressively constructed and rely on various sources
* Press, both general and specialized
* Documents from the CCFA (Comité des Constructeurs Français d'Automobiles)
* Annual reports from firms
* Previous studies, analyses (and the text).

# NOTES

1. The model relates the total production of a product since its introduction to characteristics of the competitive game and to the localization of production around the world. The cycle comprises four phases: introduction, development, maturity and decline.
2. There are several versions: in the United States Sloan revised the Fordian model to apply it to General Motors and mass production was then adapted to Europe with specific characteristics (Sloan 1963; Altshuler *et al.* 1984; Roos 1990).
3. Sachwald (1989a) gives a table showing large differences between results.
4. This, in turn, is due to the theoretical origin of the notion of economies of scale; economic theory defines economies of scale in relation to the production function, and the notion of economies of scope does not fundamentally alter the approach (Sachwald 1989a).
5. Marfels (1988) gives a table for production concentration for the different countries and up to 1986.
6. The automobile sector was thus a clear example of intra-industry trade; on this question see in particular Sachwald (1989a).
7. At least of solvent demand; needs are still enormous in developing countries and in Eastern Europe.
8. See section 3.2.3 for comments on this notion and on its applicability to the automobile industry. See also the discussion of the product cycle model in Chapter 7 on chemicals.
9. There have been some other entries, like that of Korea or Latin American countries, but, despite some forecasts, their role has remained minor.
10. Statistics from the annual bulletin from CCFA (see bibliography).
11. The MIT's International Automobile Program has been the most important effort at understanding the differences between the production systems in the world automobile industry. For results from the programme, see in particular Altshuler *et al.* (1984): Krafcik (1988); Womack, Jones and Roos (1990).

12. What follows is not a definition or a precise description of the lean production process, but rather a broad description in order to contrast it with mass production. Several elements of lean production are discussed in the text; for a more complete description, see Womack, Jones and Roos (1990).

13. See Jones (1988). For suppliers, see Chapter 4 in this volume.

14. Volpato (1983) has used a similar notion by qualifying the automobile as a 'neo-infant industry'.

15. More detailed indications on the position of the different firms will be given when discussing strategies (section 3.4).

16. On the difficulties of estimating the degree of vertical integration, see in particular Banville and Chanaron (1991); Ruigrok, Tulder and Baven (1991).

17. J.-Y. Helmer is the Director of the automobile division of the PSA group.

18. This second point has been mentioned above in section 3.2. For a broader analysis of the whole system of production, see in particular Jacot (1990); Ruigrok, Tulder and Baven (1991).

19. For a detailed analysis these evolutions, see in particular Sachwald (1989b).

20. Free trade already exists, and the Single Market provides for technical harmonization.

21. On this agreement, see *Europolitique* (17/7/1991, 31/7/1991, 3/8/1991); *Les Echos* (17/10/1991).

22. On this point, see in particular Bélis-Bergouignan, Bordenave and Lung (1991), Ruigrok, Tulder and Baven (1991).

23. One should note that Honda was already a strong exporter and had a cooperative agreement in the UK; see below.

24. Nissan also produces vans and trucks in Spain.

25. MIT's automobile programme was a case study, see Womack (1988).

26. Performances are between those of Toyota in Japan and GM in the US (Womack 1988).

27. The ambitions of the association were high and other cooperations were explored, in research in particular; see Loubet (1990).

28. According to C. Zettergerg, chief executive at Volvo, about 75 per cent of the savings are related to product development and the supply of components (*Financial Times* 31/4/1992).

29. See for example, *Financial Times* (1/5/1992); *Business Week* (25/5/1992); *Le Nouvel Economiste* (22/5/1992).

30. Ambitions in the field of trucks were also important, but, the relationship was much tighter in the case of cars (*Le Nouvel Economiste* 22/5/1992).

31. See a list of cooperations in CCFA (1991).

32. In this respect one should also consider components, see Chapter 4.

33. See *Le Figaro* (8/12/1989); *Financial Times* (23/1/1990).

34. The database probably underestimates the number of licences since it does not deal with developing countries (except for Korea). See the presentation of the database in the appendix.

35. In 1966, VW and Daimler-Benz signed a cooperative research agreement to study pollution and electric propulsion.

36. Or globalized, according to a now fashionable term. The qualitative difference between internationalization and globalization would require a detailed discussion. The text returns to this point in the conclusion. For a more detailed discussion, see in particular Bélis-Bergouignan, Bordenave and Lung (1991).

37. It has been the case with VW for example; the case of Renault has already been mentioned.

38. Even if there are a number of problems in achieving this classification; see the appendix on the database.

39. This is a common problem in the analysis of long-term cooperative agreements; see the appendix on the database.

40. For a more detailed and formal demonstration of the interest of transaction cost analysis for cooperative agreements, see Sachwald (1990a) for the automobile case.

41. The alliances between American, Japanese and Korean firms could be analysed along this line.

42. The number of agreements has to be considered together with the number of firms; they are quite few in the automobile industry.

43. With the possible exception of the alliance between Daimler and Mitsubishi, the scope of which remains to be confirmed.

44. See the example of the Renault/Volvo alliance which has the American market on its agenda.

# BIBLIOGRAPHY

Abernathy, W. (1978), *The Productivity Dilemma: Roadblock to Innovation in the Automobile Industry*, Johns Hopkins University Press, Baltimore.

Altshuler, A., Anderson, M., Jones, D., Roos, D. and Womack, J. (1984), *The future of the Automobile*, MIT Press, Cambridge.

Banville, E. de and Chanaron, J.-J. (1991), *Vers un système automobile européen*, Economica, Paris.

Bélis-Bergouignan, M.-C., Bordenave, G. and Lung, Y. (1991), 'Ford: une stratégie trans-régionale', *Annales des Mines*, October.

Bertodo, R. (1990), 'The collaborative Vortex: Anatomy of a Euro-Japanese Alliance', *Japanese Motor Business*, Economist Intelligence Unit, London, June.

Caput, B. (1989), *L'industrie automobile européenne à la veille du Grand Marché Unique*, Banque de l'Union européenne, January.

CCFA (Comité des Constructeurs Français d'Automobiles) (1991), *Répertoire mondial des activités de production et d'assemblage de véhicules automobiles*, Paris.

Gerwin, D. and Tarondeau, J.-C. (1984), 'La flexibilité dans les processus de production: le cas de l'automobile', *Revue Française de Gestion*, July.

Helmer, J.-U. (1991), 'L'industrie automobile européenne est-elle condamnée?', *Annales des Mines*, October.

Jacot, J.-H. (sous la direction de) (1990), *Du Fordisme au Toyotisme*, La Documentation française, Paris.

Jones, D. (1988), 'Ajustement structurel dans l'industrie automobile', *STI Revue, OECD*, April.

Krafcik, J. (1988), *Comparative analysis of performance indicators at world auto assembly plants*, mimeo, MIT, 1.

Loubet, J.-L. (1990), *Automobiles Peugeot, une réussite industrielle 1945–1974*, Economica, Paris.

Marfels, C. (1988), *Recent trends of Concentration in Selected Industries of the European Community, Japan, and the United States*, Commission of the European Communities, Brussels.

Porter, M. (1986), 'Competition in Global Industries: a Conceptual Framework' in M. Porter (ed.), *Competition in Global Industries*, Harvard Business School Press, London.

Roos, P. (1990), *L'Automobile*, Economica, Paris.

Ruigrok, W. Van, Tulder, R. and Baven, G. (1991), *Cooperation, competition, coalitions and control. Globalisation and glocalisation processes in the World car industry*, FAST, EC.

Sachwald, F. (1989a), *Ajustement sectoriel et adaptation des entreprises. Le cas de l'industrie automobile*, Document de travail, CEPII, no. 89-03.

Sachwald, F. (1989b), 'Libéralisation et néo-protectionisme. Le cas de l'industrie automobile', *Politique étrangère*, no. 4, IFRI.

Sachwald, F. (1990a), 'Les accords dans l'industrie automobile: une analyse en termes de coûts de transaction', *Economie prospective internationale*, CEPII, La Documentation française, Paris, 2nd trim.

Sachwald, F. (1990b), 'Les accords dans l'industrie automobile: la poursuite de la concurrence par d'autres moyens', *Economie prospective internationale*, CEPII, La Documentation française, 1st trim.

Sachwald, F. (1990c), 'La Compétitivité européenne: nations et entreprises', in *RAMSES 91: le monde et son évolution*, IFRI/Dunod, Paris.

Sachwald, F. (1990d), 'Acuerdos de investigacion cooperativa en Europa. Las formas de la competencia a través de la innovacion', *Economia Publica*.

Sachwald, F. (1991), *Competition Policy and Competitiveness: Europe in the 80s*, Occasional Paper, Tokyo Club Foundation for Global Studies, October.

Sloan, A. P. (1963), *My Years with General Motors*, Doubleday, Garden City, New York.

Volpato, G. (1983), *L'industria automobilistica internazionale*, CEDAM.

Womack, J. (1988), 'Multinational joint ventures in the steel industry', in D. Mowery, (ed.). *International Collaborative Ventures in US Manufacturing*, Ballinger, Cambridge.

Womack, J., Jones, D. T. and Roos, D. (1990), *The Machine that Changed the World*, Rawson Associates, New York.

# 4. The Autocomponent Industry

## Etienne de Banville and Jean-Jacques Chanaron

The autocomponent industry is difficult to understand, by the very fact that it is defined with reference to cars, it is an intermediary industry. Automobile production calls upon a very broad selection of technologies; thus, the activities concerned are of considerable variety, i.e.

- automobile components in the strict sense of the term, that is, those falling within the internal engine definition;
- tyres and rubber, plastic and composite parts;
- batteries;
- glass products;
- electrical and electronic parts; and
- to some extent, unfinished components before transformation of the metals (machined, cast, forged, cut and pressed, etc.).

To build up appropriate general indicators is all the more difficult as, even though activities are becoming concentrated in bigger companies, the number of these companies remains high.[1]

A specific examination of external growth in the autocomponent sector is justified first by the subordinate position they hold as regards the car makers. Although most of the latter have begun systematically dismantling their vertically integrated structure, entrusting their suppliers with a growing role in design and manufacture of many components, the master-servant relationship has remained largely stable; any large-scale external development in the sector is ultimately 'regulated' by the car makers, who accept it or not.

Second, car makers and component suppliers are sometimes in competition. Most automobile producers have developed historically from highly integrated positions; they manufactured many of their components themselves. They are all now engaged in disintegrating their production, but are going about it in different ways; while some manufacturers have kept large component subsidiaries which they have sought to 'introduce into the market' by supplying other manufacturers (such as Fiat with Magneti Marelli, Gilardini and Teksid, PSA with ECIA, and more recently Ford), they have also sold many workshops or subsidiaries to autocomponent groups. The automobile industry itself has therefore contributed considerably to determining its upstream operations.

In spite of considerable factors of competition, car makers and suppliers will share an increasingly similar future. The upsurge in 'automobile systems', where car makers and component manufacturers or first tier suppliers are teamed, is entirely due to this. The suppliers take complete responsibility for *'functions'*, i.e. design, manufacture and delivery of subsystems ready for mounting, fulfilling one or several purposes defined by vehicle specifications: heating/air conditioning, lighting/signalling, seating, display information, ground linkage, braking, remote control, etc.

Within these systems, good medium-term relationships between firms are essential; in other words, medium-term strategic coordination between firms is vital to the establishment of partnerships.[2] Some methods for inter-enterprise coordination may be alliances, agreements and shareholdings, quite apart from partnerships as such.

This entire development is characterized both by the speed with which it is growing, and also by its sectorial breadth. It accelerated most strongly in 1990 and 1991, under the pressure of the growing Japanese presence in the European car industry, and preparation for the Single Market. On the other hand, developments in central and Eastern Europe seem to be mostly concerned with car manufacturing and not the component industry.

These inter-enterprise developments are not restricted simply to specific areas, for three overlapping reasons First, most of the 'functions' to be designed, manufactured and delivered call upon joint competence in several technological fields; alliances and agreements will therefore be of trans-sectoral nature. Second, some groups see strategic opportunities in these developments, such as going downstream, alliance with a competitor, and so on; and finally, the field of autocomponents may be just one particular area in which strategic alliances are struck between mega-industries and financial groups undertaking overall reorganization of many of their industrial interests at the same time.

## 4.1  SECTORAL CHARACTERISTICS

The European automotive component industry is a large sector. Firms independent of the car manufacturers employ nearly 1 million employees, i.e. 38 per cent of the 2.5 million jobs in the European automobile industry system (see Table 4.1).

The Germans are the leaders in the European autocomponent industry system; their share of total European turnover was some 39 per cent in 1988–89. Recent FIEV estimate put this share at a little under 50 per cent for 1991–92 (see Table 4.2).

*Table 4.1   The European automobile system in 1988, distribution of employment by activity*

|  | Number of employees, '000s | In % |
|---|---|---|
| Assembly | 100 | 4.0 |
| Production of components by car makers | 590 | 23.6 |
| Component subsidiaries of car makers | 110 | 4.4 |
| Independent component suppliers | 950 | 38.0 |
| Transformation of materials | 540 | 21.6 |
| Production of materials | 210 | 8.4 |
| Total | 2500 | 100.0 |

*Source*: CEE-Boston Consulting Group (BCG)

*Table 4.2   Independent European automotive component industry, 1988*

|  | Turnover, in ECU bn | Number of firms | Employment | Share in industrial employment (%) |
|---|---|---|---|---|
| Germany | 30.6 | 600 | 329 100 | 3.4 |
| France | 16.9 | 400 | 168 700 | 2.9 |
| Italy | 11.1 | 1000 | 138 500 | 2.5 |
| Spain | 8.8 | 450 | 147 100 | 4.7 |
| UK | 8.2 | 350 | 132 600 | 2.0 |
| Benelux | 1.8 | 230 | 17 600 | 1.0 |
| Total EC | 78.5 | 3250 | 950 000 | 2.6 |
| United States | – | – | 700 000 | – |
| Japan | – | – | 505 000 | – |
| Car makers' subsidiaries | 10.3 | – | 110 000 | – |

*Source*: CE-BCG (1991); *Financial Times*, FIEV

The European autocomponent industry was still relatively scattered in 1988. The Boston Consulting Group (BCG) study for the EC (CE-BCG 1991) counted 3200 companies, only 150 of which had more than 1000 employees. The 25 leading autocomponent groups accounted for some 55 per cent of total turnover in the industry at that time. The many mergers and takeovers between 1989 and 1992 have added considerably to the influence of the big groups (see Tables 4.3–4.5 for figures).

*Table 4.3*    Turnover of the main European component producers and of the
European subsidiaries of the American component suppliers, in $ bn*

|  | | 1990 | 1988 | 1988 |
|---|---|---|---|---|
| 1990 Rank | | Auto turnover $ bn | Auto turnover $ bn | Share in the total turnover in % |
| 1 | Michelin (F) | 10.31 | 8.07 | 100 |
| 2 | Bosch (D) | 10.12 | 7.61 | 55 |
| 3 | Philips (NL) | 4.79 | 3.79 | 5 |
| 4 | Continental (D) | 4.66 | 1.77 | 63 |
| 5 | Valéo (F) | 3.94 | 2.06 | 78 |
| 6 | Mannesmann (D) | 3.67 | na | – |
| 7 | Magneti Marelli (I) | 3.37 | 2.04 | 100 |
| 8 | ZF (D) | 3.11 | 1.95 | 76 |
| 9 | BASF (D) | 3.09 | 1.67 | 8 |
| 10 | ACG Europe (US) | 2.90 | 2.00 | 100 |
| 11 | GKN (UK) | 2.75 | 1.81 | 60 |
| 12 | SKF (S) | 2.71 | 1.78 | 58 |
| 13 | Freudengerg (D) | 2.64 | 0.61 | 34 |
| 14 | Pirelli (I) | 2.62 | 2.90 | 52 |
| 15 | Lucas (UK) | 2.45 | 2.00 | 62 |
| 16 | BTR (UK) | 1.85 | 0.82 | 12 |
| 17 | Fichtel & Sachs (D) | 1.79 | 0.60 | 80 |
| 18 | Teves (D) | 1.58 | 1.31 | 100 |
| 19 | T&N (UK) | 1.38 | 1.08 | 69 |
| 20 | VDO (D) | 1.36 | 0.86 | 80 |
| 21 | Mahle (D) | 1.28 | 0.86 | 89 |
| 22 | Pilkington (UK) | 1.17 | 0.96 | 25 |
| 23 | Epéda-BF (F) | 1.11 | 0.66 | 63 |
| 24 | Allied Signal (US) | 1.10 | 1.03 | 37 |
| 25 | BBA (UK) | 1.10 | 0.93 | 84 |
| 26 | Siemens (D) | 1.10 | 0.90 | 3 |
| 27 | ECIA (F) | 0.85 | 0.59 | 60 |
| 28 | Saint-Gobain (F) | 0.84 | 0.77 | 6 |
| 29 | Behr (D) | 0.84 | 0.77 | 100 |
| 30 | Rockwell (US) | 0.83 | 0.77 | 49 |

\*  For European firms: worldwide turnover. For American firms: European subsidia-
ries' turnover.
*Sources*: Banville and Chanaron (1991): *Financial Times*, FIEV, EIU, CCFA, *Les
Echos*.

*Table 4.4  Degree of concentration in European autocomponent industry, 1988, in %*

| Share of the total turnover realized by: | | | |
|---|---|---|---|
| First firm | First 5 firms | First 10 firms | First 25 firms |
| 8.7 | 26.5 | 37.1 | 54.1 |

*Source*: estimate from the authors based on European turnover given in CE-BCG (1991)

The mid-term forecasts of the BCG study (CE-BCG 1991) indicate a mean annual increase of some 2.7 per cent in production and consumption of automotive components, accompanied by a continuing fall in workforce figures.

*Table 4.5  Forecast for 1994 (ECU bn for production and consumption)*

| | 1988 | 1994 | Annual rate of variation, in % |
|---|---|---|---|
| Production | 78.5 | 91.9 | + 2.7 |
| Consumption | 70.9 | 83.4 | + 2.7 |
| Number of employees | 950 000 | 880 000 | – 1.3 |

*Source*: CE-BCG (1991)

### 4.1.1  Differentiated National Systems

Different industrial development in each country has led to different configurations. In the UK, the car industry system is characterized by its total dependence on the strategies of the car and autocomponent manufacturing multinationals. The supply and autocomponent sector is divided into five categories:
1. A few big groups, such as Lucas, GKN, T&N, TI Group, BTR, BBA, etc., which have found that swift internationalization and external growth have solved the problem of the drastic reduction of their internal markets.
2. Some American multinational establishments, such as Allied Bendix, Rockwell, Cummins and Perkins, and also Japanese ones (Yuasa, Mitsubishi Electric, Calsonic), whose future policy is decided elsewhere.
3. A vast number of SMEs (Small and Medium Enterprises) who have experienced the failure of national car industry and have sought to survive by reducing capacity; today they are in a disastrous position.

4. High-tech SMEs, particularly in electronics, seeking to survive today by riding the crises (such as AB Electronic).
5. Engineering and design firms in bodywork and mechanical parts, which have acquired a position as world leaders.

The German automobile sector was really built up as an essentially national system, with, first of all, a very integrated industry which remains so, exemplified by Mercedes Benz; and second, powerful autocomponent producers with wide international markets and commanding positions in many areas. Among the 34 main European autocomponent groups in 1988, including tyre manufacturers, there were thirteen German groups, of which Bosch was the world leader, and ZF, BASF, and Teves accounted for over a billion dollars of world turnover in the car industry. It is in Germany that the autocomponent sector is the most concentrated. Sixty-five per cent of the jobs in this sector are provided by firms with over 1000 employees and 4 per cent by firms with under 100 employees. These manufacturers are supplied almost exclusively by national firms: Mercedes buys 90 per cent of its components in Germany, and VAG 80 per cent.

Fiat completely dominates the autocomponent sector in Italy, and has financial control over the only large national autocomponent group, Magneti Marelli. It has succeeded in keeping control of nearly all the very many SMEs in this sector (90 per cent of firms have under 500 employees), which therefore have only one client since Fiat controls most of the Italian car industry and 88 per cent of its parts come from firms based in Italy. As for local units of American multinationals such as ITT and Rockwell in particular, they are dedicated to supplying Fiat and Iveco. The situation for trading and spare parts is set out in Box 4.1 and Table 4.6.

In France, the autocomponent industry was long structured by the two car manufacturing groups for their own benefit, and was then weakened by majority holdings (over 60 per cent of workforce) taken by American (GM-Components, Rockwell, Dana, TRW, and ITT), British (GKN and T&N), Italian (De Benedetti and Fiat) and German (Bosch, Teves, Fichtel & Sachs) groups. Some French groups are nevertheless among the European or world leaders in their field, for example Michelin, Valéo, Epéda Bertrand-Faure, and Ecia. As for SMEs, they are dependent on market fluctuations. Faced with the challenges of foreign competition, particularly from Japan, they are generally obliged to regroup or integrate larger groups if they are to survive.

*Box 4.1    Trading and Spare Parts*

For most European autocomponent producers, the spare parts market is essential since it covers almost 24% of their total market share, and is thus a damper protecting them from conjunctural fluctuations in assembly part deliveries to car assemblers.

*Table 4.6    Markets for independent autocomponent manufacturers*

|  | First equipment |  | Replacement parts |
| --- | --- | --- | --- |
| Germany | 19.5 | Germany | 4.0 |
| France | 11.2 | France | 4.0 |
| Italy | 6.8 | Italy | 2.4 |
| Spain | 8.1 | Spain | 1.1 |
| UK | 6.1 | UK | 3.0 |
| Benelux | 2.0 | Benelux | 1.3 |
| Total EC | 54.0 | Total EC | 16.9 |

*Source*: CE-BCG (1991)

This market is undergoing rapid restructuring at the present time, producing effects such as:

- increasing importance of large retailing surfaces for parts and components, including for substitute engine servicing and gear boxes; in France, general distributing giants such as Carrefour, Promodès, Auchan and so on are competing with specialist retailers such as Norauto, Feu Vert, etc.;
- increasing importance of swift repair services which initially concerned only one function, but which are now broadening their scope to exhaust systems, oil-changing, electrical equipment, shock-absorbers, paintwork etc.;
- restructuring of subsidiaries and car manufacturers' agents to adapt to competition from the pre-existing networks by developing swift, personalized service, maintenance contracts and so on;
- attempted development of networks owned by certain autocomponent manufacturers such as Lucas, Bosch, Michelin, etc.;
- growing competition from 'adaptable' parts copying original parts, particularly from Italian SMEs not listed as autocomponent manufacturers;
- continuing decline in independent repair garages incapable of financing investment in and training for new technology in vehicles and garage equipment.

In this special market, autocomponent manufacturers' strategies vary: some have strengthened their position with regard to competition on both the original and replacement part markets; some have simply left the replacement market to adaptable parts manufacturers, and have concentrated on the original equipment market; finally, some have specialized in replacement.

Exacerbated competition in this part of the automobile system, which has become of strategic importance, is occurring at a time when the car industry, with the help of the auto-component industry, is launching products which are far more reliable and long-lasting, such as tyres, spark plugs and shock-absorbers, for example. Since a contact with the client as permanent and personalized as possible has become a main aim of the European car industry's strategy, they are finding themselves more and more in competition with their suppliers in the replacement market. Thus the trade names used by autocomponent manufacturers are important, being at the heart of the competitive/cooperative relationships between the car and auto-component industries.

### 4.1.2  The Case of the Car Makers' Component Subsidiaries

While the general trend is towards disintegration on the part of the car makers, i.e., growing dependence on outside supply which can be measured as a lower added value on turnover, it is at the expense of increased strength in the autocomponent industry. At the same time, however, some manufacturers have chosen to subsidiarize and autonomize integrated activities considered as competitive.

Many car manufacturers then asked themselves what policy to adopt towards productions from their own workshops or those of subsidiaries. Two main types of attitude developed.

Ford continued to produce exclusively for itself a great variety of components, according to its former habits of dividing work up on a world scale. It is only recently that the group has envisaged supplying other car makers.

The VAG group followed a progressive policy combining negotiated reduction of the degree of integration, supply from countries where labour costs were cheaper (Spain) and support for national supply markets.

The French and, to a lesser degree, Italian car industries have organized continuous, broad disintegration (how could they do otherwise?) from the mid-1970s onwards. They differed widely as to their methods. While Renault sold many subsidiaries to different outside groups, PSA and Fiat sought to put their subsidiaries Ecia and Magneti Marelli on the market as independent autocomponent producers, following in this the example of General Motors, but having neither the latter's seniority nor its power.

Is confidentiality between the car and the autocomponent industries compatible with the stiff competition between car manufacturers? To make Ecia or Magneti Marelli a major partner when one is not Fiat or PSA is a risk few of today's car manufacturers are prepared to take. The answer is not easy. And yet the European autocomponent industry needs an answer if it is to find a structure.

### 4.1.3  Towards Global Partnership?

The 1980s were years of great change in national car industry organization — from strictly state organized industry, in which nationalized manufacturers had a privileged position, to complex interaction of industrial operators, for whom national borders no longer have great significance. With competition intensifying and taking on world dimensions, no-one today would deny that the actors in the automobile system share the same destiny. A systemic approach (Banville and Chanaron 1991) would allow integration of all the actors in design, manufacture, marketing, use and maintenance of vehicles, as in their ultimate destruction.

This common destiny must not only be recognized; it must also give rise to gradual building of generalized partnerships between suppliers and manufacturers, between manufacturers and distribution networks, between industry and consumers, and so on. It is such relationships between all the actors which will lead to the notion of global partnership. Partnership, while expressing a basically attractive notion in public eyes, entails a behavioural change, from competitive relationships 'coordinated' by market rules only, and by one dominant category of actors, to medium-term association and shared responsibility and profits; in other words, to new forms of 'non-market' coordination and organized solidarity.

Two forms of industrial partnership may be distinguished: horizontal partnership marked by alliances and joint ventures between competitors, and vertical partnership (or supply partnership) associating part, component or functional subsystem suppliers with their clients the car manufacturers. Partnership may be either *de facto* between agents, with no legal formalization, or a relationship concretized by a contract, an associative structure such as the French *groupement d'intérêt* (common interest grouping), financial links or sometimes simply charters.

The introduction of new forms of technological, industrial and commercial relationships seems unlikely to be reversed, and is linked to two sets of factors, themselves resulting from the search for improved productivity and the many attempts to catch up with Japanese productivity on the part of the rest of the world.

Factors concerning industrial organization show two complementary developments. The first is vertical disintegration. Measured using the ratio between added value and turnover, disintegration has evolved very continuously over a long period for most European car manufacturers. The result is increased external supply; the weight of suppliers in the unitary 'value' of each car produced in France thus rose from 50 to 75 per cent between 1955 and 1986 (Banville and Chanaron 1991).

The second movement concerned imitation of Japanese practices and organizational models which have gradually become accepted as obligatory references. Quite apart from concrete methods of supply such as stock turn management and 'just in time' (JIT) deliveries, it is the organizational aspects of the Japanese model which seem to be at the root of its efficiency. There are two organization models: one is specific to the car industry, the other to conglomerates. The first is a pyramid structure with the original equipment manufacturer (OEM) at the top and a hierarchy of suppliers with autocomponent suppliers delivering ready-to-mount functions in first position, suppliers in second and custom subcontractors in third position. The second is the subsidiary system, with mainly minority holdings taken by the car manufacturer in the capital of its preferred suppliers; finally, there is the quasi-integration technique operated by the Japanese *kyoryokukai*, or investment clubs, in which there is no hierarchy, but a web of technical, economic and financial cooperation.

The second type of factors results from the evolution in techniques and skills. First, new technologies in products, such as on-board electronics and new materials, and in processes, such as computer-aided production, have drawn new suppliers into the system, such as electronics engineers or chemists, with whom relationships are different from the longstanding ones set up with the metal and mechanical component branches (see also Chapter 3). Thus Philips and Siemens have become major autocomponent producers, as BASF and Du Pont are becoming in intermediary products such as fibres, resins, adhesives, paints and varnishes, and finished ones such as plastic and composite parts and subsystems.

Second, product development times and equipment design times have been reduced. They are now around seven to four years for car manufacturers and four years to eighteen months for autocomponent manufacturers.

Growing reliance on outsourcing has led to a change in the nature of relationships between car and autocomponent producers. Partnership seems to be a way of coordinating disintegration. As the most efficient organizational model, it is also becoming a norm which competition is gradually adopting.

Growing attention is being paid to environmental protection and pursuit of research into improved car security, and this is likely to increase the likelihood of big technical changes. Component suppliers are the first to experience potential or generalized innovation. In the short term, catalytic exhaust systems and electronic engine regulation devices must satisfy European standards limiting atmospheric pollution. In the medium term, restraint systems and driving aids such as map reading aids, mechanical diagnosis assistance, etc., will contribute to safety, and the big question of recuperation and recycling of plastics or more generally entire processing of the car up to elimination and recycling, will be addressed.

In the longer term, components for electrical or hybrid diesel-electrical cars, cruise-control systems, electronic navigational aid systems, etc., or generally everything connected with controlling car flow will be developed.

Autocomponent manufacturers are also much involved in large-scale technical developments such as supply of functional subassemblies ready to mount, and research into reduction of the number of constituent parts.

To confront these new challenges, autocomponent manufacturers today must develop their R&D potential to increase their capacity for technical initiative. The German groups have already integrated this new dimension to a considerable degree: 6 per cent of their turnover is invested in R&D (i.e. double that of the car manufacturers) while all their American, French, UK and even Japanese competitors only invest under 3 per cent of turnover.

### 4.1.4 Practices, Significance and Consequences of Partnership

The subcontracting system has long been in force. It combined three main criteria: the lowest price possible, for the required volumes, in the time given.

However, the main criterion was always the price in the last resort. Industrial relation practices were as follows: open orders, i.e. left entirely to the orderer's discretion and renewable by simple order form with no clear economic prospect for the supplier; open books; systematic competition; and customized work on imposed, but variable, technico-industrial specifications.

The client-orderer exercised total technological, industrial, commercial and financial domination over the supplier. All his strategic decisions applied *de facto* to the supplier. The client was the omniscient 'general practitioner' who designed a complex system product, and subcontracted manufacture of some of its parts to others (it is to be noted that the word 'parts' is used rather than 'equipment'). This is the Fordist model of inter-enterprise relationships, with division and specialization of tasks and separation between design and manufacture. Information flows downwards in a sequential hierarchy.

In its principles and practices, the partnership model contrasts with the subcontracting model. Supply criteria are more complex. Matters such as supplier credit rating and managerial stability are examined alongside the notion of minimum price. The price must enable reasonable profit to be made, ensuring the survival of the firm; this is the confidence criterion. The quantity criterion is closely linked to that of optimum quality, and thus to that of technical mastery of the product and its renewal cycle. This is the excellence criterion. As for the time criterion, it has become as important as the criteria of quality JIT and synchronous delivery, and when the part is incorporated into the car; no stocks are kept but the supplier is located within a short distance. This implies that the latter must be mobile and prepared to become international: this is the criterion of implication.

Supply relationships are no longer merely those of traders but have become those of cooperation, with functional association between design and production according to a division of labour based on skills and no longer on tasks.

If partnership relationships between manufacturer and supplier are to grow, many changes both in practices and behaviour are needed. First of all, sharing of technical, industrial and commercial responsibility is necessary. The supplier is implicated from the outset in the design process for new models and is truly able to propose innovations. The supplier no longer delivers a component but a function for which he is entirely responsible, including his own supplies.

Sharing is also necessary in productivity improvements and profits: the client and the supplier must both benefit from improved productivity. They must also share technical and economic information, facilitated where computer systems, from CAD to management of accounting and financial documents, are linked up. The flow of information is no longer unilateral, but bilateral, or even multilateral.

Partnership also signifies duration in order to establish medium-term supply relationships such as supply contracts for a particular reference, qualification by standardized procedures such as Ford Q1 or PSA-Renault, a partnership charter, membership of a club, and so on. A durable relationship requires a continuing supply flow, but it also serves to plan price falls. Qualified or privileged suppliers thus profit from a medium-term economic prospect, enabling them to envisage true development strategies. Thus, in Germany, the number of contracts over three years rose from under 5 per cent in 1987 to 35 per cent in 1990, and should exceed 60 per cent in 1995 (Table 4.7).

*Table 4.7    Share of long-term and short-term contracts in Germany*[*]

|  | 1987 | 1990 | 1995 |
|---|---|---|---|
| Long term contracts (more than 3 years) | < 5% | 35% | > 60% |
| Short term contracts (less than year) | 85% | 30% | 25% |

[*] Average for the car makers
*Source*: CE-BCG (1991)

Partnership implies confidence, an absolute requirement in a situation where sharing is over time. Where the supplier collaborates with several car manufacturers in the design of new models, he must observe complete discretion. There is thus solidarity between partners collaborating in the design and manufacture of a car model the commercial success of which will also be shared.

*Table 4.8    Evolution of inventory turnover rates (number of rotations per year)*

|  | 1984 | 1989 |
|---|---|---|
| Car makers |  |  |
| Japan | 21 | 24 |
| United States | 13 | 12 |
| Europe | 7 | 8 |
| Suppliers (OEM) |  |  |
| Japan | 18 | 22 |
| United States | 6 | 5 |
| Europe | 5 | 7 |

*Source*: CE-BCG (1991)

Partnership also means selection and ranking of suppliers; only those capable of satisfying eligibility requirements such as excellence, confidence, and implication qualify. The others are either simply eliminated or moved down to second tier. The development of partnerships therefore leads directly to net reduction in the number of suppliers and to the building of a hierarchy like the Japanese pyramidal model.

Partnership also means client diversification. The search for technological and economic excellence, i.e. the best components at the best prices, implies a search for economies of scale, which can generally be made only by supplying several clients with the same family of components.

There are several consequences of the autocomponent industry's selection criteria (Banville and Chanaron 1991). Product quality entails reliability and quality assurance; service quality means respecting deadlines and regular stock turns. If innovations and technological changes are to be made, R&D capacity is required. Finally, autocomponent manufacturers need a solid financial basis, i.e. profits, which show sustained cooperation and a capacity to internationalize.

These conditions point to powerful, profitable, inventive groups, mastering locations in several countries; this is the portrait of the ideal partner. However, discouraged by the negative aspects of subcontractual relationships, suppliers have only recently begun to conform to this ideal. Thus there has been a sudden surge in takeovers, portfolio reshuffling and alliances since 1989.

In the early 1990s, car manufacturers endeavoured mostly to choose direct suppliers. Thus the number of PSA suppliers, for instance, fell from 2000 to 650 between 1980 and 1992, those of Renault from 1850 to to 1050 between 1985 and 1991, and those of Ford Europe from 2200 to 1000 between 1980 and 1990 (Banville and Chanaron 1991).

It is therefore impossible for any new entrant of notable size to appear, except if there were external growth and diversification in a large group (like Siemens at the end of the 1980s) or a need for new technology. It does indeed seem arduous, lengthy and hazardous for a component manufacturer to become a partner with a car manufacturer, either from scratch or from a second-tier position. In other words, positions in the automobile world are becoming entrenched, and only strategic alliances or continuing financial concentration seem likely to modify them to any significant degree.

### 4.1.5 Internationalization and Globalization

From the early 1980s, the main European autocomponent groups began to internationalize their activity within the Community as well as in the United States. They wished to exploit the qualitative, and technological weaknesses of their local competitors to supply the 'Big Three'; moreover the Japanese transplants JIT deliveries required relocation near the car manufacturers' assembly units.

The prospect of the European Single Market and the location of Japanese manufacturers in Europe have been the opportunity for further strengthening of the restructuring process in the European autocomponent industry. Function suppliers have moved nearer assembly lines and set up units for synchronized deliveries; most of them seek to become 'qualified suppliers' to the Japanese car makers, envisaging eventual installations in South East Asia, in the recent footsteps of GKN, Michelin, Valéo and Allied Signal, among others.

New competition is also emerging. The Japanese autocomponent companies, subsidiaries of the car manufacturers, which have followed their main client and seek to increase their market share with local car manufacturers, have benefited from their reputation for total quality acquired under pressure from, and in collaboration with, their clients. The movement towards globalization in the autocomponent industry therefore emulates that of their clients.

The result of all these changes is considerable growth in the volume of international exchanges of automobile parts and components, which are not well recorded in customs statistics; this is because they record both 'true' imports and exports (original and replacement part delivery) and flow between car and autocomponent manufacture production units. Thus examination of component trade balances cannot be assessed separately from overall automobile balances.

The process of international concentration and development may roughly be divided into a phase of 'national concentration' within the main component-producing industry, followed by one where a policy of multi-nationalization has been developed mostly on a European scale. Almost none of the European autocomponent firms, except, perhaps, ACGE — General Motors — have yet reached the stage of true globalization, that is, global integrated management of their industrial assets and their markets. This is nevertheless their objective, and they endeavour to do so, strengthening their strong points, their 'specialities' and their skills, by aiming for excellence in one or several functions, at least on a continental scale. 'Function oligo-polies' are thus being created.

## 4.2   THE EMERGENCE OF FUNCTION OLIGOPOLIES

The main characteristic of the recent changes in the European autocomponent sector is the rapid emergence and consolidation of function oligopolies which have led to fundamental remodelling in industrial structures.

These oligopolies are characterized by the concentration of design know-how and production capacity amongst a small number of industrial groups specializing in a single technical subsystem, which is a set of preassembled parts ready for mounting on the car it was designed for and ensuring one or several of the vehicle's technical 'functions' such as braking, interior fittings, air conditioning, or signalling, for instance.[3]

Such oligopolies have arisen due to three converging trends. First, the development of outsourcing and partnerships has resulted in increased responsibilities for fewer suppliers per function. Second, car manufacturers tend to choose one or two external sources per function, thus reducing their former multi-supply practices on standing orders, which were virtually subcontracting. Third, autocomponent manufacturers are seeking optimum size and specializations, with a view to conquering first the European, then the world markets in the face of Japanese competition.

Autocomponent manufacturers' functional specialization is therefore logical both in terms of the new supply practices of the automobile industry, which has developed 'programmed' selection of excellent suppliers capable of satisfying their price and therefore volume requirements, and mastering total quality requirements, and in terms of their own suppliers seeking economies of scale.

This specialization has led to considerable external growth via takeovers and regroupings, and by many strategic alliances and industrial and techno-logical cooperation agreements.

### 4.2.1 External Growth Operations in the Autocomponent Industry

External growth operations, mergers, acquisitions and alliances became very numerous at the end of the 1980s. It is however difficult to document these operations accurately. In view of the lack and insufficiency of the documentation available from the EC and the various national and international professional organizations, it was soon considered vital to bring order to the observations compiled regularly from the economic and financial press and more rarely from documentation published by the enterprises themselves, by creating a specific sectoral database.

#### 4.2.1.1 The EUREQ base
The first problem to be solved was that of the field covered by a database on alliances and takeovers, since the enterprises supplying the automobile industry are very inadequately accounted for in the various existing lists and databases.

To overcome these difficulties, it was judged necessary to build up a specific database, using existing information relating to the enterprises concerned and various documentation such as press cuttings, annual reports, and previous publications (Banville and Chanaron 1990; 1991).

The EUREQ base includes several types of operations, concerning the main American, European and Japanese autocomponent companies targeting the European market, and concerning European autocomponent manufacturers aiming at American and Japanese markets (see Box 4.2):

- total or partial acquisition of a formerly independent firm;
- increased holding in a subsidiary already owned in part;
- creation of a common subsidiary (joint venture) owned by at least two partners;
- creation of a production unit from scratch (creation);
- other operations not requiring financial participation, such as transfers of licences and industrial or technical cooperation agreements.

*Box 4.2     The EUREQ base*

Any record in the EUREQ base has the following structure:
1.  Calendar year of operation
2.  Date of publication of the information
3.  Initiator of operation
4.  Nationality of initiator
5.  Subsidiary of initiator involved in operation
6.  Second initiator in a joint venture or agreement
7.  Third initiator in a joint venture or agreement
8.  Main target of operation
9.  Target subsidiary or division
10.  Second target of operation
11.  Country or geographical zone targeted by operation
12.  Type of agreement creation, acquisition, holding, increased holding, other
13.  Participation in target, capital in % or variation
14.  Description of content and scope of agreement
15.  Category(ies) of products concerned by operation

While operations concerning the big autocomponent manufacturers are virtually all covered, those of SMEs and the subsidiaries of diversified groups are only partly so, due to the defects in the sources chosen.

As of 31 December 1991, the EUREQ base created contained 439 operations, 261 of which were acquisitions, 100 joint ventures, 47 creations, and 17 increased participations. The latter agreements were the most difficult to take stock of, since they were little mentioned in the economic press in cases where neither the car makers nor the larger autocomponent firms such as Bosch, Nippondenso, Lucas, Magneti Marelli or Valéo were involved. The fourteen 'other' agreements in the base were either technological cooperation agreements, particularly in R&D, or transfers of licences. But because the economic and financial press showed little interest in this type of agreements, the 'others' only concerned the big groups and operations which were sufficiently spectacular to have drawn publicity. Moreover, operations concerning French enterprises are without doubt better documented than those for other European countries, particularly where the enterprise is small, and often a second-tier supplier. Movements in and out of second-rank supply of the automobile system are considerable. A satisfactory systematic solution to this problem of sectoral definition seems virtually impossible.

A second problem is equally difficult to solve — that of the period of reference. The great majority of agreements and takeovers are generally spread over time: discussions are held; then interests are bought, or joint ventures are created; then, later on, the holdings are increased, crossing various thresholds; the agreements are or are not put into effect, alliances are more or less active, and so on.

Any time limit is therefore arbitrary and it is impossible to rely solely on the date a newspaper article was published. Operations having taken place since 1988 have all been entered into EUREQ. Some important agreements dating from before 1988 have been included, although the 1987 financial year has several fairly large gaps. The industry itself maintains that external growth operations and strategic alliances in the autocomponent sector multiplied in the mid-1980s, but no reliable information to prove this is available for the years before 1987. Only operations concerning Japanese autocomponent manufacturers in Europe since 1970 have been identified.

#### 4.2.1.2 External growth operations in EUREQ

The main figures may be found in Tables 4.9–4.14. One thing must always be kept in mind when reading them: where a country is referred to on a horizontal line, it is the country in which the enterprise is financially controlled; where it is vertical, it is the host country for a creation or an alliance.

The 47 creations of new units[4] and the sixteen operations involving American and Japanese enterprises, targeting the United States and Japan, have been deducted from the 439 cases recorded in the EUREQ base. This is because counting of the operations outside Europe is in any case very fragmentary.

The total number of operations is thus 376, of which 22 date from before 1987. Between 1987 and 1991, there were 354 external growth operations and alliances.

*Table 4.9    Operations according to type, in number of operations*

|  | Acquisition | Joint venture | Capital increase | Others | Total |
|---|---|---|---|---|---|
| Germany | 45 | 24 | 4 | 4 | 77 |
| France | 85 | 16 | 2 | 1 | 104 |
| UK | 44 | 11 | 1 | 3 | 59 |
| Italy | 46 | 4 | 2 | 0 | 52 |
| Japan | 8 | 23 | 2 | 0 | 33 |
| US | 18 | 9 | 2 | 1 | 30 |
| Others | 12 | 6 | 1 | 2 | 21 |
| Total | 258 | 93 | 14 | 11 | 376 |

*Source*: EUREQ

*Table 4.10  Operations according to date*

|  | Before 1987 | 1987 | 1988 | 1989 | 1990 | 1991 | Total |
|---|---|---|---|---|---|---|---|
| Germany | 2 | 5 | 9 | 15 | 26 | 20 | 77 |
| France | 4 | 9 | 18 | 24 | 28 | 21 | 104 |
| UK | 0 | 2 | 14 | 14 | 19 | 10 | 59 |
| Italy | 4 | 7 | 10 | 12 | 17 | 2 | 52 |
| Japan | 12 | 1 | 3 | 10 | 5 | 2 | 33 |
| US | 0 | 4 | 7 | 4 | 8 | 7 | 30 |
| Others | 0 | 1 | 1 | 10 | 9 | 0 | 21 |
| Total | 22 | 29 | 62 | 89 | 112 | 62 | 376 |

*Source*: EUREQ

Tables 4.9 and 4.10 indicate how few operations are initiated in Europe by countries other than the four big European countries (Germany, France, the UK and Italy), the United States and Japan. The total absence of Spain is to be noted: it is only a 'target country', since its enterprises have no active role. The acceleration in the annual rhythm of operations in 1989 and 1990 also shows up clearly.

Among the 439 entries in the EUREQ base, the share of operations initiated by French enterprises is almost 28 per cent, while that of 'Japanese' operations is relatively small, slightly under 6 per cent.

*Table 4.11  Operations (all types) according to initiator country and target country*

|  | Germany | France | UK | Italy | Spain | Japan | US | Other Europe | Other | Total |
|---|---|---|---|---|---|---|---|---|---|---|
| Germany | 23 | 9 | 7 | 6 | 1 | 3 | 9 | 8 | 11 | 77 |
| France | 11 | 45 | 6 | 5 | 9 | 1 | 8 | 3 | 16 | 104 |
| UK | 8 | 5 | 17 | 1 | 0 | 2 | 18 | 1 | 7 | 59 |
| Italy | 2 | 10 | 4 | 23 | 6 | 0 | 2 | 3 | 2 | 52 |
| Spain | 0 | 0 | 0 | 0 | 0 | 0 | 0 | 0 | 0 | 0 |
| Japan | 3 | 5 | 13 | 1 | 5 | * | * | 0 | 6 | 33 |
| USA | 4 | 4 | 2 | 11 | 1 | * | * | 2 | 6 | 30 |
| Other | 3 | 2 | 2 | 0 | 2 | 5 | 5 | 3 | 3 | 21 |
| Total | 54 | 80 | 51 | 47 | 24 | 42 | 42 | 20 | 51 | 376 |

* Non determined
*Source*: EUREQ

Table 4.11 enables us to assess the geographical structure of the operations. The number of internal operations in each of the four main European countries shows that France and Italy are clearly occupied with internal reorganization, with 44 per cent of total operations taking place internally; Germany and the UK seem more extrovert, with only 30 per cent internal operations.

A second observation may be made with regard to the relative balance of operations between France, the UK and Germany, when these countries are considered in pairs. There are indeed almost as many operations initiated by France in Germany as there are by Germany in France, for instance. The only exception seems to be Italy, which initiates twice as many operations in other countries as others do in Italy, even though the EUREQ base tends to reduce quantities, since it considers Valéo as a French group (see Box 4.4 on Valéo).

*Table 4.12  Acquisition operations according to initiator country and target country*

|  | Germany | France | UK | Italy | Spain | Japan | US | Other Europe | Other | Total |
|---|---|---|---|---|---|---|---|---|---|---|
| Germany | 12 | 7 | 5 | 5 | 0 | 0 | 4 | 4 | 8 | 45 |
| France | 10 | 41 | 5 | 4 | 6 | 0 | 6 | 0 | 11 | 83 |
| UK | 5 | 5 | 13 | 1 | 0 | 0 | 16 | 0 | 4 | 44 |
| Italy | 1 | 7 | 4 | 23 | 6 | 0 | 2 | 2 | 1 | 46 |
| Spain | 0 | 0 | 0 | 0 | 0 | 0 | 0 | 0 | 0 | 0 |
| Japan | 1 | 1 | 5 | 1 | 0 | * | * | 0 | 6 | 8 |
| US | 2 | 3 | 1 | 10 | 0 | * | * | 1 | 6 | 18 |
| Other | 2 | 1 | 1 | 0 | 2 | 0 | 3 | 1 | 4 | 14 |
| Total | 33 | 65 | 34 | 44 | 14 | 0 | 31 | 8 | 29 | 258 |

* Non determined
*Source:* EUREQ

Table 4.12 shows that acquisition is the commonest type of operation, more so for Italy and France than for Germany, the UK or the United States. It is rare for Japan, where autocomponent manufacturers seem to prefer creations and joint ventures.

Increased holdings giving absolute control of the target firm may be added to acquisitions as such: eleven of the fifteen increased holdings observed outside the United States and Japan enabled the acquiring group to hold over 90 per cent of the target's capital.

Table 4.13 shows the strategic choice of German autocomponent manufacturers setting up joint ventures first with German, then American enterprises, while Japanese autocomponent manufacturers tend to choose UK or Spanish homologues (as indeed do Japanese vehicle manufacturers).

*Table 4.13  Joint ventures according to initiator country and target country*

|         | Germany | France | UK | Italy | Spain | Japan | US | Other Europe | Other | Total |
|---------|---------|--------|----|-------|-------|-------|----|-------------|-------|-------|
| Germany | 9 | 7 | 0 | 1 | 0 | 2 | 5 | 4 | 2 | 24 |
| France  | 1 | 4 | 1 | 1 | 2 | 0 | 2 | 2 | 3 | 16 |
| UK      | 1 | 0 | 3 | 0 | 0 | 1 | 2 | 1 | 3 | 11 |
| Italy   | 0 | 3 | 0 | 0 | 0 | 0 | 0 | 0 | 1 | 4 |
| Spain   | 0 | 0 | 0 | 0 | 0 | 0 | 0 | 0 | 0 | 0 |
| Japan   | 2 | 4 | 7 | 0 | 5 | * | * | 0 | 5 | 23 |
| US      | 0 | 1 | 1 | 0 | 0 | * | * | 1 | 6 | 9 |
| Other   | 1 | 1 | 0 | 0 | 0 | 1 | 1 | 2 | 0 | 6 |
| Total   | 14 | 14 | 12 | 2 | 7 | 4 | 10 | 10 | 19 | 93 |

* Non determined
*Source*: EUREQ

*Table 4.14  Evolution in the number of acquisitions and joint ventures, 1987–91*

|               | 1987 | 1988 | 1989 | 1990 | 1991 | Total |
|---------------|------|------|------|------|------|-------|
| Acquisitions  | 20 | 42 | 58 | 87 | 46 | 253 |
| Joint ventures| 6 | 16 | 32 | 20 | 12 | 86 |

*Source*: EUREQ

It would seem that the movement towards financial concentration distinctly accelerated in 1988, 1989 and 1990. However, the number of strategic alliances reached a peak in 1989 and fell thereafter.

The structure of the European autocomponent industry was considerably changed by these different external growth operations and multiple strategic alliances. This was due mainly to the European enterprises themselves — only 51 operations out of 376 since 1987 have involved American and Japanese groups. This confirms the hypothesis that a 'European automobile system', capable of standing up to the competition from North American and Japanese systems, is gaining power (Banville and Chanaron 1991).

The fact that only 24 operations were carried out by American auto-component manufacturers, despite their former domination in Europe, would seem to confirm the hypothesis that the sector is weakening in the United States. American autocomponent manufacturers have often found it difficult to adapt to the total quality requirements of the big car manufacturers (Womack, Jones and Roos 1991). Since the end of the 1980s, and not counting the big specialized multinationals, the American autocomponent industry has seen great changes in structure, with many SMEs failing and European and Japanese autocomponent subsidiaries gaining power.

As for the structure of the Japanese autocomponent industry, it seems to have been relatively stable in recent years (Dodwell 1990; Sleigh 1992), which shows that Japanese autocomponent manufacturers have both privileged investment abroad (in the United States and Europe) and have developed 'bilateral' relationships with car manufacturers (i.e. quasi-exclusivity). Only a major upheaval in the structure of the automobile industry could have repercussions on that of autocomponents.

### 4.2.1.3 Technological cooperation

Since it has no access to reliable information, the EUREQ base has not been able to survey technological cooperation agreements satisfactorily. In the autocomponent sector, competitive pressure and the requirements of techno-logical innovation are such that in all probability, these agreements between autocomponent manufacturers, or between autocomponent and car manufac-turers, (see Chapter 3) will multiply, particularly with the help of European research programmes. However, this process will be limited by three sectoral factors.

First of all, only medium- and large-sized autocomponent manufacturers are capable of R&D enabling them to tender for EEC offers, thus many small and medium-sized enterprises are automatically excluded. Second, because they are positioned upstream of car designers and manufacturers, they are often closer to technological development of ideas and designs produced elsewhere than to applied research before competition and innovation in the strict sense of the term. Finally, because they specialize technologically in a highly competitive climate, they often reduce their R&D cooperation. Examples of R&D and alliances are given in Box 4.3.

*Box 4.3      R&D and alliances — some significant examples**

---

**I.   MATERIALS**

1.   BRITE–EURAM

Materials, whether of metal, plastic, composites, or ceramics, and the industrial processes of their transformation and treatment, represent a major technological challenge for car and component manufacturers and for suppliers.

Industrial research into these problems has received considerable finance from the EEC through the BRITE programme in 1988 and the BRITE–EURAM programme from 1989 to 1992, amounting to ECU 560 million, which represents 43% of the total financing (some 1.3 m ECUs).

Of the 536 programmes current on 31/12/91, 73 described automobile and auto-component projects, i.e. 13.6% of the total number of projects.

Forty-one projects were led by firms supplying car manufacturers, including specialized engineering firms, and 25 others involved at least one autocomponent manufacturer as partner. Only twelve projects were led by car manufacturers.

All the projects were in cooperation. There were 31 alliances between auto-component manufacturers, 25 alliances between suppliers and car manufacturers and eight alliances between car manufacturers. Nine projects were joint ventures involving university laboratories, three of which were cooperating with autocomponent manu-facturers, three with automobile manufacturers and three with other laboratories.

2.   CARMAT

CARMAT is a EUREKA research programme (thus open to EEC and EFTA companies and universities) on optimal design of car structure using 'new' materials such as composites, ceramics and so on. Estimated cost of research is around $55 m. The leader in the research group is Peugeot SA, with Sollac (steel), ICI and DSM (plastics), Pechiney (aluminium) and the INRETS (tests).

**II.  ELECTRONICS**

PROMETHEUS (PROgraMme for European Traffic with Highest Efficiency and Unprecedented Safety) is also a EUREKA programme. It was set up in 1986 and aims at development of an intelligent, 100% safe car. As of today, all the European car manu-facturers, 56 autocomponent manufacturers, component and electronic system suppliers, and 115 university or private R&D laboratories are involved.

The average annual budget since 1989 has been ECU 90 m, two-thirds of which is financed by industry and the remaining third by the national ministries for research, technology and industry. The PROMETHEUS programme is linked to the EEC DRIVE and ATT programmes, and information is exchanged with partners in the American IVHS programme.

* The examples of agreements presented in this paragraph are not repeated in the EUREQ base.
*Source*: EEC (1992), BRITE–EUROM, Synopses of current projects 1990–1991, INRETS

Because it is heterogeneous and incomplete, particularly in that no single nomenclature of automobile components has been created, information on products, technologies and the content of the agreements and takeovers has received no specific treatment. This is why the EUREQ base does not allow new and developing function oligopolies to be pinpointed and quantified. Only individual case studies can show evidence of this essential aspect of the European autocomponent industry structure.

### 4.2.2 Some Examples of Function Oligopolies

While the EUREQ base can help to measure movements in the auto-component industry, it cannot yield a comprehensive analysis. These operations are generally motivated by the wish to grow to a certain size, function by function, sometimes within the same technological family, or to seek industrial credibility on a world scale, or at least in Europe.

Most of the big European autocomponent groups (Bosch, Lucas, Magneti Marelli in particular) had already refocused most of their activity on the functions or 'skills' deemed central, and therefore only undertook operations to 'develop' these initial positions (see Box 4.5 on Bosch); Valéo, for its part, was less advanced and was the last among them to recentre and internationalize (see Box 4.4 on Valéo).

These large autocomponent manufacturers thus acquired dominant positions in braking, shock-absorbers and ground contact, clutch, engine cooling, air-conditioning, heating, ventilation, lighting and signalling, adjustment electronics equipment and so on. On these segments, the market is divided among a few large firms. The oligopoly seems to correspond to the two conflicting requirements of these markets, i.e. progressive concentration leading to responsible partnerships in R&D, and competition giving automobile manufacturers the possibility to choose.

All the functions which constitute an automobile seem to be the object of partnerships or of oligopolies. This is why the following examples deal with less important functions than those generally mentioned, because they have undergone a lesser degree of concentration.

### 4.2.1.1 Dashboards

Formerly mounted by vehicle manufacturers on subsidiary lines, dashboards contain all the control instruments of the vehicle, plus various complementary accessories for the driver's convenience. They are more and more frequently mounted and checked at the autocomponent manufacturer's, from which they are delivered synchronously 'just in time' (JIT) to the vehicle assembly lines ready to mount. It is increasingly common to find electronics and controls in this function.

*Box 4.4    Valéo external development, 1987–91*

Valéo, a Franco-Italian group, which has become a European and then a world leader, has seen particularly dynamic external growth in the last five years. This is due to the gradual assumption of control by CERUS, a company in the de Benedetti group, which has held 39.5% of the voting rights as of early 1992.

When the turnover is examined, two development stages may be observed: diversified growth from 1986 to 1988, followed by consolidation and refocusing since 1989. These stages were characterized by growing internationalization; the group's turnover in France had fallen to 44% in 1990, as against 55% in 1987. The consolidated turnover before tax evolved as follows (in FF bn): 1986: 12.1, 1988: 16.5, 1990: 20.2, 1991: 19.9.

1.    From 1986–89, considerable external growth, technological partnerships

Not counting the sale of Isba (building components), Soma (heavy duty vehicle transmission) and Allevard Industries (steel and springs), the period was dominated by many purchases of enterprises.

In 1987 Chausson cooling/heating products and its foreign subsidiaries were taken over, together with Nieman, the subsidiary of which was sold the following year (Ronis-locks).

In 1988 the Brazilian firm Bongotti (cooling/heating equipment) was taken over; joint ventures with the Korean Pyeong-Wa (clutches) and the American Eaton (clutches); Clausor (Spain) and Tibbe KG (FRG), specialized in anti-theft devices and protection, were respectively controlled and purchased; joint venture with the American Acustar, the Chrysler autocomponent subsidiary (air conditioning).

In 1989 Cartier Systems (electronics and signalling), the Volkswagen factory at Fort Worth (air conditioning), the American firm Blackstone (engine and interior cooling and heating) and the British firm Delanair (air conditioning) were taken over.

Alongside this very fast external growth, technological partnerships were set up with Japanese groups in 1988, an agreement was concluded with Akebono for the production of brake linings in Spain; in 1989, the Mitsuba licence for alternators produced in France (l'Isle d'Abeau) for Honda/Rover was acquired; also in 1989, joint venture with Nippon-denso for ignition coils produced in Spain.

This period was not just one of successes. In 1988, Valéo attempted a public exchange offer on Epéda Bertrand Faure. This failed, due in particular to public opposition from the vehicle manufacturers, which did not wish to see too powerful an autocomponent group in France.

2.    Refocusing and consolidation since 1990

In 1990, Valéo started slimming down its operations and began to concentrate its main skills. While the group maintained the Cartier electronics and lighting activities, it sold those in electromechanical relays and plastics injection. It also sold longer-standing activities within the group, such as electromagnetic ignition and horns. The sale of its ignition activity brought the end of the joint venture with Nippondenso concluded in 1989. All the brake lining (linings and segments) activity was sold to Allied Signal Automotive.

As of 1991, concentration on Valéo's 'true' specialities, i.e. clutches, clutch plates, engine cooling, lighting and signalling, interior security and cooling/heating, electronics, ignition coils and starters, wiping systems, and distribution, were the main references in the group's industrial policy.

Activity outside France was energetically developed, particularly in Germany (where Valéo's turnover doubled between 1987 and 1991). It is under this policy that Renak clutch activity in East Germany was acquired. Similarly, since electronics only represented 4.47% of turnover in 1990, the group set up a new electronic module plant in 1992, and is developing collaboration and agreements for development and production with specialists, particularly with Motorola.

Until the mid 1980s, the European markets were very fragmented: while VDO reigned in Germany and Veglia in Italy under the control of Fiat, these firms had to face competition from France (Jaeger) and Italy (Borletti). But the Italian autocomponent manufacturer, following the takeover of Jaeger through Ufima (Union Financière Matra–Magneti Marelli) in 1987, and the merging of Borletti with Veglia, has become the dominant firm in Europe. With the Jaeger, Veglia and Borletti labels, Magneti–Marelli held some 50 per cent of the European market in 1987, as compared with VDO's 35/40 per cent.

Fierce competition developed between these two firms and new entrants, particularly Siemens. At the end of 1991, VDO (DM 2 bn consolidated turnover and 14000 employees) was seeking a buyer, and two German groups showed an interest: Siemens and Mannesmann. Finally, the second won, thus becoming one of the leading European autocomponent manufacturers, and VDO's dashboards joined Boge shock absorbers and Fichtel & Sachs' power transmission products; the European Commission gave its agreement, based on the argument that the activities of Mannesmann and VDO were not sufficiently similar (*Les Echos*, 17/12/1991).

The dashboard oligopoly is thus constituted of parts of large groups, one of which is independent of the vehicle manufacturers.

### 4.2.2.2 Rear-view mirrors

In Europe, a specific sector is growing for what is becoming the 'rear view mirror function', which must take into account both aerodynamics and the arrival of rear-viewing by camera in the near future. Certain firms have withdrawn or disappeared, like the French firm CIPA, thus concentrating the sector, or else agreements or takeovers have taken place.

At the end of 1991, three European groups of similar importance stood out. The first is Hohe, a German family enterprise. It has two constraints to face: it must become European (it is only located in Germany and Spain at the moment), and it must find a successor for its owner–manager. The second is Britax-Geco, controlled by the British group BSG International. It is located in the United States and many European locations. The third, Gilardini, is a Fiat subsidiary. In late 1989, Gilardini took a 50 per cent holding in Harman, a subsidiary of the French group, Reydel, which had bought it from the American group Beatrice Food in 1983. Harman and Gilardini each have a subsidiary in Spain: Atepsa and Taisa. While Gilardini will probably take over Harman completely in the near future, it will still have to try to mask its own status as a Fiat subsidiary and try to appear independent. Smaller challengers are to be found in Spain (Sefico, Arto Iberica/Sogefi) and Italy (Donelli).

Firms manufacturing rear-view mirrors are relatively small and the usual practice is that of total or progressive buyout of capital, for the twin purposes of attaining optimum size via external growth and developing an industrial location near the vehicle manufacturers' final assembly lines. But in future, if more technological capacity is required, then the suppliers depending on big groups will have a significant advantage.

### 4.2.2.3  Batteries — the European oligopoly

The car battery market has long been fragmented. This is due to the great diversity of battery uses, and therefore of products, and it has been encouraged by freedom of choice in replacement parts, either under own brand names or under distributors' brand names (as opposed to car manufacturers' replacement parts). It is thus a fairly easy market to penetrate. The many companies were mainly national in character. Until today, concentration occurred in fairly traditional fashion, i.e. intranational and then European takeovers occurred. Today this is still the case for the smallest producers.

But after 1990, when the large firms wished to concentrate, they encountered the European competition policy. In 1991, Brussels examined two big operations. The first occurred in the framework of the strategic agreement between Alcatel (ex CGE) and Fiat. Magneti Marelli took control over CEAc (Fulmen, Tudor and Dinin) and its subsidiaries in Germany (Sonnenschein) and Italy (Saem, Dobra). But Magneti Marelli had owned 75 per cent of the CFEC (Ducellier, Steco) in France since 1990, and would thus have controlled over 50 per cent of the French market. The Commission authorities asked them to reduce their holding in the capital of the CFEC to 10 per cent. In the second case, Brussels finally allowed the two main German (and European) firms Bosch (Bosch and Femsa) and Varta (Varta and Baroclem) to join forces via a common subsidiary held 25/75 per cent.

The future needs of electrical vehicles constitute the technical and commercial challenges which are giving rise to this dense concentration. The present structure of the European battery industry is as follows:

- there are a few major producers: Magneti Marelli, Bosch and AC Delco/ General Motors;
- a few smaller manufacturers, among which are the 'deconcentrated' CFEC, the Spanish group TS Tudor, which has taken over Chloride France, Hagen and Neste, the de Benedetti/Sogefi group which also controls the FIAMM, and the Japanese group Yuasa; and
- some smaller producers which have remained autonomous.

In this highly competitive climate in all the many commercial fields, market shares are considered as trade secrets; it is thus very difficult to give reliable data for European firms.

Thus the accumulator function offers a clear example of concentration which has reached its own economic and financial limits, and has been regulated by political intervention.

#### 4.2.2.4 The European car seat industry

The car seat has become a complete function, making use of various techniques (fashioning of metal tubing, foam, textiles, electromechanics, motorization). Most enterprises were forced to regroup in order to finance increased R&D costs and to set up near to vehicle manufacturers geographically so as to deliver in synchronous 'just in time'. Since many vehicle manufacturers are still very much integrated, car seat function seems to offer worthwhile development prospects for autocomponent manufacturers.

The main world leaders are now present in Europe. The American (Johnson Controls, Lear Siegler) or Japanese (Ikeda Bussan/Nissan, Tachi'S) have mostly set up in Europe via joint ventures. The European groups for their part have developed via majority shareholdings and takeovers. First among them is Bertrand Faure Automobile (BFA, a subsidiary of Epéda Bertrand Faure). Then there is ECIA, a subsidiary of PSA, and finally, Gilardini, a Fiat subsidiary. Another French enterprise, Roth Frères, is seeking recognition as an autocomponent manufacturer.

Although BFA took over a German firm, Schmitz, in 1971, it took nearly fifteen years for the group to develop a true external growth strategy in Europe and in North America. In 1986–87, BFA bought up three companies: a Canadian one, Case, specialized in car seat mechanisms, an Italian one, SICAM, and a Portuguese one, Molaflex. In 1989, it concluded two agreements, one with Woodbridge, a North American foam producer, to supply complete seats to GM and Chrysler; and the other with the British firm Bostrom. In 1990, it bought the French company Treca Mousse and the German company Rentrop. BFA has thus built up the leading car seat group in Europe, ahead of the German Keiper Recaro and the French ECIA.

ECIA, a subsidiary 'autonomized' by PSA as an autocomponent enterprise in 1987, has included car seats in its development projects. Initally a manufacturer of metal frameworks for Peugeot car seats, ECIA has sought by various means to become a 'complete' car seat manufacturer. In 1989 it created a common subsidiary with Treca, and in 1990 took a controlling interest in Cesa (formerly Tubauto, in the Vallourec group). Until now, ECIA's car seat activity remained not only within national limits, but also largely devoted to PSA's interests. In future years, the main question will be disintegration policy in the vehicle industry. Will the car seat autocomponent subsidiaries of the vehicle manufacturing groups (PSA and Fiat) be able to develop if they remain dependent on the latter?

#### 4.2.3 The Iron and Steel Groups Move Downstream

Examination of the EUREQ base shows a tendency for many industrial groups in iron, steel and metallurgy to make a strategic move downstream.

Mannesmann, like the Siemens group before it, has rapidly taken its place in the ranks of autocomponent manufacturers. Having bought up Fichtel & Sachs, it now groups the following activities: shock absorbers with Allinquant and Boge (which Sogefi and de Benedetti, large minority share-holders, have now left), dashboard instrumentation with VDO, and increased participation from the British TI Group.

For its part, the Hoesch group took control of firms involved in mecha-nical activities in the UK (Carlo Engineering, Camford Engineering), France (Deffontaine) and Germany (Bilstein), but was then taken over itself by the Krupp group.

Similar movements, of lesser amplitude, may be noted at Kloëckner (Peguform/Manducher), Usinor (Allevard), Cockerill (Ymos), Metall-gesellschaft (Kolbenschmidt) and Hoogovens (Neumeyer Fliepresse). The position in Italy is different, since Fiat has its own iron, steel and metallur-gical subsidiary, Teksid.

This growing interest from some iron and steel producers for car industry products, components or functions is to be associated with their search for higher added value development prospects than un- or semi-finished products. At the same time, it may contribute to the increase in function oligopolies. The developments of the next few years will no doubt confirm (or disprove) this impression.

### 4.2.4  Balance within the Automobile Systems is Achieved by the Vehicle Manufacturers

What are the limits to function oligopolies? At first view, they may be divided into economic and regulatory limits. The following section examines the economic limits. The effects of laws and regulations will be examined later.

Today the national automobile systems are being progressively replaced by continental ones, and will shortly become global. Systematization and globalization of activities and strategies are now common goals for all the actors in the automobile system. The resulting close-knit complementarity and partnership between vehicle manufacturers and direct autocomponent suppliers entails reinforced technological, industrial, and financial capacity for all players; to continue to figure in the first rank of world competition requires mobilization of greater and greater sums. In the competitive arena it is less and less true to say that automobile profitability is enough to ensure autonomy for the autocomponent industry. The first questions concern diversification; strategy for the different actors will differ depending on their degree of automobile specialization in the system, be they vehicle or auto-component manufacturers or distributors.

*Box 4.5     Bosch, world leader*

---

1.  The group

It was in 1886 that Robert Bosch opened his first 'precision mechanics and electrotechnical workshop'. The company gradually became the first auto-component manufacturer in the world entirely independent of the car makers. In 1990, Bosch was in the top ten German enterprises, with 60 manufacturing units spread over 130 countries. Fifty-one % of its turnover comes from foreign countries. In 1989, the Bosch group employed 175 000 persons, 58 000 of them foreign. The Robert Bosch Stiftung GmbH has held 90% of the shares since 1964, and has assigned its voting rights to the Robert Bosch Industrietreuhand KG company, in charge of managing the Robert Bosch company.

Assembly and spare parts account for a little over half the group's consolidated turnover. They are grouped into seven sectors or strategic functions: security equipments (ABS) and shock absorbers, diesel injection, lighting techniques, petrol injection and ignition, electrical and electronic body parts, semi-conductors and electronic central controls, starters, alternators and batteries. Bosch also plays a part in communication techniques (22% of turnover), consumer goods (household appliances, kitchens, audio and video equipment, tooling, heating and furniture 20% of turnover), and manufactured goods (hydraulic and pneumatic parts, electronic industrial equipment, metal and plastic products, and packaging machines 6% of turnover).

Bosch has invested an average 7% of annual turnover in capital goods and external growth operations from 1986–91. Its investment in R&D rose to almost 6% in 1989.

2.  External growth operations and alliances

All Bosch's acquisitions and cooperations over the past four years were linked to the group's functional specializations. The EUREQ base counted seventeen operations, five of which were acquisitions and eight joint ventures.
The most important concerned
• electrical and electronic systems and components: joint venture with Behr for electronic controls for heating and air-conditioning, with Varta for batteries, with TDK for audio systems, with Philips and Jeumont–Schneider for radio-telephones, with UEB for lamps and headlights, with the American Emerson for electrical engines (hand tools and cars); acquisition of Motometer for on-board electronic components, Signal Bau Huber for navigational assistance systems; licence for shock sensors assigned to Zexel, Japan;
• injection systems, in which Bosch is world leader joint venture with Nippon-denso in the United States, acquisition of Alpine Automotive in Austria;
• security equipment ABS licence assigned to Zvs Brno in Czechoslovakia, joint venture with Morton for inflatable bags.

Bosch's strategy is to keep or acquire a dominant position in the automobile functions in which it has specialized, and to pursue its diversification.

How can the increasing function oligopolies and the financial concentrations be regulated? Fairly numerous recent examples have illustrated the overwhelming influence of the car makers, which can give their opinion and take decisions on certain envisaged takeovers, majority shareholdings and public takeover bids. Thus, the French car industry radically opposed Valéo's attempt to take control of Epéda Bertrand Faure in 1988, the German car industry blocked possible control of Continental by Pirelli, and General Motors redirected strategy in the original part tyre market after Firestone was taken over by Bridgestone. It is not surprising that several examples from the tyre industry should be found here, since world oligopoly is well advanced in this area (Banville and Chanaron 1991b).

The concentration of function oligopolies is therefore limited by the clients. It is they who ultimately decide on concentration operations, and who can also organize their upstream operations when disintegrating; they influence concentration of suppliers by their choice of the group buying the subsidiary or the factories to be sold.

At a time when a soaring number of function oligopolies are confronted with the purchasing power of the car makers, the latter remain ultimate arbiters of industrial organization in the automobile system, of which they will remain leaders in so far as they remain designers and assemblers (production and marketing).

## 4.3   STRATEGIC GUIDELINES IN THE IMMEDIATE FUTURE

### 4.3.1  The Strategic Options

The autocomponent manufacturers' strategy largely depends on the evolution of their relationships with car makers and on the development of internationalization.

#### 4.3.1.1  Supplying strategies of car makers

While the main characteristic of relations between manufacturers and suppliers in the automobile system remains continuing disintegration by the former (increased outsourcing to the detriment of integrated manufacture or subsidiaries), this process cannot simply be recreated elsewhere. In other words, in many cases, the vertical disintegration movement is likely to slow down, and proceed by degrees according to the rhythm at which new models are launched.

Can the manufacturers which are at present the most integrated — Mercedes Benz, Fiat, GM, Ford — sustain this degree of integration? The answer is very probably 'no'. When manufacturers encounter persistent economic difficulties, as has been the case for American manufacturers at the beginning of the 1990s, they logically question the strategic value of many of their assets, and re-evaluate the usefulness of their joint ventures, and of their subsidiaries which diversify or produce equipment. Thus in early 1992, General Motors envisaged moving out of Daewoo and selling its subsidiary Allison Transmission. Very soon, Detroit Diesel — already partly transferred by GM to Penske — showed interest in the latter.

More generally, what is the future for autocomponent subsidiaries and manufacturing groups' integrated productions? Apart from the case of Ford, which until now had deliberately adopted the strategy of not supplying other manufacturers outside its Ford–Mazda–Kia global alliance (see Chapter 3), two types of case may be observed: first, that of GM, which has been able to take on the role of autocomponent manufacturer as such, due to its power and the diversity of the components produced by its subsidiaries, and which supplies many competitors in the world; second, that of Chrysler, Fiat and PSA, which have only slowly and partially turned their subsidiaries Acustar, Magneti Marelli and ECIA into large autocomponent manufacturers. Finally, there is the case of VAG, which has no autocomponent subsidiary. Disintegration, encouraged by development prospects in Germany and central Europe, and negotiated with its employee organizations, is being discussed in a climate of probable expansion, which will enable industrial choices to be made more easily.

The French groups, wondering what their chances of survival are at the end of the present decade, are testing to what degree of disintegration they can go to be still considered as 'true' car manufacturers, mastering most of the main components, and not just as assemblers mainly responsible for design.

Further, as regards some integrated activities, particularly the plastics transformation units, the choice between 'make' or 'buy' may be influenced by contradictory temporal requirements. Short- and medium-term constraints may encourage 'make' where economic and social difficulties contribute to development of internal capacities, and long-term constraints may encourage movement towards 'buy' due to specialization in skills.

Autocomponent manufacturers also depend on the manufacturers' choice between single sourcing and multiple sourcing. This question has no one final answer, since the supplier must be big enough to be reliable and autonomous, but not to such a degree that a durable monopoly is attained. All the more as the Japanese manufacturers' purchasing departments have publicly announced that they were returning to multi-sourcing for each family of products (even if mono-sourcing was maintained for one reference), thus obliging their competitors once again to change their supply strategy.

Another traditional question concerns brand image. Who gains prestige *with the consumer* from technical advances, the car manufacturer or the supplier? Should the vehicle manufacturer's brand name 'absorb' that of the autocomponent manufactuer? Or should the car manufacturer help the auto-component partner to build up his brand name?

Very often, the vehicle manufacturer tries as far as possible to 'rub out' the supplier's brand name in the replacement part market, by practising an 'original part' policy. The same Valéo alternator may thus be sold by the Valéo distributing network under its own name and under that of a car manufacturer. Two interesting examples of 'joint promotion' of vehicle and autocomponent manufacturers' brand names show both the limits and the efficiency of possible cooperation in the new vehicle market.

When Fiat equipped some of its models with 'ABS Bosch', the German autocomponent firm required that explicit, visible mention of this equipment be made on the vehicle and in the advertising. Bosch was at that time the only possible supplier, and because of its size and technological expertise, it could impose its demands. Since then, the ABS brand name has become generic; electronic braking assistance systems have been developed by other autocomponent manufacturers, and the Bosch name has disappeared from the advertisements.

Seat developed the Ibiza model during a difficult period, before Fiat, with which it had had strong technical ties, withdrew and VAG took control, with the help of experienced autocomponent manufacturers, and particularly with that of Porsche, which developed and built the engine. Seat obtained permission to mention 'Porsche system' on the car and in the advertising, and this no doubt contributed to sales of the model, since the German manufacturer is famous for its technological expertise.

The prospect of continuing disintegration in the car makers raises several important questions for autocomponent manufacturers. To whom are parts to be sold and with whom are agreements to be concluded? National auto-component manufacturers? European, American or Japanese groups? Raw material suppliers? New entrants? Diversified conglomerates? And so on.

Since they can choose their buyers or partners, the vehicle manufacturers shape the supply sector to some degree. Observation shows that attitudes vary considerably; among the French manufacturers, it would seem that Renault aims rather at dispersion of its assets to different groups — French, European, American or Japanese — thus hampering the development of French firms in burgeoning oligopolies. However, one sizeable exception to this is Financière du Valois, considered as a pole for automobile nuts, bolts and screws. Further, iron and steel groups also see here attractive opportunities for increasing downstream valorization of their semi-products and for diversification, particularly in plastics and composites.

Finally, because all first rank suppliers must supply their vehicle manufacturer clients' plants regularly, whatever their location, they have rapidly regrouped and organized transborder cooperation in Europe according to the product or function, and have sought excellence to a degree nearing monopoly.

### 4.3.1.2 Evolution of internationalization

Ten or fifteen years ago, the automobile system could be viewed as being formed more or less of a centre comprising the richer countries with vehicle manufacturers, and peripheral producers of anonymous parts or components, thus reflecting the traditional international division of work into North and South. This scheme of things never really worked, and cannot be envisaged, now or in the future, because of the increasing technological nature of the components, increasing function integration, and shorter production times as a whole. These conditions require compatible structures in the cooperating enterprises, which are difficult to envisage in less developed environments, particularly as regards the technical and economic skills of subcontractors.

Vehicle manufacturers in industrialized countries have maintained most of their potential there. They will be able to develop and guide links and exchanges with the most advanced firms in intermediary countries, which could lead to global alliances in which each participant has a place in the hierarchy. Hypothetical world distribution of work is replaced by finely tuned management, not necessarily excluding tension and conflicts, of the distribution of work in the global or European alliances. The distribution of work will be transnational, yet at the same time internal to the groups or alliance networks. Thus the Ford–Mazda–Kia alliance seeks to rationalize its supplies according to continental geographical zones, depending on the respective roles of the leaders: the medium range in Europe, top of the range in the United States, and the lower range in South East Asia. This rationalization concerns external suppliers as well as the group's part and component plants, its subsidiaries or its affiliates.

Integrated supply strategies are being set up in this framework, whether by allied or autonomous firms, operating as more or less sole suppliers. More specifically still, component supply is often an ideal vector for acquaintance, followed by cooperation between firms from different countries, provided the levels of development are fairly similar.

How could the European autocomponent industry be extended? There are two neighbouring zones which could extend and complement the European Single Market automobile zone: central and Eastern Europe, and the Maghreb.

During the past few years, development possibilities for the manufacture of automotive components in the Maghreb have been analysed, notably by the UNIDO and at the level of the Union du Maghreb Arabe (Arab Maghreb

Union). Scope for volume and variety seems limited, since many firms are in competition for these automobile markets, and so no vehicle manufacturing group has particular interest in developing its own division of work.

In central and Eastern Europe, some countries seem capable of resuming industrial work and organization, and of using the Western manufacturers, particularly the Americans in Europe, to help them participate in trade within the enlarged European automobile system. Many projects have been announced, but whether they will be carried out is not yet known. Other countries are in such economic, political and social disarray that the question of possible industrial cooperation seems premature, to say the least.

Partial extension to the east of Europe raises both positive prospects and additional problems. The positive prospects are based on the very high levels of demand for modern vehicles, which have become the symbol of these countries' opening to liberal economies and rejection of socialist planned economic options. Thus the higher echelons in each State have negotiated agreements between vehicle manufacturers: Skoda/VW, FSO/ Fiat, FSL/PSA, and soon FSM/Fiat, Lada/Fiat, and so on. It is mostly the European general producers which have become parties to these agreements, the Americans in Europe preferring to develop industrial links by setting up their own units or joint ventures producing equipment, mechanical parts or functions, and sometimes vehicles assembled from imported parts.

*Table 4.15   Eastern European operations by autocomponent manufacturers, 1989–91*

| Country | Group | Partner | Type of operation | Product |
|---|---|---|---|---|
| Hungary | Varity/US | UAMO | Joint venture | Engines |
| | GM/US | RABA | Joint venture | Engines |
| | Ford/US | na | Creation | Pumps |
| | Pirelli/It | TAURUS | Acquisition | Tyres |
| | United Tech./US | na | Creation | Cables |
| Poland | Continental/D | STOMIL | Technical agreement | Tyres |
| Czechoslovakia | Bosch/D | ZVS BRNO | Licence | ABS |
| | Lucas/UK | AUTOBRZDY | Joint venture | Spark plugs |
| | GM/US | BAZ | Joint venture | Gearboxes |
| | Kloeckner/D | PLASTIMAT | Joint venture | Plastics |
| | Continental/D | BARUM | Joint venture | Tyres |
| USSR | Pirelli/It | na | Joint venture | Tyres |

*Source*: EUREQ

Table 4.15 shows that Hungary and Czechoslovakia have attracted most of the autocomponent manufacturers' investments, mainly American and German ones, including GM. Eastern Europe does not seem to tempt either vehicle or autocomponent producers from Japan. It is also important to note that only four operations concern tyres.

### 4.3.2 Actors and Strategies

#### 4.3.2.1 The European groups
As Table 4.3 indicated, among the leading 30 European autocomponent manufacturers including tyre producers for the years 1988 and 1990, there are significant changes at the head of the list.

It is particularly to be noted that in anticipation of the considerable developments expected in automobile electronics, some of the leaders have strengthened their positions by links with industrially diversified and financially powerful groups such as Philips and Siemens.

The positions of smaller autocomponent producers are more difficult to pinpoint, because there are so many, and they are scattered geo-economically. However, there have been, and will still be, many changes with a view to reinforcing function oligopolies, it being understood that this objective may be overtaken by voluntary, sometimes swift, changes of position by the large industrial and financial groups in the autocomponent field. For concentration is both industrial and financial.

#### 4.3.2.2 The American and Japanese groups
The American and Japanese autocomponent producers are generally very dependent on the car makers, including for finance (Banville and Chanaron 1990). They often form actual conglomerates or mega groups, in which they are mere business units which are easy to leave immediately the function is no longer seen as strategic.

The speed with which the North American autcomponent industry remodelled, under the twofold pressure of the setback in the automobile market as of 1990, and the competitive and quality constraints imposed on the whole sector, has led not only to the beginnings of disengagement by the American car makers, with GM autocomponent subsidiaries abandoning many product lines, and Chrysler selling several units, but also to accelerated restructuring within the autocomponent sector itself. These changes may lead to opportunities both for the European autocomponent industry, which has indeed long been present, but also for their Japanese counterparts, already established in the United States in the wake of their car makers.

The American automotive equipment mutinationals, ACG Europe, a GM subsidiary, Rockwell, TRW, Varity, Allied Signal, and Johnson Controls, among others, have long had European subsidiaries, supplying most vehicle producers. They will no doubt pursue their strategy of winning market share and specializing according to function.

The establishment of Japanese autocomponent manufacturers in Europe (see Table 4.16) is however a recent phenomenon, still relatively small-scale: 64 productions units, 23 of which are joint ventures, were created between 1970 and 1991. Thirteen operations date from before 1985. The two years of the most notable activity were 1989 and 1990, with eighteen and fourteen operations respectively.

*Table 4.16  Establishment of Japanese autocomponent manufacturers in Europe, 1970–91*

| Operations | UK | Spain | Germany | France | Italy | Others | EC |
|---|---|---|---|---|---|---|---|
| Creation | 15 | 5 | 4 | 2 | 1 | 3 | 30 |
| Acquisition | 5 | 0 | 1 | 1 | 1 | 0 | 8 |
| Joint venture | 7 | 5 | 2 | 4 | 0 | 5 | 23 |
| Other | 1 | 0 | 0 | 0 | 0 | 2 | 3 |
| Total | 28 | 10 | 7 | 7 | 2 | 10 | 64 |

*Source*: EUREQ

Large autocomponent manufacturers, wishing to contribute all types of supplies to European vehicle manufacturers, set up a certain number of operations: NGK for spark plugs, Sumitomo for tyres (taken over from Dunlop), Nippondenso for radiators and ignition coils, Yuasa for batteries, Nippon Seiko for bearings, and Matsushita, Kenwood, Sanyo, Pioneer and Clarion for car radios.

Some plants were set up for autocomponent manufacturers to follow a Japanese vehicle manufacturer with which they had long been partners: Ikeda (seats, joint venture with Johnson Controls), Kasai (internal trim, joint venture with Reydell), Yamato Kogyo (pressing) for Nissan; Koyo Seiko (bearings), Ogihara (pressing) for Toyota; Yachiyo Kogyo (tanks, joint venture with Unipart) and Yotaka Giken (catalytic exhausts, joint venture with Unipart) for Honda.

Finally, more recent plants have been set up for JIT supply of local vehicle manufacturers Ryobi (clutch foundry parts) for Ford UK, Yazaki (wiring) in Spain, Inoue (on board instruments) and Tokei (dashboard clocks) in Germany.

The fact that the UK and Spain are mainly chosen as locations for these plants shows that the Japanese suppliers and car makers have coordinated their international strategies. The proximity standards required by JIT delivery and technological partnership, Japanese style, encourage such coordination. Moreover, the UK and Spain are among the European countries with the lowest labour costs, which is an important criterion for component mounting units. The former also has the benefit of the language, of historical antecedents, and of demonstration effects in other activities such as electronics, TP equipment, etc. Moreover, there is a favourable social and political climate (Banville, Chanaron and Guelle 1991).

In many cases, the vehicle manufacturer contributes finance to the installation of its suppliers, either because the latter are subsidiaries (this is the case of Ikeda with Nissan, and Yachiyo Kogyo with Honda, for instance), or because the vehicle manufacturer contributes finance to the unit directly; this is the case, for instance, with Yamato Kogyo, the Newcastle factory which is, like the Ikeda one, located in the supply zone for Nissan, next to the vehicle plant; it is owned by a joint venture, 80 per cent of which is owned by Nissan UK.

In future, it seems unlikely that Japanese autocomponent manufacturers will invade Europe on a similar scale as that which occurred in the United States in the 1980s. European autocomponent manufacturers are, it is true, in a better position than their American homologues, both as regards the quality of their production (in price, supply quality and punctuality), and as regards their technological mastery. The Japanese car makers will therefore be more inclined to take their supplies from local producers satisfying their high selection standards, whereas in the United States they found it difficult to appoint suitable suppliers.

Generally speaking, when a European autocomponent manufacturer satisfies the selection procedures of local vehicle producers, particularly Ford's Q1 and PSA and Renault's shared AQF, Japanese car makers consider that they can contract with them (Bosch, Valéo, Lucas, T&N, GKN, etc.). Thus, the European autocomponent manufacturers are leaders in several joint ventures: Freudenberg with NOK (60–40) in 1976, for seals, Reydel with Kasai Kogyo (80–20) in 1989 for manufacture of interior wood trim, Lucas with Sumotomo Electric (70–30) in 1990 for electrical wiring. Moreover, in many cases, licensing agreements led to shareouts according to trading areas; thus, the Japanese autocomponent manufacturers under licence to Bendix, Valéo, Bosch, Lucas and GKN, for instance, were contractually excluded from European markets.

Further, political pressure from the EEC and states also encourages supplies from local firms, in order to avoid screwdriver factories and bankruptcies in local autocomponent firms. Besides, supplies from Japanese groups to European vehicle manufacturers have not yet become the norm, and in a fierce competitive climate where there are races to launch new models, problems of secrecy and therefore confidence in the discretion of suppliers could soon be of paramount importance. And Japanese autocomponent manufacturers are almost all affiliated to Japanese vehicle manufacturers, and are members of their *Kyoryokukai*, the club in which they exchange strategic information.

Finally, the issue of optimum production levels arises because Japanese vehicle manufacturers set up in smaller units than those in the United States, and rarely 'share' the same suppliers. Furthermore, their American experiences could discourage Japanese autocomponent manufacturers, since many of them have not attained satisfactory levels of profitability since they were set up, according to the American financial press.

Japanese autocomponent manufacturers' international strategy in Europe will no doubt, therefore, be circumspect, and creations will only occur where European producers are incapable of equalling their Japanese counterparts' technical and economic performances.

Not all the experts agree that the Japanese autocomponent manufacturers' deployment in Europe will be different from that experienced in the United States. Several think that the American pattern in the 1980s will be reproduced, and that privileged links between the Japanese vehicle manufacturers and their affiliated suppliers will result in the latter flooding the European market with highly competitive products. However, the arguments which claim that such swift expansion is unlikely are sufficiently convincing to make this threat seem nebulous for the time being.

### 4.3.2.3  Is the automobile system still strategic?

More generally speaking, given that the field of action is becoming more concentrated and on global level, the main question about the automobile industry is this: will, or must, automobiles remain a 'strategic' market, or indeed the sole activity? This is what makes the question of concentrations and strategic alliances particularly interesting.

On the other hand, diversified autocomponent manufacturers such as Bosch, Epéda-Bertrand Faure, Lucas, GKN, etc., have continued to apportion their activities equally. They are thus more able periodically to revise the nature and/or scope of their engagements in the automobile system.

Since the latter is now based on a 'mature' product, the market prospects of which are situated essentially in replacement, except for a few limited geographical zones where competition is therefore very fierce (such as in the newly industrialized Asian and central European countries), certain autocomponent manufacturers may be expected to redirect their policy, moving out of the automobile system partly or entirely.

### 4.3.3  Regulation of Concentrations

There are internal limits to continued concentrations between autocomponent manufacturers (see section 4.2.4). Groups also have to take account of European institutional and political regulations with regard to competition.

It is generally because competition needs regulating, and therefore mono-polies are combated, that the national authorities in most European countries, and the European authorities, intervene where there is industrial and financial concentration. In the light of experience, the behaviour of the national agencies is generally all the more predictable as their opinion is often requested during accomplishment of these operations. The European Commission has logically sought to regulate competition at the European level (see Chapter 1). But it is criticized because in some cases its action appeared as too political. This is partly why lobbies and professional and industrial influence are proliferating in Brussels, including those for the autocomponent manufacturers!

The main technical debate centres on defining the market so as to assess the degree of competition: first of all, geographical limits (a European market, but with what limits? national markets — why some and not others? a world market?); then technical–economic limits (in the Nestlé-Perrier case, should all non-alcoholic drinks be considered or only mineral waters? should the latter include spring waters? and so on). It is here that methods appear random and unclarified. Pressure of all kinds thus comes to bear.

Above all, these procedures do not seem adapted to the case of automotive components: many important functions are produced by companies with a turnover under ECU 5 bn, which is the threshold after which the Directorate-General for competition intervenes, and they therefore fall under the control of national authorities, according to the principle of subsidiarity; any European cohesion in a unitary automobile system is thus ruled out, and overall coherence of future decisions seems in no way guaranteed at first view.

The drawbacks of industrial regulation based solely on competition appear clearly; it cannot possibly play the role of industrial policy. On the contrary, only an industrial policy could give meaning to European anti-trust regula-tions. Any industrial policy must, in any case, go beyond European borders, as the analysis of the autocomponent industry has illustrated. European auto-component manufacturers have genuine prospects worldwide, but as things stand at present, it would be better if they were helped rather than hampered by the European authorities. Thus the best vector for progress would be a European industrial policy with global relevance.

## 4.4  CONCLUSION: IS GLOBAL PARTNERSHIP POSSIBLE?

The future of the European autocomponent industry is closely linked to four groups of strategic characteristics in the automobile system.

First, its overall position is as an intermediary industry, the activity of which is inevitably regulated, both in the medium and short terms, by the client. The car manufacturers will remain ultimate arbiters of industrial organization within this sector. On the other hand, since multi-supply (of several vehicle manufacturers by the same supplier) is becoming the norm, auto-component manufacturers retain a degree of strategic autonomy.

Second, the growing complexity of technology, and the diversification of required competences to provide complete, ready-to-assemble functions, have strongly encouraged strategic agreements and alliances. This development has led to even more concentration in order to improve industrial and financial efficiency, but it has also opened the door to new actors in the sector.

Third, the autocomponent groups have not diversified their activities, preferring to specialize according to function. Given the previous trends, it seems unwise for an autocomponent group to remain too strategically dependent on a vehicle manufacturer. One solution could be strategic alliances with groups operating on other 'mega-markets'. This is even more true for vehicle manufacturers themselves if they are not integrated into diversified groups. This is the trend illustrated by the strategies of the British (Laird, BTR, TI, BBA and others) and German (Siemens, Mannesmann) conglomerates. Strategic alliances have also been concluded by Volvo and Procordia, Fiat and GGE, Daimler and Mitsubishi, etc.

Finally, an irreversible process of vertical disintegration in the car makers is incompatible with the existence of autocomponent manufacturing subsidiaries supplying competitors, as in the case of Fiat and Magneti Marelli, PSA and ECIA, Chrysler and Acustar, GM and ACG/ACGE. Future restructuring of the sector will be a function of this, since continuing ambiguity in the strategic positioning of these entities will soon become impossible. One possible solution could be total or partial takeover by diversified autocomponent groups independent of, or at least only partly dependent on, the vehicle manufacturers. However, the vehicle manufacturers are opposed to the constitution of over-powerful autocomponent groups, dominating several major function oligopolies simultaneously. This long-term prospect will no doubt be an important reason for possible new entries into the industry.

It is in the light of these four factors that industrial development will occur in the coming years. The search for security in an ever more hazardous automobile activity will logically lead to regrouping and strategic alliances. In such a context, all-encompassing, in other words worldwide, partnerships will be the answer.[5]

While there is no simple answer to the question of global partnership, due to the continuing, and indeed increasing, competition between the three main regional automobile systems, significant progress should nevertheless be possible within Europe, for Europe has considerable overall advantages which merely need suitable organization.

A European industrial 'policy' should focus on constituting a true European *automobile system*. It should organize coordination and coherence between the different actors: suppliers, autocomponent manufacturers and car manufacturers, of course, and also the system's downstream sectors, such as the distribution networks, the maintenance and repair networks, and finally, the national and European authorities, many of whose decisions are of great importance for the automobile system.

In a recent communication, the European Commission has recognized the important role of the component suppliers for the competitiveness of the European automobile industry.[6] The Commission has reasserted the importance of the achievement of the Single Market which should create favourable conditions to enhance European competitiveness. It nevertheless agreed with the need for complementary policies with respect to research and training. It also encouraged car makers and suppliers to better coordinate their activities — particularly R&D.

The Commission has thus recognized the problems of adaptation with which the European car industry is confronted. The Commission should diversify its policy to strengthen the competitiveness of the European automobile industry. Indeed, so far, it has dealt mostly with two related aspects: deregulation to achieve the Single Market and competition policy (see Chapter 1 for a general discussion).

## NOTES

1. On the definition of the sector, see also the appendix to this chapter.
2. Partnership is used in this text as a translation of the French term: *partenariat*.
3. While the automobile industry agrees on such overall definitions of function, there are no nomenclatures which are agreed on by both the automobile and auto-component industries.
4. Which are often direct investments from Japanese enterprises with internal growth.
5. From this point of view, competition policy could generate uncertainties and trigger 'political' reactions to certain alliances — at the national or European level.
6. *L'industrie automobile européenne: situation, enjeux et propositions d'action*, COM(92) 166, Bruxelles 8/5/1992.

## APPENDIX: What is an Autocomponent Manufacturer?

The French understanding of an autocomponent manufacturer is of a company mainly producing parts, equipment and components which increasingly comprise complete functions designed for mounting and equipping vehicles. Most of these companies belong to a professional union under the heading of the French Fédération des Industries d'Equipement des Véhicules (Federation of autocomponent manufacturers, FIEV).

This definition does not, however, enable definite pinpointing of a stable group of agents; not only is membership of a professional union voluntary, and not necessarily continuous, but some firms such as Michelin, more particularly, have never wished to be considered as mere autocomponent manufacturers. Conversely, some firms would welcome a definition as auto-component manufacturers, which they would consider more flattering.

Other definitions, conceived by French institutions, have added to these historical notions: mechanical and metallurgical firms do not adhere to the FIEV, although their main market is the automobile. Finally, large industrial groups are also important suppliers to the automobile industry, but have very varied clientèles.

## BIBLIOGRAPHY

Banville, E. de (1989), 'Le développement du partenariat industriel', *Revue d'Econo- mie Industrielle*, no. 47, pp125–136.

Banville, E. de and Chanaron, J.-J. (1985), 'Le système automobile français: de la sous-traitance au partenariat?', CPE Etude no. 56, March.

Banville, E. de and Chanaron, J.-J. (1987), 'Les techniques de CAO et le système auto- mobile', CPE Etude no. 85, April.

Banville, E. de and Chanaron, J.-J. (1988), 'Stratégies technologiques et développe- ment du partenariat industriel', Colloque sur le génie industriel, Nancy, 12–14 December.

Banville, E. de and Chanaron, J.-J. (1990), in H. Jacot (ed.), *Du fordisme au toyotisme*, La Documentation Française, Paris.

Banville, E. de and Chanaron, J.-J. (1991a), *Vers un système automobile européen*, CPE-Economica, Paris.

Banville, E. de and Chanaron, J.-J. (1991b), 'Pneumatiques: concentration et crise', in M. Fouquin and D. Pineye, *Economie mondiale: de Berlin à Bagdad*, Economica, Paris.

Banville, E. de, Chanaron, J.-J. and Guelle, F. (1991), 'Les groupes japonais à la conquête de l'Europe?', in J.-P. Gilly (ed.), *L'Europe industrielle horizon 93*, tome 1, pp115–136.

Braxton Associés (1992), 'Concentrations', *Le Journal de l'Automobile*, 31 January.

Chanaron, J.-J. (1991), 'Automobile: le temps des méga-alliances stratégiques', in M. Fouquin and D. Pineye, *Economie mondiale: de Berlin à Bagdad*, Paris, Economica.

Chanaron, J.-J. (1992), 'Rapport du MIT, Comparer ce qui est comparable', *Le Journal de l'Automobile*, no. 328, 20 December, pp18–25.

CE-Boston Consulting Group (1991), *The competitive challenge facing the European automotive component industry*, CEE, Brussels.

Commission Technique de la Sous-Traitance (1986), 'Le partenariat industriel: sa signification et ses conséquences pour les sous-traitants', Livre Blanc, Ministère de l'Industrie, des P&T et du Tourisme, September.

Dodwell, O. (1990), *Structure of the Japanese Autoparts Industry*, Tokyo.

*Financial Times* (1991), 'Automotive Components', *FT Survey*, 27 March.

Sleigh, P. A. C. (1992), *The European Automobile Component Industry*, Economist Intelligence Unit, London.

Womack, J. P., Jones, D. T. and Roos, D. (1991), *The Machine that Changed the World*, Rawson Associates, New York.

# 5. The Semiconductor Industry

## Mike Hobday

Semiconductors (SCs) represent the physical building blocks for all electronic goods and systems. SCs, or 'chips', are the main hardware input for consumer electronics, telecommunications, computers, informatics systems, office automation and other information technology products. More traditional industries such as aerospace, defence, instrumentation, medical equipment and automotives are today critically dependent on the application of SC technology.

In the world context, European countries have lagged behind the US and Japan, both in SCs and electronics systems. In 1990 European firms produced only 13 per cent of total SC output, 10 per cent of computer output and 16 per cent of consumer goods output (ICE 1991 pp2–37).

This weak competitive position is of great concern to European policy makers. Information technology is one of the key technologies of the future. In economic terms electronics hardware represents around 4.4 per cent of European GDP. It is predicted to reach 6.7 per cent of GDP by 1993 (CEC 1989 p1). Europe's poor performance has led to a burgeoning balance of trade deficit in electronics. This grew from a positive balance in 1975 to a deficit of $21.9 bn in 1987 (CEC 1989). In SCs the balance of trade deficit was around $4.2 bn in 1988 and forecast to reach $7.0 bn in 1994.

In order to build up the electronics industry the European Community (EC) embarked on a series of technology support programmes (e.g. ESPRIT 1, 2 and 3 and RACE) during the mid-1980s. The EC also assisted the Eureka Programme. Most of these programmes subsidized SC research and development (R&D) in the belief that SCs were vital to Europe's long-term performance in information technology. The programmes aimed to strengthen firms' technical competences in SCs and thereby improve their competitive performance.

This chapter has two objectives: first, to assess the build-up of competences by European-owned[1] chip producers during the 1980s, focusing mainly on technological competences; and second, to examine the impact of EC support policies on Europe's SC industry. The method used is to analyse the external operations (EOs) of European firms during the 1980s. EOs are defined as technical joint ventures, mergers, acquisitions and other equity operations.

EOs include second sourcing arrangements, joint manufacture, licensing contracts and joint ventures for future technology development. The chapter looks both at intra-European ventures and agreements with overseas companies.

EOs represent only one dimension of European firms' competence accumulation. However, as the chapter shows, technical EOs are particularly important in the SC industry. The data provide useful insights into the growing technological competence of Europe's chip industry during the 1980s.

The chapter is structured as follows. Section 5.1 introduces the industry and technology of SCs. It looks briefly at market concentration, capital and R&D costs and the historical importance of EOs to the SC industry. Section 5.2 examines the overall state of the European chip industry touching on production, consumption, trade, firm strategies and EC policies.

Section 5.3 is the core of the chapter. It analyses a sample of 161 European EOs carried out during the 1980s, including 120 technical agreements and 41 mergers, acquisitions and joint ventures. The data are divided into two periods corresponding roughly to before and after the start of the European Programmes in 1984. EOs are examined according to trends over time, motivations, choice of partner and direction of technology flow. Section 5.3 shows that European firms' main external source of technology is US companies. The chapter therefore looks at the data to see whether EC policies may have distorted the 'natural' pattern of technology flow by subsidizing an increase in intra-EC EOs at the expense of external European alliances.

Section 5.4 attempts to place European EOs within the international context by comparing them with some of the major US and Japanese alliances. It also looks at other issues of critical importance, including the orientation of European firms towards the US. It questions the rationale of near-market EC support to European-owned firms and touches on the impact of the industry recession which began in 1990.

The conclusion summarizes the main points, confirming that EOs are central to the evolution of corporate competences in the European SC industry. A glossary (Appendix 1) is included to explain technical terms and abbreviations.

# 5.1  TECHNOLOGICAL AND INDUSTRIAL TRENDS

### 5.1.1  Process and Product Technology

The design and production of SCs is an extremely complex, capital-intensive activity. One report described it as one of the 'most complicated high-volume processes ever developed by man' (UNCTC 1983 p80). Although SCs appear to be manufactured in roughly the same way, slight variations in production generate devices with fundamentally different performance characteristics.

The standard 'planar' manufacturing process has five basic stages of production. These are repeated as required by the different product types:

1. The design stage: the conceptualization of the product design and process steps.
2. Mask production: a mask, or photomask (a physical pattern from which the final circuitry is made) is produced by a computer which generates patterns for each layer of circuitry. Alternatively electron-beam or X-ray lithography techniques write patterns directly on to a mask under instructions from a computer.
3. Wafer fabrication: silicon wafers (the processed silicon material from which chips are made) are manufactured from raw silicon. The silicon is purified and doped with 'n' type (negative) and 'p' type (positive) impurities to produce the special conductivity characteristics of SCs.
4. Diffusion: the circuit pattern is imprinted on the silicon, layer-by-layer, using a lithographical technique. Next, a pattern is etched into the oxide layer using either chemicals (wet etching) or hot gases (dry etching).
5. Assembly, test and quality control: the chips are connected up to the outside world with fine aluminium or gold wires. They are then given a series of electrical tests to grade the devices and to ensure their quality.

Various types of material are used to produce SCs. Silicon is the material from which most of the industry has evolved. Other materials are used in some applications, such as gallium arsenide.

Within silicon an important division is between MOS (metal oxide semi-conductor) and bipolar. These terms refer to the type of transistor used as the active element in the integrated circuit (IC).[2] During the 1960s, the TTL bipolar product range dominated the industry under the leadership of Texas Instruments. Due to its slow speed TTL is almost obsolete today.

Advances in MOS, especially CMOS (complementary MOS), produced ICs with low power consumption, simpler circuit designs, and lower cost per circuit element. CMOS enabled IC makers to achieve very large scales of integration (VLSI) with hundreds of thousands of circuit elements on a single tiny chip. The process led to the steady displacement of bipolar products in new systems during the 1970s and helped create large new markets such as calculators, electronic watches and microcomputers.

Figure 5.1 presents a simplified SC product family tree with market share and growth information. SCs are made up of discrete circuits (only one functioning element) and ICs (more than one element). ICs, which represent around 80 per cent of the total SC market, are comprised of four main groups: linear devices, memories, microcomponents and logic circuits.

*Figure 5.1 Semiconductor family tree and approximate market share and growth\**

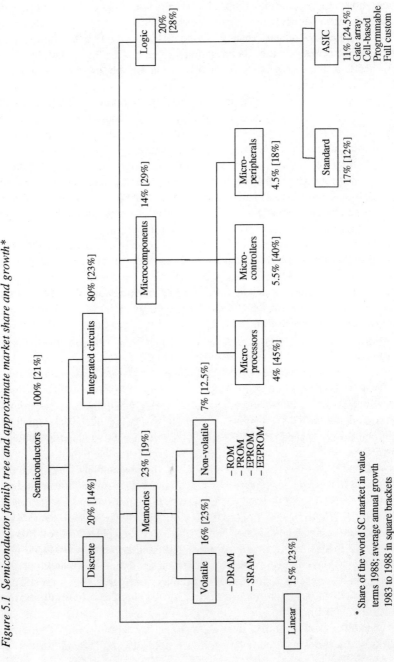

\* Share of the world SC market in value terms 1988; average annual growth 1983 to 1988 in square brackets

Linear ICs are mostly analogue (continuous wave form) circuits. They are used to modify incoming electrical signals and convert them into qualitatively different, outgoing signals. They are used in automotive, communications equipment, most entertainments products (e.g. television and radio), interface devices (e.g. keyboards and tuners) and amplification equipment. Linear account for around 15 per cent of the IC market.

The other three IC families are largely digital (on-off switches as opposed to analogue). Digital ICs carry out logical (e.g. number crunching) functions — rapidly manipulating, storing and transmitting many different kinds of data in binary digits (bits). Increasingly digital ICs are supplanting analogue ones (e.g. in television and telecommunications applications). Some digital devices contain analogue functions (and vice versa).

Memories (23 per cent of the IC market) store large quantities of data in binary code in the form of electrical charges. The two main segments of the memory market are volatile and non-volatile. Volatile memory — or RAM (random access memory) — is memory which is written in by the user and stored temporarily. If the current is switched off, the memory is lost. The two main forms of RAM are static (SRAM) and dynamic (DRAM). DRAM cells are smaller than SRAM and can store more data for any given chip size. Non-volatile — or ROM (read only memory) — is memory that is pre-programmed and cannot be altered by application software. The main types are ROM, programmable ROM (PROM), erasable PROM (EPROM), and electrically erasable PROM (EEPROM).

Microcomponents (29 per cent of the IC market) are made up of microprocessors (MPUs), microcontrollers and microperipherals. MPUs were first developed for use in calculators, combining the functions of various custom-built logic (see below) chips. The first MPU was introduced in 1971. Since then many new generations have been introduced, helping to create whole new electronic equipment sectors, including microcomputers, cash registers, computer aided design equipment, intelligent terminals and office equipment.

Logic devices process, convert and direct electronic signals. They perform arithmetic calculations (and other logic functions) in conjunction with data stored elsewhere in the IC. Standard logic ICs are produced for the mass market according to a pre-programmed circuit pattern. In contrast, ASICs (application specific integrated circuits) are customized to meet the needs of specific products and/or particular customer. ASICs include customized and semi-customized ICs such as gate arrays, cell-based chips, and programmable logic.

Semi-custom ASICs tend to be less expensive and faster to produce than fully customized circuits.

### 5.1.2  Barriers to Entry

#### 5.1.2.1  Market concentration

Overall, the SC industry is fairly concentrated, although not nearly as concentrated as say computers, where a single firm (IBM) accounts for a very large share of the world market. As Table 5.1 shows, the largest chip supplier (NEC) supplied 8.5 per cent of the world market in 1991 just ahead of Toshiba at 8.2 per cent. The top ten firms accounted for 55.6 per cent in 1991.

However, there are very significant concentrations at the product group level. In key product areas such as DRAMs and MPUs, small oligopolies of firms dominate the industry. In DRAMs four Japanese and one Korean firm accounted for 66 per cent of the market in 1990 (ICE 1991 pp6–55). In SRAMs US firms have left the high volume, low priced commodity end of the market, leaving this to Japanese firms. In 32-bit microprocessors (a key product for microcomputers) two US firms (Intel and Motorola) accounted for 81 per cent of the total market in 1990 (ICE 1991 pp6–27).

Generally, the SC industry is highly concentrated at the mass production end of the industry (e.g. standard DRAMs, SRAMs, MPUs and gate arrays) with a few firms dominating most main new IC types.

Entry into the 'big league' of mass producers is very difficult due to capital costs and technological complexity. Barriers to entry in the DRAM market are particularly daunting. As one of the main commodity chips worldwide, DRAMs are used in many electronic systems. In 1990 Europe had only one producer (Siemens) in the top twelve suppliers of one-megabit DRAMs. Eight of the others were Japanese, one was Korean and two American. Toshiba alone accounted for 20 per cent of world sales. Europe's poor showing in DRAMs was a particular cause for concern in the EC.

#### 5.1.2.2  Capital and R&D costs

One of the main barriers to entry is capital costs, especially the escalating cost of wafer fabrication lines. In the mid-1970s a 'wafer fab' cost around $30 m. By 1990 a fabrication facility cost in the region of $400 m. This could rise to $500 m by 1992 (ICE 1991 pp3–5).

Entering and staying in the industry requires huge financial resources. To compete with the US, Japanese firms spent roughly $2.5 bn per annum during the mid-1980s on capital equipment, and as much as $3.5 bn in the boom of 1984, roughly equivalent to 36 per cent of sales in 1984 and 1985 (Ferguson 1988 p60). In 1990 worldwide capital spending stood at around $11.5 bn, roughly 20.2 per cent of total chip sales (ICE 1991 pp2–62).

*Table 5.1*   *Leading merchant semiconductor manufacturers worldwide, 1990 and 1991*

| Rank 1991 | Rank 1990 | Company | 1991 Sales ($ m) | HQ* | Market share 1991, in % |
|---|---|---|---|---|---|
| 1 | 1 | NEC | 5547 | J | 8.5 |
| 2 | 2 | Toshiba | 5337 | J | 8.2 |
| 3 | 3 | Hitachi | 4351 | J | 6.7 |
| 4 | 5 | Intel | 4059 | US | 6.3 |
| 5 | 4 | Motorola | 3915 | US | 6.0 |
| 6 | 6 | Fujitsu | 3111 | J | 4.8 |
| 7 | 7 | Texas Instrument | 2573 | US | 4.2 |
| 8 | 8 | Mitsubishi | 2568 | J | 4.0 |
| 9 | 10 | Matsushita | 2421 | J | 3.7 |
| 10 | 9 | Philips | 2072 | N | 3.2 |
| 11 | 11 | National | 1697 | US | 2.6 |
| 12 | 14 | Sanyo | 1612 | J | 2.5 |
| 13 | 12 | Samsung | 1592 | K | 2.5 |
| 14 | 15 | Sharp | 1490 | J | 2.4 |
| 15 | 12 | STM | 1490 | F/I | 2.3 |
| 16 | 17 | Sony | 1426 | J | 2.2 |
| 17 | 16 | Siemens | 1258 | WG | 1.9 |
| 18 | 19 | AMD | 1185 | US | 1.8 |
| 19 | 18 | Oki | 1157 | J | 1.8 |
| 20 | 22 | Rohm | 1029 | J | 1.6 |
|  |  | Total | 64914 |  |  |

\* Headquarters (also indicates country of origin and major operations)
   J = Japan, US = United States, K = Korea, N = Netherlands, WG = West Germany,
   F/I = French/Italian
*Source*: Dataquest (quoted in *Electronics Times*, 16 January 1992, p6)

Large R&D expenditures also make entry into the mainstream of the industry extremely difficult. The historical data show that Japanese firms spent on average around 14.5 per cent of sales per annum on R&D over the period 1976–85. In contrast, US firms spent an average of only 8.5 per cent percent per annum over the same period (Ferguson 1988 p61). This partly explains the rise of Japan in relation to the US. In the past few years, roughly 24 per cent of Japan's capital spending has been allocated to new products and R&D.

The most capital and R&D intensive sectors of the business are in the new generations of mainstream product types such as DRAMs, SRAMs and MPUs. New offerings in these product groups generally require significant advances in process technology as well as product design. The move from 256-kilobit to one-megabit DRAM production, for instance, required radical improvements in wafer fabrication technology.

As discussed below, the high cost of R&D and new product development has led some of the largest US and European firms into joint ventures. For instance, Siemens and IBM joined up to produce the 64-megabit DRAM.

In contrast, firms in niche segments of the industry are able to rely more on adding value through design. In this manner relatively small firms are able to bypass the large capital and R&D thresholds which apply to volume production. Many small firms can and do enter at the niche end of the business. A large number of small US start-ups entered during the 1980s, designing and making ASICs and other specialist technologies. Niche markets are important 'windows of opportunity' which add to a country's overall capability in chips and electronic systems. Unfortunately, Europe has produced very few start-ups of the US calibre.

### 5.1.3   The Importance of EOs in the SC Industry

Throughout its history the SC industry has engaged liberally in various forms of EO. EOs have always been a widely used form of competence accumulation and corporate strategy.

Before the 1980s the main forms of EO were product licensing agreements, known as second-sourcing (SS) in the industry. SS arrangements are usually tightly defined and concern a single product. The 1980s witnessed an increase in joint ventures for future technology, strategic business partnerships, mergers and acquisitions and research collaborations.[3]

As Steinmueller (1988) shows, SS began in the US in the late 1950s. Military buyers, then the largest customers for SCs, insisted on more than one supplier for transistors and ICs. SS helped to ensure the durability of new IC designs. SS signalled confidence in a new product and competition in its supply. Later, large commercial buyers insisted that chip suppliers licensed out their technology to other producers to guarantee supplies and ensure price competition.

SS began the liberal tradition of technology licensing in the chip industry. Typically a US chip supplier would choose an SS partner either in the US or Japan. The dominant partner would transfer vital elements of the technology (e.g. lithography masters and masks) enabling an exact replica of the original device to be produced.

SS agreements proliferated. In MPUs, for example, during the period 1971–81 22 chip makers introduced 203 separate products of which 69 were originals and 134 SS products (Swann 1985). SS agreements differ in several respects from joint ventures or strategic partnerships (Steinmueller 1988). SS allows two firms each to produce a competing product independently. Conversely, technology joint ventures often favour one production facility. Joint ventures tend to develop a new technology, rather than replicate an existing product as in the case of SS. SS is therefore tightly defined at the level of product, but loosely defined at the level of corporate strategy. The opposite is usually true of joint ventures.

During the 1980s competitive conditions caused a broader range of EOs than witnessed during the 1960s and 1970s. Increasing R&D costs encouraged many firms to begin joint ventures for new technologies. To capture overseas markets some firms formed global joint marketing and technology ventures. Global alliances increased as US firms met with more competition from Japan, Korea and Europe. An overall pattern of expanding technology options, increased competition and catch up by non-US firms occurred in the 1980s.

Corporate motivations for EOs include: technology acquisition, market access, cost and risk sharing, production capacity expansion (in the case of SS) and sometimes access to capital. The steeply rising costs of devising new generations of chips led some of the largest firms into technology development agreements (e.g. IBM and Siemens in 1990). EOs both inside and outside Europe were a chief mechanism by which firms such as Siemens, Philips, SGS and Thomson hoped to catch up with world leaders in Japan and the US.

Governments too have their motives. The Japanese government sponsored a well known programme of joint technology development (the VLSI Programme) during the period 1973–80. Its motive was to encourage Japanese firms to independently develop DRAM chips. The Korean government also sponsored collaboration between the large corporations (the *Chaebol*) in DRAMs.

The US government responded to the rise of Japan by supporting a large joint venture called Sematech. This includes most large US chip suppliers. Sematech is funded by the Department of Defense and aims to restore US competitiveness in process technology.

In the case of Europe, several pan-European ventures were supported by the EC. As discussed in section 5.2, the EC and individual European countries began several R&D programmes to support domestically-owned firms.

## 5.2   The EUROPEAN SEMICONDUCTOR INDUSTRY

### 5.2.1   Europe in the World Context

Table 5.2 presents data on worldwide chip consumption. The market is fairly
large, in the region of $57 bn in 1990. Year-to-year SC growth fluctuates
considerably, but shows a healthy underlying upward trend which is
expected to continue.

*Table 5.2*   *Worldwide merchant semiconductor market by region, consumption
value in $ bn*

| Market | 1982 | % | 1989 | % | 1990 | % | 1991[*] | % |
|---|---|---|---|---|---|---|---|---|
| North America | 6.5 | 45 | 17.0 | 31 | 16.6 | 29 | 17.8 | 29 |
| Japan | 4.0 | 28 | 21.4 | 39 | 21.9 | 38 | 23.7 | 38 |
| Europe | 3.0 | 21 | 9.9 | 18 | 10.7 | 19 | 11.5 | 19 |
| Rest of the world | 0.9 | 6 | 6.8 | 12 | 8.0 | 14 | 8.8 | 14 |
| Total | 14.4 | 100 | 55.1 | 100 | 57.2 | 100 | 61.8 | 100 |

\* Forecast
*Source*: ICE (1991 pp1–18 and pp1–19)

More importantly, as noted in the introduction, SCs are the main strategic
input for each of the electronics industries. Their value far exceeds that of
the chip industry. The world electronics industry (defined as computer,
consumer, automotive, telephony, industrial and military) amounted to
around $530 bn in 1990 (ICE 1991 p1–7). Many believe that a strong
production base in SCs is needed to gain market share in the wider electronics industry.

The European market is smaller than that of the US and Japan, but is
nevertheless highly significant (an estimated $10.7 bn in 1991). Europe
accounts for just under 20 per cent of world consumption, compared with
roughly 38 per cent for Japan and 29 per cent for the US. Europe is also one
of the main competitive battlegrounds for US and Japanese firms as they
struggle for market domination.

Turning to production, since 1980 European companies' share of world
output has oscillated around a 10 per cent share. In 1980 Europe's share was
13 per cent. This dropped to 11 per cent in 1983 and 1984 and remained
around this level till 1988 (Dataquest, cited in *Wall Street Journal*, 19 June
1989).

*Table 5.3    Semiconductor production shares by geographical region\**

| Company HQ | 1988 | % | 1989 | % | 1990 | % |
|---|---|---|---|---|---|---|
| North America | 22.9 | 41.0 | 24.5 | 40.2 | 25.7 | 40.7 |
| Japan | 25.5 | 45.7 | 27.9 | 45.7 | 27.8 | 44.1 |
| Europe | 5.3 | 9.5 | 5.8 | 9.5 | 6.6 | 10.5 |
| Rrest of the world | 2.2 | 3.9 | 2.8 | 4.6 | 3.1 | 4.9 |
| Totals | 55.8 | 100 | 61.0 | 100 | 63.1 | 100 |

\*    'Region' refers to ownership of company, not location of production (e.g. world-wide production by Japanese-owned firms).
\*\*   'Merchant' denotes traded semiconductors.
*Source*: ICE (1991 pp1–8)

Recent production data by region are provided in Table 5.3. Despite the EC programmes of support (see below) European producers' share was still only 9.5 per cent of total sales (including captives) in 1988 and 1989.

This rose to 11.5 per cent in 1990, mainly due to currency fluctuations and a decline in rest of the world (ROW) memory sales. If captive in-house sales are added to world production figures Europe's performance is slightly worse. Over the past fifteen years or so Europe's share has averaged around 7 per cent to 9 per cent (ICE 1991 pp1–19). In 1990 Europe's share was approximately 10 per cent of the world total.

Korea and Taiwan account for around 87 per cent of ROW sales. According to ICE, if present growth trends continue, ROW sales will overtake European production during the 1990s (ICE 1991 pp1–9).

Comparing consumption with production, Europe's share of the world consumption has remained at around 20 per cent since 1982 (Table 5.2), while production has averaged around 10 per cent per annum (Table 5.3). Around one half of Europe's SC needs have therefore been satisfied either by imports or by production by foreign firms operating within Europe.

Trade data reflect Europe's continuing weakness in production. Europe's balance of trade in active components (which also includes optoelectronic and discrete devices) deteriorated from around –\$2.6 bn in 1984 to approximately –\$4.2 bn in 1988. The deficit is forecast to further increase to around –\$7.0 bn in 1994.

By imposing tariffs on imported SCs, European countries have encouraged US and Japanese firms to invest directly within Europe.The EC has ruled that multinationals must undertake wafer fabrication within Europe to avoid import duties. This policy, coupled with the desire of non-European firms to participate in the post-1992 pan-European market, has encouraged firms such as Texas Instruments, Fujitsu and Toshiba to expand their manufacturing presence in Europe.

Europe's weakness in chip production is also reflected in the ranking of leading companies for 1990 and 1991 (Table 5.1 above). Only one firm, Philips was in the top ten (at number 10) in 1991. STM (SGS-Thomson) ranked number 15, Siemens number 17. Over the past ten years or so Philips has been the only European firm constantly in the top ten list of firms. With Philips decision to exit the SRAM business due to financial difficulties, it is possible that Philips will fall out of the top ten in the near future. This would mean that Europe would have no indigenous producer in the top ten, Japan would have six or seven, the US three or four.

*Table 5.4    European-owned companies' sales of integrated circuits*

| Company | Headquarters | Total sales, $ m |
|---|---|---|
| Philips–Signetics | Holland | 1175 |
| SGS–Thomson** | Italy–France | 1175 |
| Siemens | FRG | 1000 |
| GEC–Plessey*** | UK | 340 |
| ITT | France | 210 |
| Telefunken | FRG | 120 |
| MHS Semiconductor (Matra) | France | 105 |
| Mietec | Belgium | 92 |
| Austria Micro Systems | Austria | 63 |
| EMM | Switzerland | 48 |
| ABB HAFO | Sweden | 42 |
| ES2 | France–UK | 29 |

**    Includes Inmos
***    Includes Marconi
*Source*: ICE (1991 pp2–39)

Table 5.4 shows total integrated circuit sales of the twelve largest European-owned suppliers of SCs. The three largest firms, Philips–Signetics, SGS–Thomson (including Inmos) and Siemens accounted for sales of $3350 m in 1990, around 75 per cent of total European-owned companies' production. Other firms are very small in comparison with the leaders in Europe.

Table 5.5 presents sales of the top twenty SC suppliers in the European market for 1991 (European and non-European owned). Seven of the leading firms are American, six are European, six are Japanese and one South Korean. The data confirm the dependence of Europe on non-European firms for SC supplies. They also show the build up of Japanese direct foreign investment in the EC, partly due to EC trade policy.

*Table 5.5    European semiconductor rankings for 1990 and 1991*

| Rank 1991 | Rank 1990 | Company | 1991 Sales ($ m) | HQ* | Market share 1991, in % |
|---|---|---|---|---|---|
| 1 | 1 | Philips | 1172 | N | 10.3 |
| 2 | 2 | Siemens | 958 | WG | 8.4 |
| 3 | 3 | SGS–Thomson | 887 | F/I | 7.8 |
| 4 | 4 | Motorola | 770 | US | 6.8 |
| 5 | 6 | Intel | 760 | US | 6.7 |
| 6 | 5 | Texas | 629 | US | 5.5 |
| 7 | 7 | Toshiba | 509 | J | 4.5 |
| 8 | 8 | NEC | 452 | J | 4.0 |
| 9 | 9 | National | 408 | US | 3.6 |
| 10 | 10 | Hitachi | 318 | J | 2.8 |
| 11 | 10 | AMD | 307 | US | 2.7 |
| 12 | 14 | Samsung | 263 | K | 2.3 |
| 13 | 11 | ITT | 240 | US | 2.1 |
| 14 | 12 | GPS | 221 | UK | 1.9 |
| 15 | 13 | Telefunken | 220 | WG | 1.9 |
| 16 | 17 | Mitsubishi | 179 | J | 1.6 |
| 17 | 16 | Harris | 150 | F | 1.3 |
| 18 | 15 | Fujitsu | 147 | J | 1.3 |
| 19 | 18 | Analog | 136 | US | 1.2 |
| 20 | 29 | Oki | 104 | J | 0.9 |

* Headquarters indicates country of origin and major operations
J = Japan, US = United States, K = Korea, N = Netherlands, WG = West Germany,
F/I = French/Italian, UK = United Kingdom
*Source*: Dataquest (cited in *Electronics Times*, 16 January 1992, p1)

One particular cause for concern for European firms is the composition of SC sales. Around 37 per cent of 1990 sales were made up of relatively mature, bipolar technology (63 per cent was in the more advanced MOS). This compares with worldwide output of 24 per cent in bipolar in 1990 and 75 per cent in MOS (ICE 1991 pp5–1). European firms are not only under-represented on the world market; too large a share of their output is in mature, rather than leading edge, technology.

### 5.2.2  European Corporate Strategies

To understand the changing position of European firms within the world SC industry it is first helpful to outline a typology of corporate strategies. Within the SC industry there are various types of corporate strategy ranging from those of the small US start-ups to those of huge Japanese corporations (*keiretsu*). Table 5.6 presents these strategies in terms of four generic types.[3]

Type 1 strategies are followed by the major US merchant producers. Sales are mainly to the external chip market, rather than for in-house needs. They are therefore 'outward-looking'. They produce both standard SCs and ASICs. Strategies can be based on cost leadership, product innovation and market agility. Under competition from larger Japanese firms, most of these firms have retreated from the high volume commodity chip markets they once dominated.

*Table 5.6    Typology of corporate strategies in semiconductors*

| Strategic type | Market orientation | Product markets | Examples |
|---|---|---|---|
| 1. Merchant volume | Outward-looking | Standard custom/ ASIC | Texas Instruments Motorola |
| 2. Merchant niche | Outward-looking | Custom/ASIC | Inmos ES2 |
| 3. Vertically integrated | Inward-looking | Standard custom/ ASIC | IBM, DEC Siemens |
| 3. Vertically integrated | Inward-looking | Standard custom/ ASIC | Fujitsu Samsung |

Type 2 firms are niche marketeers. They tend to supply ASICs and other specialist custom devices, again to the open market. Many cluster in Silicon Valley. They are small and have limited access to capital. Type 2 firms have to be highly innovative to survive. They tend either to aim for a large market share of one or two major niche products (e.g. Inmos in Transputers) or they supply a wide range of smaller niches and expect to move on quickly to new products once the majors begin competing (e.g. Plessey in ASICs). Survival of these firms depends on market agility, fast reaction to shortening product life cycles and software capabilities.

Type 3 firms include the very large vertically integrated electronics corporations of the US (e.g. IBM, DEC, AT&T and Hewlett Packard). Such firms are 'inward-looking' as they make chips largely for their in-house use, rather than the open market. Some manufacture chips in very large volumes (e.g. IBM). Others focus more on specialist/ASIC chips for systems (e.g. Ericsson). Large volume strategies are based upon process innovation and economies of scale.

Type 4 firms are relatively new, consisting mainly of Japanese and Korean corporations. Whereas they are similar in structure to type 3 firms, they are dedicated to combining open market (i.e. outward-looking) competition with in-house production. This combination strategy has proved very successful for Japanese and Korean firms. The rigours of competing in the open market prevent inertia, force companies to maintain leading edge technology and quality, and exert downward pressure on costs and prices.

Within this typology large European firms such as Siemens, Philips and GEC have traditionally been within type 3 (inward-looking, vertically integrated). Indeed, during the 1970s, Europe's large firms followed an extreme form of type 3. Not only did production focus on in-house needs, sales were often within national boundaries. Technological levels were generally behind the frontier set by US firms. Output was frequently for highly specialist chips dictated by company needs.

State procurement and subsidy in the 1970s encouraged the inward-looking strategies of the chip makers. European governments tended to support the idea of national champions by protecting and subsidizing their major firms. Nationalistic policies also encouraged the fragmentation of the European market. By the early 1980s, Europe's chip industry was technologically backward and uncompetitive, especially in mainstream markets.

However, during the 1980s several European firms attempted a resurgence in SCs via a strategic shift from type 3 to type 4. Siemens for example embarked on a large-scale corporate restructuring programme which placed great emphasis on SC (see Box 4.1). Thomson, SGS, and Philips also attempted to build up their technology capabilities to world class levels, to increase exports to international markets and become dynamic outward-looking chip suppliers. As discussed below, they were assisted in this strategic move by pan-European programmes of support by the EC.

### 5.2.3 European Government Policies in the 1980s

During the mid-1980s, the EC took a leading role in formulating R&D recovery programmes in chips. National programmes were set up which complemented the European-wide programmes. France, the UK, Italy, West Germany and the Netherlands began to channel resources directly to their leading manufacturers.

Some of the major initiatives are listed in Table 5.7. The programmes included ESPRIT, RACE, BRITE and Eureka. ESPRIT (the European Strategic Programme of Research in Information Technology) was the EC's first major R&D programme in electronics. RACE (R&D in Advanced Communications and Electronics) focused on telecommunications. Eureka was initiated by France in 1985 and included twelve Community states, six EFTA countries and Turkey.

*Table 5.7 Government technology initiatives\*, 1982–87*

| Pan-European programmes | Single country programmes |
| --- | --- |
| ESPRIT 1 | Alvey, UK |
| ESPRIT 2 | FINPRIT, Finland |
| ESPRIT 3 | Informationstechnik, W. Germany |
| BRITE | *La Filiere Electronique*, France |
| Eureka | National Microelectronics Programme, Sweden |

\* Not exhaustive; mostly concerned with information technology

ESPRIT began in February 1984. It focused primarily on so called 'pre-competitive' R&D projects. The largest sub-programme area was the Advanced Microelectronics Programme (AMP) which accounted for about 25 per cent of allocated funds (Hare, Lauchlan and Thompson 1988). The AMP's aim was to ensure a healthy supply of chips for Europe in sufficient quantity and at competitive prices (CEC 1987 p1).

The second phase of ESPRIT (ESPRIT 2) ran from 1987–92. Within ESPRIT 2, the Microelectronics and Peripherals sub-programme took over the SC work. It aimed to develop advanced ASICs and to ensure the commercial exploitation of R&D results from ESPRIT 1.

ESPRIT 3 was launched in June 1991. Its budget for SC work was reported to be £127 m (*Electronics Times*, 11 July 1991). This included £45 m for the Open Microprocessor System Initiative to develop, by 1994, world class MPUs, design tools and software to integrate RISC chips with other MPUs. A further £83 m was allocated to other SC research under ESPRIT 3. Each of the government programmes in Table 5.7 intended to improve the productivity and competitiveness of European industry. Most contained substantial SC-related R&D.

Table 5.8 reports on some of the major European government-sponsored corporate ventures in SCs. It also contains important mergers and acquisitions which occurred in the latter part of the 1980s.

Table 5.8 shows how the main European firms formed strategic alliances and engaged in takeovers to form 'European' champions. These took the place of the national champions of the 1970s. These corporate ventures were inextricably bound up with the EC policies of the period.

SGS–Thomson formed a pan-European venture (STM), while Siemens and Philips collaborated in major SC projects. Significant events in the UK included the takeovers of Ferranti by Plessey, Plessey by GEC/Siemens and Inmos by SGS/Thomson. In contrast with France, Italy, West Germany and the Netherlands, the UK's participation was limited to small scale projects in ESPRIT and JESSI.

*Table 5.8    Major European Ventures in SCs: a Selection*

| Date | Venture | Firms | Cost in $ m[*] |
|------|---------|-------|-----------|
| 1984–89 | Megaproject 1 | Siemens/Philips | 930[**] |
| 1986 | Mostek acquisition | Thomson | 120 |
| 1986 | Megaproject 2 | SGS/Thomson | 655 |
| 1987 | Merger | SGS/Thomson | – |
| 1988–95 | JESSI | Siemens/Philips Thomson/SGS/Plessey | 3700 |
| 1988 | Takeover | Ferranti SC by Plessey | – |
| 1990 | Takeover | Plessey by GEC/Siemens | – |
| 1989 | Takeover | Inmos by SGS/Thomson | – |
| 1990–91 | Joint venture | ibs-Siemens | > 1000 |

\*   Cost of programmes only
\*\*  Exchange rate $1.7 = £1.0
*Sources*: Compiled from appendices and other sources

Within Eureka one of the main programmes geared towards SCs was the 'Megaproject', the first large scale technology partnerships between Siemens and Philips. Siemens and Philips spent roughly $1bn on leading edge (sub-micron) SC technology. The Dutch and and West German governments financed approximately one third of the total cost. The Mega-project was a four-year joint R&D venture in memory chip technology (one-megabit and four-megabit DRAMs).

In 1986, SGS and Thomson jointly applied to Eureka for $255 m to support a new project in memory chips (four-megabit and sixteen-megabit EPROMs) and ASICs. In January 1987, Megaproject 2 was approved by the Eureka Commission. Each company was reported to have committed $200 m to the venture. In April 1987 the two firms launched a jointly-owned pan-European chip company (SGS–Thomson) with its headquarters in Holland and manufacturing operations in France, Italy and elsewhere.

The largest pan-European SC initiative was JESSI (the Joint European Sub-micron Silicon Initiative), set to run from 1988–95 under Eureka. Initially JESSI was a Siemens/Philips project designed to follow on from Megaproject 1 (due to end in 1989) to develop sixteen-megabit DRAMs and advanced ASICs. However, the scope of JESSI grew considerably to include the Siemens-led 64-megabit DRAM development (to reach the market by 1995) and the SGS–Thomson 64-megabit EPROM project (following on from Megaproject 2). Philips led a major project to develop leading edge (0.5 micron) SRAM technology.

JESSI's committed expenditure was in the region of £2.75 bn (roughly $4.2 bn) for an eight-year period (*Electronics Times* 27 June 1991). By June 1990 JESSI had approved 83 projects out of the 221 project proposals received from European firms, universities and research institutes.

Although JESSI was a key plank of Eureka, the EC funded part of the project under its programme umbrella called 'Framework'. Half of the cost of JESSI projects was borne by participating firms, a quarter by participating national governments and the remaining quarter by the EC. Many of the SC projects in ESPRIT 3 were linked to the Eureka/JESSI projects.

In 1990 IBM Europe was allowed into projects within the JESSI Programme. This followed a decision by the JESSI board to treat each applicant, from whatever country, on its own merits. Allowing in IBM prompted JESSI to bring forward its 64-megabit DRAM target by one year to 1994. STM began discussing the possibility of inviting foreign firms into its EPROM initiative. JESSI also forged formal links with the American SC initiative Sematech.

Undoubtedly, the ESPRIT programmes and Eureka played a large part in assisting firms in developing new strategies to catch up with their Japanese and US competitors. The programmes provided a mechanism for creating cooperation among European firms in R&D. They also helped create convergent expectations about the future and how Europe could best meet Japanese competition.

However, it is not possible to attribute European firms' strategies in SCs solely or principally to EC programmes and policies. Other influences on strategy included independent corporate responses to Japanese competition, the new opportunities provided by the electronics market and the tendency towards increasing strategic partnerships during the 1980s. EC policies tended to 'fit in' with corporate strategies. Rather than determining strategies, EC policies were bound up with firms' strategies, reinforcing and supporting European firms. The following section examines quantitative data on European companies' EOs during the 1980s and assesses the impact of the EC policies on corporate EOs.

## 5.3   EXTERNAL OPERATIONS ANALYSIS: TECHNOLOGY AND EQUITY AGREEMENTS, 1980–91

### 5.3.1   Method and Data

#### 5.3.1.1   Types of agreements
Appendix 2 describes in detail the research methods, definitions, data sources and commonly used abbreviations. Following the discussion in

section 5.1.3, the types of agreement reported are those most important to competence accumulation in the SC industry:

1. SS = second sourcing agreements (formal SS agreements for production of a specific SC device).
2. L = licensing agreements (the one way flow of technology, product or process — not necessarily one specific product).
3. TE = technology exchange (the two-way exchange of existing technology between firms).
4. JV = joint venture (refer to the joint development of new technology suitable for a range of products).

Note that various types of production agreements are contained in each of the above. Types 1 to 3 usually contain formal agreements for production. Type 4 (ventures for new technology development) may or may not contain an agreement for production at the outset.

Distribution and marketing agreements are not included as these are not usually directly related to competence accumulation in SC technology or production. Most large SC firms engage in a wide variety of distribution agreements with independent (and captive) distributors. Usually, these do not contain production process or product design arrangements, although there are some exceptions.

The above four types of agreement were chosen for two reasons: first, they include the majority of EOs which relate to competence building and technology accumulation within the SC industry; second, shifts between the four types of agreement over time are a useful indicator of changes in capability among firms. For instance, SS and L are relatively passive forms of technology acquisition (from the recipients' perspective), involving a senior and junior partner. The senior or dominant partner sells technology to a junior or weaker partner. In contrast, TE and JV represent pro-active forms of EO.

Under TE and JV arrangements both firms share their specific competences or assets to swap technologies (TE) or to develop a new technology (JV), to the benefit of both firms.

A move from SS and L towards TE and JV would suggest an increase in competence, both in relation to outside firms and in relation to previous performance. The converse would also be the case. For instance, Japanese firms began their EOs via SS agreements with US firms. Today, they are also engaged in a wide range of JVs and reverse SS agreements to US firms. This reflects the growing competence of Japanese firms in relation to US firms (and in relation to their prior abilities).

For the purposes of this chapter it is important to assess whether the share of pro-active EOs increased as European firms attempted to build up their competences in the latter half of the 1980s. If so, this would indicate an increase in relative competence on the part of European firms.

### 5.3.1.2  Direction of technology flow

The data were further categorized according to the geographical direction of technology flow. 'International technology flow' indicates whether the technology flowed into or out of Europe.

As Appendix 2 shows, the data were divided into five categories:

- E = Intra-European technology flow
- E*/EC = Intra-European technology flow sponsored by the EC or Eureka
- I = Inward (international) technology flow (to Europe from overseas)
- O = Outward (international) technology flow (to overseas from Europe)
- I/O = Technology flow both directions, in and out (both parties gained technology).

The purpose of this categorization was to ascertain the main international sources of technology to Europe and if these changed over time. Also it was useful to see whether and to what extent intra-EC ventures had increased after the onset of the European technology programmes of the mid-1980s.

### 5.3.1.3  European EOs within the international context

Other studies have examined the worldwide position of EOs in electronics and SCs. These provide a useful frame of reference, although none are not strictly comparable with the present study. Hagadoorn and Schakenraad (1990), for instance, identify 641 partnerships in microelectronics during the 1980s (the period covered by this study). They also exclude distribution agreements for the reasons expressed above. Their data included US–US, US–Japanese and Japanese-Japanese partnerships (as well as rest of the world partnerships). European partnerships are not separately identified in their study.

As discussed below, the present study identified 161 European EOs over the 1980s (25 per cent of the total identified by Hagedoorn and Schakenraad). Considering there are far fewer European SC firms compared with Japanese or US firms, this figure suggests that the EO activity of individual European companies is fairly high. In the US, for instance, there are scores of small SC firms which engage in partnerships in SCs.

### 5.3.2  External Technology Operations in SCs, 1980–91

Appendices 3 and 4 present details of European firms' external technology operations in SCs for two periods: 1980–84 and 1985–91. The two periods correspond roughly to before and after the initiation of the pan-European EC programmes in 1984. This allows for a partial examination of the impact of the programmes on firms' technology competence building.

*Table 5.9   Technical EOs, 1980–91, agreements by year*

| Year | Number of agreements |
|------|----------------------|
| 1980 | 4 |
| 1981 | 13 |
| 1982 | 11 |
| 1983 | 4 |
| 1984 | 11 |
| 1985 | 7 |
| 1986 | 8 |
| 1987 | 9 |
| 1988 | 9 |
| 1989 | 9 |
| 1990 | 16 |
| 1991 | 13 |
| Undated | 6 |
| Total | 120 |

*Source*: Appendices

Taking the two periods together, a total of 120 technical agreements were reported over the 1980-91 period (Table 5.9). These were distributed fairly randomly through time on a year-by-year basis, although more were concentrated in the latter half of the 1980s. This is consistent with the findings of other studies (e.g. Delapierre and Zimmerman 1991; Chesnais 1988) which show an increase in partnerships during the 1980s.

As would be expected the major European firms (Siemens, Thomson, SGS, Philips and GEC) accounted for most technical EOs in both periods. The pan-European ventures SGS–Thomson (STM) and ES2 became very active during the second period. Other firms typically engaged in one or two ventures, with a small number undertaking three or four technical EOs each.

A total of 48 technical agreements were reported over the first five-year period, 1980–84, averaging nearly ten per annum. As Table 5.10 shows, most agreements were with US firms (29 or 60 per cent). Ten (21 per cent) were with Japanese firms; only four were intra-European. In addition, three took place with South Korea, one with Hong Kong and one with Canada. The fact that European electronics firms turn outwards to non-European (especially US) firms is confirmed by Mytelka (1991 pp182–183) in a summary of the findings of databases on partnerships covering a range of industries.

*European Integration and Competitiveness*

*Table 5.10  Analysis by Partner Country; 1980–84*

| Partner country | Number of agreements | % |
|---|---|---|
| United States | 29 | 60 |
| Japan | 10 | 21 |
| Intra-European | 4 | 8 |
| Other | 5 | 10 |
| Total | 48 | 100 |

*Sources*: Appendices

Table 5.11 looks at the direction of technology flow over the period 1980–84. The largest category of technology flow was into Europe (23 or 50 per cent) from non-European firms. The next main category was joint technology flows in and out of Europe (13 or 28 per cent). Only four intra-European ventures occurred out of 46, of which one was sponsored by the EC (the Philips–Siemens Megaproject). Only six cases (13 per cent) were one-direction flows out of Europe.

*Table 5.11  Analysis by direction of technology flow, 1980–84*

| Direction | Code | Number | % |
|---|---|---|---|
| Into Europe | (I) | 23 | 50 |
| Jointly with non-European | (1/0) | 13 | 28 |
| Intra-European | (E) | 4 | 9 |
| Out of Europe | (0) | 6 | 13 |
| Total accounted for | | 46 | – |
| Not accounted for | (n/a) | 2 | – |

*Sources*: Appendices

Clearly technical EOs were already a significant feature of European SC technology developments in the early 1980s. European firms gained access to important new product technologies (e.g. MPUs, custom chips, gate arrays and memories) and processes (e.g. CMOS). Domestic European firms relied mainly on US firms for technology, although Japanese companies such as NEC and Toshiba also supplied technology.

Second sourcing was not the main function of technical EOs, although some European firms second sourced US products. A look at the individual agreements (not presented here) confirms that during the early 1980s

European firms' strategies were designed mainly to meet the needs of in-house systems (e.g. MPUs for telecommunications) rather than the merchant market. This corresponds to the inward-looking, type 3 approach in the classification in section 5.2.2 and contrasts with the outward-looking market strategies of Japanese system firms.

Europe was the main beneficiary in terms of technology acquisition. Very few ventures involved outflows of technology from Europe. Most EOs resulted in technology flowing into Europe (50 per cent). Inflows and joint developments together amounted to 78 per cent of all agreements.

Left to the market European firms tended to form technical agreements outside Europe, rather than within. This reflected the technological and commercial lead of US firms over European companies. Europe's firms acted on the belief that the best option for technological acquisition was via foreign EOs, rather than intra-European ones.

Over the period 1980–84 the US was a valuable source of support for the competence building activities of Europe's SC and electronics systems developers.

### 5.3.3  External Technology Operations in SCs, 1985–91

During the seven-year period 1985–91 total agreements numbered 74. This represents an average of ten per year, a slight increase over the earlier period 1980–84 (eight per annum).

*Table 5.12  Analysis by Partner Country: 1985–91*

| Partner Country | Number of agreements | % |
|---|---|---|
| United States | 34 | 47 |
| Japan | 17 | 23 |
| Intra-European | 22[*] | 30 |
| Other | 0 | – |
| Total | 73[**] | |

* of which 7 EC-sponsored
** one of which was a three way agreement
*Sources*: Appendices

As Table 5.12 shows, the largest category of agreements was with US firms (as in the early 1980s). However, the share of US agreements declined from 60 per cent to 47 per cent from the earlier period. Another difference between the two periods was the large increase in intra-European EOs. These increased from only 8 per cent in 1980–84 to 30 per cent in 1985–91. Intra-European ventures therefore overtook Japanese ones as the second largest category of technical EOs.

Part of the reason for the increase in intra-European ventures was EC financial support and political pursuasion under the EC R&D programmes (Mytelka 1991). Seven of the 22 agreements were EC-sponsored. Removing EC projects reduces the intra-EC share to 21 per cent of the total, roughly equivalent to the Japanese share. This still represents an increase in intra-EC ventures over the period 1980-84. The residual increase was probably due to market rationalization, EC policy effect, and as argued below, the increasing competence of EC firms.

### 5.3.3.1  EC programmes and the 'natural pattern' of technology flow

Given the beneficial flows of technology from the US to Europe in the early 1980s, a critical question must be asked about EC policies for increased intra-European collaboration: did EC subsidies distort the 'natural pattern' of inward technology flows from the US to Europe? Put another way: did the EC subsidize sup-optimal intra-EC partnerships into existence and thereby damage the competence building of European firms?

It is not possible to fully answer this question from the data alone, as what would have occurred in the absence of the programmes is impossible to judge. However, the following three factors indicate that the EC programmes had a positive rather than a negative effect on competence building.

First, as noted above, EC policy did not stem EC–US technology flows. This remained the largest category in both periods. The policy may have substituted some intra-EC agreements for EC–US flows, but there remained a substantial flow.

*Table 5.13  Analysis by Direction of Technology Flow, 1985-91*

| Direction | Code* | Number | % |
|---|---|---|---|
| In to Europe | (I) | 9 | 13 |
| Jointly with non-European | (I/0) | 40 | 56 |
| Intra-European | (E) | 20* | 28 |
| Out of Europe | (0) | 3 | 4 |
| Total accounted for | | 72 | |

*  Of which seven were EC-sponsored
*Sources*: Appendices

Second, during the latter period there was a large shift away from inward flows towards joint development projects, reflecting an increased confidence of European firms compared with the early period. Table 5.13 shows inward technology flows for 1985–91 (down from 50 per cent to 13 per cent compared with 1980–84). This was compensated for by an increase in joint technology developments (I/O) both with European firms (up from 9 per cent to 28 per cent) and non-European firms (up from 28 per cent to 56 per cent). EC supported projects accounted for seven (around 35 per cent) of the intra-European projects. Other causes of intra-European ventures were corporate efforts to rationalize the fragmented European market before 1992 and the growing capabilities of EC players.

The increase in joint developments indicates a growing technological competence on the part of European firms. This was probably due to: (a) previous inflows of technology from the US and to a lesser extent Japan; (b) the training of Europeans within US subsidiaries; and (c) EC technology strengthening programmes.

*Table 5.14  Analysis by agreement type, both periods*

| Type of agreement | 1980–84 | | 1985–91 | | Change over time (%) |
|---|---|---|---|---|---|
| Joint venture (JV) | 25 | 40% | 41 | 45% | + 5 |
| Technology exchange (TE) | 13 | 21% | 29 | 32% | + 11 |
| Licence  (L) | 13 | 21% | 17 | 19% | − 2 |
| Second source (SS) | 11 | 18% | 4 | 5% | − 13 |
| Totals | 62[*] | | 19[*] | | |

\* Totals are larger than the numbers of agreements as some agreements involved more than one type of technical arrangement.
*Sources*: Appendices

Third, examining the data according to passive versus active technology EO types also confirms that European firms increased their pro-active abilities to develop technology in the latter period. Table 5.14 shows that joint ventures (JVs) for future technology development was the largest category for both periods, followed by two-way technology exchanges (TEs). For both periods the preferred method of technical EOs was therefore JVs and TEs, rather than the narrower and more passive licensing (L) and second sourcing (SS).

Adding JVs together with TEs gives an idea of overall pro-active technology partnership. The most interesting points from Table 5.14 are: the predominance of JVs + TEs in both periods; and the increase in JVs and TEs in the latter period (from 61 per cent to 77 per cent). This indicates a shift towards pro-active technology engagement, suggesting an increase in local technological capability relative to overseas competitors in the latter half of the 1980s.

### 5.3.4  European Equity Operations

Appendix 5 lists thirteen external equity operations from 1977–84. The main point to note is that all ventures were with US firms, mostly 100 per cent takeovers. Most takeovers were of relatively small companies, except for Signetics and Fairchild, both major US chip operations. No takeovers of European by US firms occurred. Japanese firms did not engage in any of the reported equity operations.

The main motivations on the part of European companies were probably to gain access to American technology and skills as well as the large US market. Larger European chip makers clearly benefited from the open approach of the US to high-technology takeovers.

Interestingly, Siemens — not a company reputed for expansion via acquisition — engaged in more takeovers than any other European company. Like other local firms, Siemens appreciated the importance of US takeovers to its ongoing SC operations.

Appendix 6 presents post-1984 equity operations. A total of 27 mergers, acquisitions and divestitures are reported. Again, large firms accounted for most operations, although the new firm ES2 accounted for five (19 per cent) of the total. Two main types of EO can be identified: first, takeovers of US firms by European companies (ten in all); second, intra-EC mergers and acquisitions (fourteen in all). A further three were divestitures of US firms, reflecting European efforts to rid themselves of unprofitable or problematic ventures.

As far as the takeovers of US companies are concerned, most were small or weak American firms being purchased or receiving capital injections by larger European firms. Motivations, again, were probably to access chip technology and to enter the US market. As in the earlier period a wide range of chip technologies was accessed via these agreements.

Intra-European equity operations demonstrate a large-scale rationalization of European chip operations during the 1985–91 period. A new pan-European company was formed between SGS of Italy and Thomson of France, called SGS–Thomson Microelectronics (STM). Relatively small UK chip operations were taken over by GEC to form one consolidated company. The financially weak, but technologically impressive Inmos (UK) was sold to STM, strengthening its product range.

Appendix 6 also shows the creation of the new start-up ES2. This obtained substantial financial backing (in the region of $50 m) from various European firms and the Eureka Programme. Managers for ES2 were recruited from US firms such as Texas Instruments. Other US-trained European managers took prominent positions in firms such as SGS, Thomson and Plessey. As discussed elsewehere, management training within US firms was an important source of European firms' indigenous competence building the 1980s (Hobday 1992).

Among the probable causes of post-1984 intra-European mergers, acquisitions and investments were: (a) a renewed commitment on the part of firms to SC technology; (b) a belief in the benefits of economies of scale; (c) the growing competence and ambitions of domestic firms; (d) EC financial support and political encouragement; (e) rationalization of the market, before 1992. A qualitative interpretation of the direction and nature of European EOs follows in the next section.

## 5.4 QUALITATIVE ASSESSMENT: EOs, GOVERN-MENT POLICIES AND COMPETITIVENESS

This section assesses European EOs within the world SC context, comparing the general thrust of European activities with selected US and Japanese partnerships. It also examines some important issues of policy and corporate strategy by looking at the behaviour of the largest European firms. Of particular importance is whether EC policies should continue to support near-to-market activities of European-owned companies, as argued in recent EC policy documents (e.g. CEC 1991). The severe recession which besets the industry at the time of writing is also touched upon.

### 5.4.1 The International Context

Regarding the total quantity of EOs, as section 5.3 argued, European firms are fairly active, possibly equivalent to 25 per cent of total EOs in number. Given that there are very few (large or small) European firms compared with the US and Japan, this indicates that individual European firms are very actively engaged in EOs (both equity and technology operations).

To try to put the technological and marketing thrust of European EOs in context, Table 5.15 presents a selection of large-scale, ongoing US–Japanese alliances.[4] US–Japanese ventures reflect these two countries' market leadership positions and their specific technological competences in mainstream chips. Most US and Japanese SC leaders are engaged in complementary partnerships either to gain each others' technology, or to gain access to each others' markets.[5]

For instance Motorola has traded some of its core competence in MPUs in return for DRAM technology from Toshiba. This enabled Motorola to re-enter the DRAM business through a jointly owned manufacturing unit (Tohoku Semiconductor) located in Japan. Toshiba has ten to twelve major alliances with foreign companies (including Siemens) as part of its corporate strategy (*Electronic Business*, 8 April 1991, p32). Hitachi too has several international partnerships, including one with Texas Instruments to jointly manufacture sixteen-megabit DRAMs.

*Table 5.15  A selection of major ongoing US–Japanese alliances in semi-
          conductors*

| US firm | Japanese firm | Joint activity in semiconductors |
|---|---|---|
| Motorola | Toshiba | Motorola to access DRAM manufacturing. Toshiba to gain MPU design/process capability/investment. |
| Texas | Hitachi | Joint development of 16-megabit DRAMs |
| AT&T | NEC | AT&T to access manufacturing technology. NEC to acquire custom technology expertise |
| AMD | Sony | Joint development of specialized memory chips |
| LSI | Kawasaki | Joint venture for the manufacture of ASICs (55% owned by LSI) |
| Intel | NMB | NMB to manufacture Intel's 'flash' memory ICs |
| MIPS | NEC | NEC to make MIPS' RISC microprocessors |

*Source*: *Business Week* (17 June 1991, pp64–66)

Apart from the large-scale projects carried out by Siemens, Philips and STM there are few, if any, other European firms engaged in EOs of the scale and ambition of US and Japanese alliances.

A survey of 455 leading US electronics firms shows that most SC executives rank corporate alliances high in their strategic plans. The study by Ernst and Young (reported in *Electronic Business*, 30 March 1992) concludes that external partnerships became a normal part of business during the 1980s. The tendency towards EOs is likely to increase in the 1990s. The survey shows that the main motive in SCs is to access technology and to improve product development. Market access is also important, but secondary to technology. A large proportion of US firms form alliances with Japanese firms in order to gain access to their chip technology.

As argued in section 5.3, European firms' external ventures follow the same basic motives as those of US and Japanese firms: to access technology and markets. The majority of European EOs is oriented towards the US, rather than within Europe or towards Japan. Hagedoorn and Schakenraad (1990) illustrate two important US-European clusters centred around Motorola and Intel. These clusters reflect the latter firms' oligopolistic lead in MPUs. Large European (and American and Japanese) firms queued up to form partnerships to secure advanced MPU technology.

Mytelka (1991), in a study of European alliances, expresses some concern over the outward orientation of European firms in electronics. However, what the evidence seems to show is that the outward orientation is a fairly natural, historical set of linkages which enable European firms to gain access to superior US (and to a lesser extent Japanese) technology, as well as the US market. Given their lag in SCs, European firms are forced to 'manage' their technological dependency by EOs. In areas where US and Japanese firms lead, intra-EC partnerships could well be suboptimal. European firms tend to chose partners in the US because they appear to be able to satisfy their technological appetite, both for systems chips and in the case of Siemens–IBM, for DRAM technology. In some cases Japanese firms offer Europe the most advanced technology. This is again reflected in the EO data, especially post-1984 (e.g. Toshiba–Siemens).

Overall, the EO data reflect European companies' relatively weak positions on the world stage, their ongoing technological needs and their strategies to catch up with the world leaders.

### 5.4.2 Corporate Strategies vs Government Policies in Near-Market Areas

When there is conflict between corporate strategy and EC policy, the evidence in SCs indicates that firm strategy takes priority over government policy. This is an important point as it suggests that governments and the EC should be very cautious about attempting to influence the direction of corporate strategy.

Indeed, the cases of Siemens and Philips indicate that large firms keep their technology options open — despite their expressed commitments to EC policies and pan-European partnerships such as JESSI. For example, EC policy clearly wanted to build pan-European alliances in chips. However, this did not not inhibit Siemens from beginning a very large joint venture with IBM for 64-megabit DRAMs in 1990 (costed at over $1 bn). Siemens decided that its best option was to form a venture with IBM rather than with STM of Europe. Indeed, Siemens rejected an EC policy idea (also favoured by STM) of building a giant European chip operation through a merger between STM's and Siemens' chip operations. Earlier, Siemens accessed DRAM technology from Toshiba of Japan, again despite its involvement in European DRAM programmes. Also in conflict with EC policy aims, Philips decided to withdraw from a large SRAM project in JESSI after making losses in its SC division.

With respect to EC policy, these events indicate that large firms retain sovereignty over decision making, regardless of EC policies, wishes and subsidies. This is, of course, quite proper. Only firms are in a position within a market to take strategic decisions (rightly or wrongly). However, these cases strongly suggest that the EC should be very wary of influencing near-market decision making among firms.

Recent policy documents from the EC argue that R&D projects should get closer to the market to ensure the exploitation of research (e.g. CEC 1991). Some academic analysts such as Delapierre and Zimmerman (1991) also suggest a strong state role in support of European electronics.

However, the above examples of Siemens and Philips 'going their own way' indicates that near-market/exploitation support is highly risky. Firms may decide to opt out of ventures as market circumstances change.[6]

A further reason for questioning support for near-market projects is the opportunity cost involved due to limited budgets.[7] Less risky areas which could suffer as a result of the opportunity cost of large, near-market projects include: basic and longer-term research, firm-university programmes, long-term standards projects, human resources development and training and infrastructure projects. As genuine pre-competitive areas these do not fall foul of GATT regulations on firm subsidies.

### 5.4.3  The Reorientation of Europe's SC Industry

Ultimately the impact of SC strategies (corporate and government) will be judged by Europe's share of SCs in the international market. To date, the efforts of European firms have not significantly increased Europe's overall market share, although they may have helped stop a further erosion. At the individual firm level, some initial advances were made in the world SC league. Siemens moved up from number 20 in 1988 to number 15 in 1989, registering a growth of 32 per cent over 1988.

This growth was more rapid than all other international suppliers other than Samsung of South Korea, and was mainly due to sales of one-megabit DRAMs. However, partly due to a fall off in DRAM sales, by 1991 Siemens had fallen back to position 17 in the world league (Table 5.1).

STM registered a growth of 20 per cent in 1989 compared with 1988. This was again one of the fastest growth rates recorded. STM maintained its 1990 position at number 12 in 1991. Following its rationalization in SCs, Philips may well fall in the world league in the future.

Despite disappointing results in world market shares, there can be little doubt that during the latter half of the 1980s the leading European firms committed themselves to outward-looking strategies and heavy investments in leading edge chip technology. Europe may well have fallen much further behind in market shares and in technology if these efforts had not been made.

As argued in section 5.2, corporate efforts in SCs cannot be ascribed to EC policy alone. Indeed, as the case of Siemens shows (see Box 5.1), a large-scale attempt at renovation had begun throughout the organization, independently of EC policy initiatives. Another important initiative was the takeover of Inmos by STM which strengthened STM's position in the advanced MPU business.

*Box 5.1     Siemens: a case of determination and renovation in semiconductors*

Siemens is a very large conglomerate and one of Europe's major high technology hopes for the future. In 1991 the company recorded sales of $45.6 bn and boasted 402 000 employees.

The company's main product lines are:

| | |
|---|---|
| Computers | $7.6 bn |
| Public communications | $7.1 bn |
| Industrial and building systems | $5.5 bn |
| Medical engineering | $4.6 bn |
| Industrial automation | $3.6 bn |
| Private communications | $3.2 bn |
| Power generation | $3.1 bn |
| Semiconductors | $1.3 bn |
| Other lines | $13.3 bn |
| Total | $49.3 bn (includes intradivisional sales) |

Like other international electronics companies, Siemens is currently suffering from the recession in SCs and other sectors. In 1991 sales were $1.3 bn, making SCs Siemens' smallest division.

In chips, the company ranks only sixteenth in the world. But it is determined to catch up technologically, to capture a large share of the world DRAM market and to use SCs to strengthen its electronics systems activities overall.

Although Siemens is still losing money in SCs, today the corporation is in far better shape than it was in the early 1980s. At this time the company was highly centralized, far too focused on the local market and, in SCs, technologically backward especially in mainstream areas such as DRAMs and MPUs. Siemens' weaknesses in chips were reflected in very low market shares and low exports, especially to the important US market.

In the mid-1980s the company increased its spending on SC technology, adopted a more aggressive marketing stance and began to establish a broad catalogue of mainstream SC products. The company overall restructured from seven to sixteen divisions and decentralized much of its decision making and its R&D. The organizational upheaval which began in 1988 under chief executive officer (CEO) Kaske is now being carried forward by new CEO Von Pierer. Von Pierer wants to break down Siemens further into smaller more agile units, headed by young entrepre-neurial managers. Where necessary the divisions must link up with foreign suppliers of advanced technology.

The renovation in SCs began before 1988. In 1986 Siemens hired Ulrich Schumacher, then 30, to a top job in the SC division, bypassing ranks of senior managers. By 1989 Schumacher had been promoted three times. At 33 he is now marketing director of memory chips, responsible for $300 m in sales.

Siemens invested heavily in its own SC technology. It also hedged its bets by forming joint ventures with leading technology suppliers worldwide. In DRAMs the company worked within Europe in ESPRIT and Eureka with companies such as Philips (see text). However, it also licensed in Toshiba's DRAM technology from Japan. In MPUs Siemens developed its own 32-bit RISC processor. However, the product it took to the market was the series 3000 MPU from Mips Computer Systems Inc. — a leading US supplier.

Siemens intends to be taken seriously as a world leader in SCs. There are some signs of success. In 1989 sales of SCs grew by 32%, faster than all other major producers except Samsung of Korea. Most of Siemens' sales were in mainstream one-megabit DRAMs. In fact, DRAMs accounted for around 50% of Siemens' SC sales in 1989 — a respectable 2.1% share of the world DRAM market.

By the end of the 1990s Siemens hopes to capture a 5% share of the DRAM market. In 1990 it began a major collaboration with IBM — the world's largest producer of chips and computers — to produce 16- and 64-megabit DRAMs. The two companies agreed to share equally the estimated $1 bn costs. For Siemens such an agreement would have been inconceivable in the early 1980s. It testifies to the renovation of the company in this field.

Nevertheless, writing in 1992, the companies' problems are huge. It is still losing money heavily, not only in SCs but also in 50 out of its 300 other businesses, with a further 150 only breaking even. The rejuvenation of its bureaucratic structures still has a long way to go. The company suffers from the traditional 'middle management' problem — ranks of cautious, career bureaucrats worried about taking initiatives and even more worried about taking risks and embracing change. Siemens' productivity is also low. Revenues per worker are only 56% of those of GE in the US.

Despite the problems, Siemens has forged ahead technologically and could well meet its targets. SC renovation is the key to meeting Siemens' broader international electronics systems objectives. If it is successful, Siemens will become the undisputed European electronics leader by the year 2000.

Overall, the new European strategies resemble that of their Japanese, rather than their American counterparts (type 4 rather than type 3 strategies). Firms have integrated backwards into mainstream chip manufacturing in order to supply the merchant market as well as their in-house needs. This is a significant shift in strategy compared with the 1970s when most European chip output was for in-house systems requirements.

### 5.4.4  The Current Market Recession

Despite the optimism of the mid-1980s, prospects for the early 1990s currently look bleak due to the severe market recession which began in 1990. Recession and financial difficulties led some observers to seriously question the health of European industry and the benefits of EC policies (Jonquières 1990).

Philips, the largest electronics producer in Europe, introduced a plan to cut 15 per cent of its workforce in 1990 as a result of falling profitability. The components division (mostly SCs) announced large-scale redundancies after losing $74 m in 1989. STM reported around $60 m loss in 1990, while Siemens continued to lose money on SCs.

Such problems beset not only SC makers but most of Europe's big electronics producers. For example, in 1990 the UK's largest computer firm ICL was taken over by Fujitsu of Japan. In the same year, ICL's parent company, STC, was taken over by the Canadian firm, Northern Telecom. Nixdorf of West Germany suffered losses and was taken over by Siemens in 1989. Norsk Data of Norway (previously one of the most promising computer firms in Europe) ran into difficulties as did Olivetti of Italy. Bull, the French computer manufacturer, forecast a loss of $578 m in 1990.

At the present time it is impossible to predict the outcome of these difficulties. However, three factors help put the current problems in context. First, most US and Japanese firms also face serious difficulties due to recession and declining profitability. The market downturn is testing not only for European companies.

Second, European firms are both larger and technologically stronger than they otherwise would have been if the restructuring of the late 1980s had not occurred. They are therefore better placed to survive the present difficulties — especially if they prove to be short-lived.

Third, if European firms are able to survive the current recession and maintain their newly gained capabilities, then they could well recover their profitability during the next market upturn. Indeed, one of the key reasons for the success of Japanese and Korean electronics companies has been their ability to maintain comparatively high technology investments during recessions.

Seen in the context of the regular cycles of boom and slump in electronics, the current difficulties are an inevitable test of the competences and technological commitment of European firms.

## 5.5 CONCLUSION

During the 1980s Europe's SC manufacturers adopted outward-looking strategies and committed themselves to long-term investments in technology. The data show that technological competences improved in relation to non-European firms. In the latter half of the 1980s there was a large shift away from one-way inward (international) flows of technology towards joint, two-way technology ventures with foreign firms. This reflected a growing competence and confidence among European firms. Firms adopted increasingly 'pro-active' forms of technical EOs (joint ventures and technology exchanges) as opposed to 'passive' forms of technical EOs (second sourcing and licensing).

Throughout the 1980s US and, to a lesser extent, Japanese firms continued to be an important source of competence for European-owned companies, both via technical EOs and by takeovers of US companies.

Europe's domestic firms continued to benefit from the US's relatively open approach to high technology takeovers. Conversely, there were no significant takeovers of European chip firms by US or Japanese companies.

Intra-European equity EOs show a fundamental restructuring of Europe's SC industry. The 'national champions' of the 1970s gave way to pan-European champions, now led by Siemens of Germany and STM of France and Italy. Philips of the Netherlands reduced its commitment to SCs due to financial difficulties in 1990. The UK failed to produce a locally-owned chip maker of the scale or competence of the European leaders.

The EC programmes of the 1980s supported and coincided with European firms' new dynamic strategies. Although EC support was bound up with firms' strategies, European companies followed their own directions, withdrew from large-scale projects when market circumstances dictated, and formed alliances with non-European firms in areas of EC promotion.

This chapter has argued that the EC should think again about close-to-market subsidies for European-owned chip companies. The near-market projects are intrinsically high cost and high risk. Firms can and do change their strategies mid-stream, leaving projects in difficulty.

European-owned firms are now large enough and technologically strong enough to 'stand on their own two feet'. EC policy support for longer term investments in basic R&D, training, standards projects and university-firm linkages are less costly and less risky. By improving the overall technological infrastructure and skill base, such projects offer wider gains to the community as a whole, benefiting European-owned firms and making foreign investment from abroad more attractive.

Today's chip industry is inherently global in nature. Europe can and does benefit from direct foreign investment by the US and Japan.

An open door, outward-looking EC policy could encourage more direct investment from the US and Japan and encourage new entrants from South Korea and Taiwan.

Finally, at the time of writing, recession and financial difficulties beset Europe's SC operations. Many are pessimistic about the future of European-owned electronics firms. Nevertheless, the EO evidence shows an improved technological and marketing competence on the part of European companies. Europe's leading electronics firms have successfully reversed their 1970s image of inertia and technological backwardness. They are therefore in a stronger position to weather the current recession and survive as contenders in the global marketplace.

## NOTES

1. Throughout the chapter the term 'European firms' indicates European-owned firms. The chapter recognizes the vital role of foreign chip firms within Europe but the focus of the discussion is on the activities of European-owned firms.
2. An IC is a SC with more than one functioning element. In the industry, as in this chapter, the terms SC and IC are used interchangeably.
3. The strategic types are not mutually exclusive; overlap exists. There are many ways of outlining strategies in the SC industry.
4. US firms are also engaged in EOs with each other, both under the framework of Sematech and in private initiatives. Japanese firms are less involved in near-market initiatives within Japan either in government-sponsored or private ventures, despite popular belief.
5. One new trend is for US merchant firms to form partnerships with Japanese companies to gain financial capital. For example, large US firms including Texas Instruments, LSI Logic, Harris Semiconductor and VLSI Technology have linked up with Japanese steel firms to access capital (Dataquest information, cited in *Electronic Business* 8 April 1991 p30). Steel companies including Kawasaki Steel, Kobe Steel, NKK and Nippon have entered the chip business in areas such as ASICs and high-speed SRAMs by these means.
6. This also occurred during the UK Alvey Programme for SCs (the VLSI Programme), where a large firm, GEC, withdrew from large-scale near-to-market SC projects (Guy and Georghiou 1991).
7. Other more fundamental economic objections to near-to-market support include: (a) that it is contrary to the fair trading principles of GATT and the Treaty of Rome; (b) unlike pre-competitive R&D it does not have the economic justification of externality benefits; and (c) by establishing subsidy as normal practice the EC could stimulate a 'subsidy race' between the EC, Japan and the US.

# APPENDIX 1: Glossary of Technical Terms and Abbreviations

*Analogue*: electromagnetic wave form analagous to a continuously variable quantity such as temperature. Digital on the other hand, is transmitted in discrete, separate pulses using techniques such as pulse code modulation (also see *Digital*).

*ASIC*: Application Specific Integrated Circuits are design-intensive semi-conductors which allow the user to closely specify the design of the final circuit. They are to be contrasted with standard ICs, such as memory devices (e.g. DRAMs).

*Cell-based*: (see *Standard cell technology*).

*Chip*: (see *SC–semiconductor*).

*Custom (or full custom) technology*: an ASIC which is crafted, by hand, to meet the design needs of an individual user.

*Digital*: a discrete or discontinuous signal transmitted in intervals. Modern computers are based on digital technology because of its superiority over analogue in terms of speed, reliability, and low cost per bit of information.

*DRAM*: Dynamic Random Access Memory — a general purpose IC used to store large quantities of information in binary code in the form of electrical charges. DRAM electrons are constantly in motion and have to be refreshed by special circuits (see *SRAM*).

*EEPROM*: electrically erasable programmable read only memory — a standard memory chip which can be reprogrammed using software. Often used in combination with microprocessors.

*Gate array*: an ASIC which is mass produced until the final stage of manu-facture. The customer then specifies a particular design and the array is put through the final interconnect stage of prduction.

*IC*: integrated circuit — any semiconductor component with more than one functioning element. Also known as a chip, a microelectronic device and a semiconductor component.

*Megabit*: refers to the number of bits of information which can be stored on one silicon chip (one-megabit = one million).

*Memory*: a family of semiconductors used to store large quantities of infor-mation (see DRAM).

*MPU*: microprocessor — a complex type of semiconductor used to perform the central functions of microcomputers.

*PLD*: programmable logic device — an ASIC which is produced as a standard component but with 'fusible links' between the circuit elements on the chip. Using software, the user programmes (or fuses) the PLD according to a specific design.

*RISC*: reduced instruction set computers. A form of microprocessor IC which operates very quickly due to substantially reduced numbers of logic operations within the chip.

*SC*: semiconductor — the material commonly used in the production of ICs, having special electrical conducting properties.

*SRAM*: static random access memory. Unlike DRAMs, SRAMs do not require constant refreshing with special circuits, hence the term static. SRAMs tend to be cheaper than DRAMs and are often used in electronic watches and calculators.

*Standard cell technology*: a widely used ASIC. A range of pre-designed logic and memory functions is stored on a computer and recalled according to a user's design requirement.

*TTL*: transistor–transistor logic. A standard logic IC where one transistor is connected directly to another (rather than via a resistor or diode).

*VLSI*: very large scale integration technology allows for one million (one-megabit) or more circuit elements to be condensed on to one tiny chip.

## APPENDIX 2: Method, Data Sources and Definitions

The method used for the data analysis is an extended version of the method used by Haklisch and Pouletty (1986) who carried out an international study of the SC industry up to the year 1984. Primary data on technical and equity EOs for the period 1985-91 were gathered from industry journals and data-bases. Earlier data were derived from the original data presented in Haklisch and Pouletty (1986).

### Nature and Size of Sample

The data deal only with published ventures. Non-reported (e.g. minor, confidential or secret agreements) are not included. EOs reported are self-selected and important in the sense that firms publicized their reasonably assumed that: most important European ventures are included; and a fairly large proportion of all important ventures are included.

Unless reported in the press the data exclude R&D agreements entered into under EC programmes such as ESPRIT and European programmes such as Eureka. The reasoning is that if they are reported then they constitute ventures directly 'important' to the strategy of the firm concerned. An account of the scale and impact of state intervention via the EC programmes in firms' activities is provided by Mytelka (1991).

## Distribution and Marketing Agreements

Distribution and marketing agreements were not included as these generally are not entered into for the purposes of competence accumulation in SCs. Such agreements are very large in number and taken as 'given' in the industry. Other studies of SCs and information technology also exclude distribution agreements for similar reasons (e.g. Hagadoorn and Schakenraad 1990; Haklisch and Pouletty 1986).

## Data Collection: Method and Scope

Data for 1985–91 were gathered via an initial database search (Predicast, Prompt and Textiline). These proved unsuitable for the exact categorization needed (see below). Therefore a detailed examination of industry journals was undertaken. The main sources were *Electronics Times*, *Electronics Weekly*, *Electronics Business*. Information was also gathered via interviews with industrialists.

## Data Categorization Method

The data were classified into four main types of technical agreements of relevance to the SC industry: SS, L, TE and UV. Definitions sometimes overlapped and therefore all were not mutually exclusive (e.g. many JVs involve TE and sometimes L as well).

### External technical operations, definitions and codes

SS = second sourcing agreements, refers to a specific, formal SS agreement; may occur within or in conjunction with a TE or JV; refers to current technology.

L = one way flow of technology (product or process); similar to SS but not necessarily one specific product; can refer to a process or group of products; refers to current technology.

TE = technology exchange; refers to a two-way technology exchange agreement; broader than an SS but can specify a specific product, process or family of either; refers to current technology.

JV = joint venture (sometimes known as a strategic partnership); refers to the development of a generic process technology suitable for a range of products (or a major new product design); refers to future technology development.

### International direction of technology flow

International technology flow refers to the principal direction of technology flow, in or out of Europe. Each agreement was assessed by the author according to principal technology recipient and donor. In many cases both parties gained from technology flows.

The five categories used are as follows:

| | | |
|---|---|---|
| E | = | Intra-European technology flow |
| E*/EC | = | Intra-European technology flow sponsored by the EC or Eureka |
| I | = | Inward (international) technology flow (to Europe from overseas) |
| O | = | Outward (international) technology flow (to overseas from Europe) |
| I/O | = | Technical flow both directions, in and out (both parties gained technology) |

## Other Points

Intra-European technical EOs are not double counted but treated as one agreement. Thus Philips agreements with Siemens are listed under Germany–Siemens or Netherlands–Philips and not in both sections.

## Other Abbreviations Commonly Used

### Technical codes

| | | |
|---|---|---|
| ASIC | = | Application specific integrated circuit |
| IC | = | Integrated circuit |
| CMOS | = | Complementary metal oxide SC (see section 5.1) |
| MPU | = | Microprocessor unit |
| PLAs | = | Programmable logic arrays |
| SC | = | Semiconductor |
| VLSI | = | Very large scale integrated circuit |

### Country codes

| | | |
|---|---|---|
| G | = | Germany |
| HK | = | Hong Kong |
| J | = | Japan |
| N | = | Netherlands |
| NW | = | Norway |
| PE | = | Pan European |
| SK | = | South Korea |
| UK | = | United Kingdom |
| US | = | United States |

# APPENDIX 3: European Firms' External Technology Operations in Semiconductors, 1980-84

| European firm | Partner | Year | Technology area | Type of agreement | Technology direction |
|---|---|---|---|---|---|
| *Germany* | | | | | |
| AEG-Telefunken | Mostek (US) | 1982 | CMOS, custom VLSI | JV | I |
| | Mostek (US) | 1983 | n.a. | JV | I/O |
| Nixdorf | Ferranti(UK) | 1981 | n.a. | TE | E |
| Siemens | AMD (US) | 1984 | CMOS, custom | JV, TE | I |
| | Fuji (J) | n.a. | n.a. | JV, L | I |
| | Intel (US) | 1982 | MPU for telecom | JV, SS | I/O |
| | Intel (US) | 1984 | MPU for telecom | JV, TE | I/O |
| | Philips (N) | 1982 | Sub-micron-CMOS | JV, TE | E |
| | Philips (N) | 1984 | Memories, CMOS | JV, TE | E*/EC |
| | Zilog (US) | 1981 | MPU | SS | I |
| | | | | | |
| *France* | | | | | |
| Bull | Trilogy (US) | 1982 | Wafer technology | L | I |
| Matra | Citel-L (US) | 1983 | CMOS, custom, gate arrays | TE | O |
| | GCA (US) | 1982 | SC equipment | JV, TE | I/O |
| | Harris (US) | 1980 | Custom ICs | JV | I |
| | Intel (US) | 1981 | CMOS, MPUs | SS, TE | I |
| | NEC (J) | n.a. | MPUs | TE, SS | I |
| | Tandy (J) | 1981 | TRS-80 | JV | I |
| Schlumberger/ | Goldstar (SK) | 1984 | Memories | L | O |
| Fairchild | National (US) | 1982 | MPUs, peripherals | JV,SS | I |
| | Hitachi (J) | 1982 | Memories, MPUs | JV | I/O |
| | Philips (N) | 1982 | Bipolar logic design | JV | E |
| | Sanyo (J) | 1981 | MPUs | L | O |
| | VLSI (US) | 1981 | Gate arrays | JV, TE, SS | I/O |
| Thomson CSF | AMD (US) | n.a. | MPUs, peripherals | SS | I |
| | GI (US) | n.a. | MPUs, peripherals | SS | I |
| | Motorola (US) | 1981 | MPUs, peripherals | SS, L | I |
| | Motorola (US) | 1984 | MPUs, peripherals | SS | I |
| | Oki (J) | 1984 | Gate arrays | SS, TE | I/O |

| European firm | Partner | Year | Technology area | Type of agreement | Technology direction |
|---|---|---|---|---|---|
| *Italy* | | | | | |
| Olivetti | Goldstar (SK) | 1984 | Software | JV, L | O |
| | Linear technology (US) | 1982 | Linear circuits | JV | I |
| | VLSI (US) | n.a. | n.a. | n.a. | n.a. |
| | Zilog (US) | 1980 | MPUs, peripherals | n.a. | n.a. |
| SGS-ATES | IBM (US) | 1983 | ICs | JV | I/O |
| | LSI Logic (US) | 1980s | Gate arrays | L | I |
| | Toshiba (J) | 1981 | CMOS | JV, L | I |
| | Toshiba (J) | 1984 | CMOS | JV | I |
| | Zilog (US) | 1981 | CMOS | SS | I |
| | | | | | |
| *Netherlands* | | | | | |
| Philips ou (incl. Signetics) | AMD (US) | 1981 | MPUs, process tech. | TE | I |
| | Intel (US) | 1982 | MPUs, process tech. | TE | I/O |
| | Motorola (US) | 1981 | MPUs, peripherals | SS, JV | I |
| | RCA (US) | 1982 | CMOS logic | JV | I/O |
| | Texas Inst. (US) | 1984 | Chip design | JV | I/O |
| | | | | | |
| *United Kingdom* | | | | | |
| GEC | Fairchild (US) | 1978–9 | IC manuf. | JV | I |
| | Mitel (Canada) | 1981 | Cellmos | L | I |
| Ferranti | SC Devices (HK) | 1983 | Custom, gate arrays | JV | I/O |
| ICL | Fujitsu (J) | 1981 | CMOS, ECL, etc. | JV | I/O |
| Inmos | Hyundai (SK) | 1984 | 256k DRAM | L | O |
| | NMB (J) | 1984 | 256K DRAM | L | O |

*Source*: see Appendix 2

# APPENDIX 4: European Firms' External Technology Operations in Semiconductors, 1984–91[*]

| European firm | Partner | Year | Technology area | Type of agreement | Technology direction |
|---|---|---|---|---|---|
| *Belgium* | | | | | |
| UCB Electronics | JSR (J) | 1990 | Photoresist for DRAMs | JV | O |
| | | | | | |
| *Finland* | | | | | |
| Micronas | AMD (US) | 1987 | Telecom chips | JV, TE | I/O |
| | | | | | |
| *Germany* | | | | | |
| AEG–Telefunken | Siliconix (US) | 1988 | Power SCs | TE | I |
| | Deutsche Aerospace | | | | |
| | DASA (FRG) | 1991 | ASICs | JV | E |
| | Hitachi (J) | 1990 | Chip on glass | TE | I/O |
| | Mitsubishi (J) | 1990 | Automotive chips | JV | I/O |
| Siemens | Motorola (US) | 1986 | VLSI, telecom ICS | JV | I/O |
| | Toshiba (J) | 1986 | MOS process | L | I |
| | AMD (US) | 1988 | ISDN chips | JV, SS | I/O |
| | MIPS (US) | 1989 | 32-bit RISC MPU | TE | I |
| | IBM (US) | 1990 | 64 M-bit DRAMs, EPROMs | JV | I/O |
| | IDT (US) | 1990 | R300 microcontrollers | JV | I/O |
| | IBM (US) | 1991 | 16 M-bit DRAMs | JV/TE | I/O |
| | Toshiba (J) | 1991 | Wafers for ASICs | TE | I/O |
| | | | | | |
| *France* | | | | | |
| Matra/MHS[**] | NEC (J) | 1987 | CMOS MPUs | SS,TE | I/O |
| (Matra Harris SC) | Cypress SC (US) | 1986 | CMOS process | SS,TE | I/O |
| Thomson CSF | Oki (J) | 1985 | CMOS gate arrays | SS, TE, JV | I/O |
| | Telefunken (G) | 1984 | 32-bit MPUs | SS, TE | I/O |
| | Hitachi (J) | 1985 | Telecom chips | SS, TE | I/O |
| | Dallas (US) | 1986 | Late definition SC | SS, TE | I/O |
| | Motorola (US) | 1989 | RISC MPUs (military) | L | |
| | Valid (US) | 1990 | Design automation | JV | I/O |
| TCM (a Thomson CSF subsidiary) | Vitesse (US) | 1990 | ASICs, Logic, RAM | TE | I/O |

| European firm | Partner | Year | Technology area | Type of agreement | Technology direction |
|---|---|---|---|---|---|
| *Italy* | | | | | |
| SGS-ATES*** | AT&T (US) | 1989 | Telecom ICS | TE | I |
| | Siliconix (US) | 1986 | Power MOS | TE, JV | I/O |
| | Lattice (UK) | 1987 | PLAs | SS, TE | E |
| *Netherlands* | | | | | |
| Philips/Signetics | Siemens (G) | 1985 | Telecom CMOS | SS | E |
| | Hitachi (J) | 1985 | MPU peripherals | SS, TE | I/O |
| | VLSI (US) | 1988 | ASIC design/mfr. | SS, TE | I/O |
| | Racal–Redac (UK) | 1989 | CMOS, array design | JV | E |
| | Sun Microsyst (US) | 1989 | SPARC RISC chips | L | I |
| | Seeq (US) | 1990 | Flash, EEPROM | TE | I/O |
| | Texas Instr. (US) | 1990 | Bicmos, CMOS telecom | TE, JV | I/O |
| | Texas Instr. (US) | 1990 | Bicmos logic chips | JV | I/O |
| | Matsushita (J) | 1991 | Microcontroller mfr. | L | I |
| Philips Interactive Media Systems | NMB (J) | 1989 | Full motion video ICs | JV | I/O |
| *Norway* | | | | | |
| Nordic VLSI | GE (US) | 1988 | Custom ASIC | JV | I/O |
| *United Kingdom* | | | | | |
| GEC/Plessey | SGS–Thomson (PE) | 1991 | Semi-custom ICs CMOS (cell-based) | JV | E*/EC |
| (GPS) | Thomson Milit. | 1990 | COMOS 'SOS' process | JV | E*/EC |
| (GPS) | AT&E (US) | n/a | Telecom decoder IC | L | O |
| (GPS) | Music SC (UK) | 1991 | CMOS 'CAM' chips | JV | E |
| (GPS) | Simtek (UK) | 1991 | SRAM, EEPROM | L | I |
| (GEC) | GTE (US) | 1985 | Custom gate arrays | SS, JV | I/O |
| (Plessey) | Thomson (FR) | 1986 | ASIC macrocells | JV | E*/EC |
| (GEC) | McDonnell Douglas | 1987 | SOS processor | SS | O |
| (GEC Plessey Telecom) | AMD (US) | 1989 | IC design, ISDN IC | JV | I/O |
| (Plessey) | Philips (N) and Nordic VLSI (NW) | 1987 | Satellite TV chip | JV | I/O |
| (Plessey) | Pilkington (UK) | 1988 | Erasable PLAs Non volatile | L | E |
| (Plessey) | Simtek (US) | 1989 | EEPROM | JV | I/O |

| European firm | Partner | Year | Technology area | Type of agreement | Technology direction |
|---|---|---|---|---|---|
| ICL | Fujitsu (J) | 1990 | SC design and dev. | TE | I/O |
| Inmos | Siemens (G) | 1988 | Complex VLSI mfr | JV | E/EC* |
| Pilkington ME | Toshiba (J) | 1989 | SRAM-based arrays | JV | I/O |
| | Toshiba (J) | 1990 | Semicustom logic | JV | I/O |
| Pilkington Communication Systems | National (US) | 1990 | Data interface ICs | JV | I/O |
| *Sweden* | | | | | |
| Aga | Nippon Sanso (J) | 1991 | SC gas equipment | JV | I/O |
| Electrolux | Imp (US) | 1987 | Analogue ASICs | TE | I |
| *Pan-European* | | | | | |
| ES2 | Lattice (UK) | 1985 | Design tools | JV | E |
| | Microtech (UK) | 1987 | Military custom ICs | JV | E |
| | VLSI Techn. (US) | 1991 | Custom ICs | TE | I/O |
| | Advanced Risc (US) | 1991 | 32 bit RISC | TE | I/O |
| | Etec Systems (US) | 1991 | Gate arrays, E-beam | TE | I/O |
| SGS–Thomson Micr 11 | Anamartic (UK) | 1987 | Wafer scale memory | JV | I/O |
| (STM) | Sieko Epson (J) | 1991 | SRAMs, Graphics IC | TE | I/O |
| | CNET (French Telecom) | 1991 | Submicron research | JV | E |
| | Alcatel (Fr) | 1987 | Telecom chips | JV | E |
| | National (US) | 1986 | ISDN U-interface IC | JV | I/O |
| | Oki (J) | 1988 | DRAM modules | TE | I |
| | Philips (N) | 1988 | SCs (JESSI) | JV | E*/EC |
| | Siemens (FG) | 1988 | SCs (JESSI) | JV | E*/EC |
| | CNET (FR) | 1989 | Sub-micron SC (JESSI) | JV | E*/EC |
| | Siemens (FG) | 1990 | Microcontrollers | SS | E |
| Innovative Silicon Techn. (subsid. of STM) | ZYMOS (US) | 1990 | Semi-standard PC ICs | TE, JV | I/O |

\*  Data up to December 1991
E\*/EC  Supported by ESPRIT or Eureka (including JESSI)
\*\*  Harris (US) has 20% stake in MHS until 1989 when it sold the share to 'new partners', including Daimler Benz (FG)
\*\*\*  See Pan-European (SGS–Thomson) for post 1987 EOs
*Source*:  see Appendix 2

## APPENDIX 5: European Firms' External Equity Operations in Semiconductors, 1977–84

This appendix proposes only a selection of these operations

| Country/European firm | Year | External firm/country | Equity share (%) |
|---|---|---|---|
| *Germany* | | | |
| Siemens | 1980 | Threshold Tech. (US) | 100 |
| | 1979 | Databit (US) | 100 |
| | 1977 | AMD (US) | 20 |
| | 1977 | Litronix (US) | 100 |
| | 1979 | Microwave SC (US) | 100 |
| | | | |
| *France* | | | |
| CIT-Alcatel | 1980 | Semiprocess (US) | 25 |
| Schlumberger | 1979 | Fairchild (US) | 100 |
| | 1978 | Membrain (US) | 100 |
| | 1982 | Acutest (US) | 100 |
| Thomson CSF | 1979 | Solid State Scientific (US) | 100 |
| | | | |
| *UK* | | | |
| Ferranti | 1977 | Interdesign (US) | 100 |
| GEC | 1982 | Circuit Tech. (US) | 100 |
| | | | |
| *Netherlands* | | | |
| Philips | 1982 | Amperex (US) | 100 |
| | 1979 | Signetics (US) | 100 |

*Source*: Derived from data presented in Haklisch and Pouletty (1986)

# APPENDIX 6: European Firms' Equity Operations in Semiconductors, 1985–91

| Country /European firm | Year | External firm/ country | Technology area | Event |
|---|---|---|---|---|
| *Austria* | | | | |
| Austria Microsystems | 1987 | Gould AMI (US) | SCs, ASICs | Austria M. took full control of joint venture by buying Gould's 51% share |
| *Germany* | | | | |
| Telefunken/AEG (AEG is 80% owned by Daimler Benz) | 1988 | Siliconix (US) | Power SCs for auto's | AEG/T, a subsid. of D-Benz acquired 39% of Siliconix. AEG to gain automative tech. |
| | 1990 | Silliconix (US) | Power, auto, computer chips | AEG provided $15 m bankruptcy rescue package. Shareholding raised from 39% to 80%. |
| | 1991 | Deutsche Aerospace (DASA) (FG) | Fast SRAMs, ASICs, other electronics | Full merger of DASA/AEG el. activities. DASA subsids include Telefunken Systemtechnik, Dialog SC Eurosil + AEG shares in MHS and Siliconix |
| Siemens* | 1991 | AMD (US) | Telecom chips | Siemens sold its 10% share in AMD |
| *France* | | | | |
| MHS (Matra Harris Semiconducteur) | 1989 | Harris (US) | CMOS manufacture | Harris sold its 20% share in MHS (renamed Matra MHS) MHS was created in 1979 |
| Schlumberger (Fairchild) | 1987 | National (US) | SC manuf. and design | After 8 years of ownership and substantial losses, Sch. sold Fairchild to National. |
| Thomson CSF | 1985 | Mostek (US) | SC manuf. and design | United Technologies accepted $71 m from Thomson CSF for its chip subsid., Mostek. |
| | 1987 | SGS (Italy) | SC manuf. and design | Full merger (50–50 owned) of SC activities forming SGS–Thomson Microelectronics (SIM) in April. 1987 sales appx. $800 m (3% of world mkt) SGS occupy15 of 21 senior management positions. |
| Thomson ventures | 1990 | Vitesse (US) | ASICs, logic, RAM chips | Equity investment giving Thomson access to Vitesse IC product technology. |

| Country /European firm | Year | External firm/ country | Technology area | Event |
|---|---|---|---|---|
| *Hungary* | | | | |
| Interchip | 1990 | NCM (US) | SC manufacture | National Council of Ind. Co-op (+ several firms) formed Hungary's first independent chip maker with $60 m start-up funds. Tech. from NCM of Silicon Valley |
| *Netherlands* | | | | |
| Two Dutch venture capital firms | 1987 | Sierra (US) | Cell based SC manuf. and design | Sierra to form European JV in Holland |
| *UK* | | | | |
| Cambridge Instr. | 1986 | Riechert Jung (G) | SC products | Merger to form a company within Cambridge Instr. |
| Plessey | 1987 | Ferranti SC (UK) | ASIC production gate arrays | Plessey acquired 100% of Ferranti's chip activities at cost of £30 m; merged company sales £130 m. |
| GEC | 1989 | Plessey SC (UK) | ASICs, custom | GEC–Siemens complete hostile 100% takeover of Plessey. New chip company GPS (GEC-P1 SCs) formed from Plessey SC and GEC's Marconi (MEDL) and GEC Caswell (R&D), new firm's sales £200 m (employ. 3900). |
| Inmos | 1989 | SGS–Thomson (STM) (PE) | 32-bit MPUs Transputer | STM acquired 100% of Inmos from Thorn–EMI of UK. |
| IPS (Integrated Power SC) | 1987 | Liquidation | Power SC | Investors withdrew backing due to losses. |
| Semafab | 1987 | GI (US) | CMOS wafer fab. | Semafab. purchased GI's wafer fab. plant in Scotland; is 60% owned by Semelab (a UK distributor). |
| Zetec | 1989 | Mngmt, buy-out | Discrete SCs | Zetec, the UK's largest discrete SC maker was sold by Plessey for £2.5 m (was part of Ferranti). |
| *Pan-European* | | | | |
| ES2 | 1985 | New start-up | Custom ICs, SC design | Pan-European start-up company European industry funded £25 m. Further £20 m from capital spending grants (e.g. £15 m from French govt for factory). Also unspecified bank loans. |

| Country /European Firm | Year | External firm/ country | Technology area | Event |
|---|---|---|---|---|
| | 1987 | Lattice Logic (UK) | SC design | Acquisition by ES2 of Lattice (Lattice main shareholders Ferranti and Cambridge. Instr.) |
| | 1989 | Aerospatiale (PE) | | Aero. became 9th corporate shareholder in ES2 (equiv. to BAe, ABB or Bull). Ind. partners own 50% of ES2. |
| | 1989 | Siemens (FRG) | | Shareholding purchased by Siemens. |
| | 1990 | Cadence (US) | Silicon design tools | A joint company (Eucad) was formed to develop design tools. |
| SGS–Thomson (STM) | 1989 | CNET (France) | Sub-micron ICs | Joint company formed betw. French Atomic Energy Comm. R&D lab. (CNET) and STM for R&D for 0.5 miron SCs. |
| | 1991 | Microwave (US) (Siemens owned) | Defence, telecom SCs | STM purchased non Ga-As activitities of US-based Microwave from Siemens. |
| | 1991 | 2 US facilities[*] | Design, DRAM dev. | Inmos's fav. facilities consolidation. |

[*] Divestitures
*Source*: see Appendix 2

# BIBLIOGRAPHY

CEC (1987), *The ESPRIT Programme: Project Synopses,* Sub-programme 1, Advanced Microelectronics, Directorate General XIII, Telecommunications, Information Industries and Innovation, Commission of European Communities, Brussels.

CEC (1989), *The Review of ESPRIT 1984 to 1988: the Report of the ESPRIT Review Board,* Executive Version, Commission of European Communities, Brussels, May.

CEC (1991), *The European Electronics and Information Technology Industry: State of Play, Issues at Stake and Proposals for Action,* Communication from the Commision SEC (91) 565 final, 3 April, Brussels.

Chesnais, F. (1988), 'Technical Cooperation Agreements between Independent Firms, Novel Issues for Economic Analyses and the Formulation of National Technological Policies' *STI Revue,* no. 4, pp51–121.

Delapierre, M. and Zimmerman, J.-B. (1991), 'Towards a New Europeanism: French Firms in Strategic Partnerships', in Lynn K. Mytelka (ed.) *Strategic Partnerships and the World Economy,* Pinter, London.

*Electronics Times,* various issues.

*Electronic Business,* various issues.

*The European,* various issues.

*Financial Times,* various issues.

Ferguson, C. H. (1988), 'From the People who brought you Voodoo Economics: Beyond Entrepreneurialism to US competitiveness', *Harvard Business Review,* May–June.

*The Guardian,* various issues.

Guy, K. and Georghiou, L. (1991), *Evaluation of the Alvey Programme for Advanced Information Technology.* A Report by Science Policy Research Unit, University of Sussex, and Programme of Policy Research in Engineering, Science and Technology, University of Manchester, HMSO, London.

Hagedoorn, J. and Schakenraad, J. (1990), *Leading Companies and the Structure of Strategic Alliances in Core Technologies,* Mimeo, MERIT, University of Limburg, Maastricht.

Haklisch, C. S and Pouletty, P. (1986), *Technical Alliances in the Semiconductor Industry,* Center for Science and Technology Policy, New York University.

Hare, P., Lauchlan, J. and Thompson, M. (1988), *An Assessment of ESPRIT in the UK,* Technological Change Research Centre, Heriot-Watt University, 31–35 Grassmarket, Edinburgh.

Hobday, M. G. (1992), 'The European Electronics Industry: Technology and Structural Change' *Technovation,* vol. 12, no. 2, pp75–97.

ICE (1991), *Mid-Term 1991 Status and Forecast of the IC Industry,* Integrated Circuit Engineering Corporation, Scottsdale, Arizona.

Jonquières, G. (1990), 'Shadows over the Sunrise Sector', *Financial Times,* 25 July.

Mytelka, L. K. (1991), 'States, Strategic alliances and International Oligopolies: the European ESPRIT Programme', in Lynn Mytelka (ed.) *Strategic Partnerships and the World Economy,* Pinter, London.

UNCTC (1983), *Transnational Corporations in the International Semiconductor Industry,* United Nations Center on Transnational Corporations, New York.

Steinmueller, W. E. (1988), 'International Joint Ventures in the Integrated Circuit Industry', in D. C. Mowery (ed.) *International Collaborative Ventures in US Manufacturing*, Ballinger, Cambridge.

Swann, G. M. P. (1985), 'Product Competition in Microprocessors', *The Journal of Industrial Economics,* Vol. XXXIV, September.

UNCTC (1983), *Transnational Corporations in the International Semiconductor Industry*, United Nations Center on Transnational Corporations, New York.

*Wall Street Journal,* 19 June 1989.

# 6. The Consumer Electronic Industry

## Martin D. H. Bloom

The past decade has been a remarkable one for the European consumer electronics industry, a period of great consolidation and rationalization, with its markets changing from isolated national markets to a global market with international access to components and products and competition from Japanese producers. Perhaps the main theme for this chapter is to be found in the response of the European industry to these changes as it restructured around Philips, Thomson and Nokia, with varying degrees of support from national governments and the European Commission. These are the only truly multinational indigenous producers that remain in Europe.[1]

This chapter is a study of the consumer electronics industry, and specifically the video sector — comprising colour television, video recorder and camcorder — which accounts for around two thirds of the market. It considers: the background to the sector, representing the external environment within which companies in the industry have had to compete; the resources necessary for effective competition; and the impact of the actions of the European Commission.

After identifying the main elements, case studies will provide a comparison between the strategies of Philips, Thomson and Nokia, providing an analysis of the way in which the only three companies that can be regarded as still seriously involved in this sector have attempted to build their television and video operations and sought to take control of the resources necessary to respond to the changing nature of competitiveness in the sector. (No attempt is made to document the numerous withdrawals from the market that have occurred.) The different approaches and degree of success of these companies are highlighted, reinforcing the analysis of the external factors that provide competitiveness in the sector and giving indications for future success. In all cases acquisitions have been a key method for expanding colour television production geographically, while they have employed a variety of approaches for video recorders and other products. A brief analysis of the development of high definition television (HDTV) provides indications as to likely future factors.

## 6.1   INDUSTRY BACKGROUND

### 6.1.1   General Presentation

The largest markets for the consumer electronics industry within the European Community are Germany, France and the United Kingdom. Overall, a little over half of consumption is supplied by imports from outside the European Community and 18 per cent of production exported. The sector's most important product is colour television, absorbing 33 per cent of consumers' expenditure on consumer electronics products, while video products in total account for almost 60 per cent (see Table 6.1).

*Table 6.1   Share of some products in the total demand for consumer electronics products in 1989 (US, Japan and EC\*)*

| Product | Share, in % |
|---|---|
| Colour televisions | 33 |
| Video cassette recorders | 19 |
| Camcorders | 7 |
| Audio products | 41 |

\*   In the European Community itself, video products are believed to account for an even higher percentage of expenditure on consumer electronics products.
*Source*: BIS Mackintosh in *Panorama of EC Industries 1991–92*, pp12–38.

During the past ten years, there has been growth in the market, though this has not been consistent (see Table 6.2). Perhaps the most important development was the introduction of the video cassette recorder and, more recently, the video camcorder. The greatest growth in the colour television market has been for televisions with a small screen size, the share of the market taken by televisions with a screen size of 42 cm. or less increasing from 13 per cent in 1980 to over 40 per cent in 1988, though it fell to 36 per cent in 1990.[2]

The European video electronics sector is suffering from saturated markets and overcapacity. Most European households already possess a television set and sales are largely replacement sales or the purchase of additional sets (Table 6.3). At the end of 1990, the level varied from 82 per cent of households in Italy with a colour television set to 95 per cent in the United Kingdom and Denmark. The level of penetration of VCRs in the market is at a much lower level, varying from only 28 per cent in Italy to 60 per cent in the United Kingdom. Official estimates for 1989 for Japan and the United States were 70 per cent and 65 per cent, respectively, which are regarded as close to saturation point. The introduction of the camcorder has led to rapid growth for this sector and could influence future VCR sales; penetration in Europe is still fairly low.

*Table 6.2   Market growth 1980–89, in million units*

|      | Colour televisions | Video cassette recorders | Camcorders |
|------|--------------------|--------------------------|------------|
| 1980 | 9.9  | 1.1 | –   |
| 1981 | 10.1 | 2.5 | –   |
| 1982 | 11.3 | 5.0 | 0.3 |
| 1983 | 11.5 | 5.1 | 0.2 |
| 1984 | 12.5 | 4.9 | 0.3 |
| 1985 | 12.9 | 5.4 | 0.3 |
| 1986 | 14.9 | 6.5 | 0.4 |
| 1987 | 16.1 | 8.2 | 0.8 |
| 1988 | 18.4 | 9.7 | 1.1 |
| 1989 | 18.2 | 9.8 | 1.8 |

*Source*: EACEM, quoted in European Commission (1991)

*Table 6.3   Household penetration levels, 1990*

|         | Colour televisions | Video cassette recorders | Camcorders |
|---------|--------------------|--------------------------|------------|
| Belgium | 90 | 42 | 6 |
| Denmark | 95 | 35 | 4 |
| France  | 92 | 43 | 6 |
| Germany | 91 | 51 | 7 |
| Holland | 94 | 49 | 9 |
| Italy   | 82 | 28 | 5 |
| UK      | 95 | 60 | 4 |

*Note*:   Estimates from BIS Mackintosh, quoted in *Financial Times*, 30 October 1990, put the penetration of video recorders at a higher level.
*Source*: EACEM, quoted in European Commission (1992)

These changes have taken place against a background of growing inroads made by the Japanese producers from the early 1970s. Linked to this was the way in which new products — VCRs and camcorders — provided the Japanese with entry points into both the North American and European markets. The situation has been exacerbated by imports from South Korea and from other Asian producers; initially this was largely proxy production heavily dependent on Japanese components and subcontracting, though this is slowly changing.[3]

The political response by the Europeans has also been influenced by the experience of the virtual elimination of the indigenous North American television set producers, only Zenith now remaining. Philips and Thomson adopted a strategy of persuading national governments and later the European Commission to attempt to deny market access to Japanese and Korean producers. The result has been an increase in Japanese production within Europe, especially in the United Kingdom and Germany, with some production of audio products in France. Imports are still a major factor for audio products and for the newer video products such as camcorders. By contrast, an estimated 68 per cent of the colour televisions and 59 per cent of the video recorders sold in the European Community in 1990 were produced locally.[4] For the structure of the EC consumer electronics market in 1990, see Table 6.4.

*Table 6.4    Structure of the EC consumer electronics market, 1990*

|                             | Sales in ECU bn |
| --------------------------- | --------------- |
| European market             | 23              |
| European production         | 13              |
| of which: European-owned    | 9               |
| of which: Foreign-owned     | 4°              |
| Imports                     | 12*             |
| of which: from Japan        | 5               |
| of which: from Korea        | 1               |
| Exports                     | 2               |

°    3.3 from Japanese-owned firms
*    Which represent 52% of the European market
*Source*: Calculated from EACEM and BIS Mackintosh estimates

These inroads by Japanese producers have enabled them to take control of around 40 per cent of the European consumer electronics market, over a third of this figure coming from their European plants, the remainder from imports. Yet the data for European manufacturers — their European production controlling just over a third of the market — underestimate their position. Considerable imports from the overseas plants of Philips and Thomson — in Austria, in the United States and in a number of Asian countries, including Japan — suggest that they still retain over half of the European consumer electronics market, even after taking into account that some of their European production is exported. In addition, there is strong competition between the Japanese companies themselves, with ten Japanese companies establishing European production facilities for video cassette recorders (see Table 6.5). Nevertheless, European production has been affected, with employment levels in the industry falling almost continuously from 160000 at the start of the decade to 121000 at the end, with a slight increase in 1989 possibly reflecting expansion or establishment of Japanese plants.[5]

Table 6.5   *Japanese VCR production capacity in Europe, 1989–90, in thousands*

| Firms | Production, in '000 units | Localizations |
|---|---|---|
| JVC | 1000 | Germany |
| Sony | 700* | Germany, France, Spain |
| Matsushita | 600 | Germany, France, Spain |
| Hitachi | 600 | Germany, UK |
| Sanyo | 500 | Germany, Spain |
| Sharp | 450 | UK |
| Mitsubishi Electric | 420 | UK |
| Akai Electric | 310 | France |
| Toshiba | 300 | Germany, UK |
| Funai Electric | 240 | Germany, UK |

\* Including 8 mm camcorder production
*Source*: *Japan Industrial Journal*, 18 June 1990

Figures for sales of video equipment (televisions, video recorders and camcorders) are provided in Table 6.6. Where it has not been possible from published sources to calculate sales of video equipment specifically, data are provided for consumer electronics sales in total. The published figures for Philips include considerable sales of audio, domestic appliances and personal care products (a similar problem to that with the figures for Toshiba, Hitachi, Mitsubishi Electric and NEC). Philips' sales of video equipment are likely to be a little more than those of Thomson Consumer Electronics, while Nokia is far behind. Of particular note is the number of Japanese companies with a presence in the sector, Matsushita Electric and Sony by far the most important for sales of video equipment.

*Table 6.6   Company sales of video equipment in 1990*

|  | Sales in $bn |
|---|---|
| Philips (excluding PolyGram)* | 12 |
| Thomson | 5 |
| Nokia | 1 |
| Matsushita Electric | 12 |
| Sony | 12 |
| Toshiba* | 10 |
| Hitachi* | 7 |
| Mitsubishi Electric* | 5 |
| JVC | 4 |
| Sanyo Electric | 2 |
| Sharp | 2 |
| NEC* | 2 |
| Akaï | 0.5 |

*Note*:   Sales of televisions, VCRs, camcorders and/or related equipment, except for *
which includes sales of audio, domestic appliances and/or personal care products.
*Source*: Company annual reports, and *Japan Company Handbook*, First Section, Summer 1991.

### 6.1.2   Resources for Success

The question arises as to what special elements have been necessary to compete effectively in the sector and the degree to which all these elements have been successfully captured by the European companies. This is the focus of this section, while a later section postulates how the balance of these special elements might change in the future in the light of the introduction of some form of high definition television.

Ownership of certain resources is necessary for operating in the consumer electronics industry. These are related to market share, to production facilities and to technology. For the latter, component technologies are of considerable relevance.

#### 6.1.2.1   Market share and production facilities

One of the more important ways by which companies come to possess market share is through the ownership of brands, especially where market share is not restricted by non-economic means and the market can be supplied through imports. Brands can be acquired or developed, though the latter takes time. When each country was regarded as a separate market, or where trade restrictions limited market access to certain companies, market share and ownership of production facilities were essentially interrelated. Thus, to enter a restricted market, production facilities had to be established or acquired in that market. Incompatible broadcast standards, with PAL in Germany and the United Kingdom and SECAM in France, reinforced the need for local production facilities in the television and video sectors.[6]

Philips and Thomson adopted a strategy of persuading national governments and later the European Commission to attempt to deny market access to Japanese and Korean producers. The result has been an increase in Japanese production within Europe, as mentioned above.

While this chapter considers the European markets, there may be a requirement for global market access for successful competition in the European consumer electronics industry. In this context, the Japanese and North American markets are the most important. Until now, the Japanese and North American markets have benefited from a common television standard, a factor not just for colour television products but also for video recorders, and this may place Europe behind in product launches. Improvements to the VHS system, for example, with better signal-to-noise ratios and the incorporation of digital frame stores, resulted in an NTSC version of S-VHS for the Japanese and American markets. A PAL version for most European markets took longer. The NTSC version appeared in the United States in 1987, while the PAL version was only introduced into Europe in the second half of 1988.

The Japanese market may have another important role for product development. The market for consumer electronics products in Japan is more advanced than elsewhere, partly as a result of lower spending on housing by young Japanese and a greater percentage of expenditure on consumer durables and luxury items. Japanese companies often use their home market as a launching pad for new product introductions, new products often appearing there one or two years before their launch in European or North American markets. Even when a product is launched simultaneously, the greater receptivity by the Japanese consumer may provide much higher sales levels for those companies supplying the Japanese market. This gives them time to develop their production processes and marketing strategies and refine the product, and their lower production costs and higher product quality may be beneficial when they come to tackle overseas markets.

Acquisition has been the preferred route by the surviving European producers of colour televisions to capture market share and production facilities within Europe, whereas the Japanese have — with certain exceptions — invariably established new production facilities, though sometimes by buying factories closed by their European competitors. Sanyo, for example, bought Pye's television factory at Lowestoft, while Mitsubishi bought a factory in Scotland from Tandberg. The exceptions have been few. In 1975, Sony acquired Wega and Sanyo acquired Fisher HiFi, both German companies. Hitachi and Toshiba were initially forced into joint ventures in the

United Kingdom that they did not seek, with GEC and Rank, respectively, joint ventures that did not last. The most important joint venture was that for video recorder assembly between JVC, initially with Telefunken and Thorn–EMI, later with Thomson. Matsushita established a joint venture for video recorder assembly with Blaupunkt.

### 6.1.2.2 Components and technology

In the consumer electronics industry, much of the technology is embodied in the components; in fact, the product may owe its existence to the particular combination of components used. There are also technologies underpinning some of the generic product types, as with optical discs, a product that has links with both audio and video sectors, as well as with the computer industry.

There is a range of possibilities relating to control over the components supply.[7] At one extreme, the problem can be bypassed. It is possible to purchase consumer electronics products on an OEM basis, without any production — or even product design — required. Next, it is possible to purchase all the necessary components, assembling these oneself. At the other extreme, a company may produce all its own components, before assembling these into the finished product.

Each of these options has benefits and drawbacks. Where a company has limited technological capabilities, entering a market late such as Nokia in video recorders and camcorders, purchase of finished products on an OEM basis may be the only way to retain a presence in the sector and provide a complete product range. This usually provides a lower degree of profit for the individual product.

For products such as video recorders, where the Japanese companies largely control the component technologies, access to components may be a problem, even where there is a joint venture to assemble the product. Often the Japanese are not prepared to supply the individual components, only sub-assemblies. In the mid-1980s, for example, Korean companies were unable to obtain the glass bonding bars that are processed into the chip cores used in video recorder heads. In these cases, bought-in components tend to have a high value-added, and therefore represent a high proportion of ex-factory costs for most electronics products, providing smaller margins and less flexibility from changes in exchange rates or in other costs. Purchasing components from a competitor also provides him with details of production volumes and even model types, extremely useful commercial information that enables changes in the market and changes in a company's product strategy to be identified. That most Japanese companies producing in Europe are dependent on television tubes and some other components from Philips and Thomson indicates that these problems are much more complex.

At the other extreme, producing all components in-house may provide greater control over product development. But it may require enormous capital expenditure for production, as with television picture tubes and certain types of semiconductors, while it may be difficult to keep up with the latest component technologies. Component design is important for another reason. A key factor in the success of Japanese consumer electronics producers has been their ability to integrate components. Any simplification had an enormous impact. This not only reduced the cost of the product through the use of fewer components, but also simplified the production of that product, enabling the use of automated insertion machines.

Obviously it is not always essential — or even possible — to provide all components for consumer electronics products in-house. The enormous capital costs in developing the new generation of semiconductors and the scale of production force even the Japanese producers to sell these in the open market. It is the more specialist semiconductors that will become important for the new generation of televisions and other consumer electronics equipment, and here design is the key, outside foundries being available to produce these.

The way in which these various resources are managed is an important determinant of whether capture by the company concerned is effective. Acquisitions, for example, do not guarantee the creation of a viable international consumer electronics group. Among the greatest challenges for Philips, Thomson and Nokia were to integrate their later acquisitions with the existing activities into a coherent corporate entity, especially their European operations. In each case, the process has taken longer than anticipated. Philips and Thomson have the added problem of having significant activities in the North American market.

### 6.1.3 A European Community of Interests

The balance between the various resources a company needs will change over time. Various forces will influence these changes. An important influence on the environment within which these changes have occurred has been the establishment of the European Community and the activities of the European Commission.

The removal of internal tariff barriers within the European Community in 1968, and the entry of the UK in 1973, provided the conditions to open up European markets and to enable a company to rationalize its European activities. At that time, Philips and the American company ITT were the only consumer electronics companies with a substantial proportion of their production in more than one European country, and the incentives to rationalize were not yet there. The imposition of separate broadcasting standards for colour television, and initially the use of patents to protect these markets, did much to maintain the previous situation. It was the reality of Japanese competition, more than anything else, that resulted in the achievement of a single market — at least for the consumer electronics industry.

The use of voluntary trade restraint by national governments, followed by initiatives at the European Community level, attempted to assist European firms retain these benefits.[8] In this they failed, though French government actions managed to restrict Japanese penetration while strengthening the domestic industry.

Nevertheless, the influence of the European Commission in persuading those Japanese assemblers establishing facilities in the European Community to purchase a high proportion of their components from within Europe has been beneficial to European components producers, especially Philips and Thomson. These two companies provide television tubes to all the Japanese producers assembling television sets in Europe, with the notable exception of Sony. In addition, Grundig provides components to Matsushita's video recorder joint venture in Germany.

Attempts to impose common European HDTV standards on satellite broadcasters combined with the provision of research funds — mostly Eureka rather than the European Commission — are considered in section 6.3.


## 6.2   THE SURVIVORS

This section considers the strategies adopted by Philips, Thomson and Nokia in the consumer electronics industry, with special reference to the video (television, video recorder and camcorder) sector.

### 6.2.1  Philips

Philips has been an international company almost from its beginning, with exports of considerable importance. The restrictive trade policies of the 1930s, as high tariffs were placed on finished and semi-finished goods, forced Philips to establish local production facilities throughout Europe. Thus while national markets remained separate entities in the postwar period, Philips and ITT were the sole transnationals active in the European consumer electronics industry. Fifty-seven per cent of Philips' employees were based outside the Netherlands in 1948.[9] Table 6.7 summarizes Philips' acquisitions, mergers and cooperative agreements from 1952–91.

#### 6.2.1.1  Television
Philips' prewar inheritance, with local production in the most important markets for television, made it ideally placed to benefit from the growth that was then occurring as television overtook radio as the prime product of the

sector. Acquisitions have been an important element in the expansion of Philips' European television activities in more recent years, especially in Germany and in the United Kingdom. It purchased 60 per cent of Pye in 1967, taking complete control over its radio and television interests in 1977.[10] This strengthened Philips' position in the UK market.

*Table 6.7    Philips: acquisitions, mergers and cooperative agreements, 1952–91*

| Partner | Type of operation | Date |
|---|---|---|
| Matsushita Electronics Corp. | 35:65 joint venture with Matsushita | 1952 |
| Pye (UK) | Acquisition of 60% of company | 1967 |
| Loewe Opta (Germany) | Secret acquisition of controlling stake | 1973 |
| Magnavox (US) | Acquisition | 1974 |
| Pye (UK) | Total control of radio and television interests | 1977 |
| Grundig (Germany) | Acquisition of 24.5% | 1979 |
| GTE–Sylvania (US) | Acquisition from GTE | 1981 |
| Marantz (Japan) | Share increased to 50% | 1981 |
| Grundig (Germany) | Share increased; took management control | 1984 |
| Videlec | Acquired remaining 50% share | 1984 |
| Loewe Opta (Germany) | Divestment | 1985 |
| Grundig (Germany) | Licensed video head cylinder technology from Matsushita | 1988 |
| CD–I standard | Agreement with Sony | 1988 |
| Airvision | Joint venture with Warner Brothers | 1988 |
| Marantz (Japan) | Share increased to 51% and took control | 1990 |
| JVC Malaysia | Acquisition of 50% | 1990 |
| Bang and Olufsen (Denmark) | Acquisition of 25% | 1990 |
| D2B Systems | Joint venture with Matsushita | 1990 |
| Photo CD | Jointly developed with Eastman Kodak | 1991 |

Philips attempted to acquire Grundig in 1979, but was restricted by the Federal Cartel Office from taking management control. It took a 24.5 per cent share and first option over the rest. After Thomson tried unsuccessfully to purchase Grundig, Philips was able to increase its share to 31.6 per cent in 1984 and to take management control.[11] An additional 20 per cent is owned by German and Swiss banks, the remainder by the Grundig family and foundations. In response to this acquisition, the Cartel Office gave Philips a year to sell its 15 per cent stake in Loewe Opta; it later transpired that Philips had had majority control through a secret network of investments at least since 1973.[12] These changes made Philips the world's largest producer of television sets, just ahead of Matsushita.

The expansion of Philips' television activities in Europe continues; it acquired 25 per cent of the Danish producer Bang and Olufsen in 1990. It has also moved to expand its activities outside Europe. North American Philips acquired Magnavox in 1974. The Sylvania and Philco consumer activities of GTE were added in 1981.

### 6.2.1.2  Video recorders

Philips has had a long experience with video recorders, bringing out its first consumer model in the 1970s. In the early 1980s, Philips tried unsuccessfully to establish its V-2000 video recorder in the marketplace. Some success in Germany and Austria could not be translated into success elsewhere. Thorn–EMI adopted JVC's VHS format, tying up the extremely important rental channels in the United Kingdom. Thomson refused to take a licence for V-2000; it also joined JVC, albeit through its acquisition of Telefunken after the French government blocked a direct involvement. Thus Philips found the British and French markets difficult to penetrate, while there was increasing pressure in the German market. Philips was forced to license the VHS format, its first VHS video recorder appearing in 1984, and the final decision to end production of the V-2000 was made in 1985.

Philips produced its early video recorders in Austria, and this is now its European production centre. In addition, Grundig, with whom it developed the V-2000, is producing video recorders in Nuremberg. Production for North American markets is located in Asia. Philips invested f80 m (around $47 m) in Marantz Japan in 1986 to enable it to start limited production of video recorders. Full-scale production followed, while that for VHS and S-VHS camcorders started in 1990. Philips' share in Marantz was increased to 51 per cent in 1990, giving it majority control. Philips acquired a 50 per cent share in JVC's Malaysian video recorder assembly subsidiary in the same year, and annual production was increased from 300000 to one million units, mostly for export to the United States.[13] Video recorders for the North American market and VHS and S-VHS camcorders for both Europe and North America had previously been purchased from Matsushita on an OEM basis, as are 8 mm camcorders.

At the same time that Philips was launching its video recorders on consumer markets, it was also actively involved with video discs. Its so-called Video Long Play record player or 'LaserVision' was launched regionally in the United States in 1978. That and similar products were unsuccessful. Video technology continues to develop, and video discs are again becoming a reality. The Compact Disc–Interactive (CD–I) standard is being pioneered by Philips and Sony. Agreement was reached at the end of 1988, the first professional machines marketed at the end of 1989 and the first consumer machines at the end of 1991. Photo CD, a still version developed with Eastman Kodak, was released in 1992. This is being promoted as a complement to existing 35mm film, with the customer having to go to a special shop where the negatives or slides are transferred to a compact disc.[14] The resultant 5-inch compact disc, with a capacity of 100 photographs, can be played back through a television set using a special player or a CD–I player.

Philips has established a joint company with Matsushita, D2B Systems, to promote a new standard known as a domestic data bus that will enable a range of consumer electronics equipment from different manufacturers to be operated from a single remote control handset.[15] The company is 75 per cent owned by Philips and 25 per cent by Matsushita, and both Sony and Thomson have agreed to support the new standard, which might eventually be extended to a wide range of home appliances.

### 6.2.1.3 Components and technology

A key factor in the success of Philips in the early postwar period was its control over components supply, a similar factor for the Japanese electronics companies more recently. Philips had a high degree of vertical integration, with control over components production, not only transistors but also the electronic tubes used in its televisions. From 1952, it also produced the glass for these, having one of Europe's largest custom glass-blowing facilities.

Philips is constantly moving to upgrade the range and quality of its video components activities. Acquisitions and joint ventures have been an essential part of this strategy. It has 35 per cent of a components joint venture established in 1952 in Japan with Matsushita, Matsushita Electronics Corporation, which produces television tubes and semiconductors. There have been periodic reports during the past few years that Matsushita and Philips are to collaborate in new large-size high-resolution flat screen technology, possibly including joint production facilities in Europe.[16] Philips has denied this, suggesting that its own technology is sufficient if the demand for these arises.[17] Philips and Matsushita also have a joint company in Belgium which produces batteries.

The situation is complicated by the considerable interchange of components between manufacturers. Grundig, for example, produces video head cylinders using technology from Matsushita, which incorporates these into the deck mechanisms it assembles in its own company in Germany, and some of these are then sold to Grundig.[18]

Philips is placing considerable emphasis on technology for LCDs. In 1984, Philips acquired Brown, Boveri's 50 per cent share in their joint company Videlec, which had been established to develop and produce

LCDs. In the following year, construction of a pilot facility for LCDs was started in Heerlen, the Netherlands and LCD research was intensified, the first production appearing at the end of 1988. Philips also has a production centre in Hong Kong. Philips has now started construction of an LCD plant in Eindhoven to produce 35 cm (14-inch) LCD screens, with the first commercial products expected towards the end of 1993.[19] Wider LCD screens will follow.

Philips has started incorporating LCDs into its products. In 1989, it brought out a 7.5 cm (3-inch) LCD colour television set and also as a video recorder with a similar size LCD incorporated as a monitor. The previous year, it formed its Airvision joint venture with Warner Brothers to produce entertainment and information systems incorporating LCDs for use on aeroplanes and on other forms of public transport, while its Carvision version for automobiles followed in 1989.

This commitment to component research and production has continued, though enormous losses, especially in the semiconductor field, have led to a re-evaluation of these activities. At the same time as Philips announced that it was stopping development work on one-megabit S-RAMs, it also ended production at Heerlen of direct driven LCDs for laptop computers, though it is continuing production of LCD cell and modules in Heerlen and Hong Kong.[20] It also decided to end production of CCDs in Hamburg, retaining limited production in Eindhoven for its own internal use. Philips has been able to acquire the component technologies or the components themselves necessary for it to produce video recorders and camcorders. With its close links with Matsushita, and its strong research base, this should not be a constraint in its ambitions in the consumer electronics industry. As long as this continues, a move towards a higher level of bought-in components may occur.

### 6.2.1.4 Rationalization and integration

Perhaps the greatest problem for Philips has been its historical success in an industry that was until recently nationally based. Its facilities in each European country were operated as independent operations, with considerable duplication and little coordination. They were not only separate for business purposes, but were integrated into the local political and institutional environment.

The 1980s were a decade of successive reorganizations for Philips in Europe as each successive president of the company attempted to deal with the problems, with the early rationalization concentrating especially in the consumer electronics activities and their components. These rationalizations have had a dramatic impact on Philips. From a high of 412000 employees in 1974, the Philips Group had 240000 at the end of 1991, a fall of just over

40 per cent. With the exception of the period between 1982 and 1987 when employment was stable — even with a slight growth — there has been a progressive decline throughout the period, with particularly sharp falls in employment in 1975, 1981, 1988, 1990 and 1991.

One of the main results of these rationalizations, which included selling a number of product divisions, has been to make consumer products a greater focus of the group. Consumer electronics went through a period of decline during the early 1980s, its share of net sales progressively falling to a low of 22 per cent. The second half of the 1980s saw it progressively increase to 31 per cent in 1988, though a change in the composition of the division makes an absolute comparison difficult. Several of the remnants of divisions that had been largely sold were combined with consumer electronics into a new consumer products division; these now comprise 45 per cent of total sales and 76 per cent of group income from operations, before restructuring costs were added. This new focus will make the decisions Philips takes concerning high definition television of crucial importance to the future of the group.

Concomitant with the rationalization of employment in Europe, production by Philips in Asia — especially in Singapore, Taiwan, Hong Kong and, from 1985, China — was increasing during the late 1970s and 1980s, as production of audio and low-cost video items were moved there, as well as of components. It had 27000 employees in Asia in 1988, and almost a quarter of its products came from Asia, 8 per cent from its own factories, the remaining 16 per cent bought in.

### 6.2.2 Thomson Consumer Electronics

The recent history of Thomson has been a combination of successive acquisitions, reorganizations and divestments, the divestments usually being of whole business areas. Recent French government proposals indicate that the final shape of the group has still to emerge. Table 6.8 summarizes Thomson's acquisitions, mergers and cooperative agreements from 1966–89.

By the early 1970s, the Thomson Group had brought together a large part of France's domestically-controlled production of televisions and radios, as well as of domestic appliances. The Thomson-Houston company acquired Bonnet in 1962, merged with Hotchkiss-Brandt in 1966 and acquired the Calret Group in 1968.[21] A reorganization of France's electrical engineering industry saw Thomson concentrating on electronics and domestic appliances; its Alsthom heavy equipment subsidiary was transferred to CGE.

*Table 6.8*     *Thomson Consumer Electronics: acquisitions, mergers and cooperative agreements, 1966–89*

| Partner | Type of operation | Date |
|---|---|---|
| Hotchkiss–Brandt (France) | Merger | 1966 |
| Nordmende (Germany) | Acquisition | 1978 |
| Saba (Germany) | Acquisition from GTE | 1981 |
| Dual (Germany) | Acquisition | 1982 |
| Grundig (Germany) | Failed acquisition attempt | 1982 |
| Telefunken (Germany) | Acquisition | 1983 |
| Ferguson (UK) | Acquisition | 1987 |
| GE/RCA (US) | Acquisition (of consumer electronics division) | 1987 |
| J2T (Germany/France/UK) | Acquisition with JVC of Thorn-EMI's share | 1987 |
| Dual (Germany) | Divestment | 1988 |
| Corning (in France) | Joint venture (80:20) for CRT bulb glass | 1989 |
| Toshiba (in Singapore) | Joint venture (51:49) for VCR assembly | 1989 |

At this stage, its consumer electronics operations remained largely concentrated in the French market. Thomson had little overseas manufacture and only 15 per cent of production was exported in 1974, mostly televisions to West Germany and Spain, and televisions and audio equipment to Singapore.[22] Thomson established assembly of black and white televisions and of radios in Singapore in 1977. For the next six years, acquisitions in Germany became the focus. Thomson acquired 46 per cent of the German television set producer Nordmende in 1978, increasing its share to 76 per cent the following year. Even then, just under 13 per cent of its employees were based overseas. Thomson acquired Saba from GTE in 1981.

The group was nationalized in 1982 as part of a large-scale restructuring of French industry, and Alain Gomez became chairman, a position he has held through its most expansionist period. As part of its policy to concentrate on sectors in which it could develop strong international positions and to withdraw from others, it directed its activities to defence, consumer electronics, and semiconductors. To this end, Thomson took over the defence, components and consumer electronics activities of CGE, while its telecommunications and wire and cable activities were transferred to CGE and its computer activities to CII–Honeywell–Bull.[23] Thomson's semiconductor operations were merged with those of SGS in 1987. One business it was precluded from divesting by the French government of the time was its medical electronics business, a key part in its later deal with General Electric.

It now had the capital to fund its overseas acquisition drive. Its next attempt at major overseas acquisition was not successful. It failed to acquire 75 per cent of Germany's largest consumer electronics company Grundig in 1982. This was partly due to resistance from Philips, though the circumstances were complex (see Cawson *et al.* 1990). Almost immediately afterwards, it acquired Telefunken. Four years later, it turned its attention to the UK market. Thomson acquired Ferguson from Thorn–EMI for £90 m in June 1987, making it the largest colour television producer in the United Kingdom with 16 per cent of the market. Previously, its share of the UK market had been minimal.

Thomson's largest and most significant acquisition was that of the consumer electronics activities of General Electric in July 1987; General Electric received between $500 m and $1 bn and Thomson's medical equipment activities.[24] The acquisition included 31000 employees, over two-thirds of whom were overseas, six manufacturing plants in the United States and the General Electric and RCA brands, the former only for the next ten years.[25] The acquisition made Thomson the market leader in the United States with a 23 per cent share of the colour television market, and doubled its worldwide consumer electronics turnover. General Electric had purchased RCA in 1986 but had soon realized that it would be difficult to return the consumer electronics activities to profit. As part of the deal, a joint company was established to undertake research in consumer electronics activities and to own and license RCA's extensive patents. The latter bring in about $200 m each year.[26]

While Thomson had developed its own video disc technology in the early 1980s, it has been particularly weak in video-recorder technology. It adopted a joint venture strategy to enter this sector, as a result of which it has the largest market share of the North American market and is the second largest in Europe. An agreement with JVC in 1981 for Thomson to join the J2T consortium with JVC, Thorn–EMI and Telefunken to assemble video recorders in Europe was blocked by the French government.[27] Under the agreement, Thomson would have held a 25 per cent share, and video camera production would have taken place in France to supplement video recorder production in Germany and video disc equipment production in the United Kingdom. JVC deliberately chose the strongest indigenous competitor to Philips in the three largest European markets in order to establish its standard rather than either the Sony Betamax or the Philips V-2000.[28] It was Thomson's preference for the VHS technology over the Philips V-2000 technology that was ultimately responsible for its failure to persuade Philips to allow it to acquire Grundig.[29] Thomson eventually joined the J2T consortium through the acquisition of Ferguson, and later Thomson and JVC acquired Thorn–EMI's share of their J2T video recorder joint venture for £6.5 m.[30]

More recently, Thomson has entered into another joint venture, this time with Toshiba, to assemble one million video recorders in Singapore. Thomson owns 51 per cent of the joint venture, and will receive about half the production.[31]

After its nationalization, the French government requested Thomson to establish production of hi-fi and other audio equipment in France as a means of expanding employment; previously it had imported such equipment from Asian producers.[32] Thomson acquired the German audio equipment company Dual in 1982. The policy was not successful. Its hi-fi plant in Moulins was closed in 1986.[33] Dual was sold to the German computer group Schneider the following year.[34]

The French government has now introduced plans to restructure Thomson once more. Thomson Consumer Electronics and its 45 per cent share in SGS Thomson is to be merged with the industrial activities of the state nuclear energy agency, Commissariat à L'Energie Atomique, to form Thomson CEA Industries. Alain Gomez will run the then independent Thomson-CSF. While there are few industrial linkages between the two sectors, consumer electronics and nuclear power, it would provide Thomson with the funds at a time when it is losing money and looking to invest heavily in high definition television.

### 6.2.2.1 Components and technology

Thomson produces many of its own components for its television set production. Outside this sector, it is extremely weak in component production, and this could become a major problem with a range of new video disc and audio products about to be launched and a greater integration apparent between video and audio technologies.

Thomson is a large-scale producer of television tubes, the largest in the United States and second largest in Europe. Its European operations originated in Vidéocolor, a joint venture forced upon RCA to produce SECAM tubes in France.[35] Later, its television tube output was concentrated at a plant in Italy.[36] These activities were strengthened by the purchase of Telefunken's television tube activities, while its acquisition of Ferguson provided it with a significant new outlet for its production of television tubes.[37] Almost half of its production is sold to customers outside the group, including several of the Japanese manufacturers assembling sets in Europe.

Thomson is now investing heavily in very large tubes, including those with a 16:9 format, building production lines at Anagni in Italy and Ohio in the United States in 1990 at a cost of $200 m. This is in anticipation that HDTV will change the composition of demand towards large screen sets. In order to obtain control over the quality of glass production for the Anagni plant, which was totally dependent on outside suppliers, Thomson acquired a majority holding of Corning's television glass manufacturing facility in France in 1989. Vidéocolor took an 80 per cent share in a new company, Vidéoglass, into which Corning France placed its television bulb glass manufacturing plant at Bagneaux; Corning retained 20 per cent of the new company.[38]

Some of its component work is undertaken within Thomson-CSF. Preference is usually given to defense applications rather than for consumer markets, and the benefit to Thomson Consumer Electronics is often peripheral, placing its efforts behind those of its main Japanese competitors. This is certainly the case with LCD screens. The relevance of the components activities of Thomson–CSF to Thomson Consumer Electronics will undoubtedly be diminished significantly in the future. Thomson–CSF has started to reduce its involvement with components not directly connected with its core military markets, while the company is to be separated from the Thomson Group under the new French government proposals.

Thomson's involvement with video recorders is through joint ventures, and its involvement with the components for these is limited to assembling video recorder deck mechanisms at the J2T facility at Tonnerre in France from parts provided by JVC.[39] The J2T joint venture — initially between JVC, Telefunken and Thorn–EMI and now between JVC and Thomson — shows clearly one of the problems arising from lack of control over components. J2T has been extremely successful in terms of volume growth and market penetration, its production of video recorders growing to 850000 machines in 1987. It now produces one million video recorders. Despite that, profitability was only around 1 per cent of its sales in 1987.[40] According to Thomson, the J2T plants are unlikely to remain commercially viable without a continuation of duty protection. It has been suggested that Thomson may have its own video recorder capabilities by the end of 1995, though this may not lead to immediate production and is unlikely to be based on its own components.[41]

### 6.2.2.2 Rationalization and integration

The nationalization of Thomson led to a restructuring, with its consumer products being concentrated in a new company, Thomson Grand Public, with Vidéocolor becoming one of its subsidiaries. Thomson found it extremely difficult to rationalize this division in the light of government regulations making it almost impossible to reduce its workforce.[42] By contrast, the series of acquisitions that led to the internationalization of Thomson's consumer electronics activities have provided considerable potential for rationalization overseas. Ferguson's two production facilities in the United Kingdom, for example, have both been closed, as has its research facility and the J2T video recorder plant in Newhaven.

Thomson's consumer electronics activities were completely restructured after its acquisition of General Electric's consumer electronics operations. In 1988, the acquired businesses were integrated with Thomson Grand Public to create Thomson Consumer Electronics, 100 per cent owned by Thomson S.A.

Thomson is also looking towards low cost production of televisions, a strategy first pursued in its opening production facilities in Singapore in 1977. As part of this strategy, Thomson opened a small screen television plant in Thailand in 1990 for supplying European and North American markets with televisions built around a common chassis; it has an annual capacity of one million sets. Its video recorder joint venture with Toshiba has a similar rationale, as well as emphasizing Thomson's weakness with video recorder components. Early in 1991, Thomson instituted a four-year restructuring plan and productivity drive aimed at reducing the losses that had increased during the previous two years.

### 6.2.3  Nokia

The involvement of Nokia in the consumer electronics industry shows how rapidly industrial structures can change and how companies with no involvement in an industry can become prominent within a short period of time. It has adopted a strategy of acquisitions of companies and of the international management to run them.

Nokia's entry into the industry has been remarkable. A traditional Finnish company whose activities were heavily centred on forest products, rubber, and wire and cable, and mostly in Finland, transformed itself within a little over a decade into a significant international electronics company with over 70 per cent of sales and 50 per cent of employment overseas.[43] It recognized the need for change after the oil crisis in 1973, though the pace intensified after the appointment of Kari Kairamo as chief executive in 1977. His strategy was to build up a major presence in a number of individual sectors, each of which were international businesses with growth potential. It is, for example, the world's second largest cellular telephone manufacturer as a result of its acquisition of Mobira in the late 1970s and of Technophone in 1991. The early 1980s saw Nokia's large-scale diversification, with electronics a main focus. Table 6.9 summarizes Nokia's acquisitions, mergers and cooperative agreements from 1984–92.

*Table 6.9   Nokia: acquisitions, mergers and cooperative agreements, 1984–92*

| Partner | Type of operation | Date |
| --- | --- | --- |
| Luxor (Sweden) | Acquisition of 70% | 1984 |
| Salora (Finland) | Acquisition of 58% | 1984 |
| Océanic (France) | Acquisition | 1987 |
| Standard Elektrik Lorenz (Germany) | Acquisition (of video and audio division) | 1987 |
| Selectronic (Hungary) | 35% joint venture acquired as part of SEL | 1987 |
| Luxor (Sweden) | Share increased to 90% | 1988 |
| Salora (Finland) | Share increased to 99.99% | 1988 |
| Toshiba (in Scandinavia) | Distribution agreement for Toshiba products | 1988 |
| Luxor (Sweden) | Share increased to 100% | 1989 |
| Salora (Finland) | Share increased to 100% | 1989 |
| Rundfunk Fernsehen (Germany) | Licence for assembly of televisions | 1990 |
| Nokia Smurfit (Ireland) | 50:50 joint venture for marketing | 1990 |
| Finlux (Finland) | Acquisition | 1992 |

A re-evaluation of the group's strategy was already underway when Simo Vuorilehto became chairman and chief executive following Dr Kairamo's death in December 1988. The group was reorganized into six independent product divisions and efforts were concentrated on fewer sectors. This was a period of consolidation, with amalgamations and disposals. Significant disposals continued into 1991 with the sale of Nokia Data to ICL and of Nokia's share of a tissue joint venture to James River and Ferruzzi.

These disposals reinforced its commitment to electronics, and especially to consumer electronics, its largest business unit which now accounts for 34 per cent of sales. It is Europe's third largest consumer electronics manufacturer, after Philips and Thomson. Luxor of Sweden and Salora of Finland were acquired in 1984 and Océanic of France and the video and audio division of Standard Elektrik Lorenz (SEL) of Germany in 1987. Both Océanic and SEL had originally been ITT subsidiaries; Nokia acquired Océanic, and its related companies Sonolor and Televisso, from Electrolux in August 1987 and the consumer electronics and some components activities of SEL from Alcatel in December.

The Océanic acquisition provided Nokia with access to the French market, giving it a 15 per cent share of sales of colour television sets, together with annual production facilities for 200000 television sets and a small R&D centre.[44] The acquisition of SEL's activities was by far the most important, providing access to the important German market and almost doubling Nokia's television capacity of one million sets — from 1.3 m to 2.5 million sets. SEL also produced 1.7 m picture tubes and 350000 video recorders.[45] In addition to factories in Germany, SEL had television assembly plants in Spain and Portugal, and joint ventures in Hungary (Selectronic), Malaysia (with Sanyo Electric) and Italy. The SEL acquisition resulted in a more than doubling of sales of the Consumer Electronics Division and a trebling in the number of employees.

In order to strengthen its product range, Nokia agreed in August 1988 to distribute Toshiba colour televisions and video recorders, among other products, in Scandinavia.[46] In 1990, Nokia licensed the former East German manufacturer, Kombinat Rundfunk Fernsehen Telekommunikation (RTF), to assemble television sets; Nokia supplies the components. RTF has a capacity for 500000 sets, though the collapse of Eastern European markets has restricted production to below 300000 sets.[47] The Treuhand is at present looking for a purchaser for RTF, while Nokia was not prepared to allow RTF to use the Graetz name after 1991. Nokia also established a sales joint venture in Ireland with Smurfit. Finlux, a Finnish company with an annual production of 250000 sets, was acquired in 1992.

### 6.2.3.1 Components and technology

Nokia has taken a different approach to Philips and Thomson, largely forced upon it as a result of its more recent entry into the sector. It is much more prepared to buy in components for assembly. Nokia had, for example, relied on Japanese television tubes for some of its Scandinavian television sets, at least until its acquisition of SEL. This acquisition strengthened Nokia's components activities considerably, including as it did SEL's television tube and loudspeaker manufacturing operations. Moreover, SEL was highly advanced technologically, and had introduced several sets incorporating its digital circuitry, with advanced features.

Nokia is continuing to strengthen its components technology. In 1991, a design centre for integrated circuits was opened near Paris. Finlux, its 1992 acquisition, has experience of flat panel displays, remote controls and NICAM stereo television technology, among other areas. Nokia had previously been developing liquid-crystal technology in collaboration with Stuttgart University. Nokia has also developed its active sideband optimum (ASO) technology for video recorders, which it is now attempting to license to its competitors in order to establish the standard in the marketplace.

### 6.2.3.2 Rationalization and integration

At the time of its acquisition, the Salora–Luxor Group were in the process of expanding existing production facilities and adding new ones. From 1988, one of Nokia's greatest challenges was to integrate its latter acquisitions with the earlier ones, and towards this end Nokia Graetz was formed to operate the SEL acquisitions and a new head office for the consumer electronics division was established in Geneva. The death of Timo Koski early in 1988 was a setback; he had headed the electronics division and had been responsible for the implementation of its strategy. Jacques Noels, then a senior vice president of Thomson and previously chairman and chief executive of the French operations of Texas Instrument, became president and chief executive of Nokia Consumer Electronics in June 1988.[48] There were other obstacles to be overcome. Nokia had only acquired 58 per cent of Salora in 1984; most of the remainder was held by the shipbuilding company Hollming who wanted Salora to develop as an independent operation.[49] Integrating this company had to wait until Nokia had increased its holding in Salora to 100 per cent in 1989.

As a result of these various acquisitions, Nokia had 125 different television models selling under more than ten different brand names. This presented problems both for production and for marketing. By 1991, the number of television chassis had been reduced from seventeen to three, and the model range had been reduced by half.[50] Nokia had always suffered from a lack of brand recognition, even in Scandinavia, a problem already confronted in its mobile telephone operations. The brand names were also consolidated. Its new international Euro-Model range was named ITT–Nokia — and renamed Nokia in 1991. Other brands that will be retained include Finlux, Luxor, Oceanic, Salora, and Schaub Lorenz. In each of its markets, no more than three brands were to be sold.

Continuing losses by the Consumer Electronics Division and a 17 per cent fall in net sales in 1991 forced further rationalization. Following the acquisition of Finlux, television manufacturing is to be concentrated in Bochum in Germany and in Finland. In 1988, Nokia had television production facilities in Finland, Sweden, France and Germany, and television assembly in Spain and Portugal.

## 6.3   INTO THE FUTURE HIGH DEFINITION TELEVISION[51]

### 6.3.1  Background

This section provides a short case history of high definition television (HDTV), considering the main parameters involved in its introduction and the ways in which it could influence the future development of the consumer electronics industry. As there are still many uncertainties, no definitive conclusion will be drawn on whether and how high definition television will progress in Europe, though the main factors that will determine this are set out.

The European television sector is suffering from saturated markets and overcapacity. The dominance of Japanese manufacturers in product development and components for VCRs and camcorders, which have been among the few growth sectors remaining, have denied European companies — assembling under licence and dependent on Japanese components — the profits that would help support the television manufacturing side of their businesses. It is against this situation, at a time of recession in several of the key markets such as in the United Kingdom, with overcapacity at the same time as sales of televisions are actually falling, that the introduction of high definition television is taking place.

To overcome the saturation of the television market worldwide, manufacturers — Japanese as well as European — have been keen to introduce a significant new technology that could revitalize the market. High definition television has been identified as just such a step in technological development for television broadcasting. It has been the revolution that the consumer electronics companies have been desperately seeking, and this desperation underlies many of the problems that have accompanied its commercialization so far. It was also seen as a large potential market for the semiconductor industry. The European situation had the added aim to deny Japanese manufacturers the dominance of the European market that would have ensued from adoption of Japanese standards.

The predominant television standards at present are the NTSC system used in the United States and Japan, the PAL system used in much of Europe and the SECAM standard used in France. A significant difference relates to the number of scanning lines in each picture frame — 525 lines with NTSC, 625 lines with PAL, and 819 lines with SECAM. The range of HDTV standards that have been proposed are likewise diverse. Work on a Japanese HDTV system began at NHK in 1968. Its 1125/60 Multiple Sub-Nyquist Encoding (MUSE) system, also known as Hi-Vision, was announced in 1981. Since then, Europe and the United States have tried to catch up with Japanese developments.

The European Multiplexed Analogue Components (MAC) system provides for a 1250/50 format — 1250 scanning lines (broadcast at 625 lines) at 50 Hz with 25 frames per second. The resolution of the screen will be greater than for PAL — 700000 pixels, compared to 120000. Two features of particular relevance are the adoption of a cinema-style 16:9 screen aspect ratio and the incorporation of digital sound with the use of eight sound channels. There are two intermediate standards, D-MAC in the United Kingdom and D2-MAC in France and Germany. D-MAC was originally developed by the Independent Broadcasting Authority in the United Kingdom. Both of these provide a 625-line picture at a picture resolution of only 50 per cent greater than the existing PAL system. D-MAC provides eight sound channels against only four for D2-MAC. The latter has a narrower bandwidth which can be compressed for transmitting through cable.

The Federal Communications Commission (FCC) is expected to make its decision on an HDTV broadcast standard for the United States in early 1993 on the basis of tests undertaken on five candidates and completed in 1992. Compatibility with existing NTSC transmissions is an essential part of this, and priority will be given to existing broadcasters. Digital signal transmission is almost certain to be a facet of the chosen system, with advanced compression algorithms used to transmit the picture on a 6 MHz channel. Neither MUSE nor MAC use digital signal transmissions, and thereby require much wider bandwidths for full-feature HDTV transmissions.

### 6.3.2  Introducing High Definition Television in Europe

The proposed introduction of high definition television broadcasting within Europe requires a number of elements.

### 6.3.2.1  Support by governments and by the European Commission
The ability of European manufacturers to create a European standard for HDTV owes much to the support of governments and the European Commission. This commitment was shown at the meeting of the heads of state at the end of 1988. Two years before that, the all-important Eureka research programme, Eureka-95 HDTV, was launched, while the European Commission has also played a role.

The EU95 HDTV project within Eureka brings together the main equipment providers, and has been led by Philips and Thomson in a cooperative research programme. It started in 1986, the first phase concerned with standards proposals and equipment feasibility tests. The second phase, which started in July 1990, is the most important. It is concerned with implementation, and specifically with pilot use and then market introduction of the wide-screen versions of D2-MAC equipment. The final phase will be the full broadcast in HD-MAC format; on present indications, its introduction will depend heavily on the success of the second phase. There is also a part of the JESSI semiconductor programme that is involved with developing special semiconductors for HDTV use.

The European Commission's role has been threefold. First, it adopted a broadcasting directive to try to force the adoption of the D-MAC and D2-MAC standards for satellite broadcasting. The Astra telecommunications satellite, which was outside the directive's coverage, was used for television broadcasts, and using the PAL system. This forced a re-evaluation of the directive, which expired at the end of 1991. The initial proposals for its revision, backed by the equipment producers, became highly controversial, with a compromise proposal eventually adopted. Under this, D2-MAC broadcasts will only be necessary on wide-screen broadcasts or on new satellite services from 1995. More significantly, it was agreed that financial measures would be offered to induce broadcasters to use the D2-MAC standard in parallel to their PAL or SECAM broadcasts. This marks a new direction which mirrors certain aspects of the FCC policy in the United States, though the details have still to be worked out.

Second, the European Commission accepted the provision of French state aid to Thomson, part of which was to assist in the funding of HDTV.

Finally, the European Commission incorporated into several community research and other programmes elements relevant to the overall HDTV programme. The two most important are RACE 1080 and Vision 1250. The former is a $51 m programme concerned with cameras and other HDTV broadcast equipment. Its participants are solely Philips or Thomson subsidiaries. Vision 1250 was established in July 1990 to build upon the work of RACE 1080 by promoting the HD-MAC standard within Europe. It is composed of the main equipment manufacturers, broadcasters, and television and film producers. Its activities include provision of HDTV production facilities and assistance to broadcasters and other programme makers in adopting the new standards.

### 6.3.2.2 Satellite and cable broadcasts

As mentioned, the compromises that are necessary in terrestrial broadcasting of the MAC standard due to the smaller bandwidth available provide few benefits for the viewer or for the broadcaster. It is in satellite broadcasting where the greatest benefits lie, with cable somewhere in between. HDTV in Japan was devised with satellite transmission in mind for these reasons. In Europe too, the development of the MAC standards has been inextricably bound up with the future of satellite television.

Each European country has a separate broadcasting structure, and political involvement is to some extent present in its administration, whether to control it or to liberalize it. Direct broadcasting by satellite (DBS) in Europe is even more influenced by political concerns. It is not solely a broadcasting medium. It impinges on several other sectors that have important public profiles, especially aerospace (for satellite manufacture) and the Ariane programme for launching the satellites. As a result, political considerations have accompanied the DBS programmes in the United Kingdom, France and Germany. Moreover, its importance to the introduction of HDTV has brought the European Commission into the frame.

The introduction of satellite broadcasting has suffered a number of setbacks that slowed its introduction. In the United Kingdom, there were problems of financing DBS, while technical problems with the launch vehicle and the satellites themselves hindered the French and German programmes.

When the BSB service was finally introduced in the UK, using the D-MAC standard, it had been preceded by Sky Television, which was broadcast in

PAL on a low-power telecommunications satellite which was outside the scope of the European Commission's broadcasting directive. After a short time, Sky took over the struggling BSB, stopping the D-MAC broadcasts and marking an end to the first attempt to introduce MAC into the United Kingdom. Germany also wanted to renege on its commitment to D2-MAC broadcasts from its satellites, though intervention by the French president brought them back into line.

It will be decisions by the consumer that will determine the success of D2-MAC for French and German satellite television. Success, if it comes, will take time. Changes in cable technology, with the potential from moves to UHF signals and the future introduction of broadband ISDN, creates additional uncertainty and possible opportunities.

### 6.3.2.3 Equipment, components and software

A television is no longer an isolated product but part of an interrelated range of audiovisual entertainment equipment, of which the video recorder and the camcorder are important elements. The initial plans by Thomson, in particular, centre on HDTV sets. There are no plans for upgrading the video recorder or camcorder, S-VHS being seen as sufficient for the moment.

The development of new equipment suitable for high definition television use requires changes in many of the components. While there might be some differences between the components required for equipment used for the US system, using as it does compressed digital signal transmission, as compared with the systems adopted in Japan and Europe, many of these components will be common. It has become clear that neither Thomson nor Nokia, nor probably Philips, have the range of component technologies necessary for improving the equipment to the required standard. They will be dependent on Japanese component suppliers to an even greater extent than before. Even for HDTV set production, both Philips and Thomson recognize that within two years of the start of HD-MAC broadcasting, licences for the equipment will be available to the Japanese producers.

An area of particular concern is the large screens necessary to show the consumer visible differences from traditional television pictures. Research into large LCD screens is proving more difficult, the main problem being the ability to obtain high yields in a situation where each pixel is controlled by a transistor or a diode and each of these has to be working effectively. Again, the research activities of Japanese companies in this area are better funded and wider-ranging than those in Europe.

As the market develops, video software might become a factor influencing the speed of adoption and assisting the profitability of the companies involved. Certainly, the acquisition of Columbia Pictures for $4.6 bn by Sony in 1989, MCA for $6 bn by Matsushita, and a 12.5 per cent share of Time Warner Entertainments by Toshiba and C. Itoh for $1 bn and a 12.5 per cent share of the interest payments on $7 bn of debt, would be of considerable importance if it gave these companies a way of influencing the introduction of new standards of broadcasting or of consumer equipment. Thomson and Nokia have no involvement in this area. Neither Philips nor its 79 per cent subsidiary PolyGram have the resources to make such an investment, though PolyGram announced in September 1991 that it is to invest $200 m in expanding its film activities. Philips is also aiming to build up an international retail group for video software as a means of obtaining greater control over the software and increasing the potential for new video formats. It has made investments in Belgium, Holland, the United Kingdom and the United States, and others are likely.

### 6.3.2.3 Consumer acceptance

This is essential for the introduction of HDTV. Of special relevance is the degree to which the new HDTV standards will be purely relevant to a replacement market, or whether viewers will regard this as a significant new facility that would justify an acceleration of the replacement cycle and an upgrading. Linked to this is whether the consumer would only want higher quality if the price of the equipment were not too different from that for existing sets, and here there may be differences in various countries. Another factor of relevance is the possibility of improving PAL, and this option has become known as PAL Plus. This might reduce the benefit to the consumer of D2-MAC, whose position as an intermediate standard is already being questioned.


## 6.4   CONCLUSIONS

### 6.4.1   The Survivors

Each of the European colour television producers has followed a different strategy. This is partly a reflection of the historical timing and speed of change in these companies' strategies. Nothing about their present position within the industry was inevitable, and the European consumer electronics industry in 1992 could have had a very different complexion. Both Philips and Thomson considered withdrawing from the consumer electronics sector during the past decade, while Nokia's entry owed much to a remarkable chief executive. The withdrawal of companies such as ITT, GTE and Thorn–EMI, was crucial to the process, as was the complex way in which the futures of both Telefunken and Grundig were resolved.

At the beginning of this process of consolidation, Philips was the only one of the three that was a transnational, with operations throughout Europe. This was a hindrance in many ways, as the rationalization of large numbers of small television assembly plants and even smaller components plants took the better part of two decades. Philips was prepared to make acquisitions, though these do not appear to have followed any coherent strategy, and there was certainly no urgency to integrate them into the group until forced to do so. Alone among the three companies, it has two significant manufacturing joint ventures in Japan, one for components and one for finished products.

Philips' main strength has been the wide spread of its activities and the depth of its technology. This has on occasion resulted in failed products, as with its V-2000 video recorder, or in products that have succeeded, but for others more than for Philips, as with the cassette recorder. Nevertheless, this has given it considerable negotiating power to enable it to continue to license the technology of others. Cross-licensing is a way for all companies in the sector to reduce their risk, though some get preference. The close relationship Philips has had with Matsushita for many years has been especially important in this regard. Its involvement in the music business through PolyGram is another strength for the company.

Thomson's expansion strategy has been largely country based. It was only when Thomson was well established in the French market, having absorbed most of the indigenous producers, that it ventured overseas. Then, it was preoccupied with the German market for some years as there followed four acquisitions, and the attempted acquisition of Grundig, followed by the divestment of Dual some years later. The acquisition of the UK's largest television set manufacturer, Ferguson, was followed soon afterwards by its largest move, the acquisition of the consumer electronics activities of General Electric. The challenge for Thomson was to rationalize these activities and integrate them into a global company. It was less daunting than the task facing Philips but has taken longer than expected.

Its strategy for video recorders, camcorders and related products was very different, and represents what could become an important weakness for Thomson. It is dependent on JVC for its video recorder technology, with assembly in a joint venture between the two. More recently, it established another video recorder joint venture, this time with Toshiba in Singapore. Camcorders are purchased on an OEM basis from the Far East. This denies Thomson the profits that would have followed had it been able to master the technology, and makes its television activities more vulnerable to any change in the market environment. With many of the new television facilities, such as PIP (i.e., the ability to see more than one programme on the screen at any time), controlled through the video recorder, this increases its vulnerability.

Nokia came late to the market; it was only in 1987 that it expanded its production into France and Germany, having previously been preoccupied with Scandinavia. Its main operational problem was to integrate these companies into an effective unit. Continuing problems in its German activities, and falling market share generally, are making it difficult for the group to build on this position. That it has to rely largely on a higher level of bought-in components — forced upon it by the nature of its expansion — could make it vulnerable in the future, though it is strengthening this side of its activities.

Returning to the resources necessary for survival in the industry, Philips and Thomson have acquired market share, especially with their North American activities, and production facilities followed their acquisitions. The Japanese market presents a different situation. Philips has some production capabilities for the Japanese market through its Marantz subsidiary, while neither Thomson nor Nokia have any significant presence there. Thomson is weaker than Philips in non-television production, in components and in the basic technologies underpinning new products. Its weaknesses in these are heightened by its limited involvement in the Japanese market.

Despite this, each company has been able to overcome its main weaknesses and seems to have reached a level of viability — at least in terms of today's technologies and products.

### 6.4.2 High Definition Television

The introduction of high definition television requires a number of separate — and in some cases independent — elements to be successfully introduced before it will take-off. Some of the decisions have been forced on the promoters of the systems. The wide bandwidth necessary for the analogue MAC standard dictated the use of satellite transmission to obtain the greatest benefits. That required creating a new market, using special receiving equipment and new channels with untried programme formats. Broadcasts through cable or terrestrial routes were possible, but the difference of quality was not perceptible to the viewer. Even with satellite, large-screen televisions are necessary for the viewer to see a difference. The LCD screens that are proposed to reduce the enormous sizes needed for large-screen CRTs have still to be developed. It should not be forgotten that the introduction of colour television in the United States took over fifteen years before the market began to accept the new technology.

The attempts to introduce HDTV in Europe will increasingly highlight the weaknesses of European producers. In the case of Thomson and Nokia, their weaknesses in components, in non-television equipment and video software, are prominent. Whereas one of the aims of the European MAC programme was to promote greater collaboration between Philips and Thomson in maintaining a viable European consumer electronics sector, the result could be to push Philips closer to Matsushita to maintain an involvement in future video standards and peripheral equipment, such as camcorders, together with the components needed to produce them.

Should HDTV take much longer to develop in Europe than envisaged, it is possible that Nokia will withdraw from the consumer electronics sector. It is certainly the weakest European producer, with a lower market share and dependency on Japanese components. If it follows its previous strategies, its withdrawal could be through merging into a joint venture with another producer before selling out completely.

The impact of HDTV on the involvement of Philips and Thomson in the consumer electronics industry is less certain, and may be influenced by events in North America, where both are actively involved in the FCC deliberations on a digital HDTV standard for the United States. It is not inconceivable that an American standard could eventually (though not in this century) be adopted for both Europe and Japan should HD-MAC and MUSE prove to be commercial disasters — assuming of course that the chosen American system is introduced successfully. Both Philips and Thomson recognize that a digital standard will eventually come and will replace HD-MAC. The uncertainty relates to the timing. Their involvement in the North American and European markets enables them to retain a foot in both camps.

As to the role and success of government and European Community actions, it is too soon to come to a definitive conclusion. Certainly the adoption of HDTV as a key element of industrial policy was not clearly thought out at the beginning. It developed slowly, with the different elements coming together as the disparate technological and political aspects changed. The next twelve months will be again important as all parties involved have to recognize the implications of the slow adoption of D2-MAC for the introduction of HD-MAC. Many believed that such an intermediate step was not justified, and that HD-MAC should have been the only standard. The failure of the broadcasting directive to impose a solution on the new medium of satellite broadcasting implies that more subtle and more clearly thought-out policies are needed.

### 6.4.3  External Growth Strategies

In the context of the balance between external growth strategies and internally generated strategies, acquisitions have been an essential part of the strategies for acquiring production facilities and market share in the television sector for each of the companies. In most cases, these acquisitions were followed by rationalization of the group's overall television production facilities, suggesting that acquisition of market share provided the rationale for these. Several of these acquisitions also resulted in acquisition of facilities for video recorder production and in television tubes.

Philips is by far the most international of the companies, largely for historical reasons. The more recent expansion of Philips' television manufacturing operations has been through acquisitions — especially in the United States, Germany and the United Kingdom. More recently, it acquired a small share in a Danish producer.

Thomson and Nokia have followed a geographical strategy. Thomson consolidated its position in France through mergers and acquisitions before making a number of acquisitions in Germany, followed by an acquisition in the United Kingdom and a large-scale acquisition in the United States. The acquisition in the United Kingdom has turned out to be the acquisition of market share rather than production facilities, as all the production (and research) facilities acquired have since been closed, including the J2T video recorder assembly plant. Nokia consolidated its position in Scandinavian markets through acquisition before acquiring companies in France and Germany.

In video recorders, Philips produced its own equipment in Austria and acquired Grundig's facilities, while purchasing others on an OEM basis from Matsushita. More recently, VCR production has begun at Marantz in Japan, following which Philips acquired majority control, while a 50 per cent share was acquired in JVC's video recorder assembly operation in Malaysia. Thomson acquired video recorder production facilities through its acquisition of GE/RCA in the United States and entered an existing joint venture with JVC, later establishing a joint venture with Toshiba in Singapore. Thomson purchases camcorders on an OEM basis. Nokia obtained the video recorder production facilities of Standard Elektrik Lorenz (SEL) by acquisition, while it entered into a distribution agreement with Toshiba for Scandinavian markets.

In components, Philips has a long-standing components joint venture with Matsushita, which produces television tubes, among other products. Grundig produces video head cylinders using technology from Matsushita; Matsushita then incorporates these into deck mechanisms, some of which are sold to Grundig. It also acquired Brown, Boveri's 50 per cent share in a joint company established to develop and produce LCDs, and formed a joint venture with Warner Brothers to produce entertainment and information systems incorporating LCDs for use on aeroplanes. Philips has a much stronger technological base than Thomson and Nokia. This is reflected in its various technical joint ventures, whether for standards such as CD-I or D2B, or for equipment, such as Photo CD.

Thomson produces many of its own components for television set production. Its initial television tube production was as part of a joint venture with RCA, while it also obtained some production facilities through its acquisition of Telefunken. Thomson's most important remaining collaboration in the component field is its joint venture with Corning for CRT bulb glass. Nokia buys in many of its components, though it acquired television tube and loudspeaker production through its SEL acquisition and is expanding these facilities. Its acquisition of Finlux has strengthened its components activities further.

Overall, the European companies have followed a strategy of controlling their own production facilities where possible. Acquisition has been a key element for television set production and for some television tube production. Where this has not been possible, joint ventures have been pursued, as with the various Philips and Thomson joint ventures for video recorder assembly. Purchasing components and some equipment such as camcorders from Japanese competitors is still necessary, especially for Nokia. Philips' long-standing component joint venture with Matsushita is particularly important in enabling it to maintain access to component technologies, while the depth of its own technology is also relevant.

High definition television offers a contrast to this. No one European company has the capabilities to develop and promote a new HDTV system alone. The public nature of broadcasting, and the enormous sums and risks involved, have forced collaboration between the three equipment producers — Philips, Thomson and Nokia — as well as with the terrestrial and satellite broadcasting organizations. This has been in terms of setting standards and undertaking pre-competitive research. The European Community, together with the French and German governments, and the Eureka research programmes, have had an active role to play in terms of funding research and introducing satellite broadcasting regulation. In addition, Philips has acquired a number of retailers involved in video software as a means of obtaining greater control over the software.

These programmes have specifically excluded the Japanese companies. The next stage will see a change of emphasis externally. The need for an involvement with whichever standard is adopted in the United States and the need for access to Japanese component technologies will be obvious. This will result in both Thomson and Philips taking out licences for US equipment, should these be available. At the same time, Philips will undoubtedly increase its links with Matsushita for peripheral equipment and the components required.

# NOTES

1. An example of the withdrawal from the video sector, Blaupunkt, the Robert Bosch subsidiary, stopped producing colour televisions in 1985. While it has a joint venture for video recorder assembly with Matsushita, this must be regarded as more of a financial investment than a serious attempt to remain in the consumer electronics sector. The main rationale of this company is in the production of car radios.
2. EACEM data in European Commission (1992), pp12–17.
3. A detailed analysis of the development of the Korean electronics industry and its dependence on Japanese components and OEM agreements may be found in Bloom (1992).
4. EACEM data in European Commission (1992), pp12–17, 18

5. EACEM data in European Commission (1992), pp12–19.
6. For many years, 405-line VHF monochrome broadcasts coexisted side by side with 625-line UHF colour broadcasts in the United Kingdom.
7. A more detailed treatment appears in Bloom (1992), pp68–74, 89–91.
8. The best treatment of the political framework within which the consumer electronics industry in France, Germany and the United Kingdom has operated, including the international trading regime that has been created, appears in Cawson *et al.* (1990).
9. *Philips* (1955), p30.
10. Geddes and Bussey (1991), pp380, 410.
11. The background to the purchase is complex. The so-called Grundig/Thomson-Brandt Affair is considered in some depth in Cawson *et al.* (1990), pp279–281, 297–307, and in Pearce and Sutton (1985), pp154–64.
12. A company in which BMW has a 30 per cent share took a 26 per cent share holding in Loewe Opta; in November 1985 BMW took an additional 23 per cent share itself as a prelude for technological cooperation. 'BMW Lifts Loewe Opta Stake', *Financial Times*, 29 November 1985, p22.
13. *Nihon Keizai Shimbun*, 2 June 1990, p8.
14. *HFD-Retailing Home Furnishings*, 2 September 1991, p61; *Computergram*, 2 October 1991.
15. 'NV Philips, Matsushita Plan Domestic Digital Bus Venture', *Wall Street Journal and Dow Jones News Wire*, 13 June 1990.
16. 'Matsushita Electric, Philips To Establish Joint European CRT Production Base', *Nihon Keizai Shimbun*, 10 June 1989, p1; 'Matsushita Offers Know-How To Philips — Troubled Firm Needs Technology Boost', *Nikkei Weekly*, 21 September 1991.
17. 'Philips Denies It Is To Make Matsushita's TV Picture Tubes In Britain', *Financial Times*, 14 September 1991, p4.
18. 'Survey of Japan', *Financial Times*, 11 July 1988, pVIII.
19. 'Philips To Invest in Flat LCD Screens', *Financieele Dagblad* (Amsterdam), 12 October 1991.
20. *Wall Street Journal and Dow Jones News Wire*, 4 September 1990.
21. Stopford, Dunning and Haberich (1980), p1040.
22. Savary (1984), pp20, 23, 26n, 60, 68.
23. Savary (1984), pp163–6, 182–4. The political background to the asset swap with CGE is provided in Cawson *et al.* (1990), pp128–36.
24. Paul Betts and Anatole Kaletsky, 'Thomson Buys GE Consumer Electronics Arm', *Financial Times*, 23 July 1987, p1.
25. *1988 U.S. Industrial Outlook*, International Trade Administration, U.S. Department of Commerce, January 1988, 47–6.
26. *Business Week (International)*, 10 August 1987, p15.
27. Turner, (1987), pp43–46.
28. Cawson *et al.* (1990), p255.
29. 'Europe's High-Tech Struggle', *Newsweek*, 28 March 1983, pp9–10.
30. *Financial Times*, 9 November 1987, p8, and 10 December 1987, p29.
31. 'Toshiba, Thomson SA Unit Plan To Build Singapore Plant', *Wall Street Journal*, 1 December 1989.
32. Ballance and Sinclair (1983), p139.
33. Cawson *et al.* (1990), p278.
34. Haig Simonian, 'Schneider To Buy 50 Per Cent Stake In Dual', *Financial Times*, 25 August 1987, p21; Andrew Fisher, 'Schneiders Program Expansion: The ambitions of a German computer group', *Financial Times*, 12 August 1988, p22.
35. Cawson *et al.* (1990), pp265–6.
36. Guy de Jonquières (1985), 'Consumer Electronics: Why Europe Is So Rattled', *Financial Times*, 7 May, p20.
37. Guy de Jonquières (1987), 'Against The Odds: The Thomson-Thorn EMI Deal', *Financial Times*, 19 June, p20.
38. 'Corning To Transfer French TV Bulb Assets to French Firm', *Wall Street Journal and Dow Jones News Wire*, 24 April 1989.
39. Pearce and Sutton (1985), p163.

40. Terry Dodsworth (1987), 'Thorn-EMI To Pull Out of Video Venture', *Financial Times*, 9 November, p8.
41. Jacques Vannier (1990), Head of Planning and Strategy at Thomson, quoted in 'Technology: Power game with too much to lose — Thomson's part in the HDTV standards battle', *Financial Times*, 17 July, p12.
42. Cawson *et al.* (1990), pp277–8.
43. In 1977, only 26 per cent of Nokia's sales were from exports and 9 per cent from overseas subsidiaries. See Stopford (1982) p790.
44. *Financial Times*, 1 September 1987, p21.
45. *Financial Times*, 16 December 1987, p23.
46. *Financial Times Business Reports — Media Monitor*, 1 September 1988.
47. *Frankfurter Allgemeine Zeitung*, 7 September 1991, p16.
48. *Financial Times*, 23 June 1988, p15. (He left the group at the end of 1991.)
49. *Financial Times*, 30 December 1988, p15.
50. *The Economist* (London), 9 February 1991, vol. 318, no. 7693.
51. This section benefited from interviews with a number of European organizations involved with HDTV.

# APPENDIX: Glossary

*Camcorder*: Combined camera and video recorder

*CD–I*: Compact disc-interactive

*CRT*: Cathode ray tube

*CTV*: Colour television

*DBS*: Direct broadcast by satellite

*EACEM*: European Association of Consumer Electronics Manufacturers

*FCC*: United States' Federal Communications Commission

*JVC*: Japan Victor Corporation. Matsushita Electric Industrial has a 52.4 per cent share in this company.

*LCD*: Liquid crystal display

*MAC*: Multiplexed analogue components. The full HD-MAC system is a European HDTV standard providing for 1250 scanning lines (broadcast at 625 lines) at 50 Hz. with 25 frames per second. It adopts a 16:9 screen aspect ratio and incorporates digital sound using eight sound channels. D2-MAC and (in the UK) D-MAC were introduced as intermediate MAC standards towards a full-function HD-MAC standard. They both provide for 625 scanning lines, D-MAC providing eight sound channels, D2-MAC only four sound channels and thereby a narrower bandwidth.

*MUSE*: Multiple sub-nyquist encoding. The MUSE system — also known as Hi-Vision — is a Japanese HDTV standard providing for 1125 scanning lines at 60 Hz.

*NTSC*: National Television Systems Committee. The NTSC television broadcasting standard is used in the United States and Japan. It provides 525 scanning lines.

*OEM*: Original equipment manufacture. OEM occurs when a company arranges for an item to be produced with its logo or brand name on it, even though that company is not the producer. It is a type of subcontracting relationship. It is especially prominent in the consumer electronics industry where retailers like to promote their image or manufacturers want to extend their product range. It is equivalent to own brand merchandise in food retailing.

*PAL*: Phase alternating lines. The PAL television broadcasting standard is used in much of Europe. It provides 625 scanning lines.

*SECAM*: Séquentiel couleur à mémoire. The SECAM television broadcasting standard is used in France. It provides 819 scanning lines.

*S-VHS*: Super-VHS. This is an improvement over VHS. It records monochrome and colour signal components separately. The tape uses metal alloy particles rather than the iron oxide of standard tape. The shorter wavelengths that are possible are used to increase the frequency range of the recording, thereby improving quality.

*VCR*: Video cassette recorder

*VHS*: Video home system. The dominant video recorder format, VHS was developed by JVC. The initial machines were two-head helical-scanning using azimuth recording and half-inch tape in a cassette.

*VHS-C*: A format developed for use in camcorders. The main difference is the smaller cassette which contains less tape.

## BIBLIOGRAPHY

Ballance, R. and Sinclair, S. (1983), *Collapse and Survival: Industry Strategies in a Changing World,* George Allen and Unwin, London.

Bloom, M. D. H. (1992), *Technological Change and the Korean Electronics Industry,* OECD Development Centre, Paris.

Cawson, A., Morgan, K., Webber, D., Holmes P. and Stevens, A. (1990), *Hostile Brothers. Competition and Closure in the European Electronics Industry,* Clarendon Press, Oxfod.

European Commission (1991), *Panorama of EC Industries 1991–2*, Commission of the European Communities, Brussels.

European Commission (1992), *Panorama of EC Industry. Statistical Supplement 1992*, Commission of the European Communities, Brussels.

Geddes, K. and Bussey G. (1991), *The Setmakers. A History of the Radio and Television Industry,* BREMA, London.

*Japan Company Handbook,* First Section, Summer 1991, Toyo Keizai Inc., Tokyo.

Pearce, J. and Sutton, J. (1985), *Protection and Industrial Policy in Europe,* Routledge and Kegan Paul, for The Royal Institute of International Affairs, London.

*Philips. N.V. Philips Gloeilampenfabrieken*, A Study Prepared by Smith, Barney & Co., New York, 1955.

Savary, J. (1984), *French Multinationals,* Pinter, London.

Stopford, J. M., Dunning, J. H. and Haberich, K. O. (1980), *The World Directory of Multinational Enterprises,* Macmillan, London.

Stopford, J. M (1982), *The World Directory of Multinational Enterprises 1982–3,* Macmillan, London.

Turner, L. (1982), Consumer Electronics: The Colour Television Case in Louis Turner and Neil McMullen (eds), *The Newly Industrializing Countries: Trade and Adjustment* (George Allen and Unwin for the Royal Institute of International Affairs, London, pp48–68.

Turner, L. (ed.) (1987), *Industrial Collaboration With Japan,* Chatham House Papers Number 34, Routledge and Kegan Paul, London.

*1988 U.S. Industrial Outlook*, International Trade Administration, U.S. Department of Commerce, January 1988.

# 7. The Chemical Industry*

## Frédérique Sachwald

The chemical industry is one of the largest in the industrial countries. It is a traditional industry which is dominated by very large firms but also populated by numerous smaller specialized firms. At the beginning of the 1980s, the chemical industry underwent a serious crisis, followed by restructuring and new strategic moves. The industry has had to adapt to the evolution of the competitive game due to the interaction of several factors: the entry of new competitors, the acceleration of the rhythm of innovation in some segments and the challenge of stricter environmental regulations.

The largest firms have simultaneously concentrated on fewer activities and become more internationalized. They have largely resorted to acquisitions and other external growth operations to implement their strategies; the chemical industry has been one of the most active within the merger wave of the 1980s.[1] Europe has traditionally held a strong competitive position in chemicals,[2] which could have been threatened by the evolution of the competitive game. This chapter shows that European companies have retained their rank in the chemical industry.

This chapter is divided into three parts. It starts with an analysis of the characteristics of the industry and of the competitive game. Section 7.2 explains the background of the crisis at the beginning of the 1980s and questions the notion of mature industry. It also assesses the competitive position, particularly that of Europe. Section 7.3 analyses the development of firms' strategies to adapt to these changes. It focuses on external growth operations (M&A and joint ventures) which have been extremely numerous in this industry. Two segments (paints and agrochemicals) and two companies (ICI and Rhône-Poulenc) are studied more closely.

## 7.1  CHARACTERISTICS OF THE INDUSTRY

The chemical industry is an important component of industrial activity, however its frontiers are fuzzy and it is important to define them. The main

---

\* The author would like to thank the Union des Industries Chimiques (UIC), and in particular Mr Carrère who has provided me with valuable information. She also wishes to acknowledge the help of Eurostaf which gave her one of their reports.

specific characteristics of the industry, which relate to its complexity, have important consequences for its structure and economics.

### 7.1.1  Definition

Chemistry is the science of molecules and the chemical industry can be defined as the industry which transforms materials by manipulating molecules. Such a definition shows how wide the industry can be. Historically, producers have progressively explored new areas and feedstocks.[3] There is no single definition of the chemical industry and it is interesting to discuss the boundaries of the industry and to detail somewhat the products which are included.

The simplest way to define the industry is probably to resort to one of the statistical classifications in use. The American industrial classification (SIC) includes the following segments: industrial inorganic chemicals, industrial organic chemicals, plastics materials and synthetics, drugs, soaps, cleaners and toilet goods, paints and allied products, agricultural chemicals, miscellaneous chemical products. The international classification of products for external trade (SITC) considers the following groups of products within its chemical category (section 5): organic chemicals, inorganic chemicals, products for dyeing and tanning, medical and pharmaceutical products, oils and products for perfumes, toilet and cleaning, fertilizers, explosives, artificial plastics, ethers, resins, etc., and other chemical products. In its annual bulletin of trade in chemical products, the United Nations adopts a wider definition of the chemical industry. To the SITC chemicals, it adds the following products: synthetic rubber and rubber substitutes, synthetic and regenerated artificial fibres, yarn of continuous synthetic fibres, yarn of continuous regenerated fibres, and photographic and cinematographic supplies.

These examples of definition show the diversity of the industry and the difficulty in precisely defining its boundaries. This is critical for a number of chemical dependent products, such as pharmaceuticals, detergents or toiletries and cosmetics. With a definition comparable to those given above, the chemical industry is one of the largest in industrial countries. In 1990, the world chemical production amounted to $1130 bn. It represents about 10 per cent of industrial value added in the EC, the percentage being equivalent for the United States and lower for Japan. The importance and the diversity of the chemical industry can also be illustrated by listing the destinations of the products. Table 7.1 gives the final destination of the chemical products.

Table 7.2 provides another disaggregation of the industry; it shows the relative importance of the different segments within the industry.

*Table 7.1    Final destination of chemicals, in %*

| | |
|---|---|
| Consumer goods | 27.4 |
| Services (hospital, transportation, research centres) | 19.2 |
| Agriculture | 10.3 |
| Textiles/clothes | 6.6 |
| Metal industry | 6.5 |
| Construction | 5.7 |
| Paper/printing | 3.9 |
| Electric and electronic industries | 3.8 |
| Car industry | 3.6 |
| Food industry | 3.1 |
| Mechanical construction | 2.4 |
| Other industries | 7.5 |

*Source*: CEFIC (Comité Européen des Fédérations de l'Industrie Chimique)

*Table 7.2    Importance of the different segments in the European chemical industry in 1989, in %*

| Composition of industry, turnover in %, 1989 | |
|---|---|
| Organic chemicals | 19 |
| Pharmaceuticals | 17 |
| Inorganic chemicals | 8 |
| Plastics | 7 |
| Perfumes, cosmetics | 7 |
| Paints, varnishes | 6 |
| Fibres | 4 |
| Adhesives | 1 |
| Fertilizers | 2 |
| Agrochemicals | 2 |
| Other | 23 |

*Note*: This composition can vary a great deal from year to year. In 1988, plastics accounted for 13% and fertilizers for 7%.
*Source*: CEFIC, DRI Europe

This chapter deals with the chemical industry as defined above, but does not analyse pharmaceuticals in detail. The case of pharmaceuticals is particularly interesting to consider when dealing with the definition of the chemical industry. From the technical point of view, pharmaceuticals certainly belong to chemicals. They are connected to segments of the chemical industry mainly through the industrial organic route. Since the end of the nineteenth century, pharmaceuticals have traditionally drawn from the same science and technology base; now, both pharmaceutical and chemical firms are becoming interested in biotechnology. But pharmaceuticals have strong specific characteristics which explain why this study chose to isolate it in a separate chapter (Chapter 8).

### 7.1.2  Complexity

The diversity and complexity of the industry is largely due to the fact that chemistry transforms basic feedstocks first into intermediate products and then makes further changes. Some high value products result from numerous transformations which may take place in different firms. The technical interdependences can be illustrated with the petrochemical chain which represents 40 per cent of chemical production.[4] Figure A.1 in the appendix sketches the chain going from gas or crude petroleum to several stages of intermediaries and to petrochemical-dependent products. It focuses on the uses of the four main basic petrochemical products: ethylene, propylene (the two simplest olefins), butadiene (diolefin) and benzene (the simplest aromatic compound).

Technical chains result in strong interdependences between the stages of the industry. As a result, the industry is itself one of its main clients; more than 25 per cent of the product shipments are consumed within the industry, the proportion being higher for petrochemicals (Bozdogan 1989). More generally, chemicals are largely consumed by industries; about half the output is used as intermediate materials (Table 7.1 above).

The chemical interdependences can entail production constraints. Upstream in particular, technical relationships require the different units of transformation to be located quite close to one another. Beside cost considerations, producers are constrained by the fact that some products are dangerous. Ethylene for example is difficult to transport in bulk in liquid form. More generally, the location of petroleum chemical facilities has always been subject to a number of limiting factors due to the combination of technical relationships and of pollution and transportation problems. Production units should not be too far from important consumption centres, but their location also has to take into consideration the access to raw material resources (Waddams 1978; Molle and Wever 1984). Localization and configuration of production units are also constrained by the size of basic chemical units (see below).

The chemical industry is characterized by numerous possibilities of substitution. First, different raw materials can be used to produce certain molecules. Second, in a number of cases, different products can be used for the same application. Figure A.2 in the appendix for example shows several routes to produce such key molecules as acrylonitrile or vinyl acetate. There are also different routes to produce more finished products such as Nylon 6/6; as is often the case, each route has been developed by a different firm (Spitz 1988). The substitutability of finished products is very common for plastics. Pipes can be produced with polyvinyl chloride (PVC), with high density polyethylene (HDPE) or polyphenylethers (PPO). To illustrate substitution, one can also use the example of materials, and performance material in particular. The end user requires the material to possess a number of characteristics, in terms of resistance to heat or solvents, for example. Different plastics or composite materials present specific 'packages' of such characteristics and can thus be quite finely adapted to needs (Cohendet, Ledoux et Zuscovitch 1988).

The complexity of the industry results from the above technical characteristics, which are reinforced by the fact that it encompasses thousands of products.

### 7.1.3  Structure and Organization of the Industry

In order to analyse the relationship between the technical characteristics of the industry and the competitive game, it is useful to distinguish relevant groups within the industry. The groupings used above referred to products according either to their origin (organic and non-organic chemicals) or to their final destination (pharmaceuticals, agrochemicals, etc.). A complementary classification groups products according to their degree of transformation which corresponds to specific technical conditions, which themselves impact on the organization of firms and the competitive game.

There are several ways to take the degree of transformation of products into account. Generally, the degree of transformation, or the length of the production chain, is correlated with the price of the product and with its degree of differentiation. However, this is not an exact rule. Let us retain the price per kilo and the degree of differentiation. From this point of view, chemicals can be classified into three broad categories. Commodities are traditionally defined as goods produced in large quantities, at rather low price per ton and not differentiated. Manufacturers offer similar products which correspond to widely recognized specifications. Specialities, on the contrary, are characterized by their final destination, their function. They are produced in relatively small quantities and command a high price. Differentiation largely rests on formulation, which means that the research effort is oriented towards applications. Since they fulfil a specific function, they can be tailored to the clients' needs and incorporate a service element. There are for example numerous additives and chemicals 'for' plastics, papers, paints, food or petrochemical products. Along the production chain, fine chemicals are 'between' commodities and formulation or specialities (a number of specialities are formulated using fine chemicals). Quantities are small and high prices correspond to high value-added and important research efforts. The composition of products is specified, but many molecules are protected by patents. Table 7.3 summarizes the above distinctions.

*Table 7.3    Main characteristics of the different types of products within the chemical industry*

| Characteristics | Basic chemicals | Fine chemicals | Specialities |
|---|---|---|---|
| Product life cycle* | Long | Medium | Short/medium |
| Scope in number of products | Several hundred | Thousands | More than 10000 |
| Production level* | >10000 | <10000 t/year | Very variable |
| Price* | <5$US/kg | >5$US/kg | >5$US/kg |
| Product differentiation | None | Very low | Very high |
| Value added | Low | High | High |
| Capital intensity | High | Medium | Medium/low |
| Objectives for the R&D department | Process improvement | Process development | Application/product |
| Key success factors** | | | |
| Cost level | ××× | ×× | × |
| Technical service | – | ×× | ××× |
| Strong relationships with clients | – | ××× | ××× |

\*    Typically, there may be exceptions
\*\*   Relative importance: × weak; ×× medium; ××× high
*Source*: Eurostaf (1991)

The classification in the table is useful because the products have specific technical and economic characteristics, however, the categories cannot always be clearly separated.[5]

### 7.1.3.1  A capital intensive industry

Traditionally, the chemical industry is highly capital-intensive. In 1985, the stock of fixed capital per full-time equivalent employee in the American chemical industry was $92300, compared with $42900 for manufacturing as a whole (Bozdogan 1989). The production of basic chemicals is particularly capital-intensive, one of the reasons being the large size of production units.

After the Second World War, petrochemicals grew very fast. Plant size also tended to grow. At first, increasing capacity often only involved the duplication of reaction systems, by building two reaction trains instead of one, for example. By the early 1960s, a number of firms were working on the concept of large single-train plants.[6] The stake here is of course econo-mies of scale. In the 1960s the industry had become more competitive with new entrants, and cost competition had become a more important issue. Firms worked on scaling up equipment sizes and it became possible to build large single-train plants for many petrochemical products so as to exploit economies of scale. Table 7.4 shows typical cost reductions due to larger scale of production for bulk chemicals.

*Table 7.4   Typical economics of manufacture for a bulk organic chemical product (in cents/lb)*

| Costs | Small plant[*] | Large plant[*] ('single train') |
|---|---|---|
| *Variable costs* | | |
| Raw materials | 5.2 | 5.2 |
| Utilities | 1.0 | 0.7 |
| Other (e.g. catalyst) | 0.5 | 0.5 |
| Total variable costs | 6.7 | 6.4 |
| *Fixed costs* | | |
| Labour | 0.6 | 0.2 |
| Maintenance | 1.6 | 0.8 |
| Depreciation | 4.0 | 2.0 |
| Overheads | 2.0 | 1.0 |
| Total fixed costs | 8.2 | 4.0 |
| *Total production costs* (before return on investment) | 14.9 | 10.4 |

\* For this fictitious example, the 'small' plant has been assumed to have a capacity of 100 000 000 lb/yr and an investment cost of $40 000 000 while the 'large' plant has a capacity of 600 000 000 lb/yr and an investment cost of $110 000 000.
*Source*: Spitz (1988)

The single-train concept was first applied to the two most important petro-chemicals, ammonia and ethylene. Then its diffusion was promoted by engineering contractors who could make the latest technology available to the entire industry. Figure A.3 in the appendix shows the large increase in the size of ethylene plant capacity.

In order to update this figure, one should note that 1 bn lb/year ethylene plants have been built, but economies of scale do not make it interesting to go beyond this figure and in this respect technology has stabilized. Moreover, very large units can become financially risky in a cyclical industry since they reduce flexibility; costs may be lower in smaller units for which capacity utilization can stay higher.[7] In the chemical industry, economies of experience also meant substantial reductions in costs as total production of a product grew over the years.

Some of the segments of the chemical industry are also very research-intensive; in the United States in 1985, company-funded R&D expenditures accounted for 4.7 per cent of sales, while the same ratio was 2.8 per cent for manufacturing as a whole. The chemical industry is generally classified as 'moderately research intensive', with a ratio of R&D expenditures to production equal to 2.3 per cent in 1980.[8] Research intensity tends to be the greatest for certain fine chemicals and specialities, pharmaceuticals being the most prominent example, where in 1980 the ratio of R&D expenditures to production was 8.7 per cent, which makes it the fourth most research-intensive sector (after aerospace, computers and electronic components). Moreover, research intensity tends to increase in pharmaceuticals as in various fields of the chemical industry. New sectors which are more or less directly related to chemicals, such as biotechnology and composite materials, also require important research efforts.

### 7.1.3.2  A cyclical industry

Since chemicals are largely intermediary products, the industry tends to be cyclical. Table 7.1 above shows that a large part of the outlets for chemicals are themselves quite sensitive to the level of general demand; construction and automobiles are often mentioned in this respect, but it is also the case of other activities like metalwork. This explains the strong correlation between the level of gross domestic product per head and the chemical consumption per head (Blunden 1986).

For a quite long period after the Second World War the cyclical character has been obscured by the substitution of petrochemical products to traditional products. This was more particularly the case for plastics and synthetic fibres which penetrated both industrial and domestic activities. Table 7.5 shows both the dependence of chemicals on general economic activity and the quicker growth rate of petrochemicals and plastics in particular.

The surge in demand for plastics, synthetic fibres and other petrochemicals has had a perverse effect. Producers, especially in Europe, where penetration of substitutes to natural products was more recent, started to expect very high petrochemical growth rates. But in the 1970s, the chemical industry was particularly hit by the oil crisis. It first suffered as a cyclical industry, and the blow was reinforced by its dependence on petroleum feedstocks and the fact that the rate of penetration of petrochemicals started to slow at the end of the 1960s.

*Table 7.5   Average annual rate of growth in Western Europe, in %*

|  | 1960–73 | 1980–88 |
|---|---|---|
| GNP (OECD) | 5.5 | 2.9 |
| Hydrocarbons | 7.0 | 1.0 |
| Chemicals (OECD) | 10.0 | 3.3* |
| of which:  petrochemicals | 15.0 | 3.5 |
| of which:  plastics | 15.0 | 5.0 |
| synthetic fibres | 20.0 | 3.5 |
| synthetic rubber | 10.0 | 1.5 |
| nitrogen fertilizers | 8.0 | 1.0 |

\*   Western Europe
*Source*: Masseron (1991)

### 7.1.3.3  The competitive game

The technical characteristics which have been underlined above influence the pattern of competition in the industry. Two aspects are discussed below: first, the allocation of the chemical production around the world and, second, the question of concentration.

Chemical production is concentrated in industrial countries. Table 7.6 shows that countries from the Triad account for more than 70 per cent of world production. Table 7.7 lists the main exporting countries.

*Table 7.6   Distribution of world chemical production, in % for 1989*

| | |
|---|---|
| EEC | 28.1 |
| Other Europe | 3.1 |
| North America | 23.3 |
| Planned economies | 15.7 |
| Japan | 14.6 |
| Rest of the world | 15.3 |

*Source*: CE (1991)

The intermediary character of the chemical industry explains its location. Historically, demands from other industries have been a strong incentive to innovation (Landes 1969). Today, the presence of sophisticated industries and demanding clients is widely recognized as an asset for innovation and competitiveness (see Chapter 2). These remarks also help to explain the structure of the industry. The chemical industry really took off in the nineteenth century, largely from the production of dyestuff.[9] Some of the pioneer firms developed their expertise in coal-chemistry and became strong innovators; a number of these firms are still among the first chemical producers in the world (Chandler 1990). Moreover, in the past, the industry has been prone to cartels. The 1930s and IG Farben may be far away; during the 1980s, some firms have been condemned for cooperation by the European Commission competition authority.

*Table 7.7    Main chemical-exporting countries, in $bn and %*

| Exporting countries | Share in world exports, % | | | Value, $bn |
|---|---|---|---|---|
| | 1970 | 1980 | 1990 | 1990 |
| Germany | 20.7 | 19.3 | 20.1 | 69.3 |
| United States | 17.8 | 16.7 | 14.6 | 50.5 |
| France | 9.4 | 11.2 | 11.3 | 39.0 |
| UK | 10.1 | 9.8 | 9.0 | 31.2 |
| Netherlands | 7.5 | 8.0 | 7.2 | 24.9 |
| Japan | 8.0 | 6.8 | 7.3 | 25.2 |
| Belgium | 5.8 | 6.0 | 6.6 | 22.7 |
| Switzerland | 1.4 | 1.7 | 1.9 | 6.5 |
| Italy | 6.3 | 6.6 | 6.6 | 22.9 |
| Canada | 3.5 | 3.2 | 3.1 | 10.8 |
| Spain | 0.9 | 1.9 | 2.5 | 8.5 |
| Sweden | 1.5 | 1.5 | 1.8 | 6.3 |
| China | 0.8 | 1.1 | 1.9 | 6.5 |
| Total | 93.7 | 93.8 | 93.9 | 324.3 |

*Source*: GATT (1989–90)

The discussion of the structure of the industry is difficult because some important producers are not in fact chemical firms. The largest chemical firms are among the largest firms in the world, but some are divisions of petroleum companies and in Japan, most of the chemical companies are part of large diversified groups. Table 7.8 lists the 40 largest chemical industry groups.

*Table 7.8    The 40 largest chemical groups in 1989 and their sales in chemicals ($m)*

| Groups (Nationality) | Chemical sales | Global sales | % in chemicals | Total employment |
|---|---|---|---|---|
| 1. Hoechst (D) | 25 763 | 27 091 | 95.1 | 169 295 |
| 2. Bayer (D) | 25 557 | 25 557 | 100.0 | 170 200 |
| 3. BASF (D) | 24 710 | 28 105 | 87.9 | 136 990 |
| 4. Du Pont de Nemours (US) | 21 402 | 35 534 | 60.2 | 145 787 |
| 5. ICI (UK) | 21 159 | 21 159 | 100.0 | 133 800 |
| 6. Dow chemical (US) | 17 000 | 17 000 | 96.6 | 62 100 |
| 7. Unilever (UK–NL) | 14 105 | 34 628 | 40.7 | 300 000 |
| 8. Procter and Gamble (US) | 13 000 | 21 398 | 60.7 | 79 000 |
| 9. Rhône–Poulenc (F) | 12 608 | 12 608 | 100.0 | 86 024 |
| 10. Ciba–Geigy (CH) | 12 188 | 13 316 | 91.5 | 92 553 |
| 11. Enimont (I) | 12 054 | 12 054 | 100.0 | 52 656 |
| 12. Royal Dutch/Shell (UK/NL) | 11 024 | 83 805 | 13.1 | 135 000 |
| 13. Exxon (US) | 10 559 | 95 173 | 11.1 | 104 000 |
| 14. Elf Aquitaine (F) | 9 824 | 25 848 | 38 | 78 179 |
| 15. Akzo (NL) | 9 299 | 9 788 | 95.0 | 70 900 |
| 16. Union carbide (US) | 8 744 | 8 744 | 100.0 | 45 987 |
| 17. Monsanto (US) | 8 681 | 8 681 | 100.0 | 42 179 |
| 18. Bristol-Myers Squibb (US) | 7 962 | 9 189 | 86.6 | 54 100 |
| 19. Eastman Kodak (US) | 7 531 | 18 398 | 40.9 | 137 750 |
| 20. Solvay (B) | 7 181 | 7 181 | 100.0 | 45 011 |
| 21. Sandoz (CH) | 7 180 | 8 075 | 88.9 | 50 655 |
| 22. Smithkline Beecham (UK–US) | 7 088 | 7 867 | 90.1 | 62 800 |
| 23. Henkel (D) | 6 870 | 6 870 | 100.0 | 38 145 |
| 24. Merck and Co. (US) | 6 550 | 6 550 | 100.0 | 34 500 |
| 25. Roche (CH) | 6 329 | 6 342 | 99.9 | 50 203 |
| 26. Mitsubishi Kasei (J) | 6 108 | 7 306 | 83.6 | – |
| 27. 3M (US) | 6 000 | 11 990 | 50.0 | 87 584 |
| 28. Sumitomo Chemical (J) | 5 949 | 6 536 | 91.0 | 12 537 |
| 29. Pfizer (US) | 5 671 | 5 671 | 100.0 | 42 100 |
| 30. Asahi Chemical Industry (J) | 5 600 | 7 449 | 75.2 | 25 931 |
| 31. Norsk Hydro (N) | 5 531 | 10 025 | 55.2 | 32 782 |
| 32. American Home Products (US) | 5 323 | 6 747 | 78.9 | 50 816 |
| 33. Hüls (D) | 5 273 | 5 273 | 100.0 | 31 289 |
| 34. Occidental petroleum (UK) | 5 203 | 20 068 | 25.9 | 53 500 |
| 35. British Petroleum (UK) | 5 053 | 47 618 | 10.6 | 118 000 |
| 36. DSM (NL) | 5 027 | 5 628 | 98.3 | 29 500 |
| 37. Johnson and Johnson (US) | 5 000 | 9 757 | 51.2 | – |
| 38. Formosa Plastics (Taïwan) | 5 000 | 6 300 | 79.4 | – |
| 39. American Cyanamid (US) | 4 825 | 4 825 | 100.0 | 33 000 |
| 40. Colgate–Palmolive (US) | 4 750 | 5 039 | 94.3 | – |

*Note:*    Different classifications do not include the same companies. This one is quite comprehensive and gives oil companies and consumer products groups which have substantial chemical operations.

*Source*: *Chimie actualités*, November 1990

Despite these large firms, the chemical industry as a whole is not among the most concentrated; the question is rather the extent to which these firms dominate the industry (Cook and Sharp 1991). The first ten chemical groups account for 17 per cent of world chemical sales, the first twenty for 25 per cent and the first 100 for 50 per cent (Fourtou 1989). At the regional level, concentration is also moderate for chemicals as a whole. Table 7.9 gives the degree of concentration for the first one, four and ten firms in the industrial regions.

*Table 7.9*   *Concentration in sales for chemicals and allied products, share of firms in %, 1975–86[a]*

|  | First firm | First four firms | First ten firms |
|---|---|---|---|
| *European Community* | | | |
| 1975 | 5.9 | 19.0 | 34.1 |
| 1980 | 4.9 | 17.8 | 30.2 |
| 1986 | 4.0 | 15.0 | 26.2 |
| *United States* | | | |
| 1975 | 5.8 | 14.3 | 23.1 |
| 1980 | 5.8 | 14.3 | 22.0 |
| 1986 | 5.4 | 13.8 | 22.3 |
| *Japan* | | | |
| 1975 | 5.0 | 14.1 | 25.4 |
| 1980 | 3.8 | 13.2 | 25.6 |
| 1986 | 3.4 | 12.4 | 23.7 |

[a]   1975–84
*Source*: CEC (1988)

The degree of concentration is thus much lower than in the automobile industry for example, both at the global level and for regions or countries.[10] However, the concentration is quite high in certain specific market segments. The MIT report (Bozdogan 1989) gives precise figures for the United States. It calculates that the eight largest firms account for at least 50 per cent of the total value of shipments in fourteen out of the 28 market segments which correspond to broad product categories.

The degree of concentration is lower in the larger segments of the industry, like industrial organic chemicals, plastics, pharmaceuticals or paints. These less concentrated segments represent more than 60 per cent of the American chemical industry in the mid-1980s. More generally, the high degree of substitutability mentioned above is a source of competition.

The degree of concentration in the different segments and the above discussion of the technical characteristics of the industry lead to the conclusion that the competitive game differs according to markets within chemicals. The American data show that concentration is higher in smaller and more specific markets. This is of course due to the sheer size of markets, but also to the fact that the larger ones correspond to non-differentiated products. For commodities, the absence of differentiation and low barriers to entry command price competition. Basic chemicals is a capital intensive business, but the technology is quite stable and has been disseminated by licences and engineering companies (Spitz 1988). In such circumstances, the advantage to low cost resources can be crucial to successful entry. For specialities and some fine chemicals, the name of the game is differentiation, which means that innovation can be the route to entry — the development of start-ups in biotechnology can serve as an illustration. These considerations of the competitive game will be elaborated below with the discussion of firms' strategies to enter specific markets.

## 7.2 CRISIS AND QUESTIONS TO THE INDUSTRY

The characteristics of the industry as they have been examined above largely remain but, since the 1970s, some have been altered and the competitive game has evolved. This section deals with these changes in order to understand and discuss firms' strategies in the 1980s (section 7.3).

### 7.2.1 A Mature Industry?

At the end of the 1970s, an image of mature industry, or even of decline was attached to chemicals, and to petrochemicals in particular. The relevance of the notion of mature industry is discussed in general in Sachwald (1989); here, it is used as a way to deal with the elements of the crisis in chemicals.

The notion of maturity is linked to that of a 'product life cycle'. The S-shape of the life cycle is well known, it sketches the volume of the market for a product (or an industry) under consideration as time passes. The fundamental variable is thus the rate of growth of demand. The S-shape is determined by a set of factors which differ from product to product; examples are given in Figure 7.1.

*Figure 7.1    Current positions along the life cycle for the main plastics*

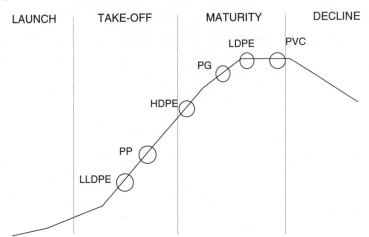

*Source*: Groupe Ferruzzi, quoted in Eurostaf (1991)

The notion of the product life cycle is of course more relevant in analysing the evolution of products than sets of products or industries and, in general, predictions from the cycle are least reliable for the last part of the product life. When a product has reached maturity, that is to say when its penetration, or sales volume, ceases to grow, it is not necessarily condemned to disappear, or even to become marginal. This is so because a mature sector may be able to enter a renewal phase, which depends crucially on its ability to innovate from its technical base. On this point, see Chapter 3.

In order to judge the degree of maturity of the chemical industry, it is important to examine the elements which the life cycle model identifies as characteristic. An industry is supposed to enter the decline phase when the rate of growth slows down, production capacity corresponds to market size and the degree of competition, (including international competition) tends to increase and profits fall. Innovations tend to be few. According to the model, the process of production evolves along the cycle. When the rate of growth slows down, the process of production is supposed to be stabilized and well known. This means that knowledge of the process is less of a barrier to entry and that new firms can enter the market. Since the 1970s, the chemical industry has experienced some of these evolutions, but not all of them to the same degree and some sub-sectors experience different conditions.

From the point of view of the process of production, basic chemicals show signs of maturity or even decline. The process is well known both among chemical companies and among specialized engineering firms. As seen above (section 7.1.3.1), this process is scale-intensive and competition affects price. Since the end of the 1960s, this configuration has led to investment battles and a cyclical tendency to overcapacity. Apart from technical characteristics, it can be explained by the high rate of growth of the industry which had been remarkable; petrochemicals had become 'too attractive' (Spitz 1988). This attractiveness led to three sources of overcapacity in the 1970s. First, chemical companies were struck by 'the large-plant syndrome' (Spitz 1988; Landau 1989), which meant that new investments were gigantic and could represent a substantial increase in total capacity. Second, high prospective profits attracted firms from other sectors, mostly oil companies because of the technical links, but also firms engaged in diverse industries (W. R. Grace from shipping, Beaunit from textiles for example). Third, developing countries wanted to enter chemicals, especially when they had access to low cost raw materials. These developments have led to a decrease in the rate of return (Spitz 1988; Landau 1989).

In these circumstances, a dramatic modification of the cost structure was bound to have severe consequences for the industry. The oil shocks dramatically increased the pressure on the industry and led to a serious crisis at the beginning of the 1980s. Producers with access to low cost energy were of course favoured and their share in total production increased. Figure 7.2 shows the progression of Eastern Europe countries and developing countries, essentially from the Middle East, as producers of polymers.

*Figure 7.2    Evolution of polymer production*

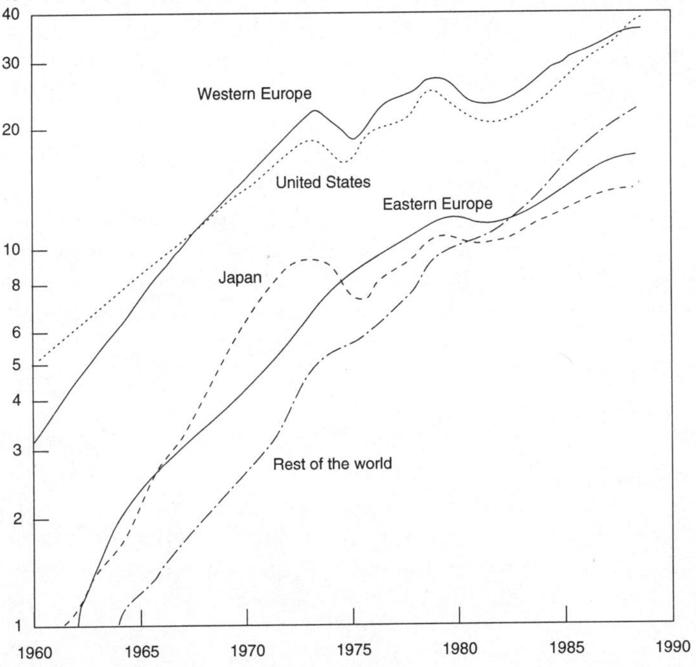

*Source:* Masseron (1991)

This aroused concerns in developed countries during the 1980s (Blunden 1986), but the threat has progressed relatively slowly. Moreover, a number of these new projects were established in collaboration with traditional producers, through joint ventures in particular (El Kadiri 1989). The most recent developments are discussed in section 7.2.3.2.

From the point of view of products, a large part of the industry also corresponds to the description of maturity. Petrochemicals in general and plastics in particular exemplify the process. Plastics have enjoyed high rates of growth as they progressively substituted for natural materials. But by the early 1970s, the possibilities of substitution were largely exhausted. In 1970, 85 per cent of the market for cleansers went to synthetic detergents, but this progression was stopped because consumers prefer traditional soaps. The rate of replacement of natural rubber by synthetics peaked in 1972 below 80 per cent. By 1973, synthetic fibres had taken over 70 per cent of the fibre market and their progression stopped (Bennett and Kline 1987).

So, by the 1970s, the chemical industry could be described as mature both in terms of process and products; competition, both domestic and international, had also become tougher. Other elements of diagnosis are less clear-cut, namely the rate of innovation and the fact that the industry is not homogeneous.

It is particularly difficult to evaluate the rate of innovation in so diverse an industry. Moreover, authors disagree on this question. Some consider that it had substantially slowed down by the end of the 1960s (Sharp and West 1982, Bennett and Kline 1987). According to Bennett and Kline, out of the 63 major innovations which they identify between 1930 and the early 1980s, 40 were introduced in the 1930s and 1940s, 20 during the next two decades and only three since then. Others, on the contrary, underline a number of process innovations as well as some new fields for product innovation, such as technical plastics and composite materials (Spitz 1988; Landau 1989). They consider that some process innovations have been somewhat wasted by the fact that their inventor has licensed widely, thus creating more competition and preventing a better return on investment in research. The case of the Unipol technology for producing linear low density polyethylene (LLDPE) is considered as exemplary in this respect. Anyhow, it is important to insist on the diversity of the industry; some sub-sectors for which innovation is an important factor in the competitive game invest heavily in research.

Finally, the role of innovation in the competitive process can be judged by the evolution of R&D spending. It seems that there was a relative decline in this during the 1970s, but the tendency has been reversed in the 1980s (Bennett and Kline 1987; Landau 1989).

## 7.2.2 Environmental Concerns and Constraints

After the oil shocks, the chemical industry was confronted with the need to reduce its energy and materials consumption. It did achieve good results in this respect (OECD 1985). But since the 1980s, the environmental challenge has been looming larger.

The chemical industry is of course one of the most affected by environmental regulations. Precise specifications differ according to countries, but the tendency is general. In Europe, the Commission wants to harmonize the rules since firms from the countries which have stricter regulations are disadvantaged. But as a whole, Europe is considered as behind the United States in the implementation of regulations.

German chemical groups have started to complain about the costs of environmental legislation. More generally, spending on the environment tends to cut into capital investment.[11] Chemical companies progressively integrate environmental thinking into their organization so that it costs less than cleaning at the end of the process. Besides environmental costs are a source of differentiation and the theme of ecology has been heavily exploited, both to market specific products and for institutional communication.

To end this brief section on environmental concerns in the chemical industry, one should mention the preoccupation with biotechnology, which progressively gives rise to new rules and constrains firms (from Germany and Switzerland in particular).

## 7.2.3 Evolution of Competitive Positions

Developed countries still dominate the chemical industry.[12] This section details the European position and provides some prospective data on the evolution of production in developing countries.

### 7.2.3.1 Europe maintains its strong position

As a producer, Europe is in a dominant position. In 1989, Western Europe accounted for 30 per cent of world production (EEC 28 per cent) and Eastern Europe another 15 per cent; North America accounts for 24 per cent and Japan 17 per cent.[13] European domination is even stronger in terms of exports; in 1990, the main chemical producers from the EEC[14] accounted for 50 per cent of world exports, Switzerland for 2 per cent and Sweden for 2 per cent (see Table 7.7).

The large chemical companies are multinational and their positions are not exactly consistent with that of their country of origin. European companies are heavily represented on top of the list given in Table 7.8 (section 7.1.3.3). There are four European firms among the five first ones and six among the first ten. In terms of turnover, European firms represent 65 per cent of the first ten firms.[15] These companies have important international operations and they do not necessarily contribute heavily to export from the country of origin; this is especially the case for small countries such as Switzerland.

Since the chemical industry is already largely internationalized, and beyond regional areas, no dramatic effects are expected from the Single Market. The most important factors have been the evolution of regulation with respect to environmental concerns and standards.[16]

### 7.2.3.2 Recent evolutions

During the 1980s, industrial countries maintained their dominance, but new entrants have progressed and will again in the near future. Producers from developing countries are on much more dynamic markets. Table 7.10 shows that demand will rise rapidly in developing countries in the future and that production will rise even more rapidly. This is particularly the case for Latin America and the Far East. Korea for example has an impressive programme of investment in ethylene.[17]

*Table 7.10  Forecasts for demand and production in world chemicals, annual rate of growth, in %*

|  | Production | | Demand | |
|---|---|---|---|---|
|  | 1989–95 | 1995–2000 | 1989–95 | 1995–2000 |
| Western Europe | 2.9 | 3.2 | 3.0 | 3.2 |
| North America | 3.0 | 3.1 | 3.4 | 3.8 |
| Latin America | 6.5 | 8.9 | 5.0 | 7.0 |
| Eastern Europe | 3.1 | 4.3 | 3.0 | 5.0 |
| Asia/Australia | 1.6 | 3.3 | 3.4 | 3.6 |
| Africa | 4.4 | 4.4 | 3.5 | 3.5 |
| Far East* | 5.8 | 7.8 | 5.1 | 5.7 |
| Indian sub-continent | 6.3 | 7.1 | 6.0 | 6.5 |

\* Except China
*Source*: Eurostaf (1991)

Developing countries concentrate on commodities and thus the evolution of their share is more impressive on those markets (Figure 7.2). Investment from developing countries constitutes a source of preoccupation because overcapacities are building up for the 1990s as a consequence of the good rates of growth during the second half of the 1980s. Moreover, reform and investment in Eastern Europe may add to the difficulties in basic chemicals.

## 7.3  FIRMS' STRATEGIES

### 7.3.1  Broad Strategic Options

At the beginning of the 1980s, the chemical industry was in a tough crisis. The first priority was to rationalize production and increase productivity. This programme entailed reduction in capacity and technical improvements, in regard to energy consumption in particular. The restructuring phase started earlier in the United States and was quicker (Bower 1986; Bozdogan 1989). Besides capacity reductions and sales of certain activities, American companies have tended to retreat from Europe where they had a number of operations (Bennett and Kline 1987; Spitz 1988). Instead, American companies undertook production in countries where feedstock sources were cheap, often with a local partner.

After this phase of restructuring, firms have been able to implement strategies which mostly aimed at reducing vulnerability to economic cycles. After 1985, firms followed similar strategies which consisted of two main elements: portfolio reshuffling and deeper internationalization. In many cases, these moves are tightly complementary.

The objective of reduced dependence on cyclical chemicals made it necessary to diversify away from basic chemicals and look for high value-added products. The latter were considered as less risky; during the 1970s and the beginning of the 1980s, speciality chemicals continued to report high profitability. In a number of cases, specialities also realized higher prospective growth rates. There was thus a quite general move towards fine and speciality chemicals. As seen above, these chemical products require a high degree of innovativeness and good adaptation to specific needs; some are service-intensive. This means that markets are highly fragmented, but also that the diffusion of products often has to be worldwide in order to cover research costs. In speciality chemicals in particular, a number of markets tend to globalize. In such cases the objective is to choose an area and try to be among the first producers on a worldwide basis.

Internationalization is also considered as increasingly necessary as innovation and market adaptation become more important in the competitive game. The objective is to be present on sophisticated markets in order to be well informed, both about the newest technical developments and about potential clients' needs. This may require delocalized production, but also delocalized research facilities. Thus, European producers tend to open research laboratories in the United States for some specific fields; European and American firms open R&D facilities in Japan, both to follow technological developments and to be nearer to new clients who themselves tend to internationalize, particularly in the automobile industry.

These tendencies have not been uniform; the degree of differentiation depended on the point of departure of firms. In a few cases, like that of Bayer, the portfolio had been worked on during the 1970s and changes were less necessary. Besides, some firms like BASF regard vertical integration as a positive feature of their structure. Du Pont de Nemours presents a quite specific profile in this respect since it is now both a chemical company and an oil company.[18] Moreover, the implementation of these strategic moves has been only partly successful. Oil companies have had difficulties in adapting their high-volume production habits to the requirements of specialized operations. Arco for example eventually sold its speciality business (Bennett and Kline 1987).

Finally, speciality chemicals represent a limited share of the sector; during the 1980s in the United States they made up about 22 per cent of the sales of industrial chemicals. With relatively limited opportunities in specialities, chemical companies also sought openings in other sectors: first, in chemically based consumer goods; second, in new technologies such as biotechnology or advanced materials; and third in systems and equipment. Here again, there are differences in firms' choices. A number of European firms have been operating pharmaceutical operations for a long time, but for American firms it was less often the case and the move has been rather recent.

The different aspects of the definition and implementation of these strategic operations will be discussed below. Section 7.3.2 relies on general data to show the role of external growth in firms' strategies; sections 7.3.3 and 7.3.4 provide more details through case studies of subsectors and firms.

### 7.3.2  Intense Redefinition of Firms' Boundaries

The above developments allow us to distinguish three periods since the beginning of the 1980s. The beginning of the decade was devoted to restructuring; after 1985, portfolio reshuffling was very actively pursued and, since 1990, the end of the growth period has triggered a new restructuring episode. All three periods have required development of firms' assets and external growth operations have been intensely used with this objective in mind.

The 1980s have seen a new wave of mergers, and the chemical industry was one of the most, if not the most, active.[19] Mergers and acquisitions in the chemical industry have been so numerous that data collection is an arduous task. Box 7.1 briefly describes the method which has been used here.

*Box 7.1    Summary of the databases Chem-MA and Chem-JV*

Two databases have been constituted, one for mergers and acquisitions and one for joint ventures, both for the period 1980–91. They both rely on four types of sources: general press and financial press, the professional press, annual reports from companies and studies by other authors. Interviews with companies have been used as a complement in a few cases. For these different sources, there is a bias in favour of European companies' operations, as more accessible. There is in particular a weak representation of American sources for domestic operations; this is also the case for Japanese sources, but it is less of a problem since external growth is much less active there (for joint ventures, observation is easier since they are often with non-Japanese partners).

Both bases consider the chemical sector as it has been defined in the text (section 7.1). Operations between pharmaceuticals companies are probably underestimated (for the pharmaceutical sector in detail, see Chapter 8).

*Mergers and acquisitions* (Chem-MA)

Acquisitions of more than 30 per cent of the capital have been recorded in this category; most of the time, the acquisition is above 50 per cent. The base gives the date of the operation, the names of the two firms, their parent companies and their nationalities. Information on the fields concerned in the acquisition is codified. When available, the price of the transaction is given. One area is devoted to a more extensive or detailed description of the operation, and one to the sources which have been used.

*Joint ventures* (Chem-JV)

Joint ventures are defined as common subsidiaries. The structure of the base is similar to that of the other base. In addition, the percentage owned by each firm in the venture is given when known.

Chem-MA records 2443 M&A between 1980 and 1991. This figure is lower than those given by some other sources. In particular, some sources have given more than 1000 for one year.[20] The best way to explain these differences would of course be to compare the bases, but this has not been possible. The following explanations are offered. First, there is a question of definition of the types of operations. Chem-MA only considers mergers and acquisitions since joint ventures are in Chem-JV. Second, the very high figures which have appeared in the press or in some articles usually refer to the years when M&A were most numerous, between 1985 and 1989. Operations have been much fewer at the beginning of the decade, and information is much more difficult to collect for these years. Third, the base should be augmented by a number of acquisitions within the pharmaceutical sector (see Box 7.1). Fourth, the base has a bias against the operations within the United States. This may be the weakest point. It seems that operations in which one European firm is involved are well covered; for the United States, only the important ones may be taken into account. As a consequence the share of firms acquired in the United States is probably underestimated. As a whole, the most important operations are recorded and those by large firms are well covered (annual reports have been used).

Table 7.11 gives the number of M&A per year. It shows that the years
1985–89 have seen the most numerous operations; the period corresponds to
renewed growth and to the strategy of diversification towards specialities. In
1990, the combination of the Gulf War and of the slowing down of growth
explain the sharp reduction in the number of operations. The figure for 1991
may be somewhat misleading. There have been a number of operations as
part of the new restructuring phase, but this is also the year for which the
collection of information has been the best.

*Table 7.11  Number of mergers and acquisitions in the chemical industry per year,
1980–91*

| 1980 | 1981 | 1982 | 1983 | 1984 | 1985 |
|------|------|------|------|------|------|
| 57 | 44 | 64 | 84 | 88 | 235 |

| 1986 | 1987 | 1988 | 1989 | 1990 | 1991 |
|------|------|------|------|------|------|
| 255 | 266 | 345 | 358 | 269 | 350 |

*Note*: Out of the 2443 operations, there are 28 for which the date is not known.
*Source*: Calculations from Chem-MA

Table 7.12 gives the geographical distribution of mergers and acquisitions.
European firms appear very active. They have acquired numerous operations
in the United States; more information would probably be needed to compare
these acquisitions with those internal to the United States.[21] European firms
have also been active within their region.

*Table 7.12  Geographical distribution of mergers and acquisitions, 1980–91*

| Firms acquired in[*] | Number | Nationality of acquiring firms[°] | Number |
|------|------|------|------|
| US | 627 | US | 379 |
| of which by US | 157 | France | 433 |
| by EC | 331 | UK | 420 |
| EC | 1354 | Germany | 267 |
| of which by EC | 918 | Netherlands | 148 |
| Japan | 12 | Sweden | 77 |
| Asia (except Japan) | 24 | Japan | 66 |
|  |  | Asia (except Japan) | 2 |

[*]  The nationality given is that of the acquired company and not that of the parent
company.
[°]  Nationality of the parent company.
*Source*: calculation from Chem-MA

Joint ventures have also been actively used to implement firms' strate-gies.[22] Table 7.13 shows the evolution of joint ventures in the chemical since 1980.

*Table 7.13  Number of joint ventures in the chemical industry, 1980–91*

| 1980 | 1981 | 1982 | 1983 | 1984 | 1985 |
|------|------|------|------|------|------|
| 5 | 14 | 11 | 12 | 17 | 28 |

| 1986 | 1987 | 1988 | 1989 | 1990 | 1991 |
|------|------|------|------|------|------|
| 30 | 48 | 43 | 70 | 86 | 102 |

*Note*: Out of the 638 operations, there are 172 for which the date is not known.
*Source*: calculations from Chem-JV

According to Table 7.13, the number of joint ventures has been increasing over the decade, more consistently than mergers and acquisitions (Table 7.12). Table 7.14 gives the geographical distribution of joint ventures.

*Table 7.14  Geographical distribution of joint ventures in chemicals*

| JV between | Number | % |
|------------|--------|---|
| US–Japan | 46 | 7.2 |
| US–EC | 87 | 13.6 |
| EC–Japan | 86 | 13.5 |
| US–Asia | 15 | 2.4 |
| US–EFTA | 17 | 2.7 |
| EC–EC | 101 | 15.8 |
| EC–EFTA | 4 | 3.8 |
| Japan–Asia | 6 | 0.9 |
| EC–Asia | 43 | 6.7 |
| East | 2 | 6.6 |
| Total* | 467 | – |

\*  A number of JVs in the base are not attributable to one of the above zones (the general total is 638).
*Source*: calculations from Chem-JV

Japan appears much more active in joint ventures than in acquisitions. Japanese companies take part in 29 per cent of the joint ventures (138).[23] Firms from Asia–Pacific (apart from Japan) are also quite active; they parti-cipate in 14 per cent of the joint ventures. American firms participate in 35 per cent of the total.

EC firms participate in 341 joint ventures, which constitutes 73 per cent of the total. However, intra-European operations are relatiively few. There are 101 intra-EC joint ventures (22 per cent), but about a third of them are actually domestic. For France, the UK and Germany, domestic joint ventures represent around 10 per cent of the total and intra-EC ones around 20 per cent. Domestic operations are less important for Japanese companies (7 per cent) and more for American companies (22 per cent).

There is about the same number of Euro-Japanese joint ventures (86) as Euro-American joint ventures (87). In the case of the Japanese companies which had not been very active in Europe in the past, it corresponds to an attempt to create a production foothold in Europe and benefit from the Single Market (EC 1991). More generally, Japan and developing countries are much better represented by joint ventures than by acquisitions, which corresponds to competitive positions and strategies as they have been analysed above. Traditional producing countries want access to cheap resources, in the Gulf in particular, while the new producers from the region look for technical and commercial support. Japan, which has so far been a weak player on the international scene, uses joint ventures to penetrate European and American markets.

*Table 7.15  Sectoral distribution of mergers and acquisitions, 1980–91*

| Field of acquisition | Number[*] | Percentage of total |
|---|---|---|
| Basic chemical | 338 | 12.2 |
| Plastic and fibres | 371 | 13.4 |
| Specialities | 659 | 23.9 |
| of which paint and varnishes | 146 | 5.3 |
| Agrochemicals[**] | 228 | 8.3 |
| Fine chemicals | 134 | 4.8 |
| Consumer products | 273 | 9.9 |
| Pharmaceuticals | 394 | 14.3 |
| Biotechnology | 89 | 3.2 |
| Advanced materials[***] | 2 | 3.3 |
| Others | 185 | 6.7 |

[*]  Because the acquired companies have often more than one field of activity, the base allows each acquisition to concern two fields; the second one may be empty of course. The total number of fields in the base is 2763 (not counting 118 records for which the field is not known); this figure is used to calculate the percentages.

[**]  Including fertilizers.

[***]  Technical plastics have been classified as plastics.

*Source*: calculations from Chem-MA

Cooperative agreements complement the above external growth operations. Information is even patchier on these cooperations and this research
did not attempt a systematic collection of data. It seems however that the
resources sought in these agreements mostly relate to research and distribution, which could explain why the most active area appears to be
pharmaceuticals.[24] Table 7.15 gives the sectoral distribution of acquisitions.

These figures correspond to those of other sources better than for geographical distribution; this may be because restructuring and diversification into
specialities have followed similar routes on both sides of the Atlantic. Petrochemicals, including plastics, have motivated a great number of
acquisitions. The explanation lies both in the importance of the sector within
chemicals and in the need for restructuring at the beginning of the period
(and again in 1991). Rationalization in petrochemicals has resorted to a
number of transaction types. There have been a number of swaps, such as
the exchange of ICI's low density polyethylene for BP's PVC in 1982.
Restructuring in this sector has also been conducted through joint ventures
(in Europe, some have come under the scrutiny of the Commission's competition policy). As a result, the number of firms in each petrochemical product
market has been reduced (Cook and Sharp 1991); however, the resulting
degree of concentration and competition should take into account the new
entrants from developing countries.

The sectoral distribution of joint ventures is slightly different, as shown in
Table 7.16. These operations have been more numerous in basic chemicals
and for plastics and fibres, where they have been used to reduce capacities.

*Table 7.16 Sectoral distribution of joint ventures*

| Field | Number | % |
|---|---|---|
| Basic chemicals | 154 | 21.0 |
| Plastics and fibres | 191 | 26.1 |
| Chemical specialities | 102 | 13.9 |
| of which paints and varnishes | 19 | 2.6 |
| Agrochemicals | 46 | 6.3 |
| Fine chemicals | 19 | 2.6 |
| Consumer products | 50 | 6.8 |
| Pharmaceuticals | 80 | 10.9 |
| Biotechnology | 17 | 2.3 |
| Advanced materials | 36 | 4.9 |
| Others | 29 | 4.0 |

*Source*: calculations from Chem-JV

Specialities (including pharmaceuticals) have been widely targeted for diversification purposes and thus represent a high share of external growth operations (Tables 7.15 and 7.16).

### 7.3.3  Subsector Case Studies

#### 7.3.3.1  Paints and varnishes

This area is particularly interesting to analyse as an example of speciality chemicals. It is one of the most recession-resistant and during the 1980s it has experienced numerous acquisitions. As a consequence, it tends to become more concentrated.

Paints and varnishes can be divided into two broad categories, for which both production techniques and competition are quite different (EEC 1991; Ghellinck 1991). The first category comprises architectural paints which are used for decoration of buildings and homes.[25] Decorative paints are produced in large volumes and often sold directly to customers. Superstores have gained more importance in distribution and competition has intensified. Moreover, the limited number of brands on offer in stores constitutes barriers to entry and make it necessary to possess well known brands on the different markets.

The second category comprises industrial paints and coatings which impart special properties to manufactured goods. These products have to satisfy specific needs such as those of the automobile or aeronautics industries. Paints for automobiles is a very demanding segment. It requires high technological standards both to provide good properties to vehicles and to adapt to different modes of application. Moreover, this market requires just-in-time supplies and rapid technical services. PPG, which is the leader on this market, has a satellite production plant at Flint so that General Motors does not need to carry paints stocks (*Financial Times* 27/3/1991). Specific properties are also required for metal boxes. Industrial paints correspond to typical speciality chemicals in that firms have to both specialize quite narrowly on particular products and internationalize their activity.

Research aims at solving increasingly demanding industrial clients. It is also strongly influenced by anti-pollution concerns and regulations. Both present and prospective regulations on the control of emissions from volatile solvents used extensively in paints induce research on water-based paints and powder coatings. The powder coatings market is the fastest growing paint market, with about 15 per cent annual volume increases over the 1980s. At first this success was due to the durability and toughness of powders which make them ideal for coating domestic appliances and various metal surfaces. More recently, powders have benefited from environmental concerns since they do not contain solvents.

In 1988, decorative paints represented 52 per cent of world sales, paints for automobiles 11 per cent and coatings for metal boxes 3 per cent (EEC 1991). The structure of the paint sector resembles that of the whole chemical industry. It is dominated by a dozen large companies but quite numerous small companies occupy specific segments on regional or local markets. Table 7.17 gives the ranking of the first ten world paint companies.

*Table 7.17  World paint companies ranked by sales in million litres*

| Groups | Country of origin | 1987 | 1990 |
|---|---|---|---|
| Imperial Chemical Industry (ICI) | United Kingdom | 720 | 805 |
| Sherwin Williams | United States | 300 | 533 |
| PPG | United States | 450 | 515 |
| BASF | Germany | 440 | 500 |
| Akzo | Netherlands | 270 | 490 |
| Nippon paint | Japan | 220 | 350 |
| Casco Nobel | Sweden | n.a. | 350 |
| Courtaulds | United Kingdom | 175 | 380 |
| Kansai | Japan | 210 | 280 |
| Du Pont | United States | 200 | 265 |
| Total, 10 majors | – | – | 4388 |
| World market (1988) | – | – | 16000 |

*Sources: Financial Times* (27/3/1991); EEC (1991)

In order to specialize in certain areas or to penetrate new markets and increase size, firms have largely resorted to acquisitions of paints and varnishes operations. Over the 1980s, the European Commission (EEC 91) recorded 200 acquisitions; our own database Chem-MA gives 146 acquisitions. The large companies which have chosen to include this area in their speciality businesses have sought strong positions and have made numerous acquisitions for this purpose. The most active have been Akzo, ICI, PPG and Courtaulds with respectively 18, 21, 9 and 19 acquisitions in the sector of paints and varnishes between 1980 and 1991 (figures from the database).

As a result, the sector has become more concentrated; in 1980 the first ten companies in paints and varnishes totalled 20 per cent of the world market; in 1989, their market share had grown to 30 per cent (EEC 1991). Concentration is even stronger in certain segments which can be considered as oligopolies, like that of paints for boats.

Acquisitions have had two main motives: first, to reinforce specialization in specific areas such as automobile or marine paints, and second, to penetrate foreign markets and become more internationalized. In the domain of paints for automobiles,[26] for example, the leaders have actively sought acquisitions to reinforce their positions (Table 7.18).

*Table 7.18  Acquisitions in the field of automobile paints by market leaders*

| Company | Home base | Sales, million litres | Number of acquisitions | In countries |
|---|---|---|---|---|
| PPG | US | 189 | 7 | Spain, Italy, Germany UK, Canada, Denmark |
| BASF | Germany | 124 | 4 | UK, US, Argentina, Mexico |
| Du Pont | US | 90 | 2 | US, Spain |
| Kansai | Japan | 83 | 0 | – |
| Nippon | Japan | 81 | 0 | – |
| ICI | UK | 39 | 5 | Ireland, Spain, US, Germany, France |
| Akzo | NL | 30 | 3 | US, Belgium |
| Total world | | 268 | | |

*Sources*: *Financial Times* (27/3/1991), own database for acquisitions (see appendix)

Table 7.18 shows a revealing geographical pattern of acquisitions. The leaders are the most active, they are also the most internationalized. PPG and BASF are actually the only two world players. Their followers are quite small and operate mainly on regional markets. No acquisition is recorded for Japanese producers, but they have links with other producers. Nippon Paints uses PPG's leading technology for electrocoating in Asia-Pacific markets (*Financial Times* 27/12/1991).[27] In July 1991, Kansai established a joint venture with Du Pont to produce automobile coatings, aiming at Japanese car producers in the United States. The Japanese producers need these international links because they are still heavily dependent on their domestic market. They have benefited from the strength of the Japanese car makers and the related large share of automobile paints in Japan,[28] but this can become a weakness when the automobile market slows down.

In the automobile paints sector and in paints in general, acquisitions have increased the degree of internationalization of firms. A number of large foreign acquisitions have opened the door to globalization for BASF (Inmont in 1985) and ICI (Glidden in 1986) for example. These operations as well as other more numerous smaller ones have engendered integration problems. These management problems are typical; they can be all the more serious in the case of large, numerous and international acquisitions like during the 1980s wave. For leaders, the challenge was to go from the agglomeration of acquisitions around the world to global management. At the beginning of the 1990s there are still only four world players in paints and coatings: ICI, PPG, BASF and Courtaulds. PPG has sought acquisitions outside the United States in order to avoid strong cyclical effects, on the hypothesis that economic cycles are not exactly simultaneous on different markets. It was also important to achieve economies of scale in the niche of car paint. Courtauld's internationalization has been a consequence of its choice to dominate the world market for marine paints; it now controls a third of the market.

### 7.3.3.2 Fertilizers and agrochemicals

Fertilizers and agrochemicals both address the agricultural sector, but with different products. As a consequence the characteristics of markets as well as the leading firms differ. In both cases, acquisitions have been quite numerous during the 1980s, with 77 concerning activities in fertilizers and 162 activities in agrochemicals.

Fertilizers are quite basic chemical products; their price largely depends on that of raw materials. This explains part of the difficulties of European producers during the 1980s. They have been confronted by cost disadvantages *vis-à-vis* competitors in North America and the Middle East[29] as well as by evolution in agriculture and environmental pressures. For the European fertilizer industry, the 1980s has been a restructuring decade. A number of firms have exited, capacity and employment have been reduced. But firms have also invested in new more productive sites and in research on environmental problems. The number of leading players has been reduced from 30 to seven companies which account for 80 per cent of regional output (*Financial Times* 10/12/91).

The leading companies have bought a number of businesses during the decade. Table 7.19 shows that the leader, Norsk Hydro, has been the most active. Its acquisitions take place in Europe. This can be explained by the combination of heavy weight and relatively low value added of fertilizers. Scandinavian countries benefit from access to low cost raw materials; they build on this advantage to expand their market share and reap economies of scale.[30] Thus it appears that acquisitions have been used as a rationalization instrument during the decade.

Exits have also occurred through acquisitions. Rhône-Poulenc for example has sold a number of units in fertilizers. In 1990, ICI announced that it would sell its loss-making UK fertilizer business to Kemira. The deal was later blocked by the Monopolies and Mergers Commission and ICI decided to run the plants. But the attempt was revealing: after a decade of restructuring, profitability in the European fertilizer industry is still weak.

*Table 7.19  European leaders in fertilizers and their acquisitions, 1980–91, sales in ECU m*

| Company | Country of origin | Sales in 1989 | Number of acquisitions | Acquisitions in |
|---------|-------------------|---------------|------------------------|-----------------|
| Norsk Hydro | Norway | 2540 | 10 | Sweden, UK, Germany, France, NL |
| ICI | UK | 1266 | 6 | UK, Australia, Ireland, Canada |
| Kemira | Finland | 1182 | 7 | NL, Belgium, UK, Sweden, Denmark |
| Orkem | France | 966 | 7 | France |
| Enimont | Italy | 907 | 0 | – |
| BASF | Germany | 883 | 4 | Belgium, Germany, France |
| FESA ENFERSA | Spain | 655 | 2 | Mergers of two Spanish producers |
| EMC | France | 632 | 1 | France |

*Source*: Eurostaf 1991, own database for acquisitions

After a sharp decline, EEC production has been stable since 1986 at around 50 m tons, which represents about 15 per cent of world production; the share of fertilizers in European chemical production declined to a mere 2 per cent in 1989. A growing proportion of the EEC market has been taken up by imports, the share of which grew from 10 per cent in 1980 to 16 per cent in 1989 (EEC 1991). The trade balance of the Community became negative in 1986.[31]

Agrochemicals are mostly pesticides, including herbicides (46 per cent of the world market),[32] insecticides (28 per cent) and fungicides (19 per cent). They also comprise a small but growing proportion of products to regulate plant growth (7 per cent).

Agrochemicals belong to specialities; as opposed to fertilizers, they are high value added and innovative. In this sector, patents are an important aspect of the competitive game. With the need for innovation and environmental concerns, R&D costs have tended to increase. In 1987, the investment needed to launch a new product was estimated at $30 m, the development period being five to seven years long (Ghellinck 1991). Moreover, the growing importance of biotechnology induces firms to acquire the relevant knowledge base. R&D spending averages 8 to 9 per cent of sales and biotechnology tends to increase its importance in research programmes (EEC 1991). Progress in biotechnology also explains why a number of chemical companies diversify their agrochemical businesses into seeds; this has been the case with ICI and Sandoz for example.

Despite their characteristics as specialities, agrochemicals remain heavily dependent on demand from agriculture, which means that the prospective rate of growth is limited. In these conditions, competition is tough and during the 1980s, agrochemicals underwent a period of restructuring. The sector has become more concentrated, with the ten top players producing more than 75 per cent of agrochemicals in 1990.

Rationalization and specialization have largely occurred through acquisitions, in particular in the United States. For example, acquisitions have taken ICI from the eleventh to the second place in a decade.[33]

*Table 7.20  Leaders in agrochemicals and their acquisitions, 1980–91[a], sales in $m*

| Company | Country of origin | Sales in 1989 | Number of acquisitions | Acquisitions in |
|---|---|---|---|---|
| Ciba–Geigy | CH | 2900 | 7 | Swizerland, US, France, Canada, UK |
| ICI | UK | 2000 | 9 | US, UK, Belgium |
| Bayer | D | 2100 | 1 | Denmark |
| Rhône-Poulenc | F | 1860 | 19 | US, France, Sweden, Belgium, Spain, Aust., Mexico |
| Du Pont | US | 1750 | 4 | US, France, Italy, Germany, Aust., Mexico |
| Monsanto | US | 1500 | 5 | Germany, US |
| Dow Elanco | US | 1500 | 3 | France, UK, US |
| Hoechst | D | 1330 | 7 | Spain, US, Aust., Netherlands, Mexico |
| BASF | D | 1220 | 3 | France, US, Germany |
| Schering | D | 890 | 1 | UK |

[a]  Acquisitions relate to traditional agrochemicals and seeds, which may be linked to biotechnology.
*Source*: Eurostaf (1991), database Chem-MA for acquisitions

Table 7.20 shows that leaders in agrochemicals have actively used acquisitions in order to strengthen their portfolio. Rhône-Poulenc made nineteen acquisitions of this type and ICI nine, each buying an important company — respectively Union Carbide's agrochemicals and Stauffer.

### 7.3.4  Firms' Case Studies

The analysis of specific subsectors within chemicals shows that different firms are leaders and that the main actors on the acquisitions and joint ventures scenes vary. It is thus important to complement the above observations with firms' case studies to analyse strategies and the instruments used to control competences. For example, the comparison between Bayer and Rhône-Poulenc is quite striking. Bayer reorganized its portfolio during the 1970s and was already quite internationalized at the beginning of the 1980s. Rhône-Poulenc on the contrary has been quite active in acquisitions during the 1980s in order to reach these objectives. The analysis of firms' strategies also enables us to observe how acquisitions have been matched by numerous divestitures.

#### 7.3.4.1  Rhône-Poulenc

Throughout its history, Rhône-Poulenc has had several quite different product portfolios (Cayez 1985). In particular, it has had important textile operations. At the beginning of the 1960s, textiles represented more than 50 per cent of sales and pharmaceuticals 13 per cent. Given the difficulties in textiles from the 1960s, the objective has been to find new areas in which to compete. During the 1960s, Rhône-Poulenc followed a then widely accepted idea: that the size of a firm was an asset in itself for competing in the new European common market. As a consequence, it acquired a number of chemical firms in various fields without paying enough attention to consistency.

In 1977, a thorough strategic analysis showed that the structure of Rhône-Poulenc had to be seriously revised. First, the group was much too diversified, so that, despite a large global size, it was not a strong competitor in any field. Second, textiles still held too large a share of sales; the shares of petrochemicals, commodity plastics and fertilizers were also too dominant, given the fact that Rhône-Poulenc had no cheap sources of raw materials. Third, Rhône-Poulenc remained insufficiently internationalized; it had a strong subsidiary in Brazil but was nearly absent from the United States and Japan, and weak in Germany. These weaknesses interacted with a low global productivity.

Rhône-Poulenc's strategy during the 1980s flows from the 1977 diagnosis. During the decade, it actively redefined its portfolio and became more internationalized, in the United States particularly. The choice of the activities to keep and strengthen was based on several criteria: the firm already had sufficient assets in the field, the rate of growth was high and, in order to benefit from the strong technical culture of the group, success largely relied on R&D. Three areas emerged: pharmaceuticals, agrochemicals and the fine chemicals in which Rhône-Poulenc already had strong positions such as rare earths, silicones, biochemicals and some synthetic intermediaries (Carré 1987). For textile activities, which could not be sold, and most chemicals, the industrial basis had to be strengthened through investments and restructuring.

*Table 7.21  Evolution of Rhône-Poulenc's sales by type of activities, % of total sales*

|  | 1979 | 1985 | 1989 | 1990** |
|---|---|---|---|---|
| Chemicals° | 39.3 | 42.2 | 44.4 | 17.3 |
| Specialities (1990) | – | – | – | 17.3 |
| Health | 14.7 | 20.8 | 24.3 | 29.2 |
| Agrochemicals | 6.6 | 11.5 | 15.0 | 12.5 |
| Fertilizers* | 10.5 | – | – | – |
| Fibres°° | 15.8 | 20.5 | 14.3 | 17.3 |
| Films and systems* | 4.4 | – | – | – |
| Brazil* | 7.9 | – | – | – |
| Others | 0.8 | 5.0 | 2.0 | 1.7 |

* These items have disappeared as classes of sales from 1985.
** Change in the classification in 1990
° Basic chemicals and specialities until 1989, for 1990: organic and mineral intermediary products
°° For 1990, fibres and polymers
*Sources*: DAFSA (1985), Eurostaf (1991)

Table 7.21 shows that the portfolio has evolved according to the broad choices made at the end of the 1970s. The fibre business retains a substantial part of the activity as it had been considered that they were very difficult to sell. Health and agrochemicals have substantially increased their shares, while fertilizers and films have disappeared. Within chemicals, the weight of commodities has declined to the benefit of specialities.[34]

In order to accelerate the evolution of the portfolio, some activities were stopped and Rhône-Poulenc resorted to numerous acquisitions and sales. According to the base Chem-MA, between 1980 and 1991 Rhône-Poulenc made 69 sales of activities and 107 acquisitions. Rhône-Poulenc also created a number of joint ventures (50 between 1980 and 1991, according to Chem-JV).

In 1980, Rhône-Poulenc made major divestures out of basic petrochemicals as well as some other basic operations. They were sold mainly to Elf-Aquitaine and also to Total, two French oil companies. During the first years of the decade Rhône-Poulenc also sold its fertilizers operations. Later, it sold a couple of fibre units. Acquisitions have likewise corresponded to the fields of specialization, as shown in Table 7.22.

*Table 7.22  Distribution of acquisitions by Rhône-Poulenc*

| Field of acquisitions | Number | % of total[*] |
|---|---|---|
| Pharmaceuticals° | 32 | 27.1 |
| Agrochemicals° | 21 | 7.8 |
| Specialities and fine chemicals | 25 | 21.2 |
| Advanced materials | 12 | 10.2 |
| Total for the main fields | 90 | 76.3 |

[*] The total number of acquisitions by Rhône-Poulenc between 1980 and 1991 recorded in the database is 107; percentages are calculated with respect to the number of fields for which acquisitions have been made, that is to say 118 (see also the comment below Table 7.15).
° Includes some acquisitions in the field of biotechnology; the total for biotechnology is 8.
*Source*: calculations from Chem-MA

Thus acquisitions and cessions have been important instruments to achieve the main strategic objectives: growing in size and refocusing the portfolio. At the beginning of the 1980s, Rhône-Poulenc ranked twelfth among world chemical companies; in 1990, it was seventh. Acquisitions have also been instrumental in a spectacular increase in the degree of internationalization. Table 7.23 shows the evolution of the international distribution of production.

*Table 7.23  Evolution of Rhône-Poulenc's international distribution of production, in %*

| | 1985 | 1987 | 1989 | 1990 |
|---|---|---|---|---|
| France | 60.0 | 57.7 | 51.9 | 45.7 |
| International | 40.0 | 42.3 | 48.1 | 54.3 |

*Source*: DAFSA (1985), Eurostaf (1991)

Internationalization is, quite logically, higher for sales; in 1989, sales in France represented 25 per cent of the total, exports 27 per cent and international sales 48 per cent (Rhône-Poulenc). The progress of sales in the United States has been formidable. Until 1985, the United States represented 3 per cent of sales, its share jumped to 11 per cent in 1986 after the acquisition of Union Carbide's agrochemicals; in 1989, due to other important acquisitions, it reached 19 per cent. In 1987, Rhône-Poulenc bought the basic chemicals from Stauffer; in 1989, it acquired Monsanto's active substances for aspirin and paracetamol and GAF's specialities. Rhône-Poulenc has also made smaller acquisitions in the United States, such as seeds from Clause or vanillin from Monsanto. Moreover, it bought RTZ

Chemicals in 1989, a UK company which was strongly present in the United States. Finally, Rhône-Poulenc made two important pharmaceutical acquisitions in North America. Mérieux, Rhône-Poulenc's subsidiary bought Connaught (Canada) in 1989, which strengthened its world leadership in vaccines. In 1990, Rhône-Poulenc acquired Rorer in the United States.

The numerous acquisitions by Rhône-Poulenc have had to be followed by efforts to integrate the new activities and sites. Moreover, in 1990, the results were quite deceptive since specialities had not been very successful. This has motivated a restructuring of these activities, including some divestitures. In order to better focus its activities within specialities, Rhône-Poulenc has sold Xylochimie and the citric acid from RTZ for example. Restructuring in this sector would be the most serious in the United States. In 1990, Rhône-Poulenc announced that twelve out of the 36 American specialities production units would be closed before 1992 (*Les Echos* 27/5/1990).

### 7.3.4.2 ICI

During the 1970s, ICI invested a great deal in bulk chemicals and plastics; it expected in particular demand for ethylene to continue to grow. The company has thus been quite severely affected by the oil shocks, with its petrochemical, plastic and other commodity operations making heavy losses at the beginning of the 1980s. ICI then decided to decrease the weight of commodities in its sales. The second main strategic objective for the 1980s has been to increase the degree of internationalization. Tables 7.24 and 7.25 show that ICI did progress in these two directions during the 1980s.

*Table 7.24  Distribution of ICI's sales by type of activity, in %*

|  | 1980[*] | 1986 | 1988 | 1990 |
|---|---|---|---|---|
| Pharmaceutical | 6.8 | 10.3 | 10.0 | 11.0 |
| Paints | 6.3 | 7.7 | 11.6 | 12.7 |
| Others[°] | 8.6 | 18.2 | 17.6 | 18.0 |
| Total for consumer products and specialities | 21.7 | 36.2 | 39.2 | 41.7 |
| Chemicals | 15.8 | 17.2 | 17.1 | 15.5 |
| Plastics and petrochemicals | 24.6 | 27.7 | 23.1 | 22.4 |
| Fibres | 24.6 | 27.7 | 23.1 | 22.4 |
| Explosives | 3.2 | 3.2 | 3.1 | 4.0 |
| Total industrial products | 49.7 | 54.2 | 48.6 | 47.3 |
| Agrochemicals and seeds | nd | 7.4 | 10.1 | 10.6 |
| Fertilizers | nd | 9.0 | 7.0 | 6.6 |
| Total agriculture | 16.2 | 16.4 | 17.1 | 17.2 |
| Others | 1.6 | 1.6 | 1.9 | 1.5 |

[*]  The classification changed after 1980.
[°]  Specialities and colours in 1980.
*Sources*: DAFSA (1985), Eurostaf (1991)

*Table 7.25  Geographical distribution of ICI's sales to external customers, in %*

|                            | 1981 | 1984 | 1995 | 1990 |
|----------------------------|------|------|------|------|
| UK                         | 56   | 51   | 48   | 40   |
| Continental Western Europe | 14   | 15   | 16   | 20   |
| America*                   | 14   | 17   | 19   | 24   |
| Asia-Pacific               | 14   | 15   | 13   | 13   |
| Others                     | 1    | 1    | 0    | 0    |

*  For 1982 and 1986, North America only
*Sources*: ICI annual reports

ICI largely resorted to external growth operations in order to implement its strategy during the 1980s. It bought 91 companies or operations and divested from 45; it also created 50 joint ventures. Acquisitions have been instrumental in ICI's strategy to grow in agrochemicals and paints (see section 7.3.2.2). Table 7.26 shows the distribution of ICI's acquisitions by field of operation.

*Table 7.26  Distribution of ICI's acquisitions by area, 1980–91, in %*

| Field of acquisition          | Number | % of total* |
|-------------------------------|--------|-------------|
| Specialities and fine chemicals | 48     | 42.5        |
| of which paints               | 19     | 16.8        |
| Agrochemicals                 | 16     | 14.2        |
| Plastics                      | 25     | 22.1        |
| Total for the main fields     | 89     | 78.8        |

*  The total number of acquisitions between 1980 and 1991 is 90. Percentages have been calculated with respect to the number of fields of acquisition (112); see also the note below Table 7.15.
*Source*: calculations from Chem-MA

ICI made three acquisitions in pharmaceuticals; it largely developed its business in this field through internal growth. Pharmaceuticals have become more important to ICI, but this business remains in a relatively weak position as compared with the international leaders.

Table 7.26 records relatively numerous acquisitions in plastics. This reflects their substantial share in sales and the fact that they needed to be reorganized. The other side of this reorganization is constituted by divestitures; ICI sold twelve operations related to plastics during the 1980s.[35] It divested from operations in polyethylene, but has strengthened its activities in PVC (eight acquisitions) and acrylics (three acquisitions). It also acquired operations in the field of new material and advanced plastics. The acquisition of Beatrice Chemicals in 1985 (for $750 bn) has been an important step in this field since it strengthened ICI's position in specialities and in particular in advanced plastics and composites. The development of ICI's advanced polymer composite (APC) was dependent upon establishing production and marketing capabilities in the United States (ECN 24/12/ 1984). This underlines the second main interest of Beatrice Chemicals: its nationality. This acquisition has been important in increasing the share of the United States in ICI's production and sales, even if Beatrice was present in eighteen countries (Table 7.25).

In ten years, ICI has become financially stronger, much more internationalized and less dependent on cyclical bulk chemicals. After the crisis, the company thought of getting out of bulk chemicals altogether. It did not, first, because between 1985 and 1988, commodity businesses achieved good performance, and second, because some of the new high value-added activities such as advanced materials and high-performance films have run into technical and commercial difficulties. These disappointments and the threat from Hanson Trust in 1991 have led to a new restructuring programme, including numerous divestitures.[36]

## 7.4 CONCLUSION

During the 1980s, chemical firms have tended to follow quite similar strategies in order to avoid the roller-coaster which is typical of the sector. After the restructuring phase at the beginning of the decade, they have both reshuffled their portfolio and become much more internationalized. Generally, these strategic moves have led to stronger firms, with more consistent activities, but recent events show that they were not the definitive answer. In particular, strong growth rates have again led to ambitious investments and overcapacities in petrochemicals.

The strategy of increasing the share of specialities in portfolios has also led to some disappointments. First, the fact that numerous companies have entered specialities has sometimes given that sector some of the commodities characteristics; in particular, when there were many entrants, competition was bound to increase — and margins to fall. Moreover, it seems that specialities are not really recession-proof. Second, it is difficult to alter a company's businesses; the experience of the chemical industry has shown that it is particularly difficult to change from a commodity business to a more technologically and marketing intensive one. Finally, the move towards specialities has largely occurred through external growth, which reinforces the difficulties of adaptation. Indeed, one of the main motives for

270 *European Integration and Competitiveness*

acquisition is the speed, but it also involves drawbacks since the foreign entity has to be absorbed and effectively integrated.

European companies have been very active in the restructuring and reorganization process of the decade. The evolution of European multinational chemical companies does not necessarily translate into more competitiveness for their countries of origin. The competitiveness of the European chemical industry world chemical imports has deteriorated over the 1980s.[37] This may be related to the fact that European firms have become more internationalized and in a number of cases have begun to organize for globalization.

The European chemical industry faces challenges in the 1990s. The first one is the new overcapacity period which has already spilt red ink. The second one is the adaptation to stricter environmental regulations, especially since Europe is somewhat behind the United States in their implementation. The third one is the more complete development towards globalization. The latter seems inevitable because of competition from developing countries in commodities; moreover, because of the higher growth rates of these countries, Asia has become an important investment zone.

Within Europe itself, competition should increase with the arrival of Japanese companies and the renewed interest of American companies, which are both attracted by the Single Market. The developments in Eastern Europe will also play a part in the evolution of the competitive game.

## NOTES

1. The most active, according to certain sources.
2. This is discussed in the text, see also the general appendix at the end of the book.
3. A crucial move was the replacement of coal by oil and gas as the main feedstocks, during or after the Second World War.
4. Organic chemicals represent 34.5 per cent of chemical exports by EEC Japan and the United States, plastics represent 36.2 per cent, thus organic chemicals generally constitute the majority of chemical exports by industrial countries (GATT 1989–90).
5. See in particular the discussion in DAFSA (1985).
6. Spitz (1988) details this period; he proposes case studies for ammonia and ethylene plants.
7. This sort of consideration underlines the fact that it is not necessarily efficient to exhaust all potential technical economies of scale; the same observation has been made in the case of the automobile industry; see in particular Chapter 3 in this volume and Sachwald (1989).
8. For automobiles it is 2.7 per cent, 0.6 per cent for petroleum refining and 0.2 per cent for textiles. Figures all refer to the OECD zone.
9. Before, chemicals were mostly developed to produce bleach for the textile industry.
10. See the Chapter 3 on automobiles; the first 20 groups account for 60 per cent of world production in the EEC, the first four groups account for 60 per cent of production in 1986.
11. According to the Chemical Industry Association (UK), the capital investment on environment represents 20–25 per cent of investment (*Financial Times* 10/12/1991).
12. As seen above in section 7.1.3.3; see also the general appendix.
13. Figures from the Chemical Industries Association, quoted in Eurostaf (1991).
14. Germany, France, the United Kingdom, Belgium and Luxembourg, Spain.

15. Calculation from Table 7.8.
16. In this respect, effects may be the strongest for pharmaceuticals; see Chapter 8.
17. See *Financial Times* (10/12/1991).
18. It acquired Conoco in 1981 and in 1990 its chemical turnover was only 60 per cent of the total (Annual Report 1990).
19. See Chapter 1 for general data, including data from the European Commission.
20. *European Chemical News* records 1359 external growth operations in world chemicals in 1986; CHEMTRAK, Kline and Co., quoted in Cook and Sharp (1991), gives a total of 1283 M&A for 1988.
21. According to Cook and Sharp (1991), the proportion of acquisitions related to European firms is lower.
22. On this, and for petrochemicals, see also EEC (1991).
23. As opposed to 2 per cent for acquisitions (with Japan as the nationality of the acquiring company).
24. On the fact that there are few cooperative research agreements in petrochemicals, see EC (1991), p105.
25. Decorative paints represented 54 per cent of the paints market in 1988 (EEC 1991).
26. In OEM, that is to say during manufacture, which is a different market from repair.
27. PPG developed the first commercially viable system for electrocoating in 1976.
28. Automobile paints account for 25.8 per cent of the paint market in Japan, 11 per cent of the world market and 12 per cent of the EC market (EEC 1991, *Financial Times* 27/3/1991).
29. See the statistical appendix at the end of the book.
30. Production processes are capital-intensive and continuous production is essential.
31. The EEC has adopted anti-dumping measures in the fertilizer sector.
32. Figures in parentheses are shares of the world agrochemicals market (CE 1991).
33. Quotation from an executive from ICI agrochemicals, quoted in *Financial Times* (10/12/1990) pVI.
34. After the acquisitions made in 1989, the share of basic chemicals was down to 25 per cent of sales and specialities and fine chemicals up to 23 per cent (*Usine Nouvelle* 28/9/1989).
35. Three divestitures were made through swaps, one with BP (1982), one with Atochem (1985) and one with Enka (1986).
36. With 14 divestitures, 1991 has been the most active year according to our database.
37. As measured by the market position indicator, see appendix.

# APPENDIX: Additional Figures (7.A.1 to 7.A.3)

*Figure 7.A.1 Petrochemical industry group: inter-industry relationships*

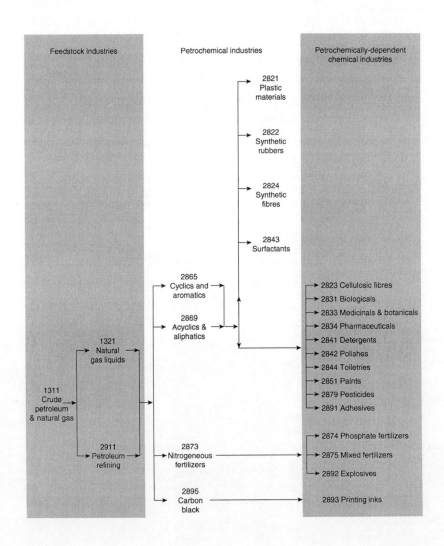

*Figure 7.A.2 Network of industry blocks related to production of key chemical molecules*

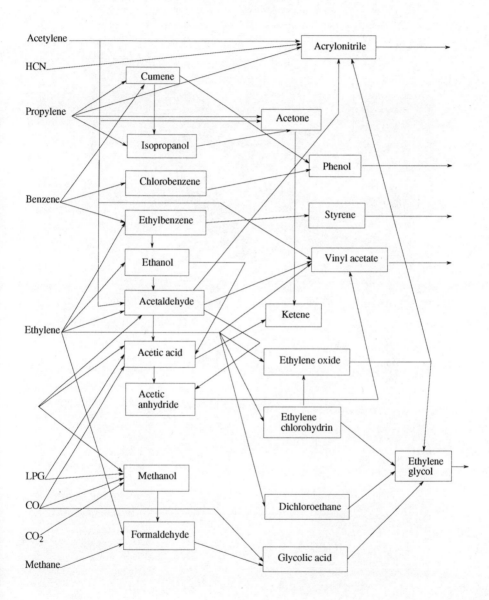

*Figure 7.A.3 Ethylene plant size, evolution*

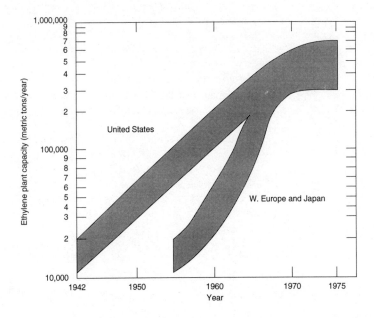

# BIBLIOGRAPHY

Bennett, M. J. and Kline, C. H. (1987), 'Chemicals: an Industry sheds its smokestack Image', *Technology Review*, Massachusetts Institute of Technology, vol. 90, no. 5, July.

Blunden, K. (rapporteur) (1986), *La Chimie, industrie multinationale,* Commissariat général du Plan, Paris, May.

Bower, J. (1986), *When Markets Quake*, Harvard Busines School Press.

Bozdogan, K. (1990), 'The Transformation of the US Chemicals Industry', in *The Working Papers of the MIT Commission on Industrial Productivity*, vol. 1, MIT Press, Cambridge.

Carré, F. (1987), 'La stratégie de Rhône-Poulenc', in *Cahiers Français*, no. 233, La Documentation Française, Paris.

Cayez, P. (1988), *Rhône-Poulenc, 1895–1975*, Armand Colin/Masson, Paris.

CE (1991), 'Industrie chimique', in *Panorama de l'Industrie Communautaire*, CE.

CEC, *Recent Trend of Concentration in Selected Industries,* Commission of the European Communities.

Chandler, A. Jr. (1990), *Scale and Scope*, Harvard University Press.

Cohendet, P., Ledoux, M. J. and Zuscovitch, E. (1988), *New Advanced Materials*, Springer-Verlag, Berlin.

Cook, P. L. and Sharp, M. L, 'The Chemical Industry',

DAFSA (1985), *Les entreprises de chimie fine et de spécialités dans le monde*, DAFSA, Paris, 3rd trim.

EC (1989), *The impact of joint ventures on competition, The case of petrochemical industry in the EEC*, EC.

El Kadiri, E. (1989), 'L'intégration vers l'aval au Moyen-Orient', *Industrie et développement international*, June.

Eurostaf (1991), *Chimie lourde, chimie de spécialités*, Collection stratégies industrielles et financières, Eurostaf, 4th trim.

*Financial Times* (1991), 'World Paints and Coatings', *FT Survey*, 27 March.

*Financial Times* (1991), 'The chemical industry', *FT Survey,* 10 December.

Fourtou, J. R. (1989), 'Les principales tendances dans les stratégies des grands groupes chimiques', *Informations chimie*, no. 312, September.

Freeman, C. and Sharp M. W. (eds), (1991), *Technology and the future of Europe*, Pinter and Publishers.

GATT (1990), *Le Commerce international 89–90*, GATT, Genève.

Ghellinck, E. de (1991), 'The chemical and pharmaceutical industries', in D.G. Mayes *The European Challenge: Industry's response to the 1992 programme*, Harvester Wheatsheaf.

Landau, R. (1989), 'The Chemical Engineer and the CPI: reading the future from the past', *Chemical Engineering Progress*, New York, September.

Landes, D. S. (1969), *The Unbound Prometheus*, Cambridge University Press.

Marfels, C. (1988), *Recent Trends of Concentration in Selected Industries of the European Community, Japan, and the United States*, Commission of the European Communities, Brussels.

Masseron, J. (1991), *L'économie des hydrocarbures*, Technip, Paris.

Molle, W. and Wever, E. (1984), *Oil refineries petrochemical industries in Western Europe*, Gower, Rotterdam.

OECD (1985), *Petrochemical industry, Energy aspects of structural change*, OECD.

Porter, M. (1990), *The competitive advantage of nations*, Macmillan, London.

Sachwald, F. (1989), *Ajustement sectoriel et adaptation des entreprises, Le cas de l'industrie automobile*, Document de travail, CEPII.

Sharp, D. H. and West, T. F. (1981), *The Chemical Industry*, Society of Chemical Industry, London.

Spitz, P. H. (1988), *Petrochemicals: the rise of an industry,* John Wiley & Sons, New York.

Waddams, A. L. (1978), *Chemicals from petroleum,* John Murray, London.

*Note*: Several articles from *European Chemical News* (*ECN*) have been used.

# 8. The Pharmaceutical Industry

## Peter de Wolf

The total West European pharmaceutical market is comparable to the North American market: both have a world market share of 32 per cent, while the Japanese world market share is 18 per cent.[1]

The pharmaceutical industry of Europe is a very strong industry comparable to its main competitors in the United States and Japan. This R&D-intensive industry has experienced a very turbulent decade, which was characterized by uncertainties about the speed of harmonization, the varying degree of state involvement and pressures on cost containment, combined with important technological developments and increasing competition, including the competition of generic substitutes as a result of patent expiration of many important drugs. In this chapter we shall try to describe and understand the changes in the structure of this industry, partly caused by factors that are inherently present in this industry (costs of innovation, short product life cycles), and partly caused by the changes in government intervention. The strategic answers of firms in this industry in terms of external operations to these challenges will be the focus of this chapter, with an accent on the evolution of mergers and acquisitions in the decade of 1980–90, in which European firms were involved.

The database on mergers and acquisitions will shed some light on those external operations that may be considered as the most strategic activities of pharmaceutical companies in order to meet the challenges of increased competition in the most important markets (Europe, the United States and Japan) as well as the challenges of biotechnology, generic competition and the developing of new markets. Also the role of strategic alliances will be illustrated as strategic weapons in gaining access to new technologies, new market segments and obtaining market presence in some countries.

Finally, we shall try to describe the competitiveness of the European pharmaceutical industry, by using some indicators of competitiveness for individual firms and for countries.

# 8.1. CHARACTERISTICS OF THE PHARMACEUTICAL INDUSTRY IN EUROPE

### 8.1.1 Description of the Sector

Pharmaceuticals form a segment within the chemical industry.[2] Box 8.1 gives a definition of pharmaceuticals. Table 8.1 provides a survey of main economic figures for various European countries, including those of the European Community. This table is composed on the basis of statistics from various tables and graphs from publications of the European Federation of Pharmaceutical Industries' Associations (EFPIA).

*Box 8.1    Definition and scope of pharmaceuticals according to Article 1 of EC Directive 65/65*

---

• Proprietary medicinal products

Any ready prepared medicinal product placed on the market under a special name and in a special pack.

• Medicinal product

Any substance or combination of substances presented for treating or preventing disease in human beings or animals. Any substance or combination of substance which may be administered to human beings or animals with a view to making a medical diagnosis or to restoring, correcting or modifying physiological functions in human beings or in animals is likewise considered a medicinal product.

• Any substance irrespective of origin. Such substances may be:

— human, e.g. human blood and human blood products;

— animal, e.g. micro-organisms, whole animals, parts of organs, animal secretions, toxins, extracts, blood products;

— vegetables, e.g. elements naturally occurring, chemical materials and chemical products obtained by chemical change or synthesis.

---

*Source*: EC Panorama, 1991

### 8.1.1.1  The role of consumers and government regulation

The demand side of drugs is characterized by some special properties which are related to the existence of health insurance systems. Prescription drugs are *prescribed* by doctors. The consumers do not make decisions concerning quantity, brand name, etc.; nor do they make price comparisons between comparable drugs. The role of consumers in terms of allocative decisions is almost absent in the pharmaceutical market.

Table 8.1   Main economic indicators of the pharmaceutical industry, 1989

| Country | Production, ECU° m | Employment, '000s | Export as % of production | Consumption,* ECU m | Consumption per capita | R&D, ECU m |
|---|---|---|---|---|---|---|
| Germany | 11 119 | 78 | 35.6 | 7 701 | 131 | 1 505 |
| France | 10 423 | 85 | 21.1 | 7 504 | 134 | 1 165 |
| Italy | 8 031 | 67 | 15.1 | 6 623 | 115 | 638 |
| Netherlands | 1 067 | 13 | 95.4 | 878 | 60 | 154 |
| Belgium | 1 244 | 17 | 81.2 | 1 017 | 103 | 134 |
| UK | 8 432 | 74 | 30.9 | 4 629 | 81 | 1 117 |
| Ireland | 495 | 5 | 92.7 | 160 | 46 | n.a. |
| Denmark | 845 | 10 | 87.2 | 374 | 73 | 95 |
| Greece | 318 | 8 | 5.7 | 359 | 36 | n.a. |
| Spain | 3 408 | 35 | 13.6 | 2 118 | 54 | 73 |
| Portugal | 432 | 10 | 15.5 | 497 | 49 | n.a. |
| EC | 45 814 | 402 | 30.0 | 31 860 | | 5 881 |
| Austria | 639 | 7 | 60.4 | 651 | 86 | n.a. |
| Switzerland | 2 621 | 27 | 90.0 | 820 | 122 | 1 200 |
| Sweden | 932 | 7 | 70.7 | 818 | 97 | 375 |
| Norway | 312 | 2 | 22.4 | 266 | 63 | 30 |
| Finland | 384 | 4 | 18.5 | 471 | 94 | 40 |
| Total | 50 702 | 449 | 34.1 | 34 886 | | 7 526 |

° Exchange rate at 1 January 1992: ECU = $1.26
* Valued at producers: prices, ECU m
*Source*: EFPIA (1990)

Of course this is true for all services of health care in general, where the right of cure and care is accepted and where the distinction between decision makers (doctors), consumers (patients) and financing organizations (private and social health costs insurance companies) generally exists. Because for prescription medicines the consumption decisions are made by the prescribing doctors, they are the primary target for the sales promotion efforts of the pharmaceutical industry, instead of the consumers. These doctors are mainly interested in the therapeutical attributes of medicines and the reputation they have amongst colleagues and hospital specialists. The price is of less concern for the doctor.

All those characteristics of the demand side result in 'strange' relationships between changes in consumption volumes and price changes of prescription medicines. It is often the case that price-inelastic demand curves may be found, but given the absence of the link between consumption and individual payment, all kinds of values of price-elasticities can be found for individual products, including many positive values (Mantel 1987). The nature of the product and the meaning for social health and welfare, in combination with many chances for monopolistic behaviour at the supply side of the industry have led to government intervention beyond the scope of competition policy, for instance to price and reimbursement regulation.

### 8.1.1.2 The OTC market

The value of this market has made it important in terms of external operations (see sections 8.3 and 8.4). The most recent figures on the market for over-the-counter medicines give an indication of turnover of about US$10 bn in 1990 at producers' prices, which is associated with a market value of $18 bn at consumers' prices. A division of the total European OTC turnover over the most important countries is shown in Table 8.2.

*Table 8.2*    *European market for self-medication, 1990; country shares in total turnover of $10 bn at producers' prices*

| Country | Share of the country, in % |
|---------|----------------------------|
| France | 35 |
| Germany | 36 |
| UK | 9 |
| Italy | 9 |
| Spain | 5 |
| Belgium | 3 |
| Pays-Bas | 2 |

*Source*: IMS

There are also substantial differences in consumption per capita of self-medication products between the various countries in Europe. France and West Germany again show the highest consumption figures. In relation to large countries like the United Kingdom and Italy, French consumption is four times as high, while the same is almost true for German consumption (see Table 8.3).

*Table 8.3*    *Turnover of self-medication medicines per capita (US$) (prescription included)*

| Country | Self-medication per capita ($) |
|---------|--------------------------------|
| France | 63.6 |
| Germany | 57.0 |
| Belgium | 35.3 |
| UK | 16.1 |
| Italy | 15.0 |
| Spain | 11.8 |
| Netherlands | 11.2 |
| Portugal | 2.3 |

As is demonstrated by Table 8.4, the main firms or groups in the self-medication market are the same as in the prescription market.

*Table 8.4    Non-prescription pharmaceuticals. The 20 main world pharmaceutical groups on the medicaments market**

| Company (nationality) | Classification | Turnover 1989 (ECU bn) |
|---|---|---|
| Merck (US) | 1 | 4 |
| Bristol Myers-Squibb (US) | 2 | 3.5 |
| Glaxo (United Kingdom) | 3 | 3.1 |
| Smith-Kline Beecham (US–UK) | 4 | 3.0 |
| Ciba-Geigy (Switzerland) | 5 | 2.9 |
| American Home Products (US) | 6 | 2.7 |
| Hoechst (BR Deutschland) | 7 | 2.5 |
| Johnson & Johnson (US) | 8 | 2.3 |
| Bayer (BR Deutschland) | 9 | 2.3 |
| Sandoz (Switzerland) | 10 | 2.1 |
| Lilly (US) | 11 | 2.1 |
| Pfizer (US) | 12 | 2.1 |
| Rhône-Poulenc-Rorer (France–US) | 13 | 2.0 |
| Roche (Switzerland) | 14 | 1.9 |
| Schering Plough (US) | 15 | 1.6 |
| Marion Merell Dow (US) | 16 | 1.6 |
| Upjohn (US) | 17 | 1.5 |
| Sanofi-Sterling (France, US) | 18 | 1.5 |
| Boehringer (BR Deutschland) | 19 | 1.5 |
| Warner Lambert (US) | 20 | 1.4 |

\*    Classification based on sales by prescription

*Source*: Sema Group Management Consultants, quoted in Commission of the EC (1991), Chapter 8, p62

### 8.1.1.3  Generic competition and parallel imports

The following reasoning sheds some light on the paradoxical situation concerning the interests of different categories of suppliers of pharmaceutical products.

As long as price competition in markets for prescription drugs does not really emerge, there will be plenty of room for generics to capture interesting market shares, unless barriers to market entry prevail, for instance strong brand loyalty of prescribing doctors, bad acceptance by consumers and pharmacists, distributional problems, etc.

The existence of considerable price differentials between European countries (see Table 8.5) are first-order conditions for the parallel imports. Secondary conditions relate to the tackling of barriers, possibly thrown up by organizations in the 'official' network, like original manufacturers and their importers, wholesalers, pharmacists, health insurance organizations and government agencies (registration procedures, etc.).

*Table 8.5   Comparison of drug prices between EC countries in 1989*

|  | Producers' price level | Wholesalers' price level | Consumers' prices at pharmacies |
|---|---|---|---|
| Netherlands | 100 | 120 | 169 |
| Germany | 83 | 97 | 137 |
| UK | 80 | 92 | 122 |
| Belgium | 59 | 67 | 97 |
| Italy | 60 | 67 | 90 |
| Portugal | 48 | 53 | 66 |
| Spain | 39 | 45 | 64 |
| France | 39 | 43 | 62 |
| Greece | 32 | 34 | 47 |

*Note*:   The index starts at the top left; the producers' price level for the most expensive country = 100
*Source*: IWI-Studien, Band (1991)

Some of these barriers have been cleared by decisions of the European Court (see for instance the Centrafarm cases). But the commercial incentive will always be the primary condition for the viability of parallel imports, that is the existence of relative high price differentials, high enough to compensate for transport costs, etc. If the disappearance of high price differentials were one of the consequences of the internal market than parallel imports would no longer be commercially interesting and would therefore vanish. However, recent evaluation of the Transparency Guideline does not show much harm to local regulation schemes and therefore not to price differentials between member states.

Market concentration as a result of defensive and offensive mergers and takeovers of European firms will certainly not lead to price competition between products of research-based firms, but probably to a smaller selection of available drugs by eliminating many 'me-too' products as the result of strategies aimed at reaping scale economies in production and promotion of the best-selling drugs. These efficiency gains of bigger concerns combined with lower costs as a result of unified registration procedures could be used to set drug prices at the end of the patent duration at such low levels that production of generics by independent firms would not be profitable. But, as we shall argue later on, the established pharmaceutical firms have strong linkages with the generic industry, so the incentives for fierce price competition are absent.

The increasing importance of the generic markets has led to many take-overs of generic firms by innovative multinationals, not only in the US with its large generic market size, but also in EC countries. The big difference between the European countries and the US for the market position of generics can be explained by the fact that pharmacists in the US have more freedom to substitute generics for branded products and have had more pressure from health insurance companies to do so. For the market share of generic firms in various countries, see Table 8.6.

*Table 8.6  Generic market shares of prescription drug sales, 1990*

| Country | As % of drug sales |
|---|---|
| Belgium | < 5 |
| Denmark | 18 |
| France | 5 |
| Ireland | n.a. |
| Spain | 2 |
| Netherlands | 12 |
| United Kingdom | 10 |
| West Germany | 15 |
| European Community | 7 |
| United States | 25 |
| Japan | 19 |

*Source*: Internal EC Document (1990)

At present, the number of independent generic manufacturers is very limited. Ratiopharm with the largest sales in Germany is a subsidiary of Merckle, Basotherm is a subsidiary of Boehringer Ingelheim and Hoechst owns an important generic supplier in the UK, A. H. Cox (Burstall 1986). Besides, the German company Stada has taken over the Dutch generic company Centrafarm and the Belgian generic company Eurogenerics.

In the United Kingdom generic consolidation has increased considerably during the last few years. The UK Harris (generics) was taken over by the US Ivax Corporation; Evans Medical and Thomas Kerfoot (both generic suppliers) were taken over by the UK Medeva Group. For France, Rhône-Poulenc's acquisition in 1988 of 68 per cent of Rorer (US) also resulted in further generic consolidation because each of these companies owned a generic subsidiary, respectively Berk and APS.[3] In addition, the medium-sized innovative French company Siegfried acquired the generic firm Dakota.

The prospects for growth of generic consumption are favourable for countries with relatively high prices, especially when we bear in mind that in the next decade many patents of important drugs expire and the pressure on governments to control expenditure on drugs will increase. The future European market for generics is estimated at about $4 bn in 1994.

### 8.1.1.4 Biotechnology and the pharmaceutical industry

The type of biotechnology that is relevant for the actual analysis of the dynamics of competition in the pharmaceutical industry is called 'genetic or protein engineering'. Genetic engineering enables researchers to create cells that can produce specific proteins. The synthesis of proteins offers applications for drugs and diagnostic products.

At present the number of approved diagnostic products is much higher (200) than the number of biotechnology-based human drugs (about ten). However, the commercial prospects for the drugs for human use are far more interesting than those for diagnostic products. A drastic increase in the number of biotech-derived drugs is expected in the next decade. Pisano (1991) has estimated that by the beginning of 1991 about 425 biotechnology-based drugs were in some stage of pre-clinical testing or human clinical trials.

Table 8.7 shows the FDA-approved biotechnology products, the date of introduction and the involved companies, in the role of developer and marketer.

*Table 8.7    FDA-approved biotechnology products*

| Product | Date | Developer | Marketer |
|---------|------|-----------|----------|
| Human insulin | 1982 | Genentech | Eli Lilly |
| Human growth hormone | 1985 | Genentech | Genentech |
| Alpha interferon | 1986 | Biogen | Schering-Plough |
| Alpha interferon | 1986 | Genentech | Hoffmann-La Roche |
| OKT3 MAb | 1986 | J&J | J&J |
| Hepatitis B vaccine | 1986 | Chiron | Merck |
| T-PA | 1987 | Genentech | Genentech |
| Human growth hormone | 1987 | Eli Lilly | Eli Lilly |
| Erythropoietin (EPO) | 1989 | Amgen | Amgen |
| Hepatitis B vaccine | 1989 | Biogen | Smith-Kline Beecham |

*Note*:    Frequency of cases: NBF (New Biotechnology Firm) developer and marketer: 3; NBF developer – established firm marketer: 5; established firm developer and marketer: 2; total cases: 10

*Source*: Pisano (1991), p242

As we are primarily interested in the linkages between established innovative pharmaceutical firms and biotechnology firms, and especially the differences in involvement between European and American companies, it is very clear that US companies dominate the biotechnology pharmaceuticals market in the US. Only the Swiss firm Hoffmann-La Roche played a role, mainly as the marketing partner of Genentech and later on as the major shareholder of Genentech. At least two German firms will be involved in the marketing of future products of biotechnology pharmaceutical product developer Immunex, namely Hoechst and Bayer via their US subsidiary cutter.

It is believed that the biotechnology discoveries will have good chances for development in relatively small newly established firms, while in the later stages of product development and in the marketing phase, alliances with large pharmaceutical companies will be necessary to raise enough capital to finance these activities.

## 8.1.2 The Role of Innovation

The pharmaceutical industry is very R&D-intensive; almost 15 per cent of turnover is invested in R&D. As was illustrated in Table 8.1 with the main economic indicators of the pharmaceutical industry in Europe, total R&D expenditure in the European Community amounts to a value of $7.3 bn (ECU 5.8 bn) in 1989. R&D in West Germany, France and the United Kingdom show the highest amounts in the EC, between ECU 1.5 bn and ECU 1.2 bn, comparable with the R&D expenditure (1.1 bn) of the Swiss pharmaceutical industry, being the highest European R&D spender in this sector outside the EC.

Table 8.8 illustrates the world division of the recent results of research in the pharmaceutical industry in terms of the numbers of new chemical entities (NCEs).

*Table 8.8   Development of new chemical entities per country, 1983–87*

| Country | Number of NCE |
|---|---|
| West Germany | 29 |
| Italy | 25 |
| France | 21 |
| Switzerland | 14 |
| United Kingdom | 12 |
| Other countries | 20 |
| United States | 64 |
| Japan | 69 |
| Total NCEs | 254 |

*Source*: International Medical Statistics (IMS)

The number of NCEs in the pharmaceutical industry in the European Community is very high in comparison with the two big rivals Japan and the United States. The total of NCEs in EC countries adds up to 87 compared to 69 for Japan and 64 for the USA. This table does not show the situation of market introductions. For instance, the long registration procedures at the American Food and Drug Administration (FDA) have meant that during the period 1983-85 only fifteen American NCEs came first on the US market. Most NCEs were first introduced on foreign markets.

Figure 8.1 shows the division of new chemical entities over the economic areas of the US, Japan and Western Europe from 1960 until 1989.

*Figure 8.1     Pharmaceuticals: new molecules by geographical source, 1960–89*

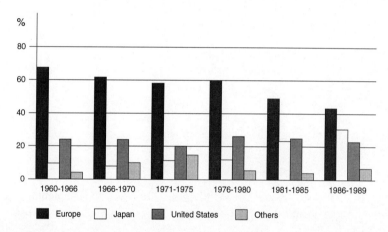

*Source*: *Scrip*

Although the European position in absolute numbers of new chemical entities is still strong, it cannot be denied that, in terms of NCE growth figures during the last fifteen years (1976–90), Japan shows the best performance. That is why representatives of European pharmaceutical producers' organizations have pleaded for an extension of effective patent protection in the European Community, in order to get equal treatment as is the case in the United States and Japan.

Pharmaceutical firms with a successful innovative drug launch every five to ten years can be considered as strong firms, capable of combining the highly profitable stages of the product life cycle of one product with those of a superseding product. The reality of innovation shows very different positions of the different manufacturers. Many European firms have only a few innovative products in their sales portfolio (Table 8.9).

*Table 8.9   Age structure of pharmaceutical companies' sales, 1987*

|  | Products older than 10 years, in % | Products 6-10 years old, in % | Products 3-5 years old, in % |
|---|---|---|---|
| Total market | 66.0 | 18.3 | 14.1 |
| Glaxo (UK) | 53.2 | 11.7 | 35.1 |
| Merck & Co. (US) | 38.7 | 11.7 | 44.4 |
| Smith-Kline (US) | 95.7 | 1.1 | 3.1 |
| Astra (S) | 66.6 | 13.7 | 19.4 |
| Janssen (B) | 41.5 | 38.0 | 20.0 |
| Beecham (UK) | 76.2 | 23.7 |  |
| Hoffmann-La Roche (Swi) | 67.1 | 16.4 | 15.8 |
| Ici-Farma (UK) | 78.0 | 9.0 | 12.3 |
| Ciba-Geigy (Swi) | 97.3 | 2.3 | 0.4 |
| Schering AG (G) | 57.8 | 39.8 | 2.4 |
| Sandoz-Wander (Swi) | 60.6 | 14.0 | 23.8 |
| Organon (Neth) | 36.0 | 61.3 | 2.6 |
| Wyeth (US) | 54.0 | 45.7 | 0.3 |
| Gist-Brocades (Neth) | 61.6 | 18.4 | 15.3 |
| Boehringer Ing. (G) | 95.3 | 2.5 | 1.0 |
| Bayer (G) | 20.1 | 41.0 | 38.8 |
| Hoechst (G) | 80.7 | 5.1 | 10.4 |
| Cedona (F) | 78.8 | 4.8 | 13.1 |
| Novo (D) | 46.8 | 38.4 | 13.6 |
| Squibb (USA) | 24.9 | 63.4 | 10.5 |

*Source*: Medical-Pharmaceutical Bulletins, Utrecht, 1989

This table also gives a clear indication of the high level of potential exposure of these research-based firms to generic competition. Some companies have been successful in defending their key products after patent expiry, but on the other hand authorities aiming at cost containment try to promote generic competition by legislation.

Older products that are essentially similar to existing licensed products could already refer to the original files of the first applicant, containing the results of clinical trials and pharmacological and toxicological tests. This abridged procedure has been provided with certain limitations via Article 1 of Directive no. 87/21 of the European Commission, that gives conditions about periods of market protection for the applicant of the original product. Only when pharmaceutical products derived from biotechnology or high-technology have been on the market for ten years will the abridged procedure be possible. Before that time, manufacturers will have to give full dossiers of tests and clinical trials, etc. The impact of this limitation on abridged procedures could be less incentive for producers to come with products. The impact on generic production after patent expiration of this time condition is not so obvious. The original first brand on the market will gain more brand loyalty in time as there will be fewer 'me-too' products, at least during the ten-year absence of abbreviated registration facilities. The higher brand loyalty could form a serious barrier to entry to 'me-too' products and generics. The promotional costs of passing these barriers could be too high for small generic firms. Only state promotion or generic-friendly regulation will be able to overcome these problems for small independent generic manufacturers. We expect a battle between real innovative firms in a highly concentrated industry and smaller generic firms, that will partly be independent and will partly be owned by pharmaceutical firms or wholesale companies. The danger exists that the market success of some independent generic firms will also mean their early end as independent firms.

### 8.1.3 Structure of the Industry

#### 8.1.3.1 Market shares, concentration and leading companies

Looking at world market figures, the pharmaceutical industry is far less concentrated than many other manufacturing industries. The world's largest drug company, Merck & Co. in the US, possesses only about 4.5 per cent of the world market, while the next three of the ranking according to world sales own market shares of about 3–3.5 per cent (*Scrip* 1990).

In 1982, the market shares of the top five sellers in eight EC countries varied between 19 per cent for Italy and 29 per cent for France, with inter-mediate positions for West Germany (24 per cent) and the United Kingdom (27 per cent) (Wolf 1987). The same five-firm concentration ratio (C-5) for the total EC market was much lower, only 15 per cent.

The larger EC countries, with significant demand, show market dominance by domestic producers. This is demonstrated in Table 8.10 with the domestic market shares in some EC countries and the names of the leading four companies in them. Despite the trend to globalization and inter-nationalization, domestic producers still have a firm grip on their home markets, which for some countries seems to demonstrate more powerful positions for their home-based firms than would be expected in the light of their relative strength in a European context.

In respect of market concentration in the pharmaceutical industry at the level of the total pharmaceutical market, we see relatively low figures of the C-4 concentration ratio in most European countries.

A comparison of these 1989 figures with national concentration levels of seven years ago (1982) tells us that the division of market share in France stays very stable. Even the market share of the first ranked company, Rhône-Poulenc, remains at the level of 9 per cent during this period.

*Table 8.10  The four leading companies in EC countries, 1989*

| Country and company | National market share, % |
|---|---|
| *France* | |
| 1. Rhône-Poulenc | 9.0 |
| 2. Sanofi | 5.7 |
| 3. Roussel Uclaf (Hoechst) | 5.4 |
| 4. Servier | 5.3 |
| Total | 25.4 |
| *Germany* | |
| 1. Hoechst | 4.0 |
| 2. Boehringer I. | 3.7 |
| 3. Bayer | 3.4 |
| 4. Merckle/Ratiopharm | 3.0 |
| Total | 14.1 |
| *United Kingdom* | |
| 1. Glaxo | 14.0 |
| 2. Smith-Kline Beecham | 5.9 |
| 3. Ciba-Geigy | 4.8 |
| 4. ICI | 4.7 |
| Total | 29.4 |

*Source*: *Scrip* (1990)

West Germany showed a decline of domestic market power of the four biggest producers to only 14 per cent, combined with a very even share-distribution amongst the four leading firms.

Most interesting in the German ranking is the Merckle-owned generic producer Ratiopharm in the fourth place according to sales, but already ranking in first place according to volumes of sales.

The domestic market share of the United Kingdom has increased to more than 29 per cent due to the enormous sales growth of Glaxo, now belonging to the top five of the world and also due to the merger of UK Smith-Kline with US Beecham. Glaxo alone with a market share of 14 per cent doubled the market share of the top company in the UK (which was 7 per cent in 1982).

Ciba-Geigy in the US ranking is the only 'outsider', when looking at the origins of the companies on the lists of the four leading companies of these big EC member states. With this exception, only national companies occupy the positions of the four leading companies in these countries.

But we must realize that domestic market shares do not tell us much about the real intensity of competition in the relevant therapeutical market segments, where position determines the strategies for price setting for the companies involved.

Pharmaceutical markets by therapeutic category show a different picture. For instance, the world market for insulin products is characterized by two big suppliers Novo-Nordisk (Denmark) and Eli Lilly (US), a third supplier, Hoechst (Germany), with a modest share of 4 per cent and a couple of firms with smaller market shares, adding up to 24 per cent (Drosten and Kammradt 1990).

Novo-Nordisk is the market leader with products derived from animal glands, while Eli Lilly is selling insulin on the basis of DNA methods, originally developed by Genentech. It took Eli Lilly many years to capture high market share for this biotech product. The picture in the EC market is still more in favour of Novo-Nordisk, as we shall see in Table 8.11, but it cannot be denied that Eli Lilly's insulin is now the fastest growing market.

*Table 8.11   Market concentration for insulin products in the European Community, 1988*

| Corporation | Sales, US$ m | Market share, % | Growth rate in 1988, % |
|---|---|---|---|
| Novo-Nordisk | 208 | 62 | 9 |
| Hoechst | 75 | 23 | 10 |
| Lilly | 44 | 13 | 46 |
| Others | 7 | 2 | 12 |
|  | 334 | 100 | – |

*Source*: Annual Reports, Novo Nordisk

### 8.1.3.2  International trade

Trade in pharmaceuticals is very important, not only as a result of differences in the national presence of pharmaceutical research institutions and pharmaceutical manufacturers, but also as a result of specialization of companies in research areas. This implies that sometimes countries with only one or two domestic companies may have a high import/consumption ratio combined with a positive trade balance due to the high value of exports of specialized medicines.

Besides, because of the multinational structure of many companies in this industry, there is a real network of production plants and sales divisions. This also creates trade flows. When we look at the total exports of EC countries in 1988, Germany ranks at first place in absolute export values (ECU 3.9 bn), followed by the United Kingdom (ECU 2.6 bn) and France (ECU 2.2 bn), but expressed as a percentage of production, the Netherlands has 95 per cent, with a second place for Ireland (93 per cent), a third for Denmark (87 per cent) and a fourth place for Belgium (81 per cent).

Thirty per cent of the production in EC countries is exported. When we subtract the EC intra-trade from this figure, we find an average export/production ratio of 13 per cent of the EC as a total (see Table 8.1).

Table 8.12 shows the market shares by corporate nationality in the pharmaceutical markets of the four largest EC countries and in the US and Japan. This table shows that the US market and the Japanese market are highly dominated by firms of domestic origin. In the EC, Germany has the highest domestic market share of 56 per cent, followed by France (49 per cent) and Italy (43 per cent), whereas the UK has a relatively modest domestic market share, which is amazing when we realize that the British pharmaceutical industry must be considered as the strongest of the EC countries (see section 8.5). Also, we see that the US–UK connection is strong: the US firms have a market share of 33 per cent in the UK market, while the UK firms have a market share of 10 per cent in the US market. Finally, it appears that German firms have succeeded in gaining a 5 per cent market share in Japan, which is the best performance of European countries.

*Table 8.12  Market shares by corporate nationality, 1989, in %*

| Supplier origin | Market | | | | | |
|---|---|---|---|---|---|---|
| | US | Japan | Germany | France | UK | Italy |
| United States | 74.0 | 10.0 | 18.0 | 23.0 | 33.0 | 22.0 |
| Japan | 2.0 | 79.0 | 1.0 | – | – | – |
| Germany | 4.0 | 5.0 | 56.0 | 11.0 | 9.5 | 15.0 |
| France | – | – | 4.0 | 49.0 | 3.5 | 3.0 |
| United Kingdom | 10.0 | 1.3 | 5.0 | 6.0 | 39.0 | 7.0 |
| Italy | 0.6 | 0.1 | 1.5 | – | | 43.0 |
| Netherlands | 0.3 | 0.2 | 1.3 | 2.0 | 1.3 | |
| Belgium | 0.2 | | 1.5 | 0.5 | 2.1 | |
| Denmark | 0.5 | 0.2 | 2.4 | | 2.1 | 0.6 |
| Sweden | 8.0 | 3.5 | 8.0 | 7.0 | 7.0 | 9.0 |
| Market coverage | 99.6 | 99.3 | 98.7 | 98.5 | 97.5 | 99.6 |

## 8.2  'COMPLETING THE INTERNAL MARKET': THE CHALLENGES

### 8.2.1  Completing the Internal Market

The Commission has kept the promises of the white paper[4] and has offered a package of proposals to the Parliament and the Council in order to attain the Single Market for medicines. The most important EC proposals had to do with:
- registration harmonization procedures;
- transparency of price regulation systems and reimbursement systems;
- supplementary patent protection.

**8.2.1.1  The harmonization of registration procedures**

The absence of harmonized registration procedures in combination with too lengthy registration periods in many countries in the European Community, are considererd as the main cost elements in the situation of a non-integrated pharmaceutical EC market. Officially registration procedures in the EC may not last longer than 120 days, but practice is still different: in West Germany and the United Kingdom for instance companies have to wait two years, and in Italy and Spain even three years, before they get their products through the registration procedure. Estimation of the total costs caused by late and varied procedures in different EC countries leads to the conclusion that harmonized registration could mean a cost decrease of 0.5 to 0.8 per cent in the pharmaceutical industry in the Common Market (Cecchini 1988).

The question of how to handle drug regulation in the European Community in an ideal and effective way cannot be answered easily. Both industry and governments are divided between policy options like mutual recognition or a central European agency. However the basic task of the European Commission is to remove all regulatory barriers to the free circulation of drugs after 1992. A single central registration for European drugs looks the less complicated way in principle to achieve this goal. The European central registration system would require consensus on the criteria on which registrations are granted throughout the Community. This consensus is not yet achieved. As long as there rests much uncertainty about pan-European standards, many pharmaceutical companies will have more trust in well-known national registration systems.

The Commission has responded by designing a system of pharmaceutical registration that takes account of the divided opinions amongst the participants and the fact that we have to cope with the heritage of national registered existing products, which can be distinguished from new pharmaceutical products. The biotech/high-tech products all use the direct access route through the EC Drug Agency (EDA), while for the other NCEs (new chemical entities) of interest to the EC market the company can choose between the central route via the EDA and the multistate procedure.

While European harmonization of regulation on registration procedures seems beneficial to innovative firms as they can reap economies of scale in production and promotion (compare the arguments of the Cecchini report), they must also reckon with the fact that these advantages are also available to the potential rivals with so-called 'me-too' products and to American and Japanese competitors.

**8.2.1.2  The role of price and reimbursement policies**

The Council Directive of 1989 on the transparency of measures regulating the pricing of medicine products for human use and their inclusion in the scope of National Health Insurance Schemes only laid down a minimum set of rules to be obeyed by member states. These rules have to do with time limits, agreements, publication of measures and options for appeal by concerned parties against the measures.

The efficacy of the transparency rules is at present being performed in order to draw conclusions on the perspectives for harmonization. Some decisions made by the European Court on matters of price regulation will probably imply that a uniform EC package of measures cannot be expected, so that the variation in price and reimbursement instruments will stay intact.[5]

There is still a great variety of national regulation instruments and legislation on matters of price controls, profit margin controls, reimbursement policies, positive and negative medicines lists and so on. If this variety persists, consumers in different countries will still be confronted with enormous price differences between identical drugs and pharmaceutical firms will have to cope with these different regimes in the EC. Thus all kinds of existing strategies, including transfer pricing, negotiations with member states, etc. will continue in the foreseeable future, unless the European Commission presents a new and creative perspective on these matters.

### 8.2.1.3 The Supplementary Protection Certificate

Under the European Patent Convention (1978) each pharmaceutical invention is entitled to a monopoly protection by patent for a period of 20 years from the date of filing. However, the new invented chemical entity (NCE) protected in this way takes a long time to evolve as a drug with market authorization.

*Table 8.13 Average years of effective patent life per patented product in top 100*

| Country | 1980, pre-1970 products | 1980, all | 1988, all | 1988, post-1980 products |
|---------|-------------------------|-----------|-----------|--------------------------|
| France  | 16.5 | 13.6 | 12.2 | 10.2 |
| Germany | 14.8 | 11.8 | 11.0 | 10.5 |
| UK      | 15.6 | 13.1 | 13.0 | 11.9 |
| USA     | 17.9 | 15.1 | 12.3 | 10.7 |
| Japan   | n.a. | n.a. | 11.2 | 11.1 |

*Source*: Redwood (1990)

These figures illustrate the erosion of effective patent life during the 1980s. It is on the basis of these kinds of patent life figures combined with the increased R&D costs of new drugs, that representatives of the pharmaceutical industry have asked for regulation to restore effective patent protection.

The European Commission took the initiative by introducing the supplementary protection certificate (the idea was of French origin) as an additional instrument of industrial property, thereby circumventing the problem of trying to get the European Patent Convention changed, a very complex and time-consuming matter. The main goal is to encourage innovative R&D in the pharmaceutical industry and research institutions in the European Community. This new instrument must be considered not only as a remedy for the considerable reduction in effective patent protection for pharmaceuticals in the EC, but also as a European reply to the regulatory changes in drugs patent protection enacted by the US Drug Price Competition and Patent Restoration Act of 1984 (the Waxman-Hatch Act) and a comparable drugs patent extension law on broadly the same principles in Japan in 1988.

The time limit of the Supplementary Protection Certificate (SPC) is not fixed, but dependent on the number of lost years of effective patent protection for each particular drug, with a maximum term of fifteen years. A further restriction is also made by the European Commission: the total duration of effective protection by the basic patent plus the certificate protection may not exceed fifteen years from the date of first market authorization in the EC.

### 8.2.1.4 Biotechnology policy

We conclude this section by giving some information on the EC programme for biotechnology after the installation of the Biotechnology Steering Committee in 1984. Two of the priorities were research and training programmes and a biotechnology regulation. The Biomolecular Engineering Programme (BEP: $15 m, 1982–86) focused on aspects of genetic engineering and enzymology. It was followed by the broader Biotechnology Action Programme (BAP: $55 m, 1985–89) and by its successor entitled BRIDGE ($100 m).

The regulations set down by the Biotechnology Regulation Inter-service Committee (since 1985) are designed to promote a harmonized regulatory approach to biotechnology.

### 8.2.2 The Challenges

Mr Kessler, President of the EFPIA, has spelt out the opportunities and challenges for the European pharmaceutical industry. In short, as opportunities he saw continuous industrial growth, scientific and technological growth and therapeutic advances. Speaking about the challenges, he posed three questions (*Health Horizons*, September 1991):

1. How effectively can the European pharmaceutical industry compete with the US and Japanese pharmaceutical industries — in Europe and in the wider international market?
2. How far are national governments in Europe ready to recognize that they have a choice between supporting the pharmaceutical industry now or watching its decline over the coming decade?
3. How skilled are European institutions — and particularly the EC — going to be in balancing competing demands for better health care and tighter cost-control?

The European pharmaceutical industry is strong.[6] But its strength depends on constant investment and determined effort. If conditions for the industry in Europe become worse, the impetus for this continued development will be lost — and so too will the industry's prospects for growth.

The pharmaceutical industry is one of the few large high-tech industries where European firms have a dominant position in the world market. Of the top ten drugs of the world, seven are made and marketed by European companies. The UK pharmaceutical industry is the most successful of the European countries, the German industry is reasonably strong and the French industry has some strong companies, in particular after the consolidation in France (see section 8.3).

Will the regulatory changes, introduced in the European Community in order to lead to a single market, be in favour of the EC-based companies or will they create a tougher trading environment with uncertain outcomes for the positions of EC firms? The chances of more intensive internal competition between European firms depend on the willingness of governments of EC countries to harmonize assortments of authorized products (varying from 3000 to 70000 authorized drugs), pricing regimes and reimbursement schemes. It seems that many European and American companies have learned to cope with the complex and differing national regulatory environments, while these have hardly been accessible to Japanese companies until now.

It seems plausible that the publication of the white paper has led many drug companies to the conclusion that the internal market will become a reality in the future. This would mean a reduction of barriers to entry to Japanese firms on the EC market. Along with the tighter cost containment programmes and the rising costs of innovation in many EC countries, these developments have led to an enormous increase in the number of external operations (mergers, acquisitions, and all kinds of strategic alliances) as responses to meet the new challenges or more intense competition between fewer but more powerful companies.

# 8.3   MERGERS AND ACQUISITIONS IN THE PHARMACEUTICAL INDUSTRY

## 8.3.1  Firms' Strategies

A number of driving forces shaping corporate strategy in the pharmaceutical industry in the last decade are mentioned in the literature, like the rising costs of innovation, the volume and price stagnation in major markets and the growing universality of practice and therapy.[7]

### 8.3.1.1  Rising costs of innovation

Cost recovery for continuous growing costs of innovation has become an important economic issue. A minimal critical mass seems needed to finance expensive innovation to generate good products and the sales expenditure to sell these products on a global scale. Rapid market penetration in the most profitable markets is needed in order to make optimal use of the effective patent protection period. Large volumes of production and efficient sales promotion can also lead to maintaining high market shares after patent protection, by making use of established brand loyalty in combination with price reduction in the case of competition by substitute products.

The main motives for many mergers and acquisitions are sought in terms of reaching the critical mass, which must be estimated at about $2 bn, according to various observers (James 1990; *Financial Times* 1991). This critical mass has been reached, for instance, as a result of the following mergers/acquisitions:

- Bristol Myers/Squibb (US)
- Smith-Kline/Beecham (US/UK)
- American Home Products/Robins (US)
- Roche/Genentech (Switzerland/US)
- Rhône-Poulenc/Rorer (France/US)
- Merrell Dow/Marion (US)

As subsidiary benefits of these external operations are seen: increase in innovation spending, increase in marketing strength, cost rationalization, acquisition of new products (including biotech products) and last but not least avoidance of hostile takeovers.

### 8.3.1.2  Globalization

We start this section with a table to show the market presence of the top fifteen pharmaceutical companies within the world's three core business areas: the US, Europe and Japan (Table 8.14).

*Table 8.14 Market presence of the top fifteen*

| Rank | Company | North America | Europe | Japan |
|------|---------|---------------|--------|-------|
| 1 | Merck & Co. | × | × | × |
| 2 | Bristol Myers/Squibb | × | × | – |
| 3 | Glaxo | × | × | – |
| 4 | Smith-Kline Beecham | × | × | × |
| 5 | Ciba-Geigy | × | × | – |
| 6 | Amho/Robins | × | × | – |
| 7 | Hoechst | – | × | – |
| 8 | Johnson & Johnson | × | × | – |
| 9 | Bayer | – | × | × |
| 10 | Sandoz | – | × | – |
| 11 | Lilly | × | – | – |
| 12 | Pfizer | × | – | – |
| 13 | Roche/Genentech | – | × | – |
| 14 | Rhône-Poulenc/Rorer | – | × | – |
| 15 | Merrell Dow/Marion | × | – | – |

*Source*: James (1990)

While the main companies participate in all three major geographic areas through licensing and joint ventures as well as their own operating companies, there is clearly a lack of a truly direct geographic presence at a level similar to their global ranking. The only exceptions are Merck & Co. and Smith-Kline Beecham.

The majority of innovative pharmaceutical companies operate in a multinational way, with the normal differences in organizational models, running from centrally controlled organization models to more autonomous local divisions. Global operating firms are those that seek to gain competitive advantages by integrating business activities on a worldwide basis (Porter 1986). This does not mean that these firms have to be present in each continent of the Triad (Ohmae 1985); the selection of the locations is also part of the global strategy which aims to gain maximum advantages from the coordination and control of activities that are geographically dispersed.

According to this definition of globalization, global firms compete with each other on a global basis; they are interested in each others' global market shares, performance indicators and external operations, aimed at gaining competitive advantage. Most pharmaceutical companies that are mentioned in this study correspond to this definition. Production activities and the later stages of product development can be found in various countries, while the earlier stages of R&D take place at the headquarters.

Clinical trials can be performed by research institutes in various countries, close to the planned markets, which is also necessary for better access to national registration authorities and for getting known in the health profession of the target countries. This is also the case for packaging and marketing; attitudes and habits of local pharmacists and physicians must be known for good access to markets. Therefore these activities may be spread over many countries.

More concentration in basic production processes in Europe may be necessary in order to reap economies of scale. In some countries, like France and Italy, the number of manufacturers is very high with the risk of inefficient production volumes. Mergers and acquisitions in these countries will unavoidably take place against the perspectives of European integration. Also unavoidable will be the abandonment of national governments' preferential treatment of foreign companies that invest in domestic production or research facilities in order to get better negotiation terms with regard to drug prices on the market. Sometimes, forms of alliances can also be understood as strategic responses of foreign companies to cope with this kind of government behaviour.

All this does not mean that there will be no room at all for smaller pharmaceutical companies. Of course, some highly specialized and innovative firms may be large and efficient enough to serve part of the European market or even a share of the global market for their specialities (e.g. Novo-Nordisk, the insulin manufacturer from Denmark, and Akzo-Pharma from the Netherlands with contraceptive products as its core business).

Most of the companies in the pharmaceutical industry are specialists, operating in specific geographical (regional or national), therapeutic or business fields. The viability of specialist strategies is a function of the sustainability of the technology or services which provide the competitive advantage in the niche position. Therapeutical specialization based on technology may be vulnerable, because the larger the therapeutical segment, the more attractive it will be to competitors.

### 8.3.1.3 Industry structure
The most remarkable fact about the pharmaceutical industry is that it has lasted almost intact since 1950 with few new firms and only a limited number of acquisitions and mergers among the leading players until the end of the 1980s. This long-term stability has persisted because normal rules of competition did not apply. Patents, trademarks and increasing regulation acted as barriers to entry.

From the mid-1980s the industry's favourable environment began to change, due to both external and internal factors. External factors were: deregulation, customer criticism on high pricing levels; and internal: the increasing cost of innovation, a declining payback, as well as the unpredictability of the timing of new product introductions; and the loss of income from major products because of the decreasing level of patent protection.

### 8.3.2 Mergers and Acquisitions

Looking at the rough data of the Predicast magazines information system,[8] we found 783 mergers and acquisitions in the pharmaceutical industry for the period of 1980–90. The countries involved in the searching process were all countries of the European Community, the United States and Japan (covering the Triad) as well as important countries as far as the pharmaceutical industry is concerned: Switzerland and Sweden.

All firms from these countries that were involved in mergers and acquisitions were divided between acquiring and acquired firms. By excluding countries that were only incidentally involved in mergers and acquisitions and that were also outside our main focus countries, we reduced the number of mergers and acquisitions in our database to 666 for the period 1980–90 (see Figure 8.2).

*Figure 8.2     Number of M&As, 1980–90 (total = 666)*

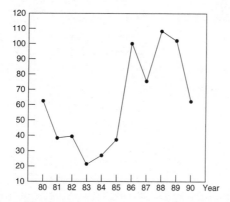

There will be a mixture of explanatory factors responsible for the evolution of the number of external operations. We mention business cycles in general, but in this sector product life cycles play a big role. The peak years after 1985 may be explained by a combination of factors relating to the renewed efforts of the European Commission to complete the internal market for drugs (white paper, etc.), the fast rising costs of innovation (including the high interest rates used to capitalize investments), many patent expiries, the fear of fierce Japanese competition on the European and American market, and the fast growing confidence in the future role of biotechnology in the pharmaceutical industry.

Table 8.15 shows that France has been the most active country involved in these types of firms' external operations. The number of mergers and acquisitions in France (150) even exceeds the number of these operations in the United States, which is 113. The United Kingdom and Germany were also very active with respectively 94 and 73 mergers and acquisitions.

Table 8.15  M&As, EC, plus US, Japan, Sweden and Switzerland*

| Acquiring country | Belgium | Denmark | France | Germany | Ireland | Italy | Japan | Netherlands | Portugal | Spain | Sweden | Switzerland | UK | US | Total |
|---|---|---|---|---|---|---|---|---|---|---|---|---|---|---|---|
| Belgium | 4 | 0 | 0 | 0 | 0 | 2 | 1 | 1 | 0 | 5 | 0 | 0 | 0 | 3 | 16 |
| Denmark | 0 | 5 | 0 | 0 | 0 | 0 | 0 | 0 | 0 | 0 | 0 | 0 | 0 | 3 | 8 |
| France | 0 | 0 | 83 | 3 | 0 | 12 | 2 | 0 | 3 | 12 | 1 | 2 | 5 | 27 | 150 |
| Germany | 2 | 2 | 4 | 27 | 1 | 3 | 2 | 4 | 0 | 5 | 0 | 2 | 6 | 15 | 73 |
| Ireland | 0 | 0 | 0 | 0 | 3 | 0 | 0 | 0 | 0 | 0 | 0 | 0 | 0 | 1 | 4 |
| Italy | 0 | 0 | 0 | 0 | 0 | 26 | 0 | 1 | 0 | 3 | 0 | 11 | 1 | 13 | 45 |
| Japan | 1 | 0 | 0 | 4 | 0 | 0 | 0 | 1 | 0 | 1 | 0 | 0 | 1 | 0 | 8 |
| Netherlands | 2 | 0 | 2 | 3 | 1 | 2 | 0 | 7 | 0 | 1 | 0 | 0 | 2 | 8 | 28 |
| Spain | 0 | 0 | 0 | 0 | 0 | 0 | 0 | 0 | 0 | 15 | 0 | 0 | 0 | 0 | 15 |
| Sweden | 1 | 3 | 3 | 0 | 0 | 5 | 1 | 3 | 0 | 4 | 27 | 0 | 0 | 17 | 64 |
| Switzerland | 3 | 0 | 5 | 2 | 1 | 0 | 1 | 0 | 0 | 1 | 0 | 13 | 4 | 18 | 48 |
| UK | 1 | 0 | 3 | 2 | 0 | 4 | 3 | 3 | 0 | 2 | 0 | 2 | 51 | 23 | 94 |
| US | 4 | 2 | 14 | 13 | 6 | 15 | 0 | 2 | 1 | 11 | 3 | 8 | 20 | 14 | 113 |
| Total | 18 | 12 | 114 | 54 | 12 | 69 | 10 | 22 | 4 | 60 | 31 | 28 | 90 | 142 | 666 |

* Rows: countries of acquiring/merging firms
  Columns: countries of acquired/merging firms

American firms show the highest absolute score of 99 cross-border M&As. France has a second place with 67 cross-border M&As, followed by Germany (46), the United Kingdom (43) and Sweden (37) and Switzerland (35) as European countries outside the EC.

Eighty-three operations or 55 per cent of the total number of French operations had a domestic scope. Even after this series of internal M&As the number of pharmaceutical firms in France is still very high.[9] The shares of internal versus cross-border M&As for some other EC countries were respectively: Germany 37 per cent, UK 54 per cent, Italy 58 per cent.

Notwithstanding the energy and finance French firms are investing in internal M&As, their foreign investments in cross-border mergers and acquisitions are considerable. Within the EC, Spain and Italy are the favourite countries for French acquisitions, with twelve operations in each of these countries. But the broader external interest of French firms is best demonstrated by the number of mergers and acquisitions between French and American firms, namely 27 operations (Table 8.16). European pharmaceutical firms in general have been very active acquirers in the US, in particular France, the United Kingdom and Germany.

*Table 8.16  Number of M&As by European firms in the US, 1980-90*

| Country | Number of M&As |
|---|---|
| France | 27 |
| UK | 23 |
| Sweden | 17 |
| Switzerland | 18 |
| Germany | 15 |
| Italy | 13 |
| Netherlands | 8 |
| Belgium | 3 |
| Denmark | 3 |
| Ireland | 1 |
| Total | 128 |

*Source*: own database

The examination of the European acquisitions in the United States show that biotech-oriented operations are important for the larger firms in the EC. And this despite the fact that there are also internal activities and links between pharmaceutical firms and universities and research institutes in European countries. For instance, in France the Louis Pasteur Institute plays a significant role. Two American firms, Squibb and Eli Lilly, had contracts for fundamental biotechnology projects with the Pasteur Institute.

The target countries of cross-border acquisitions in this period are illustrated in Table 8.17 by giving the ranking of numbers of firms in these countries, that are acquired by firms of foreign countries.

*Table 8.17  Target countries of acquisitions*

| Country | Number of acquisitions |
| --- | --- |
| USA | 128 |
| Spain | 45 |
| Italy | 43 |
| United Kingdom | 39 |
| France | 31 |
| Germany | 27 |

The United States has been by far the most popular country for acquisitions, followed by Spain. This is more particularly the case for European pharmaceutical companies. Out of the 62 acquisitions recorded in Spain, 33 were by foreign European firms and eleven by American firms; fifteen operations were domestic (acquisitions by Spanish companies). Spain is an interesting country because of the existence of low production costs, which enables exports to other European countries, and a large home market for pharmaceuticals.

Table 8.18 shows the EC companies most involved in the merger and acquisition activities during the observed period (1980–90).

*Table 8.18  EC companies most involved in M&As, 1980–90*

| Company | Number of acquisitions |
| --- | --- |
| Sanofi (F) | 41 |
| Rhône-Poulenc (F) | 28 |
| Fisons (UK) | 9 |
| Glaxo (UK) | 7 |
| Roussel-Uclaf (Hoechst) (F/G) | 7 |
| Boehringer-Ingelheim (G) | 5 |
| Montedison (I) | 5 |
| Novo (D) | 4 |
| Bayer (G) | 2 |
| Hoechst (G) | 1 |

*Source*: own database

The names of the companies in Table 8.18 are well known. They are the leading firms in their countries and most of them show ambitions to become or to remain global players in the pharmaceutical sector, at least in the product markets in which they have good reputations.

When we look at the European companies that belong to the main players in the global pharmaceutical 'game', we can try to explain their actual roles in terms of their active involvement in external operations as opposed to a more intraverted role, which means no active part in M&As, but dependence on the internal organic growth potential of the firm.

Among the world's main companies, few of them have grown without making use of merger and/or acquisitions. A comparison between the ranking of the first fifteen pharmaceutical firms according to turnover shows numerous changes between 1970 and 1980, and again between 1980 and 1989 (James 1990).

## 8.4   STRATEGIC ALLIANCES IN THE PHARMA-CEUTICAL SECTOR

The developments which triggered the wave of M&A also led to the formation of numerous strategic alliances. These developments were:
* excessively high costs of R&D and effective patent protection;
* high costs of marketing;
* accessibility of important national markets for foreign competitors;
* transparency of national regulation and the question of equal opportunities for foreign companies;
* the impact of the EC harmonization programme;
* cost containment programmes.

It seems that in the pharmaceutical industry the number of strategic alliances has grown enormously, by up to 300 to 400 a year at the end of the 1980s.[10]

The motives behind strategic alliances can be diverse and must be understood as a mixture of a time-bound estimation of several relevant forces by the firm(s) that take the initiative to start negotiations about mergers, takeovers and strategic alliances with other firms. The motives generally may be valid reasons against the background of the firms concerned to reach certain goals with regard to market penetration or the integration of new technology with marketing, and so on.

The motives for alliances may sometimes be understood by looking at the forms in which the alliances have taken place. For instance, when pharmaceutical companies have reached agreements with regard to production standards, it seems clear that the companies involved all expect to benefit from the establishment of a continental or rather a worldwide standard.

Considering the important role of R&D and innovation in the pharmaceutical industry, it is not surprising that many strategic alliances are set up to divide the high risks involved in R&D, or to exchange the innovative fruits of different successful R&D enterprises, often in combination with territorial agreements. The desired integration of technology and markets in this sector and the rising 'critical mass' needed to master both alone, not only explains the mergers in this sector, but a great number of strategic cross-licence agreements and cross-marketing agreements, besides the already known forms of R&D cooperation, production agreements and joint ventures.

The aim of entry into the world's major markets seems for many big companies of vital importance for the chances of profits high enough to finance their own R&D expenditure. Thus, it appears that co-marketing and co-promotion agreements have become very popular in this industry and probably these kinds of agreement have now exceeded the number of R&D partnerships and licensing agreements.

The rationale for establishing strategic alliances must be found in the following goals:
*   access to new technologies (in particular biotechnology);
*   access to new therapeutic categories (to get a broader product portfolio);
*   access to generic or over-the-counter (OTC) market segments;
*   access to foreign markets, which are dominated by local firms;
*   increasing the marketing power of particular products in order to combat competitive products (for instance Glaxo–Roche–Sankyo alliance to promote Zantac).

The increasing importance and further growth prospects of market segments like the generic and the over-the-counter (OTC) market have also led to strategic activities aimed at these segments. Of course, these are really different segments: the generic opportunity is the consequence of the age structure of prescription drugs, which is influenced by the expiry of many patents of well-known branded drugs with large markets during the last few years. In the next five years many more drug patents will expire, amongst which is the famous anti-ulcer drug Tagamet (with the generic name cimetedine) which held 27 per cent of its market in 1989, while the second, PEPCID from Merck and Co. only held 14 per cent. In the pharmaceutical industry in the United States and also in Japan strategic alliances have been accepted as important strategic weapons during the 1980s, while also the involvement of European companies can now be illustrated by looking at a selection of strategic alliances in the year 1987 (Table 8.19).

Looking at the future, it is expected that alliances will increase in number when Japan seeks to penetrate worldwide markets, and vice versa when European and American firms try to penetrate Japanese markets. The role of European harmonization is not so clear for the prediction of the number of European transnational alliances. The internal concentration process in the larger EC countries is mainly fed by acquisitions by the larger firms.

*Table 8.19 Selection of strategic alliances, 1987*

| Companies | Products/agreement |
|---|---|
| Upjohn and Sankyo | Co-marketing an oral cephalosporin |
| Smith-Kline and Bristol-Myers | Co-marketing Tagamet OTC in the US<br>Smith-Kline received exclusive rights to an H2 receptor antagonist |
| Abbott and Burroughs Wellcome | Co-promotion of Hytrin (once a day alpha-blocker) |
| Smith-Kline and DuPont | Co-promotion of Tagamet |
| Sandoz and Genetics Institute | Supply agreement for biotechnology products |
| Sterling and Advance Polymer Systems | Agreement for topical controlled-release OTC products |
| Johnson & Johnson and Centocor | Marketing and distribution agreement for biotechnology products |
| Squibb and McNell | Co-promotion of Capoten, co-marketing of zofenopril and a Johnson & Johnson product |
| Roche and Glaxo | Co-marketing: Cipralin, an anti-arrhythmic; inhibace and diuretic combination |
| Sandoz and Glaxo | Sandoz will develop Zantac OTC<br>Glaxo to co-market DynaCirc, a calcium channel blocker |
| Squibb and Boehringer Ingelheim | Co-marketing Squibb's second generation ACE inhibitor Fosionpril<br>Co-marketing Boehringer's PAF antagonist |
| LyphoMed and California Biotechnology | Licensing agreement for a microemulsion drug delivery technology |
| Roche and Miles | Co-marketing Baypress, long-acting calcium antagonist |
| Schering and Sandoz | Co-marketing spirapril, long-acting ACE inhibitor |

Although some authors suggest (James 1990) that increasing economic integration will lead to more transnational alliances, one could also argue that additional intra-EC co-marketing and co-promotion alliances will be needed in particular if harmonization of EC drug markets does *not* succeed, because in that case high domestic market shares with dominant positions for home-based firms can only be tackled by offering strategic deals to domestic firms.[11] To give an idea of the synergy functions that can be performed by different variants of alliances in the pharmaceutical industry, we reproduce the scheme as presented by James (1990), see Figure 8.3.

*Figure 8.3    Strategic alliances within the pharmaceutical industry*

| Functions \ Variants | Consortia | Joint venture | Equity stakes | Academia | Coperative deals | Licensing |
|---|---|---|---|---|---|---|
| Innovation | Laforne (France) | Ciba-Geigy/ Chiron: vaccines | Schering Plough: Biogen | Bristol Squibb: Oxford University | Merck & Co./ ICI | Most companies |
| Manufacture | Merckle (Germany) | Ciba-Geigy/ Sandoz: Venezuela | Searle/ Ciba-Geigy: Korea | | Chugai/ Upjohn: US | Merck & Co. in Latin America |
| Marketing | ASW (Italy) | Astral/ Syntex: Scandinavia | Roussel/ Jouveinal | | Glaxo-Roche: US | |

*Source*: James (1990), quoting from Pharma Strategy

## 8.5    THE COMPETITIVENESS OF THE EUROPEAN PHARMACEUTICAL INDUSTRY

### 8.5.1  Indicators of Competitiveness

The information on pharmaceutical companies included in all the foregoing sections of this chapter may be used to indicate the competitiveness of the European pharmaceutical industry in relation to that of the American and the Japanese pharmaceutical industry.

This section illustrates the relative positions of European pharmaceutical companies in terms of profitability and valuation levels, presence on the European market, presence in the world market (sales of top 50 products) and R&D performance. Because of the growing role of Japanese firms in this industry, a separate subsection (8.5.2) deals with Japanese competition in the European Community.

#### 8.5.1.1  Profitability
It is not easy to find figures on profits for all firms of the top 50. *Scrip*'s Review Issues show profit/sales ratios for the top ten or fifteen firms (see Table 8.20).

*Table 8.20  Profits, sales and margins for the top 50 companies, 1988*

| Rank | | Sales, $m | Profit, $m | Margin, % | R&D, $m |
|---|---|---|---|---|---|
| 1 | Merck & Co. | 5473 | 1806 | 33.0 | 669 |
| 2 | Hoechst | 4147 | 391 | 9.4 | 586 |
| 3 | American Home Prod. | 4139 | 1114 | 26.9 | 264 |
| 4 | Glaxo | 3991 | 1562 | 39.1 | 502 |
| 5 | Bayer | 3676 | 509 | 13.9 | 444 |
| 6 | Pfizer | 3453 | 902 | 26.1 | 390 |
| 7 | Ciba-Geigy | 3442 | n.a. | n.a. | 474 |
| 8 | Takeda | 3355 | 643 | 12.4 | 342 |
| 9 | Eli Lilly | 3272 | 969 | 29.6 | 541 |
| 10 | Sandoz | 3067 | n.a. | n.a. | 440 |
| 11 | Abbott | 2599 | 773 | 29.7 | 455 |
| 12 | Rhône-Poulenc | 2589 | 259 | 10.0 | 323 |
| 13 | Smith-Kline Beecham | 2541 | 487 | 19.2 | 495 |
| 14 | Warner-Lambert | 2509 | 725 | 28.9 | 231 |
| 15 | Bristol-Myers | 2509 | 565 | 22.5 | 394 |
| 16 | Roche | 2349 | n.a. | n.a. | 544 |
| 17 | Johnson & Johnson | 2338 | 789 | 33.8 | 386 |
| 18 | Sankyo | 2326 | 215 | 9.2 | 177 |
| 19 | Upjohn | 2234 | 486 | 21.8 | 380 |
| 20 | Schering-Plough | 2220 | 653 | 29.4 | 298 |
| 21 | Squibb | 2213 | 526 | 23.8 | 273 |
| 22 | ICI | 2120 | 553 | 26.1 | 307 |
| 23 | Wellcome | 2108 | 393 | 18.6 | 276 |
| 24 | Beecham | 1900 | 652.5 | 34.3 | 167 |
| 25 | Boehringer-Ingelheim | 1895 | 118.5 | 5.0 | 386 |
| 26 | Cynamid | 1831 | 284 | 15.5 | 365 |
| 27 | Tanabe | 1748 | 199 | 11.4 | 126 |
| 28 | Fujisawa | 1696 | 235 | 13.8 | 164 |
| 29 | Shionogi | 1692 | 196 | 12.0 | n.a. |
| 30 | Daiichi | 1514 | 375 | 24.8 | 148 |
| 31 | Yamanouchi | 1481 | 431.5 | 29.1 | 137 |
| 32 | Schering AG | 1480 | 198.5 | 6.7 | 232 |
| 33 | Eisai | 1406 | 262 | 18.6 | 187 |
| 34 | Syntex | 1349 | 336 | 24.9 | 245 |
| 35 | Sanofi | 1308 | 213 | 16.3 | 185 |
| 36 | Merrell-Dow | 2273 | n.a. | n.a. | n.a. |
| 37 | Sumitono | 1255 | n.a. | n.a. | n.a. |
| 38 | Akzo | 1201 | 335 | 13.9 | 149 |
| 39 | Taisho | 1110 | 296 | 26.7 | n.a. |
| 40 | Rore | 1042 | 152 | 14.6 | 103 |
| 41 | Astra | 1026 | 269 | 26.2 | 197 |
| 42 | Chugai | 999 | 152 | 15.3 | 147 |
| 43 | Monsanto | 973 | (62) | n.a. | 198 |
| 44 | Erbamont | 943 | 172 | 18.2 | 137 |
| 45 | Robins, A.H | 934 | 184 | 19.8 | 64 |
| 46 | Marion Labs | 930 | 270.5 | 29.0 | 133.5 |
| 47 | Kyowa | 927 | 204.5 | 10.0 | 110.5 |
| 48 | Boots | 885 | 160 | 18.1 | 66 |
| 49 | Solvay | 815 | n.a. | n.a. | n.a. |
| 50 | BASF | 797 | 82 | 16.8 | n.a. |

*Source*: *Chemical Insight* (1989)

The UK firms show the best results of the European firms. Glaxo had the highest margin of this league (39 per cent), in the UK followed by ICI (26 per cent) and Wellcome and Smith-Kline Beecham each with 19 per cent. German firms had lower profit margins: BASF (17 per cent), Bayer (14 per cent), Hoechst (9 per cent) and Boehringer-Ingelheim (5 per cent), while the French Rhône-Poulenc had a margin (10 per cent) comparable to the German average. Sanofi had a higher margin of 16 per cent in this year. The average profit margins of the Japanese firms are higher as a result of the relative high margins of Yamanouchi (29 per cent), Taisho (27 per cent) and Daiichi (25 per cent), while the remaining Japanese firms have figures between 9 and 18 per cent. Looking at the average margin figures, American firms are the most profitable in this league: Merck (33 per cent), Johnson & Johnson (34 per cent), Beecham (34 per cent), Eli Lilly (30 per cent), etc.

The figures for profitability and valuation levels of the top fifteen companies on the European market for 1989 are given in Table 8.21.

*Table 8.21  Profitability and valuation levels of the top fifteen companies on the European pharmaceutical market, 1989*

| | World pharm, as % of total sales, 1989 | World pharm, o.p. as % of total o.p., 1989 | Return on equity, % | Return on assets, % | Ratio 1990 |
|---|---|---|---|---|---|
| Rhône-Poulenc | 24 | 27 | 13 | 11 | 9 |
| Bayer | 18 | 30 | 14 | 13 | 7 |
| Hoechst | 18 | 23 | 18 | 15 | 7 |
| Ciba-Geigy | 30 | 51 | 10 | 8 | 8 |
| ICI | 0 | 27 | 19 | 15 | 9 |
| Sandoz | 46 | n.a. | 15 | 9 | 13 |
| Smith-Kline Beecham | 52 | 60 | nm | 25 | 16 |
| Sanofi | 53 | 90 | 10 | 8 | 14 |
| Roche | 45 | n.a. | 7 | 7 | 16 |
| Boehringer-Ingelheim | 80 | – | – | – | – |
| Glaxo | 95 | 99 | 30 | 30 | 16 |
| Merck & Co. | 83 | 90 | 41 | 35 | 20 |
| Bristol-Myers Squibb | 66 | 72 | 15 | 16 | 20 |
| Eli Lilly | 70 | 80 | 27 | 24 | 18 |
| Astra | 97 | 99 | 24 | 20 | 31 |

*Sources*: Company reports and ABN estimates, Drosten and Kammradt (1990)

Interesting information for the evaluation of the actual competitive position of pharmaceutical firms of the EC is also given in Table 8.22, where the presence of products in the top 50 world sales is shown for 1990.

*Table 8.22* *Presence of firms by country in the sales of products in the top 50 companies worldwide ($ m), 1990*

| Countries | Sales |
|---|---|
| **United Kingdom** | |
| Glaxo | 4259 |
| SB | 2255 |
| ICI | 1508 |
| Wellcome | 1039 |
| Fisons | 302 |
| | Total 9363 |
| **Germany** | |
| Bayer | 2010 |
| Hoechst | 865 |
| Schering | 750 |
| | Total 3625 |
| **United States** | |
| Merck | 3427 |
| BMS | 1798 |
| Eli Lilly | 1962 |
| Pfizer | 1383 |
| MMD | 1266 |
| | Total 9836 |
| **Japan** | |
| Daiichi | 384 |
| Yamanouchi | 290 |
| | Total 674 |
| **Switzerland** | |
| Ciba-Geigy | 1705 |
| Sandoz | 805 |
| Roche | 665 |
| | Total 3175 |

*Source*: *Scrip* Review Issue (1991)

About sixty companies in the EC are regarded as innovative companies, involved in R&D and marketing of new products. Almost thirty of these companies are subsidiaries of companies that have their original home base outside the EC. The ranking of market shares of firms in the EC pharma market of 1989 shows good positions for EC firms (Table 8.23).

*Table 8.23  The top fifteen pharmaceutical companies in the EC market, 1989*

| Company | Country of origin | Estimated market share (%) |
|---|---|---|
| Hoechst | FRG | 4.5 - 5.0 |
| Glaxo | UK | 3.5 - 4.0 |
| Smith-Kline Beecham | UK/US | 3.5 - 4.0 |
| Bayer | FRG | 3.0 - 3.5 |
| Ciba-Geigy | Switzerland | 3.0 - 3.5 |
| Merck & Co. | US | 3.0 - 3.5 |
| Bristol-Myers Squibb | US | 2.5 - 3.0 |
| Rhône-Poulenc | France | 2.5 - 3.0 |
| Boehringer Ingelheim | FRG | 2.0 - 2.5 |
| ICI | UK | 2.0 - 2.5 |
| Roche | Switzerland | 2.0 - 2.5 |
| Sandoz | Switzerland | 2.0 - 2.5 |
| Sanofi | France | 2.0 - 2.5 |
| Astra | Sweden | 1.5 - 2.0 |
| Eli Lilly | US | 1.5 - 2.0 |

*Source*: Drosten and Kammradt(1990)

### 8.5.1.2  R&D performance of European firms

According to the available information (as published annually in *Scrip*) on the numbers of products in R&D (including the licensed products) of the top 100 pharmaceutical companies worldwide, the companies of the EC show a good performance. We restrict our attention to the top 40 companies in terms of the number of products in R&D. Table 8.24 shows the performance of ten European firms.

The top 40 list of pharmaceutical companies in terms of the number of R&D drugs contains fourteen EC companies. The remaining places on the top 40 list are taken by the big US companies with a combined number of 1246 R&D drugs, the three Swiss giants (274 R&D drugs) and six Japanese firms (295 R&D drugs). So the R&D performance of the pharmaceutical companies in the European Community can be considered as very good.

*Table 8.24  Products from R&D in European firms, 1990*

| Firm | R&D drugs | Own drugs* | World rank |
|------|-----------|------------|------------|
| Smith-Kline Beecham | 148 | 118 | 1 |
| Rhône-Poulenc | 136 | 90 | 3 |
| Hoechst | 90 | 66 | 10 |
| Roussel Uclaf** | 65 | 30 | 14 |
| Erbamont | 63 | 46 | n.a. |
| Wellcome | 59 | 45 | n.a. |
| Boehringer-Ingelheim | 57 | 40 | n.a. |
| Schering AG | 53 | 43 | n.a. |
| Sanofi | 50 | 38 | n.a. |
| Glaxo | 44 | 28 | n.a. |

\*   The other drugs are under licence
\** Controlled by Hoechst
*Source*: *Scrip*

On the 1990 top ten list of companies ranked by nominal pharma R&D expenditure, six EC firms can be found, with a total R&D expenditure of $3024 m, being about 14 per cent of their combined sales. The EC firms on the 1990 top ten list of pharma R&D spending are: Glaxo, Hoechst, Smith-Kline Beecham, Bayer, Boehringer-Ingelheim and Rhône-Poulenc.

### 8.5.2  Japanese Competition: Acquisitions and Direct Investments in the EC

The first signs of the Japanese response to the expected closure of the Common Market to outsiders have been observed in the appearance of Japanese investments in Spanish and UK pharmaceutical production firms (see Table 8.25).

Japanese firms do not resort much to acquisitions but prefer strategic alliances. The number of overseas subsidiaries of Japanese pharmaceutical companies has grown from ten in 1965 to 64 in 1985. Of these, 29 were production facilities and 43 were set up to import finished products from Japan. There were 32 plants in Asia, 18 in the US, and 17 in Europe. Figures on Japanese direct investments in the EC revealed the countries in which fourteen Japanese plants were established. In Germany there were four plants, in France three, in Spain three, in Ireland two, one in Belgium and one in Italy. Besides, in Germany and the UK, there are some Japanese research centres.

*Table 8.25  Japanese acquisitions in the EC*

| Japanese firm | Year | Acquired firm |
| --- | --- | --- |
| Takeda Chem. Industries | 1980 | Grunenthal (Germany) |
| Alpha Therap. | 1982 | Lab Grifols (Spain) |
| Otsuka Pharm. | 1988 | Magnex Scient. (UK) |
| Fujisawa Pharm. | 1988 | Klinge Pharma (Germany) |
| Ajinonobo | 1989 | Omnichem (Belgium) |
| SS Pharm Co. | 1989 | Nutrichem (Germany) |
| Yamanouchi | 1990 | Drug division Gist-Brocade (NL) |
| Sankyo | 1990 | Luitpold Werk (Germany) |

*Source*: own database

### 8.5.3  Profit Potential in Europe

During the 1980s, pharmaceutical companies were challenged by many economic and political changes in Europe with different prospects for profitability. The serious route to the formation of the Single Market and the expansion of the European Community were considered as positive developments by representatives of the European pharmaceutical industry and also by managers of large pharmaceutical companies. The effect on the future sales and profitability of EC-based firms was expected to be positive. On the other hand, the slow progress of the European Commission on matters of harmonization of pricing regimes and the low chances of getting freedom of pricing for prescription drugs, combined with the serious cost-containment programmes of many European countries, have tempered the positive prospects of high profitability.

*Scrip Magazine* (May 1992) has published estimates on the profit potential in Europe, based on expected market changes in the five most important pharmaceutical markets in the EC: Germany, France, Italy, the United Kingdom and Spain, while the remaining smaller Western European countries are combined. The Eastern European countries are also seen as new challenges for many pharmaceutical companies, although they are aware of the lower incomes in these countries, forming constraints on drug prices.

The contributions of the aforementioned countries in Europe to the potential profit of the pharmaceutical industry in the 1990s are estimated in Table 8.26.

Table 8.26  *Profit potential in Europe, 1990s*

| Country | Potential profit (%) | Share of market (%) |
|---|---|---|
| Germany (Unified)* | 21 | 28 |
| United Kingdom | 14 | 10 |
| Italy | 15 | 18 |
| France | 15 | 17 |
| Spain | 8 | 7 |
| Smaller Western European countries | 20 | 15 |
| Eastern European countries | 7 | 5 |

\* Relatively high prices and profits in the Federal Republic combined with lower potential in the Democratic Republic.
*Source*: *Scrip Magazine* (1992)

An interesting conclusion from this table is that, despite the relatively low price levels of drugs in France and Italy, the profit potential of these three big markets alone accounts for 39 per cent of the profit potential of the whole European market. The home-based pharmaceutical companies and those with subsidiaries in these countries may have favourable prospects for profits, because the French and Italian markets in particular are difficult to enter, but seem to demonstrate profit potentials corresponding to their market shares.

Considering all this information brings us to the conclusion that the EC industry is still strong and must be considered as capable of coping with the new environment and with their competitors. Although the competition from Japanese firms in the future must not be underestimated, we must also not forget that the Japanese market is more open to foreign products than before, mainly as a result of the strategic alliances between US and Japanese firms and between European and Japanese firms. Almost 40 per cent of the prescription market in Japan is served by products of American or European origin.

But we must watch the progress of the Japanese pharmaceutical industry, especially in the field of technology. Spectacular new breakthroughs in this field would certainly be in favour of firms in countries that had already moved down biotechnology routes (see also Cassel 1987).

# 8.6  CONCLUSION

The pharmaceutical industry is one of the few R&D intensive industries where European companies have a dominant position in the world market.

The pharmaceutical industry in Europe is also a strong industry for a number of reasons:

1. Domestic market shares in European countries are high.
2. The total market share of European companies in the global market is high.
3. A very strong participation in external operations, in particular in mergers and acquisitions of the European companies.
4. A good performance in terms of R&D and a reasonably high involvement in biotechnology, mainly by means of acquisitions and alliances.

The changing European environment has not created serious problems for pharmaceutical firms, but the challenges in terms of increasing competition must not be underestimated.

Many managers now realize that the emergence of a centralized registration procedure in the European Community may also mean lower barriers to entry for firms that are not accustomed to coping with the different registration and pricing regimes in various European countries. The profit potential for pharmaceutical firms in the larger EC countries seems very favourable, despite the relative low drug prices in countries like France, Italy and Spain, where high volumes of consumption make for high profits.

The growing market positions of generic substitutes and self-medication drugs are no longer treated as threats by the majority of multinational innovative pharmaceutical companies but rather as opportunities that can be taken by acquiring generic firms or forming alliances. The wave of mergers and acquisitions in the European pharmaceutical industry is comparable with the wave in other industries, according to information on mergers and acquisitions in the *Panorama of EC Industries 1991–1992*. Concerning the number of strategic alliances in this sector during the last ten years, one can only guess at the numbers of these agreements. The available information must be seen as the tip of the iceberg. There is a tremendous global network of thousands of alliances in the pharmaceutical industry. The stability of these alliances and the meaning for the competitiveness of the firms involved can be evaluated in the mid-1990s. The participation of European firms in the merger and acquisition wave of the last few years of the observed decade was surprising, in particular the participation of the French firms Sanofi and Rhône-Poulenc. Besides their role in the acquisitions in France, these firms also dominated the cross-border external operations in the European Community. The data-analysis also showed a high degree of participation of EC-based pharmaceutical firms in acquisitions of biotechnology firms, in particular in the United States.

This information, supplemented by figures on market positions of products of EC firms in the world's top 50 sales and available figures on profitability of pharmaceutical figures leads us to the conclusion that the prospects for the European pharmaceutical industry are to be considered as promising. The performance of the UK pharmaceutical industry with companies like Glaxo, Smith-Kline Beecham (UK–US), Fisons and ICI belonging to the top fifteen companies of the world is strong, the larger German firms still hold firm positions and the French industry has at least two very strong firms with Sanofi and Rhône-Poulenc. The smaller countries in the EC will have room for just one highly specialized firm or for some subsidiaries of foreign-owned multinationals. The competition of Japanese firms on the European market will increase as a result of the internationalization strategy of Japanese firms, but will not become very strong in the next decade because there will still be many problems of market entry in the various member states as long as different pricing regimes exist. The high market share of Japanese drugs on the world market is mainly the result of Japan's strong home market. The Swiss pharmaceutical industry must still be considered as very strong with its three giants Roche, Ciba-Geigy and Sandoz, which have also been active in acquiring good positions in biotechnology.

## NOTES

1. The total value of the world market is about $180 bn.
2. See Chapter 7 on the chemical industry for a breakdown by type of product.
3. On Rhône-Poulenc's strategy, see also Chapter 7.
4. The report 'Completing the Internal Market', a white paper from the Commission to the European Council, was issued in 1985.
5. See also Hancher (1990) for a description of some cases of price controls and reimbursement regimes and their relation to Article 30, prohibition on quantitative import restrictions.
6. European competitiveness is discussed in section 8.5 in particular. See also the statistical appendix at the end of the book.
7. See also James (1990); Redwood (1990).
8. Predicast provides articles about the chemical/pharmaceutical industry, extracted from more than 20 magazines, including: *Europa Chemie* (German), *Scrip* (English), *Usine Nouvelle* (French), *Chemical Marketing Reporter* (English), *IMS Pharmaceutical Marketletter*, *Chimie Actualités* (French), *Cosmetics International*, *European Chemical News*, *Chemical Age*, *Informations Chimie* (French), *Chemische Industrie* (German), *Financial Times*, *Chemical Weekly*.
9. 362 in 1990 including thirteen factories of self-producing pharmacists (SNIP 1991).
10. The review *Scrip* published two volumes on 1250 strategic alliances in the pharmaceutical industry for the period 1986–90.
11. This remark in the case of pharmaceuticals corresponds to the general analysis of Chapter 1 about European joint ventures.

## BIBLIOGRAPHY

Asselt, H. Th. van (1989), *Patent Duration and Innovation*, Management Report Series, no. 32, Rotterdam.

Brown, P. (1989), 'Legal progress towards 1992: Will the legislation be realistic?' in *Researching opportunities and limitations for Health-care marketing*, EPHMRA/ ESOMAR, Amsterdam.

Bureau Européen des Unions de Consommateurs (BEUC) (1984), *The consumer and the pharmaceutical products in the European Economic Community*, Brussels.

Burstall, M. L. (1986), *Generic pharmaceuticals in Europe — Blessing or threat?*, London.

Cassel, D. (1987), *Japan: Pharma-Weltmacht der Zukunft?*, Nomos Verlag, Baden-Baden.

Cecchini, P. (1988), *The Benefits of a Single Market*, Gower, London.

*Chemical Insight* (1989), Hyde Chemical Publ., London, November.

Comanor, W. S. (1986), 'The Political Economy of the Pharmaceutical Industry', *Journal of Economic Literature*, vol. XXIV, September, pp1178–1217.

Commission of the European Communities (1991), *Panorama of EC industries 1991–92*, Brussels.

Drosten, P. and Kammradt, G. (1990), *The European Pharmaceutical Industry in the 1990's*, ABN Bank, Amsterdam.

Economists' Advisory Group (1985), *The Community's pharmaceutical industry: evolution of concentration, competition and competitivity*, London.

Economists' Advisory Group (1988), *Research on The Cost of Non-Europe*, European Commision, vol. 15.

EFPIA, *EFPIA in Figures (1990), The Pharmaceutical Industry in Europe*, several years.

EFPIA, *Information Bulletin* SPC, Brussels, June.

European Commission (1985), *Completing the Internal Market*, white paper, Brussels.

European Commission (1990), *Estimations of the Economic Effects of the Introduction of a Supplementary Protection Certificate*, Internal Document III/c/2, Brussels, 7 September.

European Generics Forum (EGF) (1991), *A Case for Balance in the Pharmaceutical Industry*, London.

*Financial Times* (1989), '*Pharmaceuticals*', Supplement, 6 November.

*Financial Times* (1991), '*Pharmaceuticals*', FT Survey, 23 July.

Hancher, L. (1990), *Regulating for Competition*, Oxford University Press.

IWI-studien (1991), *Band II, Die Österreichische Pharmawirtschaft: Ihre Rolle im Gesundheitswesen und Stellung im internationalen Vergleich*, Wien.

James, B. (1990), *The Global Pharmaceutical Industry in the 1990s, The Challenge of Change*, The Economist Intelligence Unit, London.

De Jong, H. W. (1991), 'Competition and Combination in the European Market Economy', in P. de Wolf (ed.), *Competition in Europe, Essays in honour of H. W. de Jong*, Kluwer, Dordrecht/Boston, pp265–292.

Linda, R. (1991), 'Industrial and Market Concentration in Europe', in P. de Wolf (ed.), *Competition in Europe, Essays in honour of H. W. de Jong*, Kluwer, Dordrecht/ Boston.

Mantel, A. F. (ed.) (1987), *The Dutch Pharmaceutical Market in Observation* (Dutch manuscript), Eburon, Delft.

Ohmae, K. (1985), *Triad Power: The Coming Shape of Global Competition*, The Free Press, New York.

Pisano, G. P. (1991), 'Vertical Integration and collaborative arrangements in the biotechnology industry', *Research Policy*, 20, pp237–249.

Porter, M. (ed.) (1986), *Competition in Global Industries*, Harvard Business School Press, Boston, Mass.

Redwood, H. (1990), *Pharmaceutical patent term restoration for the 1990s*, Oldwicks Press, Felixstowe.

Reuben, B. G. and Wittcoff, H. A. (1990), *Pharmaceutical Chemicals in Perspective*, Wiley, New York.

*Scrip*, Review Issues, 1988, 1989, 1990, 1991.

Sharp, M. and P. L. Cook (1991), 'Chemicals and Pharmaceuticals', in *The European Economy*, Longmans, London.

Syndicat National de l'Industrie Pharmaceutique (SNIP) (1991), *L'Industrie Pharmaceutique, ses réalités*, Paris.

Weiss, P. (1991), *Arzneimittelinnovationen in der Bundesrepublik Deutschland als unternehmerische Aufgabe und ordnungspolitisches Gestaltungsfeld*, Duisburg.

Wolf, P. de (1987), 'The Pharmaceutical Industry: Structure, Intervention and Competitive Strength', in H. W. de Jong (ed.), *The Structure of European Industry* (2nd ed.), Kluwer Academic Publishers.

Wolf, P. de (1992), 'Towards One Single Market for Drugs?', in H. W. de Jong (ed.), *The Structure of European Industry* (3rd rev. ed.), Kluwer Academic Publishers, Dordrecht/Boston.

# Conclusion: Integration and Globalization

## Frédérique Sachwald

The census and the analysis of external growth operations in several industrial sectors confirm the observations based on more general data which have
been discussed in the first chapter. First, external growth operations have
played a significant role in firms' strategies at the end of the 1980s; this
conclusion draws on the detailed data from the sectoral chapters to analyse
the relationships between these operations and the competitive position of
European firms. Second, firms' strategies have had the Single Market as but
one of their objectives; the development of globalization has been at least as
important a determinant. The question then arises as to whether this under-
mines the intra-European logic of the Single Market scheme, especially with
respect to the development of competitiveness.

## EUROPEAN FIRMS' EXTERNAL GROWTH OPERATIONS

External growth operations have generally played an important role in European firms' strategies during the 1980s. The sectoral studies have shown that
beyond this general observation, both the scope of external growth operations and the types of operation vary across industries. The differences are
attributable to the structure of the industry, to the type of competences which
are the most effective in achieving competitiveness, and to the relative
competitive position of European firms. These different factors strongly
interacted with the relative importance of the Single Market for each
industry.

Mergers and acquisitions have been very numerous in the chemical
industry, much more than in the automobile industry, for example. This is
partly due to the large difference in the number of firms, the automobile
industry being more concentrated. In this respect, one should note that
acquisitions were more numerous in the sector of automobile equipment
which was quite fragmented at the beginning of the 1980s. The chemical

industry is also prone to M&A because of the interdependences along the production chain and the extreme degree of differentiation; parts of the process of production or some products can be sold without endangering the integrity of the company. Conversely, the automobile industry has tended to use relatively more cooperative agreements, either joint ventures or even less committing agreements.[1] Cooperative research or acquisitions for technological transfer have been relatively more numerous in high-tech sectors such as electronic components and pharmaceuticals (especially in the field of biotechnology). In consumer electronics, acquisitions aim at market share, but a number of alliances also focus on technological transfers.

As argued in Chapter 2, external growth operations are used to complement the set of capabilities of firms. The sectoral studies show that external growth operations reflect the competitive positions and the strategic objectives of firms. In particular, the geographical distribution of M&A as well as alliances depends largely on the respective strengths and weaknesses of the firms involved.[2] Thus, European chemical and pharmaceutical companies are much more active *vis-à-vis* the American market than their automobile counterparts. This is due to the strength of the European chemical companies and to the fact that they aim at conquering new markets, while the automobile companies have been in a rather defensive position.[3] Conversely, Japanese automobile companies, which are in a dominant position, participate in numerous cooperative agreements, both with American and European competitors. In the chemical and the automobile cases, the Single Market has been considered as an issue of relatively limited importance since these industries are already on their way to globalization. In the case of the car industry, however, the Single Market should have a strong influence on the competitive game since it entails a common external trade policy and, eventually, more open European markets.

In the electronic components sector, European companies were very weak in the early 1980s (Tables A.2.12 and A.3.13 in the appendix). They resorted to technological agreements in order to gain competences. This strategy led to the choice of American partners, especially at the beginning of the decade. Since the second half of the 1980s, European policies in favour of intra-community cooperation have encouraged alliances between European companies with some success. These various cooperations have been instrumental in technological transfers in favour of European companies, but the strengthening of the technological base has yet to translate into improved competitiveness (Table A.3.13 in the appendix). European competitiveness in the sector of consumer electronics has been extremely weak throughout the 1980s (Table A.3.14 in the appendix). The analysis of external growth operations has shown that European firms have actively resorted to mergers and acquisitions to rationalize. Cooperative agreements are also numerous with the strongest competitors, that is to say Japanese companies. Moreover, the latter have substantially invested in the Community, while European companies have made several substantial acquisitions in the United States.

## THE SINGLE MARKET AND GLOBALIZATION

Sectoral studies underlined globalization as one of the main factors shaping firms' strategies; this development tends to reduce the relative importance of the Single Market effects. There is probably a bias in the sample of industries studied in this book; foodstuffs for example would probably show relatively more external growth operations aiming at the European market. Nevertheless, for a number of large industries, firms fight for competitiveness on global markets and consider that the European market itself is too small. Besides, in the case of high tech sectors more particularly, a presence in each of the poles of the Triad appears increasingly important, both to adapt quickly to the markets and to be in contact with the latest progress in science and technology.

The surge in foreign direct investment during the 1980s has been a significant factor in the development of globalization. The fact that a substantial part of that foreign investment aimed at controlling foreign companies has further reinforced the interpenetration of the national economies. The extension of multinational companies and the rationalization of their operations throughout the world tend to reduce the significance of trade data. In these conditions, it is more and more important to analyse both the competitiveness of firms and national competitiveness as discussed in Chapters 1 and 2. The sectoral chapters offer a number of relevant examples.

According to the market positions given in the statistical appendix, the competitiveness of Japan in consumer electronics (Table A.3.14) and in passenger cars (Table A.3.11) has decreased between 1980 and 1990, staying nevertheless at high levels. The reduction is even more striking between 1985 and 1990. The explanation largely lies in the strength of Japanese companies which have heavily invested abroad during the 1980s, and more particularly during the second half of the decade. A similar remark can be made for chemicals: the strong position of Europe in this industry has been challenged by new competitors. However, in considering the relative weakening of the European market position in chemicals (Table A.2.4 in the appendix), one should also allow for the important investments abroad and in particular in the United States. The sectoral chapters have shown that in both the Japanese automobile industry and the European chemical industry, foreign direct investment has resorted to external growth operations besides greenfield units.

The sectoral chapters also underline the fact that direct investment is not the only source of discrepancy between national competitiveness and firms' competitiveness. Cooperative agreements of various sorts play an increasingly important part in the competitive game. This is particularly the case of industries such as automobile and electronics. In these sectors, large companies tend to create networks of cooperative agreements with wide objectives. In the pharmaceutical industry, cooperative agreements are very numerous, but tend to be limited to commercial matters, and in some cases to research.

Firms have devised their strategies in order to adapt to the evolution of the competitive game, which is becoming global in a number of industries. In such conditions, it would be hazardous for Europe to focus on the sole Single Market. For example, in industries where alliances play an important part in the competitive game, and more particularly when they tend to create networks, it may become dangerous to stay isolated. This danger has been signalled in the case of the European automobile industry for example (see Chapter 3). In the sector of electronic components, alliances are numerous and European companies have had to team with both American and Japanese companies. In this perspective, the Internal Market should be considered as a larger domestic market, as a base for global competition (and not as a way to escape from it).

## EUROPEAN COMPETITIVENESS

Will the Single Market foster European competitiveness through a reorganization of firms? As explained in Chapter 1, the Single Market scheme largely aimed at completing a common market in Europe so that firms could rationalize their operations and, in particular, take advantage of economies of dimension. This book shows that firms have integrated the prospect of the Single Market into their strategies during the second half of the 1980s. But this does not automatically lead to better European competitiveness. The question can be split into two parts: will external growth operations lead to more competitive European firms? What are the relationships between the competitiveness of European firms and the competitiveness of Europe?

The sectoral chapters have shown that European firms have resorted to external growth in order to extend both their capabilities and their market reach. A large number of these operations look strategically correct, but this does not mean that they will automatically yield good results. It is too early to thoroughly evaluate the results of strategic moves which were implemented at the end of the 1980s since the integration of the new assets may be long and require substantial reorganization.[4] The management of acquisitions and alliances is known to be difficult, especially for cross-border operations. Beyond this question, it seems that firms will have to adapt not only to the Single Market but to global markets. In this respect, and given the ever rising cost of R&D, it seems particularly important for European firms to be able to get the most out of their alliances.[5] These management considerations seem crucial since external growth operations are bound to play an important part in the evolution of European companies. The wave of external growth of the 1980s ebbed in 1990–91, but the pursuit of European restructuring as well as the tendencies towards globalization will again foster M&A and alliances during the 1990s.

Beyond the analysis of external growth *per se*, the sectoral chapters have underlined the growing importance of flexibility and adaptability. These qualities depend crucially on human resources and on the relationships with business partners. European firms will have to pay more attention to these organizational aspects.[6]

European competitiveness should be considered from a different perspective since it refers to the European space and not to European companies. From this point of view, the Single Market scheme is to be seen as an important step to consolidate European industry and to achieve a true internal market. But the EC is now in a similar position as national states: it has to consider the competitiveness of its population and territory, and not only of the companies which originate from Europe and may be large multinationals.

Given the evolution of the competitive game, the quality of human resources and, in particular, the innovativeness and flexibility of the productive system have become crucial assets. The European productive structures have not yet fully adapted to this evolution. Thus both national states and the Commission should foster the required evolutions, by enhancing or revising the policies which already address human resources in general and innovation.[7] In the case of European innovation policy, the studies in this book suggest two recommendations. First, the main objective should probably not be to have European firms cooperate (and exclude non-Europeans), but to strengthen European innovativeness on a wider basis. Second, support to near-market R&D projects[8] should be considered carefully. Indeed, when they devise their R&D policy and the corresponding alliances, firms only take their own interest into account, which may not correspond to the wider objectives of public policies. The cases where national (or European) and private objectives do not coincide tend to be all the more numerous as one gets nearer to the market and as firms globalize.

# NOTES

1.  The study on the chemical industry shows that joint ventures are numerous, but alliances play a more important role in comparison with M&A in the automobile industry.
2.  The general statistical appendix gives the market position as an indicator of competitiveness for different aggregates; it provides an evaluation of European competitiveness. In the rest of this conclusion, some of the market positions are referred to in parentheses.
3.  The market position of Europe for different segments of the chemical industry are given in Tables A.2.4 and A.3.1–A.3.9 in the appendix. For automobiles, see Tables A.2.10, A.3.10 and A.3.11.
4.  The sectoral chapters have dealt with these matters in a number of cases (in the chapters on consumer electronics and automobile in particular), but do not focus on them.
5.  So far it seems that the Japanese companies get the most out of their international alliances; some examples from the sectoral chapters confirm this general impression.
6.  This conclusion does not address all the aspects of management; it focuses on the results from the sectoral chapters and thus on external growth and related questions.
7.  On these questions, see in particular the chapters on electronic components, consumer electronics, automobile and automobile components.
8.  As opposed to a strict conception of pre-competitive research. On this question see the chapters on electronic components and on automobile components (Chapters 6 and 4).

# General Appendix:
# Market Position Indicator

## Isabelle Joinovici

This appendix proposes an evaluation of the competitiveness of the main industrialized countries by using the indicator market position.[1]

The first section defines the market position indicator. The second and third sections present the positions of the different countries or areas respectively by general categories of products and by products in relation to the sectoral chapters of this book.

Calculations are based on CHELEM-International trade database (CEPII, CD ROM GSI–Eco).[2]

## A.1  DEFINITION

The market position of a country is the ratio between the trade balance of this country for the considered product and the total world trade for that product. Exports of a given product do not constitute a satisfactory indicator of competitiveness since the amount of imports may be higher. The market position indicator takes into account both imports and exports by calculating their trade balance for the different products. Trade balance is divided by world trade, to render the indicator comparable over time and between different products.

The position of the country $j$ for the product $i$, $Pij$, is defined as follows, in percentage:

$$Pij = \frac{Xij - Mij}{Wi} \times 100$$

where:
$Xij$  = exports of product $i$ by country $j$;
$Mij$  = imports of product $i$ by country $j$;
$Wi$  = product $i$ world trade (sum of world imports of product $i$).

## A.2 POSITIONS BY CATEGORIES OF PRODUCTS

*Table A.2.1*    *Positions on the international market of building materials*

|  | 1975 | 1980 | 1985 | 1990 |
|---|---|---|---|---|
| United States | −0.9 | −1.5 | −10.5 | −7.0 |
| Japan | 6.1 | 6.6 | 7.7 | 3.0 |
| EC | 21.0 | 20.1 | 21.6 | 15.1 |
| NICs | −0.4 | 0.4 | 0.7 | −0.5 |

*Table A.2.2*    *Positions on the international market of iron and steel*

|  | 1975 | 1980 | 1985 | 1990 |
|---|---|---|---|---|
| United States | −5.5 | −5.0 | −12.4 | −6.2 |
| Japan | 14.6 | 9.7 | 9.4 | 0.7 |
| EC | 10.1 | 3.7 | 8.0 | 0.1 |
| NICs | −1.7 | −1.6 | −1.0 | −3.2 |

*Table A.2.3*    *Positions on the international market of wood and paper*

|  | 1975 | 1980 | 1985 | 1990 |
|---|---|---|---|---|
| United States | −2.3 | −3.2 | −14.1 | −6.6 |
| Japan | −0.0 | 0.6 | 2.6 | −1.8 |
| EC | −7.4 | −3.0 | 2.6 | −2.4 |
| NICs | 2.0 | 3.0 | 4.5 | 3.0 |

*Table A.2.4*    *Positions on the international market of chemicals*

|  | 1975 | 1980 | 1985 | 1990 |
|---|---|---|---|---|
| United States | 7.6 | 8.6 | 3.4 | 4.2 |
| Japan | 5.1 | 2.4 | 2.1 | 1.8 |
| EC | 16.6 | 13.6 | 13.5 | 8.9 |
| NICs | −1.7 | −1.3 | −0.8 | −1.5 |
| Central Europe | −1.2 | −0.6 | −0.3 | 0.1 |
| Gulf | −2.4 | −3.4 | −2.4 | −1.2 |
| OPEC | −6.3 | −7.2 | −5.2 | −2.6 |
| Latin America | −5.6 | −4.8 | −2.3 | −2.0 |

*Table A.2.5    Positions on the international market of ores*

|  | 1975 | 1980 | 1985 | 1990 |
| --- | --- | --- | --- | --- |
| United States | –0.6 | 4.8 | 3.1 | 4.0 |
| Japan | –17.1 | –17.7 | –16.5 | –17.3 |
| EC | –25.3 | –22.9 | –18.8 | –16.2 |
| NICs | –0.9 | –2.1 | –2.9 | –5.2 |

*Table A.2.6    Positions on the international market of energy*

|  | 1975 | 1980 | 1985 | 1990 |
| --- | --- | --- | --- | --- |
| United States | –12.8 | –15.0 | –11.9 | –13.6 |
| Japan | –14.1 | –13.7 | –14.3 | –13.5 |
| EC | –26.4 | –23.6 | –19.8 | –17.6 |
| NICs | –1.5 | –3.0 | –3.4 | –3.5 |

*Table A.2.7    Positions on the international market of agricultural products*

|  | 1975 | 1980 | 1985 | 1990 |
| --- | --- | --- | --- | --- |
| United States | 18.0 | 16.2 | 8.5 | 9.6 |
| Japan | –11.0 | –10.4 | –10.0 | –10.1 |
| EC | –21.0 | –19.6 | –14.3 | –12.8 |
| NICs | –3.3 | –3.4 | –3.8 | –4.7 |

*Table A.2.8    Positions on the international market of foodstuffs*

|  | 1975 | 1980 | 1985 | 1990 |
| --- | --- | --- | --- | --- |
| United States | –4.5 | –0.4 | –4.4 | 0.7 |
| Japan | –5.5 | –5.1 | –6.2 | –9.5 |
| EC | –1.0 | 4.1 | 5.9 | 3.5 |
| NICs | 0.6 | 0.6 | 0.9 | –0.4 |

*Table A.2.9    Positions on the international market of mechanical products*

|  | 1975 | 1980 | 1985 | 1990 |
| --- | --- | --- | --- | --- |
| United States | 13.9 | 11.5 | 3.6 | 5.0 |
| Japan | 8.4 | 7.8 | 10.0 | 7.6 |
| EC | 19.8 | 16.5 | 14.6 | 10.3 |
| NICs | –2.0 | –1.7 | 0.1 | –2.0 |

*Table A.2.10   Positions on the international market of motor vehicles*

|                | 1975  | 1980  | 1985   | 1990   |
|----------------|-------|-------|--------|--------|
| United States  | −1.9  | −8.4  | −21.5  | −15.1  |
| Japan          | 13.3  | 20.6  | 24.7   | 18.0   |
| EC             | 21.1  | 14.5  | 11.4   | 7.8    |
| NICs           | −0.5  | −0.3  | 0.7    | 0.2    |

*Table A.2.11   Positions on the international market of electrical products*

|                | 1975  | 1980  | 1985   | 1990   |
|----------------|-------|-------|--------|--------|
| United States  | 8.2   | 3.2   | −5.8   | −3.0   |
| Japan          | 7.2   | 11.7  | 15.2   | 10.3   |
| EC             | 19.8  | 16.3  | 11.3   | 5.4    |
| NICs           | −1.3  | −0.6  | 2.6    | 0.9    |

*Table A.2.12   Positions on the international market of electronics*

|                | 1975  | 1980  | 1985   | 1990   |
|----------------|-------|-------|--------|--------|
| United States  | 5.0   | 3.1   | −6.0   | −4.0   |
| Japan          | 12.6  | 16.8  | 22.6   | 16.5   |
| EC             | 2.1   | −3.4  | −2.8   | −7.9   |
| NICs           | 1.3   | 2.7   | 3.2    | 4.8    |

*Table A.2.13   Positions on the international market of textiles*

|                | 1975  | 1980  | 1985   | 1990   |
|----------------|-------|-------|--------|--------|
| United States  | −6.8  | −6.6  | −19.1  | −14.4  |
| Japan          | 3.4   | 1.8   | 0.8    | −3.8   |
| EC             | 3.1   | −1.2  | 2.3    | −3.0   |
| NICs           | 10.3  | 13.2  | 16.5   | 12.8   |

*Table A.2.14   Positions on the international market of leather*

|                | 1975   | 1980   | 1985   | 1990   |
|----------------|--------|--------|--------|--------|
| United States  | −14.9  | −14.5  | −28.9  | −22.5  |
| Japan          | −0.1   | −1.3   | −1.8   | −2.7   |
| EC             | 7.3    | 0.2    | 5.3    | −0.7   |
| NICs           | 9.7    | 16.8   | 21.8   | 17.2   |

# A.3 POSITIONS BY PRODUCTS

*Table A.3.1*    *Positions on the international maket of basic inorganic chemicals (including powders and explosives, excluding fertilizers)*

|                | 1975  | 1980  | 1985  | 1990  |
| -------------- | ----- | ----- | ----- | ----- |
| United States  | 4.4   | 3.9   | 1.1   | 2.6   |
| Japan          | 2.9   | −0.9  | −3.2  | −2.9  |
| EC             | 7.9   | 2.2   | 7.0   | 7.3   |
| NICs           | −1.4  | −2.4  | −1.9  | −3.7  |

*Table A.3.2*    *Positions on the international market of fertilizers and chemical products for agriculture (insecticides, herbicides, fungicides, etc.)*

|                | 1975   | 1980   | 1985  | 1990  |
| -------------- | ------ | ------ | ----- | ----- |
| United States  | 9.2    | 12.4   | 11.3  | 9.1   |
| Japan          | 6.3    | 1.4    | 0.4   | −0.2  |
| EC             | 19.4   | 9.6    | 8.2   | 1.8   |
| NICs           | −1.8   | 1.8    | 1.3   | 0.1   |
| Latin America  | −11.4  | −11.6  | −6.6  | −3.7  |

*Table A.3.3*    *Positions on the international market of basic organic chemicals (excluding plastics and fibres)*

|                | 1975  | 1980  | 1985  | 1990  |
| -------------- | ----- | ----- | ----- | ----- |
| United States  | 10.7  | 9.8   | 4.1   | 5.7   |
| Japan          | 5.1   | 1.4   | 0.4   | 1.6   |
| EC             | 12.1  | 12.5  | 12.8  | 8.0   |
| NICs           | −3.9  | −4.1  | −3.8  | −6.3  |
| Gulf           | −1.0  | −1.1  | −0.5  | 0.5   |
| OPEC           | −3.0  | −3.5  | −2.8  | −1.2  |
| Latin America  | −7.8  | −6.6  | −3.0  | −2.8  |

*Table A.3.4*    *Positions on the international market of paints, varnishes and materials*

|               | 1975 | 1980 | 1985 | 1990 |
|---------------|------|------|------|------|
| United States | 3.7  | 3.4  | 0.1  | 1.6  |
| Japan         | 2.0  | 2.0  | 3.8  | 2.7  |
| EC            | 26.6 | 26.2 | 25.6 | 18.1 |
| NICs          | −4.6 | −4.1 | −5.2 | −4.7 |
| Gulf          | −2.8 | −3.4 | −2.9 | −1.4 |
| OPEC          | −7.8 | −8.2 | −8.4 | −4.0 |
| Latin America | −5.7 | −4.5 | −3.1 | −3.0 |

*Table A.3.5*    *Positions on the international market of toilet products, soaps and perfumes (including cleaning preparations, washing powders, cosmetics, chemical products n.e.s)*

|               | 1975 | 1980 | 1985 | 1990 |
|---------------|------|------|------|------|
| United States | 10.1 | 15.5 | 6.1  | 6.9  |
| Japan         | −0.3 | −0.3 | 0.4  | 0.7  |
| EC            | 21.0 | 19.7 | 19.6 | 17.5 |
| NICs          | −2.1 | −4.1 | −4.3 | −5.1 |
| Latin America | −5.8 | −4.7 | −3.3 | −2.7 |

*Table A.3.6*    *Positions on the international market of pharmaceutical products (including veterinary products)*

|               | 1975 | 1980  | 1985 | 1990 |
|---------------|------|-------|------|------|
| United States | 7.8  | 7.4   | 4.8  | 3.3  |
| Japan         | −3.9 | −4.6  | −4.3 | −4.3 |
| EC            | 20.1 | 20.5  | 19.6 | 14.6 |
| Gulf          | −4.9 | −5.2  | −4.3 | −3.0 |
| OPEC          | −9.9 | −11.6 | −7.9 | −5.2 |
| Latin America | −5.8 | −4.7  | −3.3 | −2.7 |

*Table A.3.7*    *Positions on the international market of plastics fibres and resins (including synthetic rubber and synthetic and artificial continuous yarns)*

|                | 1975 | 1980 | 1985 | 1990 |
|----------------|------|------|------|------|
| United States  | 9.5  | 12.0 | 6.8  | 7.2  |
| Japan          | 10.5 | 6.2  | 6.2  | 4.8  |
| EC             | 17.0 | 14.1 | 12.2 | 5.4  |
| NICs           | −2.8 | −1.7 | 0.3  | 0.5  |
| Central Europe | −3.7 | −1.5 | −0.2 | 0.2  |
| Gulf           | −2.7 | −3.0 | −1.6 | −0.5 |
| OPEC           | −6.4 | −6.5 | −4.7 | −2.4 |
| Latin America  | −5.3 | −5.0 | −2.5 | −1.9 |

*Table A.3.8*    *Positions on the international market of plastic articles (articles manufactured exclusively with plastics, excluding shoes, clothing and compounds)*

|               | 1975 | 1980 | 1985 | 1990 |
|---------------|------|------|------|------|
| United States | −2.0 | 2.9  | −6.5 | −3.4 |
| Japan         | 2.4  | 1.8  | 2.6  | 0.5  |
| EC            | 12.4 | 9.9  | 10.5 | 5.4  |
| NICs          | 10.4 | 9.2  | 12.4 | 9.3  |
| Gulf          | −3.2 | −4.2 | −3.4 | −1.3 |
| OPEC          | −5.9 | −7.9 | −4.7 | −2.0 |

*Table A.3.9*    *Positions on the international market of rubber articles (including pneumatics, excluding shoes, clothing and compounds)*

|               | 1975  | 1980  | 1985  | 1990 |
|---------------|-------|-------|-------|------|
| United States | 0.0   | −3.2  | −11.1 | −5.2 |
| Japan         | 11.5  | 12.1  | 14.4  | 11.4 |
| EC            | 23.0  | 16.8  | 13.9  | 7.0  |
| NICs          | 1.5   | 5.1   | 5.3   | 4.1  |
| Gulf          | −6.3  | −6.7  | −6.3  | −3.1 |
| OPEC          | −10.8 | −12.6 | −10.1 | −5.2 |
| Latin America | −5.6  | −5.7  | −2.6  | −2.0 |

*Table A.3.10   Positions on the international market of motor vehicle parts*

|               | 1975 | 1980 | 1985 | 1990 |
|---------------|------|------|------|------|
| United States | 13.5 | 10.0 | 2.3  | −3.5 |
| Japan         | 3.9  | 5.5  | 10.1 | 13.7 |
| EC            | 17.4 | 18.1 | 10.9 | 9.1  |
| NICs          | −0.9 | −1.2 | 0.1  | −0.8 |
| Latin America | −5.8 | −6.6 | −3.8 | −3.4 |

*Table A.3.11   Positions on the international market of passenger cars*

|               | 1975  | 1980  | 1985  | 1990  |
|---------------|-------|-------|-------|-------|
| United States | −20.0 | −21.8 | −36.0 | −22.0 |
| Japan         | 19.1  | 29.5  | 31.7  | 21.1  |
| EC            | 19.1  | 11.3  | 12.2  | 7.7   |
| NICs          | 0.1   | 0.2   | 1.0   | 1.0   |
| Latin America | −2.7  | −3.0  | −0.8  | 0.2   |

*Table A.3.12   Positions on the international market of industrial vehicles and other land transport equipment*

|               | 1975 | 1980 | 1985  | 1990 |
|---------------|------|------|-------|------|
| United States | 12.2 | −2.5 | −16.1 | −9.9 |
| Japan         | 13.1 | 19.6 | 26.3  | 14.7 |
| EC            | 27.9 | 16.8 | 9.9   | 6.2  |
| NICs          | −1.0 | −0.6 | 0.6   | −0.8 |

*Table A.3.13   Positions on the international market of active electronic components (valves and tubes, semiconductors, integrated circuits)*

|               | 1975 | 1980 | 1985 | 1990 |
|---------------|------|------|------|------|
| United States | 8.3  | −3.8 | −1.3 | −1.5 |
| Japan         | 3.9  | 11.0 | 15.7 | 16.8 |
| EC            | −2.8 | −7.1 | −5.8 | −5.3 |
| NICs          | 1.9  | 1.0  | −2.6 | −4.2 |

*Table A.3.14*  Positions on the international market of consumer electronics (radio and television receivers, phones, transmission and guidance appliances)

|  | 1975 | 1980 | 1985 | 1990 |
|---|---|---|---|---|
| United States | −17.0 | −14.6 | −37.1 | −20.3 |
| Japan | 35.4 | 43.4 | 56.9 | 26.0 |
| EC | −5.9 | −14.4 | −10.7 | −17.1 |
| NICs | 9.1 | 16.0 | 9.8 | 11.2 |

*Table A.3.15*  Positions on the international market of data processing equipment and office machinery

|  | 1975 | 1980 | 1985 | 1990 |
|---|---|---|---|---|
| United States | 15.9 | 19.3 | 7.0 | −0.9 |
| Japan | 4.1 | 5.3 | 12.4 | 12.2 |
| EC | −2.7 | −6.3 | −7.0 | −12.1 |
| NICs | 0.9 | −0.1 | 4.3 | 11.6 |

*Table A.3.16*  Positions on the international market of household appliances (including household refrigerators and electrical heating appliances, excluding lighting appliances)

|  | 1975 | 1980 | 1985 | 1990 |
|---|---|---|---|---|
| United States | 1.2 | −1.4 | −15.9 | −7.2 |
| Japan | 6.4 | 11.7 | 19.5 | 3.4 |
| EC | 15.7 | 12.3 | 7.3 | 6.0 |
| NICs | 0.9 | 4.7 | 11.5 | 6.3 |

# NOTES

1. This indicator has been established by CEPII (Centre d'Etudes Prospectives et d'Informations Internationales); see in particular Lafay *et al.* (1989).
2. The precise definition of the categories of products is given in the presentation of the database provided by CEPII.

# Index